Holistic Engagement

Holistic Engagement
Transformative Social Work Education in the 21st Century

Edited by Loretta Pyles
and
Gwendolyn J. Adam

OXFORD
UNIVERSITY PRESS

OXFORD
UNIVERSITY PRESS

Oxford University Press is a department of the University of Oxford. It furthers
the University's objective of excellence in research, scholarship, and education
by publishing worldwide.Oxford is a registered trade mark of Oxford University
Press in the UK and certain other countries.

Published in the United States of America by Oxford University Press
198 Madison Avenue, New York, NY 10016, United States of America.

Library of Congress Cataloging-in-Publication Data
Holistic engagement : transformative social work education
in the 21st century / edited by Loretta Pyles, Gwendolyn J. Adam.
    pages cm
Includes bibliographical references and index.
ISBN 978-0-19-939272-8 (alk. paper)
1. Social work education.   2. Holistic education.
I. Pyles, Loretta, editor.   II. Adam, Gwendolyn, editor.
HV11.H586 2016
361.3071—dc23
2015027013

9 8 7 6 5 4 3 2 1

Printed by Edwards Brothers, USA

To our students

CONTENTS

ACKNOWLEDGMENTS

We are sincerely grateful to the authors of this volume who have shared their pedagogical stories so candidly, revealing their inner worlds despite the challenges that such vulnerability can pose. They have been willing to revise repeatedly and go deeper when we have asked. We believe the fruits of their journeys are revealed here and make this book unique in its richness and clarity.

We are appreciative of senior editor, Dana Bliss, Andrew Dominello, and the editorial team at Oxford University Press, who have offered vital feedback and support throughout this process. The external reviewers provided new and thoughtful perspectives on our work that we have endeavored to adequately incorporate throughout the chapters.

LORETTA PYLES

Although I have been blessed with many outstanding teachers throughout the years, the pedagogy utilized in training yoga teachers at Kripalu School of Yoga and Health has had a significant impact on this book. I am grateful to the many teachers there who taught me how to hold space, let go, and integrate new insights into mind–body–spirit. I hope I have been able to transmit some of the wisdom of this dynamic tradition through these pages.

I am equally appreciative of my students, who have been willing to bravely step into classroom experiences outside of the norm. They have trusted and taken risks, with open minds and hearts. Their courage, insights, and growth are what really inspired me to do this book.

I thank the following people who have offered wisdom, inspiration, and encouragement (knowingly, and perhaps unknowingly) before and during the writing of this book: Katharine Briar-Lawson, Ed Canda, Heather Horton, Heather Larkin, Hal Lawson, Rachel Mehl, David Pettie, Salome Raheim, and Ben Shepard. I am also appreciative of the resources and support from the Capital District Contemplative Higher Education group and the SUNY Contemplative Network. Thanks to all of my comrades at CommunityLAB, especially Shanna Goldman and Angelica Clarke, who have helped me to refine some of these practices and ideas and who are constantly teaching me about social justice work. Last but not least, I have continually been moved and inspired by the authenticity, persistence, and consistently positive encouragement offered by my co-editor and co-author, Gwendolyn Adam. I have never had such a deeply fulfilling professional collaborative writing experience.

I return home to thank Ted Mehl for his fierce loyalty, unwavering support, appreciation, and love. And so as not to forget the nonhuman world, I am thankful to Alex, Joey, and Tara and for the peace and inspiration bestowed by the Helderberg and Catskill Mountains of upstate New York.

GWENDOLYN ADAM

At best, acknowledgments in textbooks list meaningful contributions to the work in a creative enough way to warrant reader interest. The challenge for the authors is to make lists without leaving folks out, recognizing that expressing gratitude fully to all people and experiences that impact us in our work efforts remains impossible. Instead of engaging in that Sisyphean challenge, I opt instead to share two stories to express my gratitude relative to my work on this project.

First, I thank Dr. Loretta Pyles, co-author and co-editor of this text. As I was interviewing for a faculty position on her team some years ago, we met for the first time at the requisite faculty interview dinner. I spent only an hour or two with her that evening and did not see her the following day during the interview and did not end up in the position. I did leave the experience feeling like I had encountered someone special. We spoke briefly of our shared passion for transforming education to value the whole person and the authentic inquiry we all need to grow. We had no additional contact. A few months later, I received an e-mail from Loretta asking if I would like to consider joining her in her book project on transformative pedagogy. Surprised, open to the unexpected, and honored by her invitation, we agreed to meet and see where our interests and intentions were complementary. In a daylong meeting without distractions and very few breaks, we co-created the core constructs for *Holistic Engagement* and articulated with precision the detailed definitions that serve as our model for transforming pedagogy. The energy of this shared process fueled our work well beyond reasonable attention span or physical comfort lost as we worked for hours on the floor surrounded by drawings and notes. I think we both experienced the powerful impact shared intention has when we least expect it.

I share the detail of this story with you because all of this happened through her willingness to be present fully that night at dinner and to reach out to connect despite very limited experience with me. Her capacity to invite collaboration and creativity, especially from a distance, surpasses my understanding and has changed me. Many folks write books together, a few develop meaningful theories together, and fewer still work collaboratively throughout intense deadlines together. I do not know anyone else who has made all of these happen without knowing the other at all. If I had known how much her work, her process, and her example could impact me, I would have signed up to be her student long ago. For the rare gift of this project and our unexpected connection, I simply say thank you, Loretta.

Second, my life story brought me to this work authentically, as a person and professional who tends to spend more time in my head than in the rest of my experience. My journey to experience and teach the whole of living continues with the support of people in my professional experiences and personal life, without whom I would have had only ideas to share in this book rather than transformational experiences that let me know there is more to living and more to teaching than just good ideas. They are my current life teachers who, from a much longer list, have directly impacted my work on this text: my courageous CCSU social work students and committed colleagues from the Committee on Well-being of Children, Youth and Communities and the Social and Emotional Learning Task Force at CCSU who, together, have welcomed my whole self as a teacher (with all those mindfulness activities) and colleague; and Sharon Alpert, Maxwell Adam, Elizabeth Weinberg, Susan Lord, Bodhi, and the unending beauty of the Berkshires of western Massachusetts, which together cultivate my whole self as a person. Because of you, I have so much more than ideas. Thank you.

ABOUT THE EDITORS

Loretta Pyles, PhD, is Associate Professor in the School of Social Welfare at the State University of New York (SUNY) at Albany. She is an engaged scholar concerned with transformative social change and holistic social work practice and pedagogy. Her scholarship has centered on the ways that individuals, organizations, and communities resist and respond to poverty, violence, and disasters in a policy context of neoliberal global capitalism and social welfare retrenchment in both the United States and the developing world. She is author of *Progressive Community Organizing: Reflective Practice in a Globalizing World* (2nd ed., Routledge, 2014). She is a certified yoga instructor and utilizes mindfulness and embodied learning in her pedagogy, both in the classroom and in the community. For more information, see http://www.lorettapyles.com.

Gwendolyn "Wendy" J. Adam, PhD, MSW, LICSW, is Associate Professor at Central Connecticut State University (CCSU), School of Education and Professional Studies. Through a variety of leadership roles in academia, federal government, and community practice, she developed experiential interdisciplinary leadership training curricula for faculty, graduate trainees, and community-based youth and family programs. She led a constituent-driven national needs assessment for maternal and child health training programs and is currently working with CCSU colleagues to co-create a social and emotional learning curriculum for state pre-service teacher training. Her current research and writing focus on cultivating engaged leadership, compassionate presence, and innovative educational methods to engage the whole learner and the whole educator.

ABOUT THE CONTRIBUTORS

Meera Bhat, BA, MA, is a PhD student at the School of Social Welfare at SUNY at Albany. Her dissertation research will focus on women's experiences of participation and empowerment in emerging social entrepreneurship practices in India. Her prior experience is in participatory research, collaborative training, and community organizing on issues of youth as well as women's health and microfinance. She is interested in participation as a means of empowering individuals in personal, societal, and political spaces and building democratic institutions that enable people to realize their capabilities. She has been involved in conducting classes, curriculum development, and research on holistic and experiential learning for social work students and community organizers internationally.

Lara Bowen, BFA, MSW, attended the BFA in Acting program at SUNY Purchase and received her MSW from SUNY Stony Brook with a specialization in Student–Community Development. She is currently pursuing her PhD in Social Welfare at SUNY at Albany, with an emphasis on the study of applied theater for social change.

Steve Burghardt, MSW, PhD, is Professor of Social Work at the Silberman School of Social Work at Hunter College, City University of New York (CUNY). His most recent book is *Macro Practice in Social Work for the 21st Century: Bridging the Macro–Micro Divide* (2nd ed., Sage, 2013).

Kate Cavanagh, LMSW, has worked at Fordham University's Dorothy Day Center for Service and Justice in the service learning program and for various nonprofits in community programs. She is a mother who is part of a large extended Italian and Irish American family, grew up in northwest New Jersey, earned her BASW at Fordham University, and completed her MSW at Hunter College, CUNY, concentrating in community organizing in 2006. While at Hunter, she attended the Undoing Racism and Community Organizing training for the first time and joined the facilitation team as a Paulo Freire Methodology popular educator at the Brecht Forum.

Mette Christiansen, MSW, practiced as a social pedagogue in Denmark before coming to the United States. After working several years as a direct care worker, she obtained her MSW and now is Director of the Concentration in Human

Services in the Department of Sociology at SUNY New Paltz. Her teaching is inspired by critical pedagogy and her extensive international practice experience working with various populations. Areas of research and professional interest include professionalization and educational socialization of human services and social workers and international social welfare.

Phillip Dybicz, PhD, LCSW, is Assistant Professor, Department of Social Work, Valdosta State University. He is a social work historian, with specialization in the history of the intellectual thought of the profession. Much of his work focuses on the contributions of postmodern thought to current social work practice.

Jack J. Lu, LCSW, is a PhD candidate and adjunct faculty at the University of Connecticut School of Social Work. His research interests include health access for Cambodian Americans, community-based participatory research, eliminating health disparities, integrative mind–body–spirit social work, and social action to empower marginalized populations. He has practiced as a clinical social worker since 2003.

Kelly Lundman, B.Ed, M.Ed, BSW, is currently employed as a Defence Social Worker at Defence Community Organisation by the Department of Defence, Australian Government. She is currently transitioning to exploring her ideas in literary fiction.

Robyn Lynn, ADCW, BA (Soc.Sc.), M.Soc.Pol, AIWCW, has had an interest in mindfulness since she took up a Buddhist form of meditation for her own well-being more than 10 years ago. Her personal experience prompted an exploration of how she could integrate the practice of meditation and the concept of mindfulness into her teaching, which led to publishing "Mindfulness in Social Work Education" in the journal *Social Work Education* (2009). In her attempts to implement mindfulness into social work education, she encountered a number of challenges and ethical dilemmas that she has researched with colleagues and practitioners in relation to their experiences and understandings of mindfulness in the ethical and value context of social work and the implications of this for practice and curriculum.

Esperanza Martell, BA, MSW, teaches community organizing and is an advisor at the Hunter College Silberman School of Social Work. She specializes in organizational development, team building, leadership skills, conflict resolution, diversity training, and alternative healing. Her life work has been as a political activist working with organizations and individuals to promote anti-oppression, sustainability, the transformation of capitalism and healing in community. She holds a BA from CUNY and an MSW from Hunter College Silberman School of Social Work.

Jo Mensinga, BSW, MA (research), IYTA, has focused on the following in her postgraduate research and publications: narrative research methodologies, field education, teaching approaches, career choice in social work, and the impact of embodied practices such as yoga in social work. Publications include "The Feeling of Being a Social Worker: Including Yoga as an Embodied Practice" in *Social Work Education* (2011) and "She Let out a Burp and Got Rid of It! Learning From a Social Worker's Stories about Bodies in Mental Health Conversations" in Francis, La Rosa, Shankaran, and Rajeev (Eds.), *Social Work Practice in Mental Health: Cross-Cultural Perspectives* (Allied Publishers, 2015).

Terry Mizrahi, PhD, is Professor in the Silberman School of Social Work at Hunter College. She chairs Community Organizing, Planning, and Development. She co-chairs the national Special Commission to Advance Macro Practice in Social Work. She is a founding member of the Association for Community Organizing and Social Administration and is past president of the National Association of Social Workers.

David Pettie, LCSW, ACSW, is Assistant Director of Field Education at SUNY at Albany School of Social Welfare. He is currently exploring professional identity formation with beginning social workers and the role of mindfulness and contemplative practices within this process. In addition, he is focusing on socialization toward masculinity, its impact on the capacity of men to be relational, and the implications for a female-dominated helping profession.

Alyson Quinn, BSW, MSW, is Instructor at University of British Columbia School of Social Work and a group, individual, and couples therapist. She has been practicing as a social worker for more than 25 years in South Africa, London, and Vancouver as an individual, couples, and group therapist. She is author of three books: *Experiential Unity Theory and Model: Reclaiming the Soul* (Aronson, 2012); *Reclaim Your Soul: Your Path to Healing* (University Press of America, 2014); and *When the River Wakes Up* (Rowman & Littlefield, 2014).

Salome Raheim, PhD, ACSW, is Professor and former Dean at the University of Connecticut School of Social Work. A meditation, yoga, and reiki practitioner, she focuses her teaching and scholarship on culturally competent practice and integrative mind–body–spirit approaches to health and healing.

Benjamin Shepard, PhD, LMSW, is Associate Professor of Human Services at City Tech/CUNY. He is also the author/editor of many books, including *Community Projects as Social Activism* (Sage, 2014) and *Rebel Friendships: "Outsider" Networks and Social Movements* (Palgrave Macmillan, 2015).

Juliana Svistova, BSW, MSW, is a part-time lecturer and a PhD candidate at the School of Social Welfare at SUNY at Albany. Her primary research focus is on issues of participation in social development policy and practice, as well as pedagogic settings.

Beth Tinning, BSW, has been employed in the human services since 1991. She has worked in organizations responding to domestic violence, sexual assault, HIV/AIDS, and homelessness. From 2007 to 2014, she was a lecturer in the Department of Social Work and Human Services, James Cook University. In January 2015, she returned to direct service delivery and is currently Child & Youth Counsellor at the Cairns Regional Domestic Violence Service.

Allison Weingarten, LMSW, is Program Director at Queens Community House in Queens, New York. She runs an after-school program for elementary school-aged children in Queens. She leads a staff team to promote social and academic development with the participants, staff members, and families through programming focused on literacy, arts, science, math, music, team sports, dance, group work, and community engagement.

Holistic Engagement

PART I

Theoretical and Empirical Foundations of Holistic Engagement

CHAPTER 1

Educating Transformative Social Workers

The Case for Holistic Pedagogies

LORETTA PYLES AND GWENDOLYN J. ADAM

INTRODUCTION

At a time when there is an increase in social disparities throughout the world, more severe fiscal austerity in policymaking, greater frequency of environmental disasters, overreliance on technology for problem-solving, and intensified fear and isolation, social workers are questioning the fundamental assumptions about the project of modernity and its impact on the individuals, organizations, and communities with which they work (Coates, 2003; Lee, Ng, Leung, & Chan, 2009; Pyles, 2014; Reisch, 2013). Contemporary thinkers, including economists, environmental scientists, neuroscientists, religious leaders, social work scholars, and others have observed that society is moving toward a tipping point and that new strategies are necessary for environmental sustainability, social equity, global peace, and public health (Coates, 2003; Hawken, 2007; Jones, 2010; Korten, 2006; Macy & Brown, 1998). As such, social work students and educators are inquiring into and interrogating the socially constructed assumptions of modernism, including a growth-oriented economic paradigm, mind–body dualism, positivistic science, and linear, mechanistic thinking about interventions and outcomes (Coates, 2003; Jones, 2010; Lee et al., 2009; Mishna & Bogo, 2007; Vick-Johnson, 2010). Importantly, social work educators and their students are also beginning to explore more deeply the causes and consequences of, as well as prevention of and solutions to, high rates of social worker burnout and stress (McGarrigle & Walsh, 2011; Moore, Bledsoe, Perry, & Robinson, 2011; University at Buffalo, n.d.).

Because of the multileveled (micro, mezzo, and macro) and multilayered (biological, psychological, social, and spiritual) dimensions of 21st-century social problems, social work educators require a unique set of knowledge, values, and skills that approach these challenges holistically. Furthermore, given the severity of the challenges faced, such as hypercapitalism and privatization of public services (Reisch, 2013), environmental devastation (Jones, 2010), and chronic, debilitating stress (Koopsen & Young, 2009), social work educators must address these challenges in manners that not only alleviate the negative effects of the problems but also tap human strengths in ways that have the potential to transform individuals, communities, and systems. This means that educators must craft opportunities that help student social workers understand and reflect on their own relationships to these issues and all of their complexity, in addition to imagining and embodying new solutions in the classroom. It is clear that social work practice and education in the 21st century demand new paradigms, innovations, and risk-taking.

We believe these transformational processes can be nurtured in the classroom through deliberate cultivation of deeper levels of questioning, awareness, and human connection. This necessitates participation of the whole self in relation to other whole selves in the context of the environment we inhabit. Such processes and practices require the creation of trusting, compassionate relationships within the classroom community so that students feel safe enough to go outside of their comfort zones. Such processes are phenomenological; there is a felt, experiential sense of the body–mind and environment (Hocking, Haskell, & Linds, 2001; Lynn, 2010). By engaging holistically in the classroom, student social workers can take their new insights and skills into the community as they practice transformative social work (Pyles, 2014).

Transformative social work is grounded at the unique crossroads of integrative healing modalities and democratic social change movements, including feminist organizing (Pyles, 2014). It seeks to bring awareness to and unravel the knots of personal suffering and social oppression, reveal individual and collective strengths, and empower people toward personal and social liberation. This kind of social work practice requires the development of holistic engagement skills and an integrative capability that allows practitioners to respond dynamically in a globalizing environment.

This chapter strives to lay the foundation for what we call "pedagogies of holistic engagement," teaching methods that affirm the skills we argue are required to transform social work education, practice, and the people with whom and communities in which we work. These skills—presence with the whole self, whole self-inquiry, empathic connection, and compassionate attention—have a growing empirical base and provide the foundation for our overall conceptual framework for holistic social work education. This framework will be explicitly articulated in the next chapter. We begin this chapter by describing and analyzing the current state of social work education, followed by an argument for why social work education is in need of transformation. We conclude this chapter by presenting some of the scholarly foundations of a holistically engaged approach to social work practice and education.

FRAMEWORKS AND ASSUMPTIONS OF SOCIAL WORK PRACTICE AND EDUCATION

Traditional social work education in the English-speaking world, especially generalist social work curricula, has been established in a series of interrelated frameworks, including the ecological approach, the biopsychosocial model, and a systems perspective (Robbins, Chatterjee, & Canda, 2011). The ecological approach emphasizes the importance of developing knowledge about the interactions between a person and his or her environment (Germain, 1973). The approach affirms that when a person or his or her environment changes, the other is impacted by the change, and thus survival depends on the other adapting to this change. One concern with this approach, from a transformative perspective, is that it implies that individuals ought to merely adapt themselves and accept the status quo rather than organizing to change oppressive social systems. Thus, social justice-oriented models of social work practice have sought to address this by emphasizing anti-oppression, empowerment, and systems change (Dominelli, 2003).

A biopsychosocial approach to a client views the problems or pathologies experienced by a person as a function of multiple factors, including biology, psychology, and various social systems, such as economic and cultural (Robbins et al., 2011). Recently, a biopsychosocial–*spiritual* approach has been put forward emphasizing the spiritual dimensions of human beings' needs and strengths (Canda & Furman, 2010). Inclusion of spirituality as a vital dimension of human behavior has only recently been incorporated into social work educational standards, and some countries have yet to include them (Australian Association of Social Workers, 2012; Council on Social Work Education, 2012; International Federation of Social Workers, 2012).

Finally, a systems perspective affirms a sense of interconnectedness and explains that change in one part of a system influences change in other parts of the system (Lee et al., 2009). By understanding how micro, mezzo, and macro systems interact and intersect, social workers are able to intervene in ways that can attend to multiple systems. However, social work education is inclined to privilege the micro and the mezzo systems (Reisch, 2013), and it tends to do so in a way that ignores more subtle forces at play, such as energy in the mind–body continuum (Lee et al., 2009).

Nonetheless, these approaches—ecological, biopsychosocial–spiritual, and a systems perspective—do share some resonance with more holistically oriented methods of social work practice and education, such as the integrative body–mind–spirit social work approach, and can offer building blocks for holistically oriented, transformative education (Lee et al., 2009). What these approaches have in common is that they reject reductionist and linear orientations to social work practice—for example, an approach that defines a person as solely a psychological being who should perform a specific set of prescribed actions to achieve stated psychological outcomes. Rather, they affirm the whole person, the role of the environment, the fact of interconnectedness, and the complexity of the human condition.

Yet, recent methods of social work practice, such as task-centered models (Epstein & Brown, 2001), as well as long-standing medical models focused on symptom amelioration, affirm a more rational–technical orientation to social work that tends to isolate specific phenomena or variables at the expense of complexity and holism (Barter, 2012). As well, the move toward evidence-based social work practice, which has advanced social work's ongoing efforts to be viewed as a legitimate profession, has been appropriately critiqued (Adams, Matto, & LeCroy, 2009). Evidence-based social work is predicated on specific epistemological assumptions that embrace positivism, or the view that there can be unbiased, certain knowledge. The positivist idea that knowledge is incremental intersects with the modernist view that science and technology will solve social problems (Coates, 2003). Furthermore, rational–technical approaches to education arguably result in technical interventions, reflecting a Eurocentric, masculine, and cognitive–behavioral bias (Barter, 2012; Kelly & Horder, 2001).

Such a belief system has led to a "best practices" agenda that "encourages social work students to demand certainty, reject an understanding and incorporation of the role of context, resist learning concepts that challenge their assumptions, and seek a 'cookbook' approach to social work practice" (Reisch, 2013, p. 721). We argue that a new paradigm for social work education would affirm the ambiguity of human lives and the social world; encourage inquiry into the origins and contexts of social problems; embrace creativity/spontaneity in social work practice; and place self-awareness, reflection, and relationships at the core of social work.

CRITIQUES OF TRADITIONAL PEDAGOGIES

Critiques of traditional pedagogies invite social work educators to consider how methods utilized in the classroom communicate how the profession conceptualizes change—in the learner and in how the learner is ultimately able to impact the world. Although social work continues to emphasize a systems perspective, prioritizing interdependent practice influences at the macro, mezzo, and micro levels, traditional pedagogies do not bring that level of emphasis to the classroom system, to the complex and layered interaction of multiple aspects of the learner with multiple aspects of the educator. By excluding vital parts of the learner, the educator and the ways these interact, we teach them to understand systems outside the classroom by ignoring the ones inside it.

Since the scientific revolution, the Academy has privileged cognitive learning in the "banking" style (Freire, 1970, 2000) as a primary method to facilitate student achievement. In this traditional educational system, which social work has largely embraced, the teacher is a disembodied, all-knowing, cognitive being depositing information into the disembodied minds of students who are empty vessels. Such an approach perpetuates the social narratives that undergird oppression, and it breeds a hegemonic, or power-over, dynamic between educators and students. This dynamic marginalizes students by failing to recognize and develop their personal power while also oppressing educators by disallowing them to bring their whole selves to their work (Barbezat & Bush, 2014; Kelly & Horder, 2001). In short, it undermines student preparedness for macro-level impact. A "banking" approach (Freire, 1970; Pyles, 2014) to cognitive learning, however, arguably produces what postmodern theorist Michel Foucault (1975) called "docile bodies," which serve to maintain the status quo of the socioeconomic order. These docile bodies are produced by controlling and disciplining people through, for example, specific physical arrangements and ordering in the classroom, such as students sitting in rows and a teacher standing at the front of the room. The problem of such docile bodies becomes perhaps even more of a challenge in this era of online and hybrid learning, as we are confronted with more barriers to human connection (Henderson, 2010). While educators grapple with blatant disconnection that this distance learner brings, there may be less dissonance with classroom pedagogy if the same "banking" styles are utilized. If both student and teacher are disembodied, with one delivering content to another, we must consider how distance pedagogies and class-based ones actually differ.

Emerging from a critique of primary/secondary education and adult education, there is a large body of literature advocating for transformative and holistic approaches to education (Hart, 2014; Hocking et al., 2001; Mezirow, 1991). Some social work educators have also been critiquing traditional approaches for many years, arguing for transformative learning and anti-oppressive education (Jones, 2010; Ross, 2007). These alternative approaches emphasize the importance of rethinking fundamental assumptions and also the facilitation of dialogic learning that can result in new paradigms and action. Although many of the approaches to transformative education have done a good job of developing social justice-oriented classrooms, we find that many, although not all, tend to emphasize the cognitive (and to some extent the emotional) dimension of students and fail to acknowledge the body, heart, and spirit dimensions (Ross, 2007). Recent literature has begun to include more holistic and integrative orientations to education, such as the approach put forward by education scholars Ryoo, Crawford, Moreno, and Mclaren (2009), who propose an educational process that "acknowledges the way students and teachers are exploited, fragmented, and Othered in schools while advocating for curricular and educational practices that are based in love and integrity in an interdependent classroom community" (p. 132).

Certainly necessary to social work education, cognitive learning often entails learning new theories; studying empirical evidence; and engaging in the important, although often elusive, practice of "critical thinking" (Gambrill & Gibbs, 2009; Kirst-Ashman, 2012). Cognition, however, especially when developed in traditional ways, represents an incomplete attempt at developing the key elements of holistic engagement. Although cognition is crucial in information management, it cannot fully account for connections between people and between people and systems. As a profession, social work purports that these relational connections facilitate health, growth, development, and healing and are crucial to mezzo and micro practice. For example, empathy requires connection with some element of one's experience emotionally and/or spiritually beyond the messages of the mind—it is a felt process that the mind can recognize but not genuinely create in the absence of body, heart, culture, and soul data input. By fostering classroom spaces where students learn and practice methods of attention, self-reflection, and conscious communication, student-practitioners have the opportunity to experience the effects that such techniques can have on their own ability to engage holistically (Lynn, 2010; Ross, 2007). In so doing, students learn the skills they need through pedagogical methods that reinforce and model the skills needed to practice at multiple levels.

THE CASE FOR A NEW APPROACH TO SOCIAL WORK EDUCATION

Several factors are converging at this particular time in history that necessitate concerted efforts toward the development of holistic engagement skills in social work practice and education. These factors are largely a function of neoliberal globalization, which prioritizes privatization, profits, and the rights of corporations, and the consequences and impacts it is having on individuals, families, organizations, communities, and larger social systems (Klein, 2002; Pyles, 2014). They are (1) the invisible suffering of globalization, (2) the commodification and compartmentalization of social work, (3) increased diversity and prevalence of non-Western cultural practices, and (4) lifestyle-oriented health risks.

The Invisible Suffering of Globalization

The first factor relates to the invisible suffering that lies behind the seemingly triumphant neoliberal global economy and how it is affecting society in complex and perhaps unknown ways. Many thinkers have noted how multinational corporations continue to displace large numbers of indigenous people and are virtually enslaving the developing world in a sweatshop system in the name of economic development (Coates, 2003; Klein, 2002; Pyles, 2014). Castells (1999) has referred to the globalizing world as a "network society," whereby multinational corporations change relentlessly, move along, form and re-form, in endless variation. Societies that are inside these networks have enhanced technological opportunities, and those outside have diminished opportunities, which has a cumulative effect. And yet, many people in the developed world are completely ignorant of this reality.

Although access to these changing technologies can potentially leave us feeling more resourced, connected, productive, and efficient, one can see that they can certainly have the opposite effect as well. Thus, "technostress" can leave us feeling more depleted, scattered, and isolated (Koopsen & Young, 2009). Unfortunately, it is something that we are hesitant to identify, name, or discuss in professional social work settings and in schools and departments of social work. Thus, challenging ourselves and helping students to develop healthy relationships with technology can be a useful and powerful remedy to the overwhelming feelings that technology can create in our professional and personal lives. For example, a university course at a small college in upstate New York called "Stress Free Computing" is helping undergraduates to navigate these dangerous waters by incorporating mindfulness and other reflective activities into course content.

Besides the personal suffering that globalization is causing for people (for those both within and outside these networks), the negative impacts of globalization on the physical environment is something that social work educators are only beginning to recognize (Coates, 2003; Jones, 2010). This is certainly ironic given that the field professes to embrace a person-in-environment perspective. Given the current ecological crisis, transformative social work educators have criticized social work's failure to consider the full meaning of "the environment"—that is, the natural world—noting that it is not enough just to "add on" the natural world in our assessments and interventions; rather, a new paradigm and approach are perhaps required (Jones, 2010). However, this oversight is understandable because the environmental devastation that surrounds us and the looming climate change threats are profoundly painful to bear in our minds, hearts, and bodies. Contemplating the devastation can leave a person feeling overwhelmed with grief, despair, and anger (Greenspan, 2003; Macy & Brown, 1998).

Many social work educators perhaps feel ill-equipped to hold space for students to experience such emotions and express them in ways that are productive for the class. Nonetheless, as educators, it is critical that we prepare ourselves so that we can create opportunities in our classrooms for students to actually *feel* this despair in body and heart, to the extent that everyone is capable. Toward this end, in an advanced master's of social work course called "Policy and Practice of International Development," I (Loretta Pyles) use activities in the classroom (meditation, journaling, conscious communication, and theater exercises) that help foster global consciousness in students. I facilitate several activities, including (1) guiding students through a somatic meditation that gives them permission to tune into feelings in their body about the plight of sweatshop workers in Bangladesh, as depicted in a film shown in class; (2) asking students to creatively embody a physical pose or gesture that reflects their feelings about global social change movements; and (3) writing about grief or other emotions they may have concerning the state of the planet and their physical environment.

Practices that facilitate student awareness of and connection with the context of their own and their clients' lives, and the global economic processes at work, can deepen their understanding of person-in-environment and help them develop a richer knowledge of the suffering caused by globalization. These awareness practices can help set the stage for an integrative and transformative social work practice that can facilitate social worker actualization of the ethical imperatives of the profession (International Federation of Social Workers, 2012). As clients present with problems of depression and loneliness and our communities become places where social capital is diminishing, the social work classroom can become a place where we overcome the sense of isolation from each other that many people in 21st-century society experience.

Commodification and Compartmentalization of Social Work

The second factor is concerned with the ways that social work practice and education arguably have become commodified and compartmentalized. Something becomes commodified, according to Marxist/critical traditions, when services, ideas, or people become commodities or goods for exchange (Kaufman, 2003). The neoliberal economic system that values privatized market-based services has made its appearance in universities and social welfare agencies through their demands for cost efficiencies. Such demands for efficiencies can be seen in the movement to outcomes-oriented, competency-based social work education (Kelly & Horder, 2001). In this regard, Barter (2012) has argued that "competence" is a weak founding principle for a values-driven profession. Predetermined tasks and routine mechanical problem-solving approaches miss the point that addressing complex social realities cannot be artificially fragmented into distinct elements, is not always measurable, and is not homogeneous (Barter, 2012): "Rather, social work is a practical–moral activity with emphasis placed on the theory/practice relationship, reflection, critical thinking, advocacy, intuition and learning through human interaction" (p. 233). Given the "McDonaldization" of society (Ritzer, 2011), we must ask ourselves whether we want to perpetuate a "McDonaldization" of social work practice and education. As Einstein said, "We can't solve problems by using the same kind of thinking we used when we created them."

Relatedly, the current social welfare services structure compartmentalizes and fragments social problems into discrete categories such as mental health, family violence, substance abuse, housing, and unemployment rather than viewing the intersectionality of such issues. Together, this structure leads to more barriers to supports and resources for vulnerable populations (Kretzmann & McKnight, 1993; Pyles, 2014). In social work practice, clients may come to be viewed as a "fee for service" rather than a biopsychosocial–spiritual human being. Social services can quickly become transactional, emphasizing outcomes over relationships, processes, and complexity. Such approaches to services make it difficult to view individuals, families, organizations, and communities holistically and support them in ways that transform.

Students require opportunities to reflect on this commodification and compartmentalization—in the substance and in the structure of their education. Holistic, transformative education, informed by the contemplative practices in higher education movement (Barbezat & Bush, 2014), in conjunction with the popular education activities and critical praxis of grassroots social movements (Adams, 1971; Freire, 1970; Pyles, 2014), offers students opportunities to be at the center of their learning process. Moving beyond the banking approach to education upends the traditional power structure of the classroom that preserves the present circumstances; such an approach becomes a means to promote personal agency (Barbezat & Bush, 2014). Contemplative pedagogy promotes this personal agency by using "forms of introspection and reflection that allow students to focus internally and find more of themselves in their courses" (Barbezat & Bush, 2014, p. 9). Whether it is improvisational theater, deep listening, or service learning, students are encouraged to strengthen their awareness of feelings, thoughts, and body sensations, as well as data from fellow students and the environment around them. These techniques offer students powerful tools that can help strengthen their knowledge of our society's personal and collective struggles and open up spaces for transformation. The educational process can then become what bell hooks (1994) referred to as "the practice of freedom" (p. 13).

Increased Diversity and Non-Western Cultural Practices

A third factor, also a consequence of globalization, is the increasing levels of diversity faced by social workers in both urban and rural communities (Lee et al., 2009). For many people from non-Western cultures, the medical model of social work, which emphasizes a "diagnose and treat" mentality and which still dominates the profession, fails to meet their needs. A medical model focusing on diagnosis of what is wrong, challenging, or problematic and eliminating it fails to invoke the complexity of human relationships, culture, context, social structure, and a number of other factors we social workers purport as crucial to understanding the human experience (Lee et al., 2009). Our practice models often settle for "find and eliminate" instead of "explore and engage."

Recent efforts in social work education have advocated for a more globalized curriculum (Gatenio Gabel & Healy, 2012); however, there is little mention in this discourse of the importance of including *non-Western* practices that originate from indigenous traditions in places such as Western Africa, Australia/ New Zealand, Southeast Asia, or the southwestern United States. Thus, there is an urgent need for the infusion of culturally competent interventions and indigenous healing modalities from throughout the world (Gray, Coates, & Yellow Bird, 2010). Such approaches may embrace a more community- or family-oriented approach to treatment and intervention, as well as affirm the inextricable links between mind, body, culture, and planet. In addition, the unseen part of the self—that is, spirit—becomes a central point of entry and intervention.

In order to be able to competently intervene with clients' spiritual selves, students must be able to understand this aspect of their own self (Canda & Furman, 2010). Integrative medicine, which affirms both scientifically based allopathic or biomedicine *and* complementary or alternative treatments, offers an important model for social work practice in this regard (Koopsen & Young, 2009; Lee et al., 2009). Such "East–West" models can better meet the needs of everyone, but especially indigenous people, such as aboriginal people in Australia, or immigrants with strong spiritual and religious backgrounds, such as Haitian vodou practitioners in Brooklyn, New York. These models contrast with Eurocentric models of social work practice that maintain hegemonic domination in a postcolonialist context, alienating more collectively oriented cultures that center family, community, spirituality, and the environment in favor of individual, cognitively oriented outcomes (Gray et al., 2010).

Thus, social work pedagogy is called to develop prospects for building on strengths, cultivating awareness, and nurturing interpersonal relationships within the classroom context. This places students on the road to a transformative social work practice that embraces democratic community building, as "the encounter of a pluralistic society is not premised on achieving agreement, but achieving relationship" (Eck, 1993, cited in Barbezat & Bush, 2014, p. 80). For example, one of the exercises I (LP) do in an advanced MSW course called "Yoga, Mindfulness and Social Work Practice" is a conscious listening practice called "Confession of Greatness." Students sit with a partner, and one person begins by saying positive things about him- or herself in terms of skills, abilities, attributes, likes, and so on. The listener is invited to close his or her eyes and just listen to the words, noticing when the mind wanders, and how the words are landing in her or him. Students then switch roles. The exercise is a powerful practice, advancing holistic engagement skills, such as deep, conscious listening; identifying strengths in self and others; building trust; and creating connection across differences.

Lifestyle-Oriented Health Risks

A fourth factor necessitating the development of holistic engagement skills concerns negative lifestyle-oriented health outcomes that manifest in a culture dominated by the "McDondaldization" phenomenon (Ritzer, 2011). As efficiency becomes more highly valued in the culture, many Westerners and now non-Westerners, as well, value efficiency when it comes to many aspects of living, including food procurement and consumption. Obesity, diabetes, heart disease, and addiction are just a few of the conditions that are plaguing our communities (McCall, 2007). In addition, rates of stress-related conditions such as low-grade anxiety, chronic fatigue syndrome, and depression have reached epidemic proportions (Koopsen & Young, 2009). If one were to address such issues by focusing solely on an individual rather than his or her environment, solely on biology rather than the social or spiritual, or expect the issue to be addressed by completing a list of tasks, interventions will fail to transform.

Holistic approaches to a problem such as heart disease go beyond the Western medical approach of linear causality (focusing solely on cholesterol levels or blood pressure) but instead bring attention to a web of causation, such as "stress and the role of the mind in perpetuating it, your emotional temperament, your connections to other people, and whether you are living life in accordance with some larger purpose" (McCall, 2007, p. 4). Thus, holistic interventions, rather than focusing on a magic, unidimensional solution, seek to work on many areas simultaneously. Furthermore, a transformative approach to these issues encourages dialogue between body and mind, self and other, individual and society. It requires being in relationship with what is painful, and allowing suffering and oppression to reveal themselves, in order to experience healing. Thus, social work students must begin this work in the safe space of a classroom at the outset of their development as social workers.

Related to these lifestyle health issues is the fact that social work practitioners experience high rates of burnout and stress themselves, as manifested in chronic aversive states, such as anxiety, and addictive behaviors, such as compulsive overeating and substance abuse. Unfortunately, there is more rhetoric around self-care in social work education and practice than there is in the practicing of it (McGarrigle & Walsh, 2011). More than ever before, self-care and personal well-being are vital to every social worker. However, social workers are seldom provided with training and supervision on techniques to regulate the emotions that arise as a result of their work (Turner, 2009). The lack of emphasis on self-care in the profession has gotten so problematic in the United States that the National Association of Social Workers (2009) has offered a policy statement on self-care affirming that "self-care is an essential component in competent, compassionate, and ethical social work practice, requiring time, energy, and commitment" (p. 269). The association argues that self-care should be integrated into every phase of social work education.

SELF-CARE AND SELF-COMPASSION

Social work students tend to be caring individuals who are already engaging in a countercultural activity by choosing to become social workers; they are seeking to make a life out of the virtue of community care in a culture that heavily resists such an idea (H. Larkin, personal communication). Even more derided than community care, however, is the idea of *self*-care: "Self-care in our culture has come to seem selfish, egoistic, a process of withdrawal, antithetical to good service" (Barzebat & Bush, 2014, p. 49). In addition, much of the self-care that does exist in the profession focuses on cognitive–behavioral approaches to managing stress, mirroring the "predominant view of conceptual knowing within social work education" (McGarrigle & Walsh, 2011, pp. 214–215). Furthermore, with the aforementioned value of productivity and efficiency, self-care can be viewed as too time-consuming or requiring too much effort.

Although social workers may have a tremendous abundance of compassion toward others, like many people, they tend to have challenges with regard to cultivating compassion toward themselves (Neff, 2012). Self-judgment and the tendency toward self-domination, alongside feelings of guilt, shame, and low self-worth, are commonly disclosed feelings of our social work students when they are given the opportunity to engage in deep self-inquiry. In this light, self-care must begin and end with self-compassion. Indeed, high levels of self-compassion are associated with greater levels of emotional well-being, physical health, and interpersonal functioning (Neff, 2012). Furthermore, self-compassion exercises have been shown to have positive effects on the functioning and well-being of therapists (Germer, 2012). According to spiritual teacher Phillip Moffitt, "the act of caring is the first true step in the power to heal" (as cited in Koopsen & Young, 2009, p. 1).

Self-compassion can be considered as honestly observing and exploring our behaviors and inner world with kindness, especially in relation to the most vulnerable parts of us. Thus, holding a compassionate container for ourselves is the beginning and ending point of mindfulness of our own experiences, and this compassionate presence prepares the ground for the ability to be more deeply present for the suffering of others. In my (LP) Yoga, Mindfulness and Social Work class, my students and I practiced a loving-kindness meditation, known as *metta* in the Buddhist tradition from which it originates, toward *ourselves*. Bringing our attention to our heart and to the feeling of having been loved unconditionally by someone in the past, we stated silently to ourselves, "May I be happy, may I be well. May I be free from fear and suffering." By engaging in the practice of sending well wishes to ourselves, we offer students a lifelong tool that they can use to strengthen their sense of self-compassion and self-care, which can nurture and sustain their abilities to engage in transformative social work practice.

EMPIRICAL FOUNDATIONS OF PEDAGOGIES OF HOLISTIC ENGAGEMENT

The premise of *holistic engagement*, in practice and in the classroom, is supported through findings in scholarly research. Current scientific research on the topics of mindfulness and neuroplasticity; environment and lifestyle-based health; and empathy, attention, and professional self-care point to the opportunity for social work educators to utilize these findings within the classroom as they prepare students to employ them in practice (Brown & Ryan, 2003; Turner, 2009). Infusing such scientific advances into the complexities of the current global context, educators have a transformative role to play in preparing professionals to practice in an integrative way. This requires an evolution beyond a modernist epistemology grounded in cognition and instead requires that educators affirm diverse ways of knowing that embrace the whole self. In turn, social workers become capable of bridging differences and adapting to changing environments in a dynamic manner. Transformative social work practice requires this kind of adaptive capability. Epstein (2003) describes the difference between competence and capability: *Competence* is what individuals know or are able to do in terms of knowledge, skills, and attitude, whereas *capability* is the extent to which an individual can adapt to changes, generate new knowledge, and continue to improve his or her performance.

Empirical Support for Holistic Engagement

Central to such an adaptive capability is the ability to be aware of self, environment, and others, which can be cultivated through mindfulness and other holistic practices, such as yoga and taiji. Mindfulness practices have been shown to be effective in developing a person's ability to adapt to changes and to adopt many of the characteristics of a holistically engaged social worker, such as presence and empathy (Brown & Ryan, 2003: Fogel, 2011). Epstein (1999) posits that mindfulness should be considered a characteristic of good clinical practice, describing how "mindfulness leads the mind back from theories, attitudes, and abstractions ... to the situation of experience itself, which prevents us from falling prey to our own prejudices, opinions, projections, and expectations" (p. 835). Turner (2009) notes that holistic/mindfulness skills training fosters clinician attention, affect regulation, attunement, and empathy, and it can assist in developing clinical sensitivity to even low levels of nonverbal attachment communication.

The research on the concept of neuroplasticity, the ability to change and heal the brain through intentional practices, and affirmed through studies of mindfulness and meditation, furthers the support for the power of the use of holistic engagement methods in practice and in the classroom (Davidson & Begley, 2012). Once thought to be fixed in early adulthood, neural networks actually demonstrate plasticity or the capacity for integration through reparative experiences (Siegel, 2007). Neurobiology research is also validating the clinical social work emphasis on the importance of the attuned therapeutic relationship in the change process (Turner, 2009).

Similarly, biological advances in the understanding of environmental influence on the epigenome, its role in activation of genes for chronic health conditions and mental illness, potentiate holistic engagement in empowering lifestyle changes to prevent or reverse chronic disease. Garland and Gaylord (2009) note the increasing call for performance-based measures of mindfulness, neurophenomenology of mindfulness, and measuring changes in mindfulness-induced gene expression because recent evidence demonstrates that mindfulness training increases antibodies and decreases proteins that lead to inflammation associated with numerous chronic health conditions. Finally, Brown and Ryan (2003) note that increases in mindfulness over time relate to declines in mood disturbance and stress across disease states, including clinical interventions with cancer patients.

Similarly, studies of yoga with a wide range of populations have shown its effectiveness on anxiety, depression, diabetes, high blood pressure, chronic pain, and so on (McCall, 2007). A recent systematic review of studies on the effect of yoga on stress found that 12 of 17 studies reviewed demonstrated positive changes in psychological or physiological outcomes related to stress (Sharma, 2014). Other mind–body practices that facilitate awareness, movement, and connection have been shown to be efficacious with a variety of populations, including older adults and at-risk youth (Koopsen & Young, 2009; McCall, 2007). The Evidenced-Based Taiji and Qigong Program has been shown to be effective for older adults in areas such as balance, immune function, emotional health, and spiritual well-being (Yang, 2008). Thus, the growing body of literature on the efficacy of mindfulness and mind–body practices provides a compelling evidence base for both holistically engaged social work practice and education.

Holistic Engagement in Social Work Education and Practice

Social work education and practice are mutually informing, recognizing that transforming students into prepared practitioners draws upon the same types of individual growth and realizations as do advances in practice. Thus, we argue that social work education must be a holistic effort that goes beyond the arena of the intellect, affirming all dimensions of the self, including the biopsychosocial–spiritual (Canda & Furman, 2010). We must teach students how to pay attention to the experiences they are having inasmuch as the ones they are observing in others and also to inquire with as much of themselves as possible in any given moment. Changing thinking and realizations of the mind alone allows a different rationale for action, but it only *partially* catalyzes the pre-requisites for human connection across differing beliefs, ideas, or worldviews.

A more integrative approach, instead, allows for connection across immeasurable differences through shared presence and "whole self" availability, actualizing the value of the dignity and worth of the person. Many of the contemplative and self-inquiry approaches utilized in practice settings have their roots in Eastern traditions and cultures, such as the yogic practices of India and the meditative practices of Buddhism; these traditions are now well-established in contemporary secularized techniques such as mindfulness-based stress reduction and the self-inquiry practices taught by people such as Eckhart Tolle (1999). They offer not only augmentation to clinical practice but also an invitation for social work educators to employ these methods in the classroom.

For example, presence and empathy are prerequisites for holistic social work practice—and are the very mechanisms through which social justice, advocacy, and action are transmitted. When the worlds of the professional and the client are immeasurably different, cognition alone cannot bridge the gaps because there is not enough context for translation of the worlds of the client into understandable languages of the professional. For example, home-based treatment experiences allow an enriched understanding of a client's experience even if dialogue remains the same. We teach social workers to *observe and note* what they see and how it likely influences various aspects of a client's experience so that, in a client's home, the social worker is fully *immersed in the family's context*—the sights, sounds, smells, intensity, temperature, and the safety offered there, or its absence. In addition, the social worker is *simultaneously immersed in his or her own reactions to that context*, including the level of noise, cleanliness, temperature, or the presence of many people just outside the door.

Indeed, we teach social workers to observe and note what they see and how it likely influences various aspects of a client's experience (Forrester, Westlake, & Glynn, 2012; Gerdes, Segal, Jackson, & Mullins, 2011). However, we do not generally emphasize recognizing the voluminous data that come from sensing and experiencing fully all in which we are immersed. We endure the discomfort in our necks and churning inside our abdomens when our work takes us to uncomfortable places. We try to ignore the reality and intensity of relief when certain clients cancel. We *manage* our experiences rather than *explore* them. We juggle, hold, and only occasionally let slip through all that our body, heart, and spirit are trying to communicate in service of doing our jobs.

Social workers need training to pay attention with their whole selves to their whole self in context. This is not easy to do. Traditional methods of social work education bring this level of detailed, attuned noticing to others, but they fail to acknowledge that this level of wholeness and complexity resides within the social worker (and, by extension, the social work educator) in that very moment also. Social work students need skill-building opportunities that will help them to understand these complexities and develop skillfulness in this type of paying attention. It does not come naturally to us as social workers; we tend to bring all of that energy and noticing to our clients or communities or causes. And yet, we also often fall very short of noticing the richness of the client's experience or the environment. Similarly, as educators we teach much about what to pay attention to while limiting the exploration of how we do this or how our students can practice doing this in classroom (Epstein, Siegel, & Silberman, 2008; Gerdes et al., 2011).

Research indicates that professionals require specific training to develop this capacity, where each part of the body is noticed in a systematic and nonjudgmental manner, and focus shifts away from the linguistic and conceptual to the nonverbal, imagistic, and somatic aspects of experience (Hick, 2009; Lynn, 2010; Siegel, 2007). Furthermore, Epstein (1999) notes the role of self-reflection in quality of professional practice, stating "this critical self-reflection enables physicians to listen attentively to patients' distress, recognize their own errors, refine their technical skills, make evidence-based decisions, and clarify their values so that they can act with compassion, technical competence, presence, and insight" (p. 833). We may teach our students the importance of self-reflection—encouraging *thinking* about responses, biases, culture, and motivations—and this is certainly important and not something we want to quit doing, but we tend not to teach *self-reflection of the whole self with the whole self.* We often remain in our minds and so do our students, leading to professionals who are developed well in one aspect of self through our traditional pedagogy, but the others linger largely untouched. In summary, it is difficult to engage in healing practices with clients and to transform the existing conditions in our communities when we are tuned into so very little of the data available to us. It is even more difficult to do this without being taught to do so.

Teaching Empathy, Practicing Presence

A primary value of social work, relationships offer individuals the connections needed to thrive and offer social workers the vehicle for fostering healing when thriving does not happen. Empathic relationships are a conduit for amelioration of damage to the self, as "clinician empathy is necessary for establishing the holding environment of the therapeutic alliance" (Turner, 2009, p. 99). Gerdes et al. (2011) proposed a model for teaching students empathy that includes activities that nurture and promote the activation of mirror neurons in difficult situations. In addition, they argue for the use of psychodrama and role playing, in addition to mindfulness techniques, to advance student empathy. Enhancing empathic capacity requires practice, specifically practicing intentional presence.

Epstein et al. (2008) state that mindfulness can be recognized and requires practice to become habitual, instilling qualities that patients value in their practitioners, such as attentiveness, interest in the clinical problem, interest in the patient as a person, clinical judgment, compassion, and presence. Improved clinical outcomes and more conscious and personally satisfying ways of practicing can be cultivated through mindfulness training. Similarly, other studies showed that through experiential mindfulness-based training, students described being more patient, aware, conscious, and able to focus (Christopher, Christopher, & Dunnagan, 2006). Krasner et al. (2009) found that provider participation in a mindful communication program was associated with short-term and sustained improvements in well-being and attitudes associated with patient-centered care. Thus, empathy serves as a vital pathway to social work connections and relies on complex aspects of engagement. Furthermore, its role in social work invites social work educators to consider not only how to enhance student understanding of these complexities but also to actively develop the students' associated skills of intention, attention, and presence.

Teaching Macro Practice, Engaging in Whole Self-Inquiry

Beyond clinical applications, this enhanced and integrative focus in education and practice has significant implications for community, organizational and institutional practice settings. Holistic social work education can advance social justice and cultural competence, as well as assist practitioners in responding to global realities in transformative and relationship-centered ways. Pyles (2014) has advocated for the use of transformative, reflective practice in community organizing, introducing a form of self-inquiry that encourages students/practitioners to ask the question, "Who am I in this moment?" Upon asking the question, the practitioner tunes into biopsychosocial–spiritual data in the self, others, and the context to gain more clarity and presence, arguably leading to more effective and sustainable practice.

Research actually supports such approaches: One study has shown that when social justice workers utilize contemplative practices to nourish themselves, their practice is more effective and sustainable (Duerr, 2002). Indeed, the idea of the contemplative organization is emerging in the nonprofit field, whereby contemplative practices are used as a technique and an organizing principle (Duerr, Nortonsmith, & Vega-Frey, 2004). For example, the US-based economic justice organization, Jobs with Justice, seeks to cultivate "organizational methods and processes that create a mindful, present, authentic, focused, honest, and listening organization that is more effective in achieving its mission" (Duerr et al., 2004, p. 5). Providing social work students, especially macro students, with opportunities to engage in such practices and build skills such as self-inquiry is more important than ever given the conflicts and cultural divides in community organizing contexts, social services cutbacks, and major organizational changes such as downsizing and mergers.

In addition to the use of contemplative practices in the macro classroom, educators are sharing the popular education techniques that originate from Latin American social movements, such as the drama exercises that come from the Theatre of the Oppressed (Boal, 1992; see also Freire, 1970; Harlap, 2014). These techniques have helped move communities toward greater clarity about oppression and how it manifests in the body, mind, heart, and spirit, revealing social justice solutions that originate from the most marginalized. Theater applications with social work students are most commonly used to teach clinical practice skills, but they also are used to enhance understanding and build skills related to oppression and social justice practice (Hafford-Letchfield, 2010; Lee, Blythe, & Goforth, 2009; Moss, 2000), including policy analysis skills and advocacy skills (Hafford-Letchfield, 2010). Thus, holistic educational practices in the macro classroom can bring the challenge of democratic participation into reality.

Teaching Social Worker Vitality and Effectiveness Through Self-Care

High rates of burnout, turnover, secondary traumatic stress, and other work-related problems can be addressed, in part, and prevented through the development of enhanced and integrated skills in social work and education (McGarrigle & Walsh, 2011; Vick-Johnson, 2010).

Christopher, Christopher, and Dunnagan (2006) developed a course teaching self-care through mindfulness practices—the application of yoga, meditation, and qigong—to counselors in training so that they could provide students with personal growth opportunities to prevent burnout. Students reported significant changes in their personal lives, stress levels, and clinical training. Another study that incorporated a self-care assignment into a social work class emphasized the importance of physical, social, and spiritual self-care as integral to the process (Moore et al., 2011). Furthermore, McGarrigle and Walsh (2011) conducted a study of a mindfulness and self-care program with human service workers and found that enhanced awareness through mindfulness practice was linked to increased self-care, which was linked to better services. The authors of the study note that "time, permission, and place of learning and practicing mindfulness-based activities" (McGarrigle & Walsh, 2011, p. 212) are necessary factors to make such mindfulness and self-care practices successful.

Stress may also harm professional effectiveness because it appears to negatively impact attention and concentration and to reduce a social worker's ability to establish strong relationships with clients, community members, and colleagues (Kinman & Grant, 2011). Findings indicate that several facets of self-care learning are important for social workers in training, including self-awareness, self-regulation or coping, and a balancing of self and other interests (Shapiro, Brown, & Biegel (2007). Ying's (2009) study demonstrated the importance of self-compassion in promoting perceived competence and mental health in social work students. Shapiro et al. (2007) suggest mindfulness-based training for mental health professionals results in significant increases in positive affect and self-compassion. Furthermore, mindfulness methods used in teaching result in student self-report of greater sense of control and adaptability of skills, as well as increased scores on empathy (Christopher et al., 2006). In summary, social worker self-care impacts the person and the practice of the social worker. These findings highlight the critical role for social work educators in preparing students to engage enough with themselves and their experiences to recognize and manage threats to well-being and attention and to learn to practice skills such as mindful presence and self-awareness during their educational programs.

OVERVIEW OF THIS BOOK

To employ holistic pedagogies requires attending to the emotions, body, mind, culture, and spirit in relation to the world around us. In addition to field internships, social work educators can and are engaging in creative pedagogy that allows students and educators (1) to inquire into and reflect on the emotions as a way to strengthen professional self-awareness; (2) to bring attention to the body as a source of oppression and liberation; (3) to analyze social problems and envision new transformative solutions; (4) to engage in cultural and artistic endeavors that facilitate deeper connections; (5) to develop more awareness and growth of the spiritual self; and (6) to learn in relationship with other students, diverse communities, and the natural world. Throughout the remaining chapters in this text, we join with innovative colleagues in social work education who are employing these and other methods toward the articulation of pedagogies of holistic engagement. Their work demonstrates the application of this shift in pedagogies at micro, mezzo, and macro practice levels, undergraduate and graduate levels, traversing the terrain of social work practice, theory, and policy.

The following are some of the key considerations that the educator–authors of this book explore:

- What role do holistic pedagogies play in developing social work practitioners who are able to respond to changing environments in creative ways?
- In what ways can holistic education deepen student connections with marginalized "others," including fellow students and clients/community members?
- What role can Freirian and popular education approaches from social movements play in transformative social work education?
- How can educators employ the arts (e.g., theater) to teach students about oppression and transformation?
- How are educators incorporating mindfulness-based and movement practices, such as meditation and yoga, into the classroom to facilitate learning

goals that embody a transformative approach to social work and human services?

- What challenges do holistic pedagogies pose in the contemporary university context as well as the current social work and human services practice environment?
- How does the construct and practice of "holistic engagement" enrich the learning environment for both learner and teacher?
- How does holistic engagement expand the roles, responsibilities, and ethical duties of educators?
- What practical methods can be employed to develop holistic engagement in educators and in students?

This book introduces social work educators to ideas and case studies concerned with the innovative concept of *holistic engagement*, including philosophical, empirical, and personal accounts. Indeed, these accounts are often at once ethnographical and auto-ethnographical as educators offer "thick descriptions" of course material, classroom spaces, and student reactions, as well as reports of their own inner and outer journeys (Geertz, 1973). New and seasoned social work educators interested in embodying integrative and transformative approaches to professional education in the classroom and beyond will find these essays particularly engaging and useful in their teaching and scholarship. The collection is organized into four parts, each designed to elucidate core aspects of holistic engagement in transformational social work education. Each section is briefly introduced next, followed by an overview of the chapters included in each section.

Part I: Theoretical and Empirical Foundations of Holistic Pedagogies lays the foundation for a conceptual framework that offers some parameters for what holistic engagement means. This is initiated through an analysis of macro and micro contexts that invite evolution of social work pedagogies. We (Loretta Pyles and Gwendolyn Adam) have set the stage for the volume in this chapter, beginning with an affirmation of what is beneficial about and a critique of current global contexts and traditional pedagogies, articulating the need for alternative ways of teaching in the current academic and human services climate. It has culminated with a review and analysis of the empirical and evidence-based literature around holistic practice and pedagogy, and it has established the need for an alternative educational conceptual framework, providing a launching point for author contributions. In Chapter 2, Adam and Pyles build on the foundations outlined in Chapter 1. The authors offer a conceptual framework for thinking about holistic engagement in social work education, informed by the science of mindfulness, popular education, and contemplative education models. The chapter sets forth core definitions of holistic engagement and introduces the skills and potential for its integration in the classroom. The authors affirm that social work education is a creative endeavor co-constructed by teachers and students requiring self-reflection toward the end of personal and social transformation.

Part II: Dialogue, Participation, and Critical Pedagogy explores the ways that honest communication is a prerequisite to self-knowledge and connections with others that are vital to holistic engagement. Contributions highlight vulnerabilities and assumptions at work in the classroom and their roles in limiting or shaping and enhancing professional development. Creative methods for catalyzing participatory action and dialogue that transforms vulnerability into empathy and understanding are presented through holistic approaches. In Chapter 3, Terry Mizrahi, Esperanza Martell, Kate Cavanagh and Allison Weingarten draw from an 18-year experience of teaching an undergraduate course that introduces students to community organizing. The authors reflect on this iterative experience that has sought to bring Freirian and feminist principles to the fore as a way to foster greater participation and empowerment of students. With a similarly strong emphasis on democratic social change, Steve Burghardt (Chapter 4) examines a 40-year teaching career discussing a process of encouraging mindfulness of discomfort in the classroom, whereby the ability to hold multiple truths and embrace vulnerability are seen as strengths in the co-creation of a democratic classroom and community. In Chapter 5, Benjamin Shepard offers a personal account of facilitating conversations that emphasize listening and supporting fellow undergraduate human services students as they navigate their own complex urban environments. The chapter explores how conversation, community engagement, and authenticity about one's whole life (including the instructor's) can transform human services' classrooms and practice. In Chapter 6, the final chapter of this section, Mette Christiansen introduces the hidden curriculum framework, which provides a lens to examine what occurs during the educational and professional socialization process; she draws from her experience using European social pedagogy and the Common Third, a shared activity used to strengthen a relationship, in an undergraduate human services program.

Part III: Theater, Arts, and the Human Spirit reveals the importance of experience in transcending the traditional limits of knowing, expanding to the full creativity and humanness of spiritual "whole self" learning as fundamental to holistic engagement. Through experiential methods of art, performance, and expression, the synergy of body, emotion, and spiritual experiences are developed as foundational for professional practice. Phillip Dybicz begins this portion of the collection in Chapter 7 by adding to the theoretical development of holistic education by introducing the postmodern theory of mimesis. Mimesis is a theory of human behavior that accounts for the creative power of human imagination, the power of heartfelt values, and the role of hope in kindling the human spirit in order to produce change. He applies these ideas to the social work classroom as a way to help develop the identity of students as social workers. In Chapter 8, Uta Walter brings her theater and social work educator backgrounds together to introduce "improvisation" as a concept central to the practice of teaching and learning social work. To this end, she explores how improvisation is part and parcel of what she considers good teaching and how principles and exercises from theater improvisation may prove useful for inspiring a playful, cooperative, and experiential form of learning that encompasses both creative and critical praxis. In Chapter 9, Juliana Svistova, Lara Bowen, and Meera Bhat explore how the use of Paulo Freire's techniques of social inquiry and Augusto Boal's activities traditionally associated with theater may be incorporated into social work education as a method of teaching to the holistic self. They seek to make a connection between a multisensory teaching model used for an undergraduate community and organizational theory class and recent advances in the neuroscience of learning. Finally, spanning the divide across this part of the text and the next part that focuses on mindfulness, David Pettie (Chapter 10) takes us through his journey of redesigning and implementing a master's level social work practice course, documenting a transition from its more traditional origins to a course emphasizing self-awareness and action methods based in psychodrama, sociometry, sociodrama, and mindfulness.

Finally, Part IV: Mindfulness and Integrative Helping develops the nexus of self and holistic engagement through contributions on mindfulness, self-awareness, and integration of self in teaching and learning. Threats and supports to grounded empathy and whole self data use orient the reader to how this holistic engagement approach shifts the sources of knowing explicitly and purposely to the self. Contributors present considerations in claiming and articulating holistic engagement methods in diverse and often skeptical settings. Chapter 11, written by Robyn Lynn, Jo Mensinga, Beth Tinning, and Kerry Lundman, begins this section with a critical reflection on often unspoken areas of philosophical and ethical ambiguity when incorporating mindfulness into social work education and training. Drawing from the journal entry of a student participating in a workshop on mindfulness-based relapse prevention, the authors use a structured critically reflective collaborative dialogue to explore this in the following contexts in order to identify the implications of this experience for social work: (1) introducing other ways of knowing into the social work profession; (2) mindfulness as a spiritual, natural, and cultural process; and (3) issues pertaining to cultural colonization or convergence. In Chapter 12, Salome Raheim and Jack J. Lu offer critical and reflective analysis of the operations of power that subjugate holistic practices and holistic education—ways of being, knowing, and learning that are outside of the dominant paradigms of the academy and biomedicine. In part, the chapter explores the authors' own journeys of "coming out" as holistic practitioners in the academy, specifically in social work education. In Chapter 13, Alyson Quinn offers an innovative social work practice model, the experiential unity theory and model, as an antidote to the culture's tendency toward disconnection and numbing. She shares her experiences with teaching this model in a social work class focused on advanced interviewing skills.

In the concluding chapter (Chapter 14), we (Pyles and Adam) integrate the previous chapters through the holistic engagement pedagogy framework; we do this by offering a matrix that cross-references the core dimensions addressed through holistic engagement and specific chapter content within the context of contemplative practices. We articulate the implications for social work pedagogy, offering recommendations for individual educators, curriculum development, social work educational leaders, and national accrediting organizational bodies, delineating opportunities and challenges. Thus, the chapter summarizes and integrates the previous chapters utilizing the holistic engagement framework and articulating a way forward, ultimately serving as a call to action for social work education.

CONCLUSION

Traditional social work higher education and its professional organizations, such as the Council on Social Work Education in the United States and similar organizations in other countries, are arguably drifting away from their values around the dignity and worth of a person, empowerment, and social justice. Instead, they are emphasizing outcomes-oriented, competency-based education, adopting market values, and silencing the inherent interconnections among mind–body–spirit–environment (Barter, 2012; Coates, 2003; Jones, 2010; Reisch, 2013). Despite this harsh reality, there are many social work educators who are making significant strides to address the global social crises we are facing by educating social work students about globalization (Gatenio Gabel & Healy, 2012; Pyles, 2014) and the environment (Coates, 2003; Jones, 2010), teaching mind–body skills in the classroom (Christopher et al., 2006; Lynn, 2010), and fostering self-care practices with students (Shapiro et al., 2007; Vick-Johnson, 2010).

In this chapter, we made a case for the need for pedagogies of holistic engagement as we have offered our own analysis of the current global context and presented empirically driven data that support holistic educational methods. It is clear that the need for pedagogies of holistic engagement that value the whole selves of educators and students within the context of the environment that surrounds them is urgent. Although social work educators are appropriately concerned with the effects that our teaching will have on future clients and communities, the words of Wendell Berry are also worth remembering: "The thing being made in a university is humanity" (as cited in Palmer & Zajonc, 2010, p. 1).

This text seeks to articulate and analyze the creative ways that social work educators are teaching holistically, in a manner that "respects and cares for the souls" of students (hooks, 1994, p. 13). It also puts forth the authors' conceptualization of a transformational model depicting how holistic pedagogies fit within current social work education. The holistic engagement model demonstrates how social work education can grow toward viewing the role of the educator and the classroom differently. Together, the empirical call for transformation, the conceptual model of holistic engagement, and the real-time examples by faculty who are already employing holistic pedagogies create a compelling path forward for social work education.

REFERENCES

Adams, F. (1971) Education for social change . . . and teaches every man to know his own. In Highlander Center (Eds.), *Highlander: An approach to education through a collection of writings* (pp. 65–75). New Market, TN: Highlander Center.

Adams, K. B., Matto, H. C., & LeCroy, C. W. (2009). Limitations of evidence-based practice for social work education: Unpacking the complexity. *Journal of Social Work Education, 45*(2), 165–186.

Australian Association of Social Workers. (2012). *Australian social work education and accreditation standards*. Retrieved from http://www.aasw.asn.au/document/item/3550.

Barbezat, D., & Bush, M. (2014). *Contemplative practices in higher education: Powerful methods to transform teaching and learning*. San Francisco, CA: Jossey-Bass.

Barter, K. (2012). Competency-based standards and regulating social work practice: Liabilities to professional sustainability. *Canadian Social Work Review, 29*(2), 229–245.

Boal, A. (1992). *Games for actors and non-actors*. New York, NY: Routledge.

Brown, K., & Ryan, R. (2003). The benefits of being present: Mindfulness and its role in psychological well-being. *Journal of Personality and Social Psychology, 84*(4), 822–848.

Canda, E., & Furman, L. (2010). *Spiritual diversity in social work practice: The heart of helping*. New York, NY: Oxford University Press.

Castells, M. (1999). *Information technology, globalization, and social development*. Geneva, Switzerland: United Nations Research Institute for Social Development.

Christopher, J., Christopher, S., & Dunnagan, T. (2006). Teaching self-care through mindfulness practices: The application of yoga, meditation, and qigong to counselor training. *Journal of Humanistic Psychology, 46*(4), 494–509.

Coates, J. (2003). Exploring the roots of the environmental crisis: Opportunity for social transformation. *Critical Social Work, 4*(1). Retrieved from http://www1.uwindsor.ca/criticalsocialwork/exploring-the-roots-of-the-environmental-crisis-opportunity-for-social-transformation.

Council on Social Work Education. (2012). *Educational policy and accreditation standards*. Retrieved from http://www.cswe.org/File.aspx?id=13780.

Davidson, R. J., & Begley, S. (2012). *The emotional life of your brain*. London, England: Plume.

Dominelli, L. (2003). *Anti-oppressive social work theory and practice*. London, England: Palgrave Macmillan.

Duerr, M. (2002). *Inviting the world to transform: Nourishing social justice work with contemplative practice*. Northampton, MA: Center for Contemplative Mind in Society. Retrieved from http://www.contemplativemind.org/admin/wp-content/uploads/2012/09/inviting.pdf.

Duerr, M., Nortonsmith, G., & Vega-Frey, J. (2004). *Creating the contemplative organization: Lessons from the field*. Northampton, MA: Center for Contemplative Mind in Society. Retrieved from http://www.contemplativemind.org/admin/wp-content/uploads/2012/09/contorgs.pdf.

Epstein, L., & Brown, L. B. (2001). *Brief treatment and a new look at the task-centered approach* (4th ed.). Boston, MA: Allyn & Bacon.

Epstein, R. (2003). Mindful practice in action (I): Technical competence, evidence-based medicine, and relationship centered care. *Families, Systems & Health, 21*(1), 1–9.

Epstein, R. (1999). Mindful practice. *Journal of the American Medical Association, 282*(9), 833–839.

Epstein, R., Siegel, D., & Silberman, J. (2008). Self-monitoring in clinical practice: A challenge for medical educators. *Journal of Continuing Education in the Health Professions, 28*(1), 5–13.

Forrester, D., Westlake, D., & Glynn, G. (2012). Parental resistance and social worker skills: Towards a theory of motivational social work. *Child and Family Social Work, 17*, 118–129. doi:10.1111/j. 1365-2206.2012.00837.x

Foucault, M. (1975). *Discipline and punish: The birth of the prison.* New York, NY: Random House.

Freire, P. (1970). *Pedagogy of the oppressed.* New York, NY: Seabury Press.

Freire, P. (2000). *Pedagogy of freedom: Ethics, democracy and civic courage.* Lanham, MD: Rowman & Littlefield.

Gambrill, E., & Gibbs, L. (2009). *Critical thinking for social work professionals: A skills-based workbook* (3rd ed.). New York, NY: Oxford University Press.

Garland, E., & Gaylord, S. (2009). Envisioning a future contemplative science of mindfulness: Fruitful methods and new content for the next wave of research. *Complementary Health Practice Review, 14*(1), 3–9.

Gatenio Gabel, S., & Healy, L. M. (2012). Introduction to the special issue: Globalization and social work education. *Journal of Social Work Education, 48*(4), 627–634.

Geertz, C. (1973). *The interpretation of cultures: Selected essays.* New York, NY: Basic Books.

Gerdes, K. E., Segal, E. A., Jackson, K. F., & Mullins, J. L. (2011). Teaching empathy: A framework rooted in social cognitive neuroscience and social justice. *Journal of Social Work Education, 47*(1), 109–131.

Germain, C. B. (1973). An ecological perspective in casework practice. *Social Casework, 54*, 323–330.

Germer, C. K. (2012). Cultivating compassion in psychotherapy. In C. K. Germer & R. D. Siegel (Eds.), *Wisdom and compassion in psychotherapy* (pp. 93–110). New York, NY: Guilford.

Gray, M., Coates, J., & Yellow Bird, M. (2010). *Indigenous social work around the world.* Surrey, England: Ashgate.

Greenspan, M. (2003). *Healing through the dark emotions: The wisdom of grief, fear and despair.* Boston, MA: Shambhala.

Hafford-Letchfield, T. (2010). A glimpse of the truth: Evaluating "debate" and "role play" as pedagogical tools for learning about sexuality issues on a law and ethics module. *Social Work Education, 29*(3), 244–258.

Harlap, Y. (2014). Preparing university educators for hot moments: Theater for educational development about difference, power and privilege. *Teaching in Higher Education, 19*(3), 217–228.

Hart, T. (2014). *The integrative mind: Transformative education for a world on fire.* Lanham, MD: Rowman & Littlefield.

Hawken, P. (2007). *Blessed unrest: How the largest social movement in the world came into being and why nobody saw it coming.* New York, NY: Viking Press.

Henderson, J. (2010). *An exploration of transformative learning in the online environment.* Paper presented at the 26th annual conference on Distance Teaching & Learning. Board of Regents of the University of Wisconsin System. Retrieved from http://www.uwex.edu/disted/conference/Resource_library/proceedings/28439_10.pdf.

Hick, S. F. (2009). Mindfulness and social work: Paying attention to ourselves, our clients and society. In S. F. Hick (Ed.), *Mindfulness and social work* (pp. 1–30). Chicago, IL: Lyceum.

Hocking, B., Haskell, J., & Linds, W. (2001). *Unfolding bodymind: Exploring possibility through education.* Brandon, VT: Foundation for Educational Renewal,

hooks, b. (1994). *Teaching to transgress: Education as the practice of freedom.* New York, NY: Routledge.

International Federation of Social Workers. (2012). *Global standards.* Retrieved from http://ifsw.org/policies/global-standards.

Jones, P. (2010). Responding to the ecological crisis: Transformative pathways for social work education. *Journal of Social Work Education, 46*(1), 67–84.

Kaufman, C. (2003). *Ideas for action: Relevant theory for radical change.* Cambridge, MA: South End Press.

Kelly, J., & Horder, W. (2001). The how and the why: Competences and holistic practice. *Social Work Education, 20*(6), 689–699.

Kinman, G., & Grant, L. (2011). Exploring stress resilience in trainee social workers: The role of emotional and social competencies. *British Journal of Social Work, 41*, 261–275.

Kirst-Ashman, K. K. (2012). *Introduction to social work & social welfare: Critical thinking perspectives.* Belmont, CA: Brooks/Cole.

Klein, N. (2002). *Fences and windows: Dispatches from the front lines of the globalization debate.* New York, NY: Picador USA.

Koopsen, C., & Young, C. (2009). *Integrative health: A holistic approach for health professionals.* Sudbury, MA: Jones & Bartlett.

Korten, D. (2006). *The great turning: From empire to earth community.* Bloomfield, CT: Kumarian Press.

Krasner, M., Epstein, R., Beckman, H., Suchman, A., Chapman, B., Mooney, C., & Quill, T. (2009). Association of an educational program in mindful communication with burnout, empathy, and attitudes among primary care physicians. *Journal of the American Medical Association, 302*(12), 1284–1293.

Kretzmann, J. P., & McKnight, J. L. (1993). *Building communities from the inside out.* Evanston, IL: Northwestern University, Center for Urban Affairs.

Lee, E. O., Blythe, B., & Goforth, K. (2009). Teaching note: Can you call it racism? An educational case study and role-play approach. *Journal of Social Work Education, 45*(1), 123–130.

Lee, M. Y., Ng, S., Leung, P. P. Y., & Chan, C. L. W. (2009). *Integrative body–mind–spirit social work: An empirically based approach to assessment and treatment.* New York, NY: Oxford University Press.

Lynn, R. (2010). Mindfulness in social work education. *Social Work Education, 29*(3), 289–304.

Macy, J., & Brown, M. Y. (1998). *Coming back to life: Practices to reconnect our lives, our world.* Gabriola Island, BC: New Society.

McCall, T. (2007). *Yoga as Medicine.* New York: Bantam Books.

McGarrigle, T., & Walsh, C. A. (2011). Mindfulness, self-care, and wellness in social work: Effects of contemplative training. *Journal of Religion & Spirituality in Social Work, 30*(3), 212–233.

Mezirow, J. (1991). *Transformative dimensions of adult learning.* San Francisco, CA: Jossey-Bass.

Mishna, F., & Bogo, M. (2007). Reflective practice in contemporary social work classrooms. *Journal of Social Work Education, 43*(3), 529–541.

Moore, S. E., Bledsoe, L. K., Perry, A., & Robinson, M. A. (2011). Social work students and self-care: A model assignment for teaching. *Journal of Social Work Education, 47*(3), 545–553.

Moss, B. (2000). The use of large-group role-play techniques in social work education. *Social Work Education, 19*(5), 471–483.

National Association of Social Workers (2009). Professional self-care and social work. *Social Work Speaks.* Washington, DC: Author.

Neff, K. D. (2012). The science of self-compassion. In C. K. Germer & R. D. Siegel (Eds.), *Wisdom and compassion in psychotherapy* (pp. 79–92). New York, NY: Guilford.

Palmer, P. J., & Zajonc, A. (2010). *The heart of higher education: A call to renewal.* San Francisco, CA: Jossey-Bass.

Pyles, L. (2014). *Progressive community organizing: Reflective practice in a globalizing world* (2nd ed.). New York, NY: Routledge.

Reisch, M. (2013). Social work education and the neo-liberal challenge: The US response to increasing global inequality. *Social Work Education, 32*(6), 715–733.

Ritzer, G. (2011). *The McDonaldization of society.* Thousand Oaks, CA: Sage.

Robbins, S. P., Chatterjee, P., & Canda, E. R. (2011). *Contemporary human behavior theory: A critical perspective for social work* (3rd ed.). Boston, MA: Allyn & Bacon.

Ross, D. (2007). Pursued by excellence: Rewards and the performance culture in higher education. *Social Work Education, 26*(5), 481–495.

Ryoo, J. J., Crawford, J., Moreno, D., & McLaren, P. (2009). Critical spiritual pedagogy: Reclaiming humanity through a pedagogy of integrity, community, and love. *Power and Education, 1*(1), 132–146.

Shapiro, S., Brown, K., & Biegel, G. (2007). Teaching self-care to caregivers: Effects of mindfulness-based stress reduction on the mental health of therapists in training. *Training and Education in Professional Psychology, 1*(2), 105–115.

Sharma, M. (2014). Yoga as alternative and complementary approach for stress management: A systematic review. *Journal of Evidenced-Based Complementary and Alternative Medicine, 19*(1), 59–67.

Siegel, D. J. (2007). *The mindful brain: Reflection and attunement in the cultivation of wellbeing.* New York, NY: Norton.

Tolle, E. (1999). *The power of now: A guide to spiritual enlightenment.* Novato, CA: New World Library.

Turner, K. (2009). Mindfulness: The present moment in clinical social work. *Clinical Social Work Journal, 37,* 95–103.

University at Buffalo. (n.d.). *Self-care starter kit.* Retrieved June 17, 2014, from http://social-work.buffalo.edu/resources/self-care-starter-kit.html.

Vick-Johnson, L. (2010). Transforming inspiration into practice: How an advanced certificate program in spirituality changed the clinical practices of its participants. *Smith College Studies in Social Work, 80,* 184–197.

Yang, Y. (2008). *Overview of best practices in Taiji.* Retrieved from http://www.chentaiji.com/articles/Best_Taiji_Practices_Aug_08.pdf.

Ying, Y. (2009). Contribution of self-compassion to competence and mental health in social work students. *Journal of Social Work Education, 45*(2), 309–323.

CHAPTER 2

A New Model for Holistic Engagement

A Foundation for Social Work Pedagogies

GWENDOLYN J. ADAM AND LORETTA PYLES

INTRODUCTION

In order to conceptualize a holistic and transformative education, we began in Chapter 1 with an analysis of the current global context in which social work education transpires, in relation to the existing evidence for holistic pedagogies. Recognizing any theoretical model for shifting aspects of social work education would need to include what we already do well, we have grappled with issues such as empathy, presence, and context in detail. We aimed to understand how we can at once recognize the limitless social justice needs beckoning, the barriers imposed by social and cultural structures, and our real human limits. Thus, we offer a provisional model that builds on traditional and emerging social work practices and pedagogies. Through this process, we include the necessary constructs to cultivate shared understandings of what it means to respond with our whole selves in dynamic contexts and how a new way of teaching, learning, and practicing is resonate with our core social work values and ethics.

In this chapter, we present a model for holistic engagement and articulate key terms, including holistic engagement and its four accompanying key skills. We offer examples from social work practice and pedagogy to illuminate these skills throughout the chapter. Then, we continue to articulate the ways that knowledge gleaned from holistic engagement, along with traditional forms of social work knowledge, can breed attunement and can develop what we call integrative capability. This is followed by an orientation to pedagogies of holistic engagement, foreshadowing what the authors in this text expand on in detail.

HOLISTIC ENGAGEMENT, ATTUNEMENT, AND INTEGRATIVE CAPABILITY

Our model fuses familiar terms in new ways, simultaneously considering the what, how, and why of social work education. We define the core construct, *holistic engagement,* as *an intentional practice of using the whole self to tune into and creatively respond within a dynamic, globalizing social work environment.* We recognize this idea as a *practice*—a developing, active, and malleable set of four skills: presence with the whole self, whole self-inquiry, empathic connection, and compassionate attention. Each of these is defined and discussed in detail.

To warrant a shift in social work education, holistic engagement and its four pillar skills are needed en route to something specific—that is, an enhanced way of practicing social work. This enhanced way of practicing requires the capacity to develop these skills in students and in ourselves as educator–practitioners. Our intentions are to examine how we can better prepare social workers to practice in a rapidly changing world—to engage, respond, and grow as they encounter the inherent and unique challenges that social work requires. Our resultant constructs include a refined definition of "attunement" so that it is understood as *a skillful means of using and synthesizing all sources of data/ways of knowing to inform and shape professional practice.* We also offer a new way of considering and assessing professional development, coining the term "integrative capability." Thus, we define integrative capability as *using the dynamic process of engaging fully, responding, and learning through dynamic attunement, experience, and context to continually improve professional practice.*

Defined and discussed in detail later, we combine these constructs—holistic engagement, attunement, and integrative capability (Figure 2.1)—with traditional social work education foci (i.e., competencies, theory, and research). This model for social work education incorporates many ways of knowing, sources, and types of data; global (i.e., both Western and non-Western) premises; a clear focus on the centrality of human relationships in context as the core of social work; and the developmental nature of professional practice in evolving and dynamic environments.

We view the retention of current, effective social work education efforts as essential, continuing to support student immersion in the history, theories, research methods, and skills development currently practiced in social work education. Immersion in these "traditional" social work topics, infused with grounded theoretical knowledge, along with existing and evolving evidence, fortifies a robust platform for building an enhanced model for social work education. From these traditional social work education foci, our model adds holistic

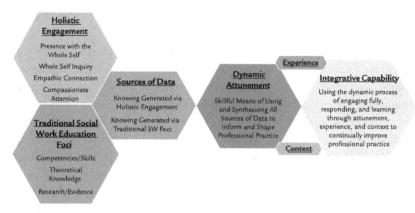

Figure 2.1:
Holistic Engagement, Dynamic Attunement, and Integrative Capability.

engagement, relying on its four skills, to produce more comprehensive ways of knowing and human transformation, which become the sustenance for attunement. Attunement, as a skillful synthesis of these ways of knowing, via experience and context, results in the lifelong development of social workers' integrative capability.

TRADITIONAL SOCIAL WORK EDUCATION FOCI

Traditional social work education incorporates knowledge, values, and skills, currently understood as building competencies. In the United States, this is upheld by the 2012 Educational and Policy Accreditation Standards of the Council on Social Work Education (CSWE), and it is upheld in Canada by the 2014 Commission on Accreditation Standards of the Canadian Association for Social Work Education (Canadian Association for Social Work Education—l'Association Canadienne pour la Formation en Travail Social, 2014; CSWE, 2012). As articulated in Chapter 1, social work has historically focused on theoretical knowledge, including such approaches as ecological systems theory and the person-in-environment perspective (Robbins, Chatterjee, & Canda, 2011). Social work theories try to explain human behavior, the nature of relationships, and the interactions people have with each other in their environment. Furthermore, social work education prioritizes the strengths perspective, acknowledging the role of individual, family, and community strengths in overall functioning and managing challenges (Saleebey, 2012). Research is of clear concern, especially with the focus during the past two decades on evidence-based practice and practice-informed research, in social work education (Grinnell & Unrau, 2010). These three areas—competencies, theoretical knowledge, and research—currently combine to construct what it is to be a competent social work professional. These are the areas we currently emphasize in social work education as we prepare students to practice successfully in the field.

However, although there are enhanced accountability activities for demonstrative competencies upon graduation, something is clearly missing in social work education. At a recent social work conference in Canada, we presented the main components of this model; one of the audience members who identified with our critique and embraced our approach bemoaned the current state of social work education, with great emotion, "We are taking the heart out of social work!" Many others around her nodded in agreement; the grief in the room was palpable. Despite increasing emphasis on field-based practice as the "signature pedagogy" of social work education, and the attendant competency-based evaluations of students' practice in the field, there are ongoing disparities in social work service and outcomes (Larrison & Korr, 2013). Despite values-driven, social justice-prioritizing, ethically informed efforts, we often still fall short in basic human connections. We believe that this has less to do with the content of social work education and more to do with the paradigm in which it is taught, specifically pedagogies that fail to develop human connections, self-reflection, and the whole person. As well, social work practice and interventions tend to preserve the status quo of society, offering initiatives that alleviate poverty rather than working toward changing social systems and perpetuating oppressive hierarchies between social workers and clients, as well as between management and staff (Reisch, 2013; Van den Berk & Pyles, 2012). We argue that this is, at least in part, because we fail to democratically engage students in their education. Democratic education demands students' (and educators') whole self participation, invites authentic exploration and analyses of the current social system, and encourages students to examine their roles in perpetuating and/or changing it (Mezirow, 1991).

Furthermore, we still see increasing rates of stress-related illnesses, vicarious traumatization, and burnout among social workers (Grant, Kinman, & Baker, 2013; Kim, Ji, & Kao, 2011; Sanchez-Moreno, Roldan, Gallardo-Peralta, & Lopez de Roda, 2014;). We continue to see, sometimes in our graduates and sometimes in ourselves, that there are limits to our current skills; there are limits to the well-intended competencies and to the knowledge that we bring, even with all of the research we now routinely access. There is still something missing.

HOLISTIC ENGAGEMENT

Holistic engagement gets at the heart of the unpredictability of connection with people in complex environments, where sometimes a thousand things can go wrong without anyone noticing or saying anything, and sometimes a thousand things can go right and we have no idea how we have just done well. At times, we seem to bring the exact same skills and efforts, yet we experience such diverse outcomes. Thus, the practice of holistic engagement can right the course of a profession in need of direction.

By definition, holistic engagement is *an intentional practice necessary to use the whole self to tune into and creatively respond within a dynamic global- izing social work environment.* Crucial to a full understanding of holistic engagement, the notion of it being a practice versus a destination informs the dynamic and fluid nature of how we engage ourselves and others in any given moment. Beyond just presence, empathy, or active listening, which are current hallmarks of social work practice (Gair, 2013; Grant, 2014), holistic engage- ment fuses these and other concepts into an active, participatory *process*—a moving, breathing, developing practice that empowers a new understanding of the dimension of connection and an integrative way to learn, intentionally and continually.

We conceptualize holistic engagement as fusion of core social work skills into an active practice and identify a malleable set of four skills: presence with the whole self, whole self-inquiry; empathic connection, and compassionate attention. Taken together, these four skills are at once the foundation and ever- changing internal systems at work when social workers engage holistically. In addition, they are the skills that social work educators are seeking to develop in the classroom through a variety of pedagogies toward transformative social work practice. Holistic engagement is not necessarily a practice that develops on a predictable trajectory. A tool to strengthen integrative capability, holistic engagement creates pathways and takes us on the journey. The following detailed exploration of each skill creates the living mosaic of possibilities and unpredict- ability holistic engagement offers.

THE FOUR KEY SKILLS OF HOLISTIC ENGAGEMENT PRACTICE

The definitions and discussion that follow begin the unfolding understanding of the four skills of holistic engagement practice. For each skill, we present a work- ing definition, followed by discussion of its application and integration into social work practice and education.

Skill 1: Presence With the Whole Self

At the heart of holistic engagement practice is showing up fully for what is, with an expanded sense of self we refer to as the whole self. Presence with the whole self is composed of three dimensions:

1. The experiences of the individual's body, mind, heart, culture, and spirit
2. The individual's awareness of and interaction with the historical and current physical, social, and energetic environments

3. How the individual's own experiences and awareness interact with other individuals' experiences and awareness

Holistic engagement practice relies on an expanded notion of the self. It redefines the self as a whole self, meaning it includes not just our thoughts but instead is concerned with ways of knowing beyond our thoughts. Larrison and Korr (2013) highlight how the process of social work practitioner development "involves the whole self—the accumulated integration of one's background, experiences, relationships, connections, and interpersonal characteristics" (p. 201) and champion the role of critical-reflective-thinking processes within learning experiences. We consider this expanded set of sources of knowing as the whole self, a rejection of the modernist dualism and rationalism that bifurcate mind and body and that privilege the mind as the primary source of knowing. This whole self includes the sources of our body, mind, heart, and spirit, and it is consistent with increasing social work emphasis on adding "spirit" to the biopsychosocial model (Senreich, 2013). Broadly considered, the whole self includes all of our physical experiences (body), thoughts (mind), emotions (heart), cultural lens of our own upbringing (culture), along with the meaning and creativity (spirit) we bring to it. It also includes how we are manifesting all of these things happening simultaneously—how we are experiencing the feelings or emotional states, our memories, and physical sensations, such as stress or discomfort or desire. It is at once using the catalyst (i.e., what we experience) and the response to the catalyst (i.e., how we notice and react to what we experience) as an integrated source of knowing.

Our conceptualization of the self goes even a step further, through our efforts to put forth an approach that embraces interconnectedness, and looks beyond the encapsulated physical and egoic self. For systems thinkers and deep ecologists, who view all things (plants, animals, air, humans, etc.) as interconnected, the Western, modernist idea of the self is limited and problematic (Robbins, Chatterjee, & Canda, 2011). Gregory Bateson (2000) referred to this conventional notion of the self as one of "the epistemological fallacies of Occidental civilization" (p. 491). Thus, for our model, the whole self includes the world and others around us.

For a very concrete example of being present with the whole self, we share the following fictitious example of a social work educator named "Rebecca" who is racing around her office trying to get ready to teach her class. Gathering her notes and books, she walks quickly and forcefully past her desk and, *bam,* she smacks her foot on the corner of the desk. As she experiences a surge of pain, she becomes furious at her desk and herself—for running late, again, and for being clumsy. With toes throbbing and time marching on toward class, she starts to cry, burdened by the weight of the stress in her life and how overwhelmed she feels. She reacts to the physical pain, the sense of judgment toward herself, the building emotions, and the haunting familiarity of this experience.

"I've been here before," she thinks, "I always do this to myself—wait until the last minute and then have to race." Her spirit sinks as the impact of her patterns become clear. She takes a breath and gets back to her preparations, limping and realizing she might not get to exercise this afternoon after all. The fusion of the physical, emotional, and mental, the dawning of the existential, each is its own unique catalyst, as well as a fused part of this complicated experience of a moment. The stubbing of the toe can trigger existential learning, if one has the capacity to be present with multiple aspects of the self in such moments. Practicing paying attention to the fullness of these sources of information and the integrated whole of how they all fit together are key sources of vital information on how we are doing, what we are doing, and how we are responding to our situation. Taken together, this is showing up with our whole self. In order for social work educators to teach such whole self presence to students, who will in turn practice this skill in the field, social work educators must begin with their own experiences.

Our notion of the whole self also includes something beyond what we tend to think of as ourselves, something we tend to consider being separate from ourselves—the physical and social environment we are in, as well as our reactions to it and our biases about it. In a sense, this separateness is understandable because we have the capacity to think about these aspects of the environment and of ourselves, meaning that we can look at these and so somehow they are not actually ourselves. Holistic engagement expands that to look at how our interaction with the energy of the physical, social environment and biases are equally important ways of knowing. In learning about our interactions, we essentially consider the ways we have responded to and continue to respond to our cultural experiences. These responses reciprocally impact all other parts of us, as we react physically, mentally, and emotionally to the minutia of immersion in complex environments and our idiosyncratic and, oftentimes, habitual and uninterrogated responses. If our biases toward the context, the physical and social environments, impact how we respond in any given situation, they become imperative to navigate if we want to bring our whole selves or understand what is getting in the way.

We also consider our knowledge of the history and politics of the place we are in at any given moment, recognizing the powerful impact close connection with the environment has on who we are and on our and others' actions. Considerations of context may include environmental, political, economic, or social factors of the physical location or institution we find ourselves in. As we consider how our interface with the context is also impacted by our interactions with and the meanings we ascribe to it, we begin to glimpse how these expanding notions of self combine to create the complex, dynamic self we bring into the social work classroom at any given moment. In the previously discussed example, Rebecca remembers that she had asked maintenance to help her move the desk because it had been sticking out for some time and tripping her up regularly. Due to the governor's new budget cuts, the university administration released main-tenance staff, making it more difficult for them to attend to all of the work orders. Thus, the context and politics that she is working in become relevant data to her as she seeks to learn from the fullness of the experience.

Finally, understanding presence with the whole self includes understand-ing how an individual's own experiences and awareness interact with another's experience and awareness. To the complexity described previously happening internally and in relationship to the energetics of the environment, we add the awareness and experience of these to the recognition that any other person with whom we interact while all of this is happening in us is also experiencing his or her own unique, complex, and fused experience of these. It requires at once pay-ing attention to ourselves and holding a space necessary to receive another who is doing the same.

In our example, as Rebecca heads for the office door, a student walks in with a question about an upcoming assignment. The student notices the shoe off, smeared makeup, and emotional state and says, "Oh, I'm so sorry, I'll come back later, or I'll just see you in class. I'm really sorry." Rebecca is aware of her own embarrassment and feels her face flush. At the same time, she notices that the student's body language reveals nervousness and awkwardness, as she pulls away from Rebecca. Rebecca has the capacity to respond to the student by telling her that she was having a difficult moment, having just stubbed her toe, and that she agreed that it would be better to connect later, perhaps during the class break. And, she adds, "You don't have to be sorry," remembering this student's particular habit of perpetually apologizing for herself. The example clearly depicts how each person was aware of multiple ways of knowing and paid attention to the other in a shared context. Showing up to one's fullest poten-tial in a given moment with the whole self means recognizing that the student's responses were just as complex as Rebecca's. By cultivating whole self presence, Rebecca was able to offer herself authentically and honestly to the student, and she was able to respond to the student in a way that was helpful and appropriate for the moment.

Being present with the whole self involves all aspects of ourselves as well as our interactions with the environment, its history and the meanings we place there, along with the infinite ways that our complex reactions to all of these interface with others immersed in their own process. When we can, albeit imperfectly, hold all three of these in awareness intentionally—self, other, and environment—we have the greatest access to our whole selves. Showing up fully with this expanded sense of self takes significant practice. While portions of this skill building are a part of social work education (primarily through attention to the internal experi-ences of the social worker), holistic engagement practice relies on this enhanced notion of presence with the whole self as one of its four pillar skills, inviting and challenging us to enrich our education to meet the complexity of the exponential ways of knowing in which we exist.

Skill 2: Whole Self-Inquiry

Learning to know these multifaceted aspects of the whole self requires *interest* in learning about these multifaceted aspects of the whole self. Given both the complexity and fluidity of the whole self experiences from moment to moment, context to context, interaction to interaction, learning to pay attention—to seek information from these parts—must be intentional, consistent, and honest in order to be meaningful. As such, we conceptualize the second skill in holistic engagement practice as "whole self-inquiry," defined as *a lifelong authentic and deliberate learning about all aspects of the whole self.*

This second important area of holistic engagement views self-inquiry in an expanded way. Whereas existing social work education efforts, including the CSWE Competency 2.1.1 in the United States, emphasize the importance of self-reflection and self-awareness as a core responsibility of the professional social worker, our expanded view of the whole self requires an evolution in how self-inquiry unfolds throughout one's career. The inclusion of heart, mind, body, and spirit as part of the self, in addition to one's interactions with the energetics of the context and the interaction with others whose whole selves are equally as complicated, invokes a level of searching, treasure hunting for the valuable nuggets of the whole self experience.

It is our belief, reinforced through the existing literature (McGarrigle & Walsh, 2011; Mishna & Bogo, 2007), that there is currently limited information on how students are being taught to pay attention. Teaching psychosocial assessment serves as a primary skills development focus in social work education; we teach students how to pay attention to specific areas of a person's life and functioning. However, curricula teaching deliberate, systematic exploration of the students' and clients' whole selves, as conceptualized previously, are not routinely taught in social work.

Self-inquiry, focused on the nuances of the whole self, is multidimensional in nature, requiring the simultaneous sensing of self, in environmental context, and in relation to others. In addition, the process of inquiry at this level of detail impacts the experience itself, leading to additional shifts in the moment's information to be gleaned from the whole self. This interdependent and iterative process invites an exquisite attention that can only be as meaningful as it is honest and authentic, and it is only as applicable as it is ongoing. Whole self-inquiry is cultivated through a lifelong developmental practice, experimenting repeatedly with paying attention to as many areas of the expanded self as one is capable of in any given moment.

Social workers have long recognized the importance of identifying biases, of looking at cultural issues and how they impact communication and connection. Indeed, there is a wealth of literature on the subject of culturally competent social work practice and teaching such skills in social work classrooms (Jani, Pierce, Ortiz, & Sowbel, 2011). However, we surmise that this process we are pointing to cannot be adequately addressed without specific, classroom-based experiences to develop self-inquiry skills. Larrison and Korr (2013) emphasize the role of purposeful experiences to foster students' "sense of who they are as developing practitioners" (p. 202). Furthermore, they advocate that "competent social work practice necessitates that emerging practitioners recognize—through self-awareness, critical reflexivity, and analytical thinking—how they make use of who they are is an integral component of one's practical and purposeful action" (p. 200).

If we aim to develop whole self-inquiry as a practice, we need to be able to model whole self-inquiry during the educational process, inasmuch as we demonstrate active listening, or utilize the strengths perspective. If our ultimate ability to engage with our whole selves is incumbent upon this inquiry, faculty and students, supervisors and supervisees must be engaged in this lifelong process. Indeed, with recent rhetorical focus on social work as a human rights profession, such a focus can only be effective when social workers continually interrogate the inner and outer terrain of their field of practice.

Developing whole self-inquiry requires that the practitioner set an intention to engage in and sustain the practice, which necessitates a strong support system along with plenty of reminders. This is why the role of the social work educator can be so powerful for students, as we can provide opportunities for them to engage in activities that may bring up discomfort and help them to develop skills for noticing and reflecting. In this regard, Rodriguez-Keyes, Schneider, and Keenan (2013) report that faculty efforts to support student self-inquiry further enhance student motivation and engagement with "essential social work curriculum by expressing care and helping students feel known in the classroom" (p. 785).

The practice also requires a tremendous amount of compassion for oneself, for as we go deeper into these practices, we tend to see things about ourselves that we may not like very much; or we may have a belief that we are not very good at the practices (Neff, 2012). The practice involved in whole self-inquiry is often uncomfortable, requiring curiosity and honesty. However, herein lies the richness of the learning, the potential growth. As we learn to tolerate and then appreciate the wealth we learn when we deliberately inquire across all of these aspects of self, we can create the spaciousness and safety required for students to initiate their practice within the classroom setting. Indeed, the connection between student and teacher becomes the venue through which the requisite safety for students, their peers, and the teacher is created.

Skill 3: Empathic Connection

Empathy is a touchstone of social work and a hallmark of the compassionate social worker (Grant, 2014). Indeed, we thrive on empathy and its power to uphold healing connections with others. As such, we prioritize relationships as the mechanism through which healing happens. However, the complexities of developing and practicing empathy are only beginning to be understood and researched (Germer & Siegel, 2012). Grant (2014) highlights that definitions of empathy are typically limited to the ability to "adopt the perspective of others in order to understand their feelings, thoughts, or actions. Such definitions do not adequately reflect the realities of empathy in the social work context or recognize its potential to lead to distress" (p. 338). Similarly, Gair (2013) points to the need for additional research on how empathy is developed via the social work class-room, beyond just an emphasis on its importance.

As we continue to build our understanding of holistic engagement, we add the skill empathic connection as a logical correlate of presence with the whole self and whole self-inquiry. Through our previous discussion, we underscored the centrality of the student–teacher connection in creating needed safety to explore unknown parts of the whole self experience.

If one can bring whole self presence to connect with another in healing rela-tionships, one likely will experience an exponential impact of that connection. If one brings only parts of oneself, the impact is limited also.

Holistic engagement relies on an unconventional definition of empathy, termed *empathic connection,* defined as *with whole self presence, intentionally join-ing with the experience of an other (individual, family, community, environment) to bear witness to that experience, while recognizing the limits of that joining.* This type of empathy requires an active engagement, and it includes recognizing one's own experiences in the moment, one's reactions to those experiences, in addition to the data we receive concerning the experiences of the other. It further requires being aware of what we are experiencing while being aware that another person is experiencing something, perhaps some version of what we sense and imagine, or perhaps not. While holding our experience in mind, we also imagine our-selves in their experience and responding as *ourselves,* based on our actual cop-ing style, but we also imagine ourselves, to the extent that we can, in *their* lives and responding how *they* would. Empathy requires all of these dimensions to be considered and to integrate all of them in a split-second opportunity to connect with another. Familiarity with this nuanced level of complexity for empathic connection is generally beyond what is currently included in traditional meth-ods of social work education (Gerdes, Segal, Jackson, & Mullins, 2011; Miehls & Moffat, 2000).

Our conceptualization of empathic connection includes some consider-ation we do not typically address relative to empathy and social work education. Specifically, *empathic connection includes recognizing our own limits.* This is impor-tant in a number of ways, especially as we are looking at the expanded whole self. We can recognize that there are places, experiences, feelings, and complexities that other people experience that we simply cannot. We honor that our experi-ences differ from others, that the history that we have experienced, our knowledge of the places, all of our individual character traits, ideas, and emotional states, are as unique as we are. Indeed, our social locations are often vastly different and for a white middle-class social worker, for example, to presume to know what it feels like to be an immigrant of color is narcissistic and only perpetuates the oppression we are working to transform. We come to the realization that connecting accurately and understanding every single one of those dimensions, given how many permutations there are potentially of each of our own complexities, is a highly unlikely connection.

This does not take away from our capacity for caring or our capacity for compassion. However, we do have to be able to hold that recognition of how complex we are as individuals and how complex they are as individuals and know that those realities affect how deeply and how completely we can connect. Grant (2014) reports findings that suggest that students require support to develop their empathic and reflective skills to "effectively manage the emotional demands of practice" (p. 338) and further recommends the use of experiential learning, including mindfulness for this purpose. We have to grapple in the educational realm with how well we can fundamentally prepare students to connect, to experience empathy, on all of those different levels while holding a commitment to the professional boundaries that are needed in the relationship.

Skill 4: Compassionate Attention

Contemplative traditions (e.g., mindfulness) embrace practices of paying attention without judgment (Barbezat & Bush, 2014; Hick, 2009). This is a particularly difficult prospect for social workers, who work in a value-laden profession that asks us to judge situations and critique injustice. We instill in ourselves and our students a commitment to social justice that extends both from our core values and what is codified in our respective national-level codes of ethics. It is our job as people and as social workers to respond to social justice issues anytime we experience them, whether or not we have a direct role in addressing those or intervening in any way at that particular time. Although this contributes to our values-driven profession by ensuring the enduring commitment to not settling for things as they are but, rather, advocating for all to experience the dignity and worth they have as beings, it does catapult us out of noticing, into action, whenever we are moved by injustice.

We recognize that we tend to abandon the moment as it is as soon as we actively try to change it. As our social justice/human dignity tripwires engage, we go from noticing, and therefore pausing long enough to connect fully in that moment, to immediately, perhaps reactively, wholeheartedly changing the moment. The balance quickly becomes very tricky because while we are reacting, we are not present in the same way. We may become caught up in our own reactions—physical, emotional, and mental—and cease to be available in the same way to connect fully with another's experience. While we react, we abandon them, ever so slightly, ironically, as we make plans for making the situation better for them. As well, this abandonment may happen due to our own intense need or habitual pattern of judging and changing the moment to be something more comfortable. Holistic engagement is concerned with connecting fully, so this abandonment issue presents a problem. If our advocacy for human rights is tethered to our recognition of and reaction to social injustices, how do we pause this reactive judgment and stay present? Is it even possible to be with others fully in their experience during the most difficult times?

Our notion of compassionate attention is built on the premise that connecting during those intense moments is a needed skill in holistic engagement and a pathway to ensuring that we remain with our clients before we act, if even just for a moment. It requires that we experience the moments, especially the outrageously unjust ones, as they are before we act upon them. Thus, we define *compassionate attention* as *seeing things as they are with a discerning capacity to suspend action or judgment en route to uninterrupted presence.*

Our work in social work education needs to include ways that students can expand in this capacity, recognizing that we, as educators, likely have not been formally supported to practice compassionate attention ourselves. Creating and strengthening "discerning capacity" for social workers to pay attention without action invites an important shift in education. It requires that we develop the skillfulness to be able to notice what is happening without changing it, rejecting it, judging it, or acting on it, when what we are seeing is uncomfortable or is not aligned with our value system.

I (GA) often tell my students that when they sign up to be social workers, they are signing up for paying attention pretty continually to social justice issues. Is it possible to be an ethical social worker and pay attention without judgment? We recognize that the importance of paying attention without judgment really lies in the elements of distraction. Because it is often in our judgment of what is or is not happening that we direct the most interest, we lose sight of what we initially experience. As social workers, having our own reaction to what we hear, including our judgment and horror in response to injustices that we see, is crucial. The way these tend to shake us up at a cellular level often bears witness to the depth of our understanding and empathy.

Paying attention without ever getting to judgment is likely not something we want to, nor is it possible to, train our students to do. However, there is a point at which that distraction of our judgment, or outrage, or motivation to action can distract us from being fully engaged in what is happening. As we are developing the notion of holistic engagement, we need to have a way to support social workers' capacities to be present in the moment in a way that includes their own judgments and emotional reactions as part of the moment but that helps them not to get too distracted by and swept up in these emotional reactions. We focus on welcoming the emotions and not shutting them down because they tend to provide important information for us to use. If we are going to be attuned professionals, we need access to this full reaction.

Part of our job in social work education is to think about what methods we can utilize to help our developing colleagues to pay attention to what arises for them in challenging or unfamiliar situations, hold them well and yet, in the moment, create a kind of spaciousness and full experience of what is happening without the need to change it *right then*. Central to this practice of holistic engagement is the ability to "let go." This means letting go of our grip on our own beliefs and emotions as well as letting go of our often tightly held egoic identities as professionals or social change agents.

Creating situations in the classroom in which students have opportunities to practice "letting go" can be useful en route to sustaining compassionate attention. When I (LP) ask my Community Building students to stand up and come into a physical pose that embodies their understanding of oppression, they are forced to confront feelings of discomfort with putting their bodies out there for everyone to see. Also, in my (LP) Yoga, Mindfulness and Social Work class, I ask students to engage in improvisational dance as a way to integrate and release after a very emotional exercise we do. Improvisational dancing in a university classroom requires a tremendous amount of "letting go" of inhibitions. Many students report how difficult it is to do but how liberating it felt once they did it. There are always a couple of students who are just not able to bring themselves to do it.

Consider the experience of being in the classroom early in the semester, inviting the new class of students to briefly introduce their own pathway to choosing social work as a profession. Hesitantly, a student of color raises her hand and begins to tell her story: "I always dreamed about becoming a nurse; I dressed up like a nurse every Halloween; I told my grandmother that I would be a nurse, as she was dying in the hospital when I was in high school, and she said 'of course you will, dear.' I worked hard, graduated with honors, and applied to the nursing program with qualifying grades, what I thought was a strong essay, and my dreams squarely intent on enrolling. I received a conditional acceptance, pending interview." She pauses. "I was told by the program director that students from 'my kind of high school' tend to struggle in the program and she thought social work would be a better fit for me, the demands weren't as difficult and she thought I'd have more 'peers' in that profession. I guess I got on the pathway to social work because the nursing program didn't like the way I looked." As we learn of this injustice in enough graphic detail to bring both tears and chills, imagining the pain, the reality that the perpetrator is a fellow educator, we may launch into rage, and sadness, and perhaps disdain for the program director. We may immediately condemn the behavior, cite the grotesque violation of educational and human rights, and reassure her that she deserved so much better. Meanwhile, here sits this student, frozen in silence that followed her spoken trauma, taking the risk to tell her real story. Are we present for the fullness of this student's experience? Perhaps we miss the uniqueness of the persons with whom we are working and *their* response because our responses are so big that they fill up the room. Our job as social work educators is to design ways for students to start to break down and inquire into the minutia of those split seconds to see the richness of their experience and to see what could be getting in the way of compassionate attention.

In our work as educators, we strive to create ways to show our students how eventually they might be able to pay attention and to sit with discomfort that might be generated *without acting*. However, it is not prudent to throw our students into the deep end without a life raft just as we would not want a new social worker to be thrown into a very challenging case alone. Sometimes, students are just not ready yet to sit with discomfort without acting, so we give them opportunities to process it in a way that is more comforting, by journaling about it, discussing it with peers, or working through difficult content through some form of artistic expression. Sitting with discomfort is difficult to trust because we often draw our energy and substantive responses from the very *judgment we experience versus the experience itself* (Van Soest, 1996). As well, our culture values both judgment and action and puts less value on nonjudgment and non-acting, so what we are teaching is in a sense countercultural, or what Buddhists refer to as "against the stream" (Levine, 2007).

In our model, we shift the contemplative emphasis from noticing without judgment to noticing without *action*—at least for a little while. If we can stay grounded in what is happening, including what is happening inside of us, our picture is much more comprehensive than if once the fireworks of judgment spark inside we abandon our client and the moment in search of justice. Compassionate attention involves all of these happening simultaneously, leaving no one's experience out. The discernment needed to do this in the moments of highest intensity presents us with a grand and challenging invitation to ourselves, our students, and for social work education.

Summary: Four Skills for Holistic Engagement

Holistic engagement requires four key skills: presence with the whole self, whole self-inquiry, empathic connection, and compassionate attention. Through this beginning discussion of the four skills, we establish the interdependent relationships between presence with the whole self and the continual learning vital to it. We note the challenges and opportunities of empathic connection, along with the growing awareness of the limits to our connection and to our presence, both impacted by various types of attention. As we continue to explore the model, these four skills empower holistic engagement, which combines with more traditional aspects of social work education, including competencies, theoretical knowledge, and research, to represent the broadest and deepest foundation for ways of knowing in social work. The sources of data in these robust ways of knowing invite social workers to expand access to a fuller, deeper, and more expansive repertoire for knowing, experiencing, and utilizing complex information and experiences to enrich the reach and impact of social work.

It is also important to remember that there are indeed limits to our ability to tune in and be present and integrate. Of course, there is so much happening in any given moment that it is impossible to be fully aware; we are not omniscient beings. There are always limits to the data points that we can become aware of. As well, we are very conditioned in our culture to distract ourselves and disso-ciate, especially when we are confronted with unpleasant experiences to which we find ourselves aversive (Hick, 2009). Thus, one finds that in a culture of dis-tracted people, mindfulness is tiring work and, in fact, not something that we can force, as it is impossible, if not counterproductive. Sometimes, it is more skill-ful to focus out rather than focus in; we may actually find that it is more skillful and compassionate to ourselves to intentionally take a step back and check out. Such skills can be taught in relation to self-care practices as students discover and perhaps rediscover ways to self-soothe, including the activities that help them to feel comforted when they are overwhelmed by sensory input (McGarrigle & Walsh, 2011).

SOURCES OF DATA/WAYS OF KNOWING

Based on the premises discussed so far, the two broad sources of data for social workers include two types of "information": (1) knowledge generated through the four skills of holistic engagement and (2) traditional social work data (compe-tencies, theoretical knowledge, and research or other evidence). We view access-ing both of these as being crucial to the kind of attunement that leads ultimately to integrative capability. Although a primary focus in this text is on introduc-ing holistic engagement and expanding social work pedagogy to develop these associated skills, we include this conceptual reference to accessing both ways of knowing because alone, either is incomplete.

Currently, most of social work education prioritizes professional competen-cies, theoretical knowledge, and research (Barter, 2012; Reisch, 2013). We aim to add holistic engagement as the other key source of data necessary to practice social work. The greatest level of attunement in social work invokes a skillful means of using all of the ways of knowing and being able to synthesize that data in a dynamic and new way. When being fully engaged with all those aspects, includ-ing the expanded self's intention and capacity to remain present while inviting the other to do the same, combines with the full richness of traditional social work education, the gateway to integrated capability is opened. It is through this fusion of all of our ways of knowing that social workers can participate in the full complexity of being human while maintaining the awareness, knowledge, and skills to do so ethically and effectively. If we can learn to bring the expectation of accessing both broad sources of knowing, we offer our students and ourselves access to the breadth and diversity of our full humanness along with the acuity, precision, and responsibility of professional social work.

If our intention is to practice with and on behalf of humans, this call to practice with ever expanding access to our own humanness makes sense, and it comes with its own new kinds of vulnerability. As we confront the limits of our existing pedagogies, which often minimize or neglect the intricacies of knowledge generated through holistic engagement, we also open ourselves to the limitless permutations we find when we actively engage with our whole selves.

DYNAMIC ATTUNEMENT

We seek a conduit to meeting clients and the systems in which they live accurately, minimizing distractions or misunderstandings, and seeking transparency with regard to preconceived notions. As we traverse the key components of our model, we purport it is the efficacy of dynamic attunement that routes our work to the places we need to go or to the places we end up going, recognizing that sometimes these are not the same. We define *dynamic attunement* as *skillful means of using and synthesizing all sources of data/ways of knowing to inform and shape professional practice*. Attunement of this dynamic sort requires action to seek out all the ways of knowing and the creativity to piece it together into a mosaic for ongoing professional growth. Dynamic attunement includes access to one's intuition, changing responses internally and in others, and adaptation to the incredible unpredictability that unscripted moments can bring.

Some notion of attunement has always been a part of social work practice and is particularly emphasized in supportive communication between parents and children (Fogel, 2011). We emphasize in our conceptualization of attunement the imperative of accessing all the ways of knowing through holistic engagement and traditional sources. Once we access all of this data intentionally, we have terrific information, but in order to utilize it to empower our practice we must catalyze its fusion, allowing the full impact of all we can learn from and with another to collide with all we can learn within and from ourselves. Facilitating this requires intention, skill, and practice.

Once we access all of this data from others, the environment, and from ourselves, attunement generates it to become something greater, with all of the potential for empowerment and change that we seek as social workers. Attunement is a proactive practice that takes energy for synthesis and integration—to retain the meaning and to safeguard the relationship. Although unique, each source of knowing is crucial to the whole, no less valuable than any other. Echoing the importance of this integration, Larrison and Korr (2011) emphasize how signature pedagogies of social work "involve the integration of practitioner knowledge, performative action, and awareness that emphasizes the development of the professional self" (p. 194).

INTEGRATIVE CAPABILITY

Our intention is to offer a potential road map or pathway that can integrate our full human experience, with multiple ways of knowing, and use all of this moment by moment to ultimately practice social work authentically. Although there is always significant suffering to be faced in social work practice, the possibilities in each of us for human growth are remarkable. If we could be fed by our challenges in the moment, nurtured by our mistakes, and reassured by what we do not fully understand, we could experience the most challenging aspects of social work as the platform for lifelong growth and development, thwarting burnout and affirming self-care in ways that the current social work literature on these subjects is only beginning to touch upon (Christopher et al., 2006; Lee, Ng, Leung, & Chan, 2009). Furthermore, Tsang (2013) highlights the crucial role of the integration needed for constructive use of social work students' life experiences, education, and work experiences and encourages social work educators to facilitate integration as part of pedagogical practices. This is especially important as we educate students of color, lesbian, gay, bisexual, transgender, and queer (LGBTQ) students, and other students of marginalized backgrounds so that these students can bring their whole selves to the class and their practice, thereby embodying the aspirations of democratic and transformative social work practice.

The attunement we described previously, the integration of all sources of knowing, from both holistic engagement and traditional sources of information, to inform and shape professional practice, sculpts a trail for just this type of ongoing evolution. As we synthesize and integrate all these ways of knowing from and about ourselves and others, we use it in ever-changing ways each time we engage again. Each experience we integrate changes us, gives us something different to draw from the very next time. If in that perpetually evolving engagement we could use all of the ways of knowing to actually *improve* professional practice, *all* of our moments offer the potential to cultivate professional growth.

We created a new construct to capture this process, termed *integrative capability*, defined as *using the dynamic process of engaging fully, responding, and learning through attunement, experience, and context to continually improve professional practice*. Integrative capability relies more on self-awareness than professional ideals; it goes beyond competencies. It is not a set arrival point; integrative capability is a process that is as dynamic as the nature of practice, and it needs to be developed during professional education and continue to be developed throughout lifelong learning.

Integrative capability fundamentally impacts the responsibilities of the social work educator in that we are now invited into this same type of professional growth, of using all of these sources of data synthesized through attunement to actually improve our practice. This includes our development as educators, as we invite students into a different kind of observation and ourselves to a different level of accountability for modeling the skills of holistic engagement in the name of integrative capability. Whereas competence, our current standard, means being able to do something well, capability means we continue to be competent *and* we take the fullness of each experience and funnel that into improved practice. Setting integrative capability as a new standard of professional accountability will require two fundamental shifts in how we prepare professional social workers. First, social work educators must embody, model, and teach the skills of holistic engagement, attunement, and integrative capability. Second, social work pedagogy must include student exposure to, and practice of, holistic engagement skills, attunement, and integrative capability. In the final section, we begin to articulate what these pedagogies can look like.

PEDAGOGIES OF HOLISTIC ENGAGEMENT

When we contemplate this idea of holistic engagement, it is clear that we are talking about a fundamental shift in what happens in the classroom. We believe everything will look, feel, and seem different if we actually shift toward these new pedagogies. The authors of this volume are offering their perspectives on and experiences with holistic pedagogies, articulating complementary theoretical grounding, as well as giving readers a sense of what such a classroom actually does look and feel like. Here, we offer some guiding orientation to social work and human service educators seeking to engage with their students in the development of holistic engagement skills and integrative capability.

We do not purport that there is a perfect way to teach holistic engagement. This is why we are referring to *pedagogies* of holistic engagement in the plural form rather than singular. We, and the authors in this volume, are aiming in holistic engagement education to cultivate an *ongoing experience of oneself* in the classroom and field, with opportunities to engage with other people in context. This process invites students into multidimensional experiences of the mind, body, heart, and spirit in relation to culture, geography, and politics.

Even our most challenging moments in the classroom can offer unparalleled learning if the intention includes engaging ourselves and our students directly in the full experience of the intensity. For example, consider teaching about human rights and the social worker role in advocacy in the current global context. As the issue of the role of military intervention in global humanitarian efforts emerges in a class discussion, students become polarized, with three students vehemently asserting the need for preemptive military action to prevent injustices and three students equally strong in their unequivocal opposition, citing civilian casualties, diversion of federal budget dollars away from a domestic agenda toward a military one, and the complex cultural considerations.

A handful of other students start shifting uncomfortably as the arguments escalate, becoming increasingly personal. "How can you even consider yourself a social worker if you won't do anything in your power to prevent genocide?!?" "How can *you* pretend that bombing villages with innocent children in them is okay as long as you kill a terrorist or two?!?" "Well, maybe you'd feel differently if some of your family members were over there!" Students start to look toward the front of the room in silent pleas to the instructor for interruption as the tension grows. "My sister *is* over there right now trying to help those people with the rest of her brave comrades!" "You're even worse, then! My dad was killed in his first tour of duty when I was in middle school! How can you want more families to go through this grief?" as the student dissolves into tears and runs out of the room. The instructor stands stunned, wondering how things went so quickly from the promise of a rallying discussion of human rights to a classroom crisis. Options for regaining *control* swirl, and she decides to invite students to take a 10-minute break. The room remains silent as students hesitate to move.

With holistic engagement, we are asking students and ourselves to enter such moments, fully and deliberately, tension and all. Instead of seeking to maintain control, we seek being and noticing all along the way, inviting experience even before all of the thinking and debating. With an awareness of the whole self, the instructor instead could enter into the discussion inviting students to notice their breathing, their hearts beating, and to consider how a planned discussion of the complex world events will engage them all with different paths having led to the discussion. She could invite the students to think about their own experiences historically, bringing to mind images from the news, their own personal or famil-ial experiences, and then write the words "human rights," "genocide," "soldier," and "social worker" on the board, asking students to silently spend 30 seconds each focused only on one word, paying attention to anything they feel. Silence is palpable. No one moves; no one talks. Together, students and teacher spend 2 full minutes engaged with these words. A few students look distracted, shift-ing uncomfortably. Two students' eyes pool with tears. When the time is up, the instructor asks, "What did you experience?" One by one, students start to share what they have noticed. "It was hard to stay focused." "I kept picturing kids scared and confused." "I felt sad." "It made me really anxious." "I missed my sister; she's over in Afghanistan now." "I miss my dad—he was killed in Iraq 11 years ago—I was in seventh grade." Students look toward the front of the room; several are in tears, as is the instructor. "This is a powerful moment we are sharing," she says, "Let's stay with it as we consider human rights and social work." Thus, pedagogies of holistic engagement embody a shift from the predictability of planned discus-sions to the unpredictability of full human experience, with the express intention of transforming ourselves together as a pathway to transforming the social con-structions and social systems that oppress and marginalize us.

Pedagogies of holistic engagement *create opportunities* for students and instructors to include their bodies, minds, emotions, and uniqueness in the experience of learning, as we participate in the democratic and creative prac-tices required to realize our social change aspirations. These pedagogies expand dimension, action, and the importance of paying attention to the minutia, internally and externally. The activities to catalyze these are the lessons themselves, not just the pathway to the richer discussions. The focus is on doing, being, experiencing, and noticing together inasmuch as it is on information exchange. A successful class session becomes one in which multiple dimensions of experience have been engaged and explored intentionally rather than one in which much content has been covered. The instructor role evolves into co-creator of experience and guide of integrating these experiences with and for her students and with and for herself.

Thus, the subjective experience of the educator becomes just as important as that of the students in any kind of pedagogy of holistic engagement. Such mindful attention can be a welcome antidote to the sense of disembodiment and disconnection that is perpetuated in our modernist, globalized culture and in social work education. We often offer our minds and our limited experience of emotions to the classroom, but we seldom attune into the minute changes in our bodies or spirits as we conduct our classes. We might notice and try to tune into similar shifts in our students. A pedagogy of holistic engagement depends on bringing all of ourselves and cultivating the fullest presence of others as often as possible and integrating what happens. Toward this end, at the beginning of all of my (LP) classes, the students and I engage in 5 minutes of quiet meditation together, the goal of which is to help us all settle in and tune into ourselves, each other, and our environment. In this meditation, I often ask students not only to notice phenomena in their own bodies and minds but also to invite their awareness into the space and people around them—for example, the sounds and smells. Bringing in such practices to academia, a traditionally disembodied patriarchal setting that embraces positivism and the empiricism of science, requires tremendous courage. I remember being terrified the first time I did this, as the voices in my head said, "They're going to hate this," "I'm going to get fired," and "This is so awkward." Although sometimes these voices still appear, I have learned that students are hungry for such opportunities, and most of them actually tend to savor the stillness.

We believe that there are many existing and still to be developed pedagogical innovations and practices in social work education that can facilitate the integrative capability we are seeking. Examples include various experiential activities, service learning, group processes, creative and other forms of artistic expression, and practices of numerous contemplative traditions, such as walking meditation and qigong. Whereas we have presented the scholarly literature on such pedagogical innovations, as well as shared some of our own experiences and perspectives, the authors in this volume utilize these and many other pedagogical innovations as they and their students are transforming social work classrooms throughout the world. It is clear that holistic and transformative education is not the easy way out. Indeed, we, as educators, may find ourselves in situations in which we must confront our own fears and comfort levels with whole self engagement, negotiate support from academic administration, deal with the demands of outcomes-based education that requires us to cover so much content, and integrate these methods into online courses. Our and these authors' experiences remind us that these obstacles can be overcome through creativity, commitment, and compassion for everyone involved.

CONCLUSION

Holistic engagement emerges as a vital connection to the continual professional growth and personal development that integrative capability offers. As we contemplate how to reach for these in ourselves and our students, we can use holistic engagement both as a tool in social work education and the collection of essential skills to be developed and practiced throughout professional practice and education. Through this process, educators and students can embody the kind of transformational social change agenda that social work so desperately needs to embody right now. We invite each of us to explore and experience fully the stories, activities, and lessons shared in the following chapters, recognizing that the more we do this, the more we open ourselves to the unparalleled richness of this moment to nurture us personally and professionally.

REFERENCES

Barbezat, D., & Bush, M. (2014). *Contemplative practices in higher education: Powerful methods to transform teaching and learning.* San Francisco, CA: Jossey-Bass.

Barter, K. (2012). Competency-based standards and regulating social work practice: Liabilities to professional sustainability. *Canadian Social Work Review, 29*(2), 229–245.

Bateson, G. (2000). *Steps to an ecology of mind.* Chicago, IL: University of Chicago Press.

Canadian Association for Social Work Education—l'Association Canadienne pour la Formation en Travail Social. (2014). *Commission on Accreditation Standards.* Retrieved from http://caswe-acfts.ca/commission-on-accreditation/coa-standards.

Christopher, J., Christopher, S., & Dunnagan, T. (2006). Teaching self-care through mindfulness practices: The application of yoga, meditation, and qigong to counselor training. *Journal of Humanistic Psychology, 46*(4), 494–509.

Council on Social Work Education. (2012). *Educational policy and accreditation standards.* Retrieved August 29, 2015 from http://www.cswe.org/Accreditation/2008EPASHandbook.aspx

Fogel, A. (2011). Embodied awareness: Neither implicit nor explicit, and not necessarily nonverbal. *Child Development Perspectives, 5*, 183–186.

Gair, S. (2013). Inducing empathy: Pondering students' (in)ability to empathize with an Aboriginal man's lament and what might be done about it. *Journal of Social Work Education, 49*(1), 136–149.

Gerdes, K., Segal, E., Jackson, F., & Mullins, J. (2011). Teaching empathy: A framework rooted in social cognitive neuroscience and social justice. *Journal of Social Work Education, 47*(1), 109–131.

Germer, C. K., & Siegel, R. D. (Eds.). (2012). *Wisdom and compassion in psychotherapy.* New York, NY: Guilford.

Grant, L. (2014). Hearts and minds: Aspects of empathy and wellbeing in social work students. *Social Work Education: The International Journal, 33*(3), 338–352.

Grant, L., Kinman, G., & Baker, S. (2013). "Put on your own oxygen mask before assisting others": Social work educators' perspectives on an "emotional curriculum." *Journal of Social Work, 13*(4), 400–418.

Grinnell, R. M., & Unrau, Y. A. (2010). *Social work research and evaluation: Foundations of evidence-based practice* (9th ed.). Oxford, England: Oxford University Press.

Hick, S. F. (2009). Mindfulness and social work: Paying attention to ourselves, our clients and society. In *Mindfulness and social work* (pp. 1–30). Chicago, IL: Lyceum.

Jani, J., Pierce, D., Ortiz, L., & Sowbel, L. (2011). Access to intersectionality, content to competence: Deconstructing social work education diversity standards. *Journal of Social Work Education, 47*(2), 283–301.

Kim, H., Ji, J., & Kao, D. (2011). Burnout and physical health among social workers: A three-year longitudinal study. *Social Work, 56*(3), 258–268.

Larrison, T., & Korr, W. (2013). Does social work have a signature pedagogy? *Journal of Social Work Education, 49*(2), 194–206.

Lee, M. Y., Ng, S., Leung, P. P. Y., & Chan, C. L. W. (2009). *Integrative body–mind–spirit social work: An empirically based approach to assessment and treatment.* New York, NY: Oxford University Press.

Levine, N. (2007). *Against the stream: A Buddhist manual for spiritual revolutionaries.* New York, NY: HarperCollins.

McGarrigle, T., & Walsh, C. A. (2011). Mindfulness, self-care, and wellness in social work: Effects of contemplative training. *Journal of Religion & Spirituality in Social Work, 30*(3), 212–233.

Miehls, D., & Moffatt, K. (2000). Constructing social work identity based on the reflexive self. *British Journal of Social Work, 30*(3), 339–348.

Mishna, F., & Bogo, M. (2007). Reflective practice in contemporary social work classrooms. *Journal of Social Work Education, 43*(3), 529–541.

Neff, K. D. (2012). The science of self-compassion. In C. K. Germer & R. D. Siegel (Eds.), *Wisdom and compassion in psychotherapy* (pp. 79–92). New York, NY: Guilford.

Reisch, M. (2013). Social work education and the neo-liberal challenge: The US response to increasing global inequality. *Social Work Education, 32*(6), 715–733.

Robbins, S. P., Chatterjee, P., & Canda, E. R. (2011). *Contemporary human behavior theory: A critical perspective for social work* (3rd ed.). Boston, MA: Allyn & Bacon.

Rodriguez-Keyes, E., Schneider, D., & Keenan, E. (2013). Being known in undergraduate social work education: The role of instructors in fostering student engagement and motivation. *Social Work Education: The International Journal, 32*(6), 785–799.

Saleebey, D. (2012). *The strengths perspective in social work practice* (6th ed.). New York, NY: Pearson.

Sanchez-Moreno, E., Roldan, I.-N. F., Gallardo-Peralta, L. P., & Lopez de Roda, A. B. (2014, September 2). Burnout, informal social support and psychological distress among social workers. *British Journal of Social Work.* doi:10.1093/bjsw/bcu084

Senreich, E. (2013). An inclusive definition of spirituality for social work education and practice. *Journal of Social Work Education, 49*(4), 548–563.

Tsang, N. (2013, January 11). Knowledge, professional and practice integration in social work education. *British Journal of Social Work.* doi:10.1093/bjsw/bcs195

Van den Berk, C., & Pyles, L. (2012). Deconstructing neoliberal community development approaches and a case for the solidarity economy. *Journal of Progressive Human Services,* 23(1), 1–17.

Van Soest, D. (1996). Impact of social work education on student attitudes and behavior concerning oppression. *Journal of Social Work Education,* 32(2), 191–202.

PART II

Dialogue, Participation, and Critical Pedagogy

CHAPTER 3

Learning in Community

A Transformative Healing Educational Model for Teaching Community Organizing

TERRY MIZRAHI, ESPERANZA MARTELL,
KATE CAVANAGH, AND ALLISON WEINGARTEN

INTRODUCTION

"Because of the language barrier, I do not talk in [other] class[es] unless circumstances demand me to speak," a student states in her Introduction to Community Organizing (C.O.) course evaluation. The student proceeds to outline the profound impact of "the instructor's teaching style in which the fellow classmates were involved in the active learning process" and the effect that the study of various materials written and published by various experts had on her personal, academic, and pre-professional development. She concludes her reflections on the course by describing how her role at her volunteer internship as part of the course went from translating documents for community outreach to becoming an active member of the organization working alongside her fellow South Asian community members "fighting for justice and equality on behalf of immigrant workers."

This is just one of the many stories from the course, an interdisciplinary Introduction to Community Organizing, which has been offered to approximately 800 undergraduate students from 1995 to 2014 at Hunter College of the City University of New York, a public university. The students, mostly women, have come from diverse racial and ethnic backgrounds. Their ages have ranged from 18 to older than 50 years. Many have work and family responsibilities in addition to being full-time students.

The C.O. course is based primarily on Freire's pedagogical theory (Freire 1970/2000, p. 69), which argues that teachers are students as well as educators and students are teachers as well as learners. Esperanza Martell worked with Terry Mizrahi, Chair of Community Organizing, Planning & Development at Silberman School of Social Work at Hunter College, on designing and then teaching the course since its inception, based on Martell's knowledge and experiences applying Paulo Freire's and feminist/womanist methodologies to adult education. Martell's role has also included mentoring a graduate community organizing teaching assistant each semester from the Silberman Master of Social Work (MSW) program who is assigned to this undergraduate learning program as a field placement while developing herself personally and professionally. Working together, the graduate assistant and Martell, as the instructor, participate in a supervisory "parallel process" in which they are constantly engaging the issues, skills, and theory taught in the class and building their relationship with each other, the undergraduate students, and the partnering community organizations (Kadushin, 1985; Williams, 1997).

This chapter models Freirian principles of teamwork through co-authorship because it was co-written by Martell and Mizrahi, along with Kate Cavanagh and Allison Weingarten, the latter two who were graduate teaching assistants in the C.O. course in 2006 and 2013, respectively. As in the classroom instruction, "parallel process" was involved in the writing of this chapter, for which we utilized the organizing skills and theory taught in the course throughout our interactions (Kadushin, 1985; Williams, 1997). In this chapter, we first provide an overview of Freire's principles that were central to our C.O. course. Then, we describe the course and include examples of "education for liberation" that it utilized as well as concepts of "holistic engagement." The perspectives of established Freirian and feminist/womanist educators and practitioners, the co-authors, the graduate teaching assistants, and alumni from the course are integrated. Lastly, both successes and challenges in applying Freirian education in the course, including grading and evaluation, are described.

The course applies Paulo Freire's idea of "education for liberation," which means a process that supports students as they analyze their knowledge and behaviors that maintain current social conditions and that challenges them to act as agents of progressive social change (Freire, 1970/2000; Pyles, 2013). Freire's concepts and techniques provide a framework for social work education that employs "holistic engagement," or utilizing students' minds, bodies, and hearts as a complement to academic writing and research. Education for liberation is a humanizing process through which students and instructors begin to break down barriers that separate people within society and connect with people authentically through shared humanity. hooks (1994), a student of Freire, believes that the concept of a radical love for humanity is at the core of social justice. Education for liberation supports students in cultivating that love and engaging love as a tool for community organizing and social change. "The heart of education as a practice of freedom is to promote growth. It's very much an act of love in that sense of love as something that promotes our spiritual and mental growth" (hooks, 1994, p. 13). hooks' framework also encompasses a feminist/womanist perspective that includes holistic principles such as self-care, process as part of the product, and the integration of the private and public spheres (Harris, 2010; Hyde, 2008, 2012; Joseph et al., 1991). We chose these approaches for our teaching because they challenge us to put into practice in the classroom these concepts and techniques that we also employ in our community work and with each other as a teaching team. It is important as instructors to incorporate our whole selves in this process, bringing our compassion, empathy, creativity, and politics into our teaching in order to best serve our students and our profession. Martell locates her rationale for teaching using a healing educational model in her biography conveyed as follows:

> My family was part of the forced economic migration of Puerto Ricans to the USA in the 1950s. I confronted and dealt with all the ills of being a poor working-class Afro/Taina in a racist, classist, and patriarchal society. My life's struggles are what make me a human rights peace activist, educator, community organizer, trainer, life-skills transformative coach, mother, and poet/artist. I have been organizing and teaching for over 40 years. The staying power of love and my life experiences are what have touched, moved, and inspired me to continue teaching from a place of love, joy, and compassion. As someone who learned to read, write, analyze, and organize through direct experience with Paulo Freire's Education for Liberation as well as womanist perspectives gained from the literature by women of color, I am committed to the liberation of all peoples.

THE CASE FOR POPULAR TRANSFORMATIVE EDUCATION IN SOCIAL WORK

The National Association of Social Workers (NASW) calls on professionals to "promote social justice and social change" (NASW, 2008). The Council on Social Work Education (CSWE, 2008) also states in its Educational Policy and Accreditation Standards that "social work's purpose is actualized through its quest for social and economic justice, the prevention of conditions that limit human rights, the elimination of poverty, and the enhancement of the quality of life for all persons" (p. 1). Therefore, social work higher learning institutions are mandated to educate social change agents who work to improve social conditions.

However, debate as to whether social work graduate programs challenge students to be instruments of transformation or educate students to maintain the current social conditions extends well beyond the university hallways into journal articles, book chapters, and scholarly debates (Mizrahi & Dodd, 2013; Pyles, 2013). In their analysis of MSW students' social activism and their perspectives on social work goals, Mizrahi and Dodd call on social work programs to "balance 'consumer demands' with the outcomes (schools) want to achieve," such as "producing social workers who value social justice and progressive social change" (p. 595).

Both NASW and CSWE assert that a social worker's vocation is to eradicate oppression, discrimination, poverty, and their root causes (CSWE, 2012; NASW, 2008). To be sure, there are progressive educators and students within social work education who have created innovative programs that pursue social activism using Freire and other radical social work scholars and practitioners (Hager, 2012; Jones, 2009; Sakamoto & Pitner, 2005). However, Rothman and Mizrahi (2014) note that the social work profession as a whole has drifted toward an imbalance between clinical and macro practice, and they call on the profession to "recalibrate," stating that "social problems require complex and sustained intervention at all levels of social work practice" (p. 91). Hager asserts that social work has neglected Freire, although his ideas could support social work educators and practitioners struggling with how to work within the nonprofit industrial complex. This idea of the nonprofit industrial complex is explained by Samimi (2010, p. 17): The "system forces nonprofits to professionalize, wherein they must focus on maintaining their funding sources rather than fulfilling their mission" to develop best practices to reduce poverty and economic inequality (Reisch, 2013a, 2013b; Sims, 2014).

Social workers have been criticized by some who claim they are trained to deliver goods and services that unwittingly perpetuate discrimination and unequal power dynamics that oppress clients (Reisch & Andrews, 2002; Specht & Courtney, 1994). In the past, much of social work education focused primarily on fixing problems using a deficit model rather than building on their strengths. Alternatively, social workers including Saleebey (1992), Cohen (1999), and others have promoted a strengths-based approach to working with clients at micro and macro levels (Brun & Rapp, 2001; Cohen, 1999; Early & GlenMaye, 2000; Graybeal, 2001). Others promote more radical social work frameworks (Reisch, 2013b), which include critically assessing practice methods with oppressed populations and promoting the profession's integrity to its mission through its pedagogy of teaching (Jones, 2009).

As a popular educator and academic in the 1970s, Paulo Freire wrote extensively on pedagogy and teaching people to respond to oppression by societal institutions and policies. In his classic work, *Pedagogy of the Oppressed* (1970/2000), he maintains that a person must first analyze the foundations of discrimination in order to unravel unjust systems. Freire radically proclaims that people such as social workers work "with," not "for," marginalized communities in order to restore their shared humanity from the dehumanizing forces of oppression. For social workers, entering into solidarity or standing alongside their clients to change their situation is required to address the social and political environments that are negatively impacting people (Freire, 1970/2000, pp. 47–49). In developing the C.O. course, while the originators agree with Freire that students cannot just learn in an ivory tower, it was challenging to build a course that embodied that idea. Early on, it was the students who felt empowered enough to insist on incorporating an assignment that connected them directly with communities so that learning could happen experientially.

According to Freire (1970/2000, p. 154), the "oppressors" control over "the oppressed" seeps into all aspects of a society, including education, social service provision, and government, where people are conditioned to perpetuate structures of inequality. Schooling is the first place where people typically encounter training in social norms. Freire terms traditional education "banking education" because teachers impart knowledge to students that is sanctioned through society and upholds social norms. In Freire's view of the "banking" system of education, students act like receptacles and internalize the information they are given without questioning the information's meaning and relevance. In this model, students and teachers do not recognize that they are also educating each other, and they also are not aware that they are the ones with the power in this situation. He believes that all the stakeholders—students, teachers, and the system itself—are impacted by banking education, and that it also taints our daily interactions with each other that reflect systemic inequalities. Sue et al. (2007) use the term "microaggressions" to describe the daily, mostly unintentional words or behaviors that communicate internalized racial stereotypes about a group (p. 273), to which we add a focus also on class and gender (Cannon, 1990).

Investigating these power dynamics, Freire established "popular education" as a method for teaching adult literacy to peasants in Latin America. Freire's (1970/2000) pedagogical theory today has been applied worldwide in social work, universities, primary and secondary schools, and in adult education (Miller, Brown, & Hopson, 2011; Sims, 2014). It redefines traditional teacher–student relationships that are dominant in Western culture (Freire, 1970/2000):

> Through dialogue, the teacher-of-the-students and the students-of-the-teacher cease to exist and a new term emerges: teacher–student with students–teachers. The teacher is no longer merely the-one-who-teaches, but one who is himself taught in dialogue with the students, who in turn while being taught also teach. (p. 80)

He challenges the traditional notion of teachers possessing all knowledge and students needing teachers to give them information. Rather, his model reminds educators that everyone, even the students, come into the classroom with knowledge based on their lived experiences that is valuable in the learning process. Martell has applied Freire's model to her community organizing experiences, believing that community members are the experts on their own experiences and that their wisdom is central to informing organizing that will make a difference in their lives and their communities. Hence, she models learning from community members and applies that approach to learning from her students as a teacher of the C.O. course. In addition, while sharing her knowledge and experience with students, she is constantly learning new concepts that inform her teaching and community practice.

As progressive social work educators and practitioners, we ask ourselves constantly how can we best educate ourselves to be progressive agents of social change at all levels. What methods do we use and how do we implement them in our institutions of higher learning as well as in community organizations? How do we navigate the tension of working for institutions that historically have acted unjustly while working to create a reality where everyone's needs are met (NASW, 2008)? In the description of the C.O. course that follows, we attempt to demonstrate how we apply and adapt Freirian as well as feminist/womanist principles.

THE "INTRODUCTION TO COMMUNITY ORGANIZING" COURSE

This C.O. course was originally designed by an interdisciplinary team of educators with input from community practitioners in 1995. It has dynamically evolved with input from the teaching assistants, students, and instructors. The course uses the urban environment of New York City as a laboratory to examine organizing and issues that arise in the work of organizers and their organizations as well as to deepen the students' analysis of power and oppression. Martell further developed the course to be experiential and to provide opportunities for students in the Freirian and feminist/womanist traditions to synthesize theory and practice ("to see, to analyze, to do"). The concepts of ritual, power, praxis, critical consciousness, and dialogue are operationalized using techniques from popular education and *Theatre of the Oppressed* (Boal, 1979). Almost every session provides some structured opportunity for small group work and interactive activities. As part of holistic engagement, the course provides an opportunity for students to participate fully in their own learning actively involving their whole selves rather than only relying on their intellect to conceptualize theory and interventions. The C.O. course employs movement, drawing, meditation, theater exercises, storytelling, music, and many more activities that challenge students to involve their body, spirit, and creativity to learn from people and the world around them.

The content of the C.O. course teaches students the beginning knowledge, skills, and values needed to achieve change through the application of readings, lectures, media presentations, and reflection on their in-class and field experiences.[1] It emphasizes the myriad roles, goals, strategies, and interactional and analytical skills used by community organizers in effecting progressive social

---

1. The Field Internship Seminar is a separate, additional, 100-hour, 3-credit course developed to complement the C.O. course and offered as a co-requisite to the Introduction to

change using the works of Hardina (2002, 2013); Pyles (2013); Bobo, Kendall, and Max (2010); and Burghardt (2013). It examines the history of organizing as a context of analyzing contemporary issues and organizations in the country and in New York City. Models of community organizing including mass mobilization, social action, grassroots empowerment, leadership development, and advocacy are identified and applied to the various organizations with which they volunteer. Special attention is paid to issues of gender, class, race and ethnicity, sexual orientation, and ability in organizing (Cannon, 1990; Mizrahi & Lombe, 2006).

The students are guided through all their assignments and given a deadline by which to complete them. They are expected to do all the readings and come prepared to discuss them in class. Reading groups are formed to facilitate discussion. At mid-semester, students do their own critical comparison and analysis paper of the major themes and learning points of the readings. They must focus on the different theories of community organizing and the major issues for organizers in the field as related to community organizing theory and practice. Here, we discuss in more detail the two major course assignments: the field experience and the community profile.

The field experience included early in the course's history was made a required component at the suggestion of students who wanted to gain some hands-on observations and experience with community practice. The purpose of this 20-hour volunteer experience is for the students to engage in praxis and reflection—that is, observing and participating in (to the extent possible) the organizing work occurring at the site (Mishna & Bogo, 2007). Under the guidance of the teaching assistant, students are expected to be proactive from the beginning, including negotiating their entry and assignment with their chosen organization.

This field assignment begins to foster leadership and personal responsibility for being accepted and also creates a relationship described as "social exchange theory," which purports that people learn and modify their behavior based on positive and negative interactions with each other (Cook & Rice, 2002; Lawler, 2001) and was applied to social work by McDonell et al. (2006). The field organization is expected to give students access to meetings, minutes, and other materials of the organization and to arrange for interviews with leaders and members.

Community Organizing course presented in this chapter. Beyond the additional field hours, they are required to take part in a 2-hour biweekly group seminar every other week, planned and led by the graduate teaching assistant under the supervision of Professor Martell. The seminar generally consists of a small group of 5–10 students. The goal of the seminar course is to further students' understanding of community organizing principles by analyzing their extended volunteer experience with a structured, supervised community organizing assignment. They keep biweekly journals, make a final presentation on different aspects of their community organizing experience including identifying the organizing models used, and write a final summary of their volunteer experiences using a suggested outline. At the end of the semester, students present their reflections on their field experiences orally in class. Field supervisors and other faculty are invited, and many attend.

In exchange for access and experience, the students' responsibility is to contribute to the work of the organization, which could include assisting in carrying out a project or event, administrative tasks, and/or providing feedback to staff or leaders on their observations.

The graduate teaching assistant, an MSW student in the community organization concentration, emphasizes to both students and organizational staff that the students are not expected to implement an organizing project in 20 hours but, rather, to gain a sense of the models and strategies in which the organization is engaged in order to whet the students' appetite with the possibility to do additional work with the organization or elsewhere in the future. From our experience, every semester since the course began, more than half the students report that they do contribute additional hours during and beyond the semester.

During the first week of the course, students are informed about choosing their 20-hour field experience requirement from one of a number of selected organizations that have been thoroughly researched for their willingness to engage in the exchange model—that is, teaching the student while utilizing the student's expertise and time. Throughout the years, many of the C.O. course alumni have gone on to C.O.-related careers, and some have become field supervisors for the course. At the second class session, all the organizations willing to accept students are invited to come into the classroom to present their organizations and possible organizing assignments to the students. Organizing staff from these organizations prepare materials and make brief presentations. Collectively, they represent the types of organizing occurring around a range of issues, including housing, labor, health, education, youth, and culture.

Vaid (1995), an LGBTQ rights activist, says storytelling or "person-to-person education" is a technique that organizers can use "to break down misunderstandings [rather] than the media oriented advertising approaches toward public education we have pursued thus far. Such political education is especially needed today, when the very idea of civil rights is under attack" (p. 305). She stresses the importance of person-to-person education in creating links across single-issue campaigns to create coalitions as well as to unite people fighting racism, classism, heterosexism, sexism, and all other forms of oppression together in the struggle for the rights and freedom of all oppressed people. The students are able to critically analyze each presentation as a "story" and to provide feedback in class and to the organization on how the representative came across to them. This creates Freirian-style dialogue that transcends the perceived power dynamics that exist in traditional education in which a guest lecturer has all the knowledge and students simply listen to absorb this knowledge. Students also begin to learn the skills involved in making formal presentations by watching more experienced organizational representatives and giving feedback to them as part of an ongoing dialogue. The organizational representatives who briefly present the highlights of their programs also benefit through social networking. They are given this opportunity to engage with other organizers, many for the first time, as they learn about the various organizations invested in different issues and using different models.

The organizations' presentations highlight community organizers as experts in their field with knowledge to contribute to students' learning; this also breaks down traditional barriers between academic/didactic learning and experiential learning. Listening to stories from representatives from organizations such as the New York Public Interest Research Group and the Child Welfare Organizing Project has the secondary benefit of exposing students and the organizers to the wealth of organizing occurring in New York City and demonstrates the interconnectedness in working for social justice across issues.

At the end of the semester, students are responsible for a presentation, an outline of the presentation, and a letter of reference from their field supervisor. This letter serves multiple purposes: It documents their activities, identifies the ways they have assisted and contributed to the organization, and provides students with a ready-made letter of reference for use in potential employment in the future. This way of evaluating a student's field performance demonstrates to the student and supervisor that this course is more than an academic exercise.

A second major assignment for the course is a community profile for which students in small groups select a geographic community in New York City (e.g., East Harlem in Manhattan or Sunset Park in Brooklyn) and identify an issue and population to study in that community, such as education or housing. For their primary research, students are asked to attend a community meeting where their group is doing their community profile. They are provided guidelines to describe and analyze the meeting in detail and are asked to use their six senses as they experience the area. The students apply an anti-oppressive and human rights lens, examining the power relations in the community and identifying how the geography and issue are impacted by racism, sexism, and other forms of oppression (Abrams & Gibson, 2007; Pyles, 2013; Sakamoto & Pitner, 2005). They are responsible for an oral presentation at the end of the semester and also a group paper/portfolio that includes photos, videos, drawing, maps, and other media.

Applying Freirian and Feminist/Womanist Concepts in the C.O. Course

Rituals and Celebrations

Creating the classroom as a sacred learning space by ritualizing our daily activities gives it meaning and makes it inspirational for the students and the instructors. The order, rhythm, and symbolism of ritual are needed to reintegrate the sacred into the learning process. Each student is unique in his or her own right. Ritual gives them the safe space to be in touch with their inner teacher and open up to share their experiences (Bobo et al., 2010; Pyles, 2013; Starhawk, 2011). In this way, they are encouraged to become teacher/learners in the tradition of "each one, teach one" (Champeau, 2011).

Throughout the semester, the class incorporates some activities in each session that have become rituals. These have been used to build community and a sense of inclusion as hooks and Freire recommend for moving forward in order to create social change. "Good News" happens at the start of each class, during which everyone has an opportunity to share about current events related to organizing in order to celebrate a victory or to acknowledge a job well done.

From the first class, Martell puts a general class agenda on the board so the students know the class flow and what is expected to be covered in the class each week. In the weekly agenda review, they are asked if they have anything to add. By the fourth week of the class, usually some students begin to ask for time on the agenda to make announcements, renegotiate presentation times, deal with class issues, and/or bring in speakers. This is part of the praxis on how to run meetings. They have the liberty of excluding Martell for a limited time for peer-led discussions. On occasion when they have used this opportunity, Martell interprets it as students demonstrating their sense of confidence and trust in the process of empowerment.

The course uses the ritual of community agreements (also known as ground rules) to create a safe space for dialogue and accountability. This process gives students a good understanding of their classmates' and instructors' expectations. For example, students in the spring 2014 class formulated the following agreement as one of their 12 guidelines for each other: "We will listen actively for understanding. We agree to disagree respectfully, suspend judgment, and learn each other's sensitivities and needs." Also, collectively writing community agreements establishes their responsibility for what happens in the class and gives them tools to hold each other and the instructor accountable, which the same spring 2014 articulated in a statement at the end of their agreements as follows: "I take full responsibility and will hold myself and the group accountable to uphold these community agreements in our work."

During the third session, the students are divided into groups of five to facilitate the agreement discussion. They are asked to make a list of what they need to feel safe in the classroom and in their workgroups. The example that Martell uses is "I (as the instructor) need you to participate to feel safe." Each group has a note taker who reports back their collective agreements to the larger group. As the instructor facilitates the dialogue, the teaching assistant is charting the responses and both are asking clarifying questions. For example, "Everybody needs to take responsibility for the class." The teaching assistant might ask, "What do you mean by responsibility?" By the end of this process, even some of the shy ones begin to speak up. In the debriefing of the exercise, someone always says, "I have never done this in a class. I learned the importance of establishing ground rules before we begin the work."

The following week, the class reviews the previous session so that students who were not in class can catch up and to refresh everyone. The written agreements and the posted charted agreements are reviewed for comparison and transparency. A new configuration of small groups edit the agreements. New students get to add their comments and ask questions. After an open dialogue, the students read the finalized agreements as a group; then everyone is asked to sign and commit to them in both the full class and in any of their small group meetings. Whenever there is an issue, the agreements are used to ground the discussion. Ground rules or shared agreements are repeated by the students each session followed by an agenda that is co-created by the instructor, the teaching assistant, and the students.

An additional opportunity for students in the course to engage in praxis, build community, and to facilitate dialogue the end of the semester is the Cultural Celebration. Students learn that celebrating victories and sharing each other's cultural customs are essential for sustainability in community organizing through working together to create their own completion event for the class. Freire (1970/2000) discusses how history and culture are integral to the human experience (p. 98) and how creating a revolutionary culture of transformation together can counteract a culture of domination and oppression (p. 180). The class celebration gives students an opportunity to acknowledge themselves for their hard work and to continue to connect with each other across race, class, gender, and other differences in their backgrounds, navigating the power dynamics they are studying and observing throughout the course.

Martell creates an affirmation circle in the last class session that precedes the celebration, during which students share their cultures through food, music, art, poems, and more. Some of the students bring friends, children, and parents. This is their celebration, and Martell says that she is always pleasantly surprised: "In the last class this year [2014], one student brought a Columbian hip hop dance instructor. The class loved it, especially the shy student." These building-community experiences result in many long-term personal relationships.

Highlighting multicultural diversity in its student body and honoring processes in completing ongoing groups are activities that social work education does well (Gutierrez, Lewis, Dessel, & Spencer, 2013). The C.O. course takes multiculturalism and group process deeper through utilizing the trust built between participants throughout the semester to share the significance of their culture for individual students and the meanings behind items such as food or dance that they are sharing. The C.O. course connects the importance of culture and the class celebration to larger struggles and victories won in community organizing.

Power

Freire (1970/2000) calls for anti-oppression pedagogy to have its groundings in analyzing power and oppression and how these forces impact people. In *Pedagogy of the Oppressed* (1970/2000), he discusses unequal relationships between colonized and colonizer as well as culture and oppression, respectively. He basically concludes that within seemingly benevolent relationships in which one group of people is offering to help or modernize a second group of people, inherent within that connection is a "power over" dynamic in which the first group dominates the second group (pp. 44–45 125–138).

Considering specifically the United States, bell hooks (1994) and Cornel West (1994) utilize Freire's philosophy and technique to examine discrimination throughout the history of the country and paint powerful pictures demonstrating how certain inequalities created our current situation and are still alive and well today. In addition, Starhawk, in *Webs of Power: Notes From the Global Uprising* (2002), distinguishes among three types of power. According to her, there is "power over;" which means institutional power; "power within," which is the personal power of the participant (student, community member, etc.); and "power with," which means collective power (pp. 6–7). Starhawk cites examples of nonhierarchical, nonviolent organizing in which power is decentralized, as with the World Trade Organization protests in Seattle that challenged "power over" (Shepard & Hayduk, 2002, pp. 52–56) and also the Occupy movement (Crass, 2013). Several social work scholars adapt and utilize these power concepts in their types of analysis as well as include them in their method of teaching and learning (Miller et al., 2011; Mullaly, 2006; Sakamoto & Pitner, 2005).

In utilizing the principles of Freire and feminists/womanists in the C.O. course, Martell attempts to demystify the "power over" concept based on the status of "instructor" granted by the academic institution. She begins this process by sharing her history and experiences as an older Puerto Rican woman of color from a working-class background. She welcomes students to do the same—that is, reflect on their experiences through the lens of social identities. This process serves to build trust as quickly as possible with students and create a safe space to allow for transformational learning.

She also attempts to reduce the power differential in the classroom by rearranging the space in which there is no front and center so students can become teachers and instructors can become learners. It starts with having everyone sit in a circle rather than rows during each class session. Martell uses open-ended questions and asks students to talk from their personal experiences using "I statements" rather than talking about another person's perspective. Most students begin to own their voice and develop critical thinking from their view of the world. Martell and the graduate assistant encourage students to contribute to conversations and validate their sharing from personal perspectives. Throughout the semester, most students begin to understand and appreciate Freire's method of teaching as interpreted by Martell. Her goal is for students to use her teachings on critical analysis and share the thought processes in their other classes and beyond, thus creating a ripple effect.

Martell uses several exercises involving the students to demonstrate and demystify power, including a power web in which students draw their definitions of power and the connections among these and also a power grid to identify those who hold power at different levels of society. One interactive activity is the "Ten Chairs," a simulation of roles that we are assigned in society and how we maintain the current social, economic, and political conditions. The purpose of the exercise, designed by Martell and based on an activity from *Popular Economics* ("The Ten Chairs," 2014), is to shed light on systems that privilege and oppress and to define the roles of gatekeepers within organizations and institutions. The instructor tells students to set up one row of 10 chairs and sit in them. At the same time, a group of six students leave the room with the teaching assistant. After the chairs are set up and students are sitting in them, the group of students who left the room are told to go back in and take the chairs away from those seated. In the meantime, the student sitting in the first chair in the row is told to take his or her chair and move to the side, sitting apart from the other nine students. The rest of the students in the class sit facing the 10 chairs as observers. As the six begin to take the chairs and bring them to the place where the single "chosen" student is sitting, they are also told to "make nice" to this chosen one. Once a chair is taken out of the line, the student whose chair was taken moves to the end of the line of chairs, usually resulting in crowding around the few chairs left. When there is a struggle about giving up a chair, or there are no more chairs left in the row, the instructor says "Freeze" and the debriefing begins.

They analyze their and others' roles in relationship to authority, power, privilege, styles of interaction, degrees of comfort, and gatekeeping roles, among other concepts. Reference is made to the other power exercises. Students are not given the rules to the game and eventually surmise that they are acting in a prescribed way. When the class debriefs the game, participants reflect on oppressive systems within society and ultimately begin to formulate how they will resist maintaining the status quo in their personal and professional lives.

Praxis and Critical Consciousness

"Praxis" is Freire's term for the process of reflection and action in order to impact social change (Freire, 1970/2000, p. 79), also known as self-reflective and critical practice by feminists/womanists and progressive social workers (Joseph et al., 1991; Mishna & Bogo, 2007; Pyles, 2013). One way praxis is put into action today is through the methodology of popular education. Freire referred to the pedagogy he created as "educacion cultural popular" (Choules, 2007, p. 162).

According to Wiggins (2011), although there is no one definition of popular education, a working definition is

> a philosophy and methodology that seeks to bring about more just and equitable social, political, and economic relations by creating settings in which people who have historically lacked power can discover and expand their knowledge and use it to eliminate societal inequities. [Popular education] maintains a shifting, sometimes uneasy relationship to hierarchical political parties and organizations. (p. 36)

For Freire, one of the key aims of social analysis is to promote the development of critical consciousness in order for people to "emerge from their silence, find their voice, capable of changing and determining the conditions in which they live" (Freire, 1970/2000, p. 36). In her work *Teaching to Transgress*, hooks (1994) speaks about Freire's influence on her development as a critical thinker. hooks discusses Freire as a catalyst for her development of critical consciousness and resistance against the "colonizing process" (p. 46). For hooks, Freire's work provided a global understanding for liberation struggles that begin with "that historical moment when one begins to think critically about the self and identity in relation to one's political circumstance" (p. 47). In social work, critical consciousness is also embedded in the core principles of social work identity and practice: self-awareness and conscious use of self (Burghardt, 2013; Jones, 2009; Sakamoto & Pitner, 2005).

hooks (1994) reminds readers that "conscientization" ("concientização") as used by Freire (1970/2000, p. 67) means the development process of critical consciousness but does not end with awareness about oppressive systems and our role in them. Rather, hooks reiterates Freire's assertion that recognizing the dehumanizing state of our current reality compels people into action. She discusses how experience verifies theory and how through joining reflection and action in praxis, people engage in an essential practice of living their politics.

The students in the C.O. course begin to critically deconstruct and gain an understanding of oppression and other social issues through exercises that stimulate dialogue and develop critical consciousness. One of these is the creation of an "oppression grid." The oppression grid uses concepts that students generate in drawing a collective map of their ideas and then discuss how they experience power in their daily lives. The oppression grid creates a visual representation of the ideologies, institutions, actions, and internalization of oppression within US society that challenges the students to reflect on their place within the grid and their role in perpetuating oppression in their daily lives. The outcome of the activity is that students analyze power and oppression through writing and drawing in order to express collective images of power. Students then have a visual tool that the instructors bring to each session to hang on the wall that they can refer to throughout the course sessions. As students are exposed to organizing campaigns and other projects/activities happening on the ground, they make connections to concepts learned in the oppression grid to the techniques and organizing models that groups and organizations employ to work in attempting to dismantle systems of power and oppression. For example, students can look at the oppression grid they created to see that an anti-police brutality campaign is addressing the "action" of racism through violence occurring in the "institution" of the criminal justice system. At the same time, they relate the campaign to the root cause of white privilege in the ideology section of the grid.

Drawing and movement-based activities are a way in which the course integrates the biopsychosocial–spiritual model of social work into the C.O. course. Artistic and kinesthetic exercises prompt students to shift from what neurobiology explains as left-brain hemisphere functioning of logical and linear thinking into right-brain hemisphere activities of processing visual, spatial, and emotional information (Miehls, 1997, pp. 83–84). Images are a way in which students can process deep, analytical information in order to connect their experiences to abstract theories (Huss, 2012).

To reinforce a critical consciousness perspective linked to the possibilities of making social change collectively, Martell engages the students interactively in the final session using the following example:

> I begin this story by giving them all a condom and ask, "What did I just give you?" They all say a condom. I say "no; it's a Life Saver!" I tell them the story of how as a youth worker in the 1970s I was known as the Condom Lady. It was against the law to give out condoms in the schools and a community center hired a white gay young man and a Puerto Rican straight young woman to give out condoms in our community and run a peer education groups. This was before HIV/AIDS. We were dealing with the epidemic of teen pregnancies and STDs. I ask them, "So what happened that you can now receive free condoms right here at the Student Health office?" Usually there is no answer. I remind them that in the 1980s and 1990s, community activists demanded health care, including free condoms. Organizations like ACT-UP (2003), which we read about this semester, not only used social action tactics like "dead-ins" but they also did legislative work, and more. They inspired a generation to organize and today we have free condoms in schools. "Yes! Organizing is hard work; yes, some organizers don't make lots of money, and yes, we have to continue to fight for our rights. But our work saves lives. I know you will never look at a condom the same way again." I make this presentation fun and uplifting. I give them information about safe sex. For some, this is the first time that they had this conversation in public. I am still "the Condom Lady."

Dialogue

Dialogue is also a way that academics such as Freire have wrestled with tough pedagogical issues. He uses the term "problem-posing" education as an alternative to

"banking" education; "problem-posing" education utilizes dialogic techniques
(rather than one-way communication) (1970/2000). His belief is that true critical reflection can only be conducted through dialogue between and among students and teachers. In *Teaching Community: A Pedagogy of Hope* (2003), hooks
encourages people "to decolonize their minds, to maintain awareness, change
behavior and create beloved community" (p. 40). Through authentic dialogue,
she asserts solidarity will emerge (hooks, 1994, p. 110).

Freire (1970/2000) proposes a method for dialogue that he calls "thematic
investigation circles" (p. 118) in which participants are broken into small groups
to critically analyze popular knowledge. Freire found that in these circles, participants "externalize a series of sentiments and opinions about themselves,
the world, and others that perhaps they would not express under other circumstances" (p. 118). By utilizing these learning circles, educators may co-educate
with participants, further breaking down the power differential between teacher
and student.

A famous dialogue between Freire and activist Myles Horton, who
founded the Highlander Education Center, has affected the way in which the
C.O. course attempts to operationalize these Freirian principles (Horton,
Freire, & Bell, 1990). Horton and Freire discuss how the purpose of education should be freedom. Their discussion explores how people have been conditioned to fear freedom and change; however, it is in being free and taking risks
that real transformation and progress occur. They speak of this as "the paradox
of education" (p. 220). Education for liberation and social change is dynamic
and unpredictable. The process takes time, might be met with resistance, and
certainly calls for reflection and reinvention. Freire and Horton believe, as
does Boal in *Theatre of the Oppressed* (1979), that educators must understand
how educational institutions have been used to perpetuate systems of oppression. Only then can educators truly transform education to be an instrument
of social change.

The course is organized into Freirian small group learning circles (Lee,
1996) in which students analyze their experiences; generate themes through
posing problems in a question form; codify common themes that occur on a personal, cultural, and institutional level; and use the themes to generate steps for
taking action. Every class session begins and ends with a "talking circle" in which
students dialogue with each other about current events relevant to the course and
about concepts and techniques they learned. During the talking circles, Martell
participates alongside students. Eventually, students, to varying degrees, stop
looking to her to provide validation for their input and reflections. Instead, the
class creates a less hierarchical investigation into course themes where everyone's
views, experiences, and knowledge are valued as important learning tools.

Students are organized in learning circles for two of the assignments discussed
previously; the first is to jointly organize and present a unit of the course syllabus

through analysis and synthesis of readings. The second is to work together on the community profile. Working in small groups throughout the semester also allows students the opportunity to analyze and discuss the community organizing concepts presented in the lecture and readings. The discussion is initiated with an exercise or series of questions relevant to the day's syllabus topic. Initially, it is the faculty and graduate assistant who develop the topical questions. Later, students are given the opportunity to produce their own questions based on assigned readings.

In addition, the small groups initiate students into actual community organizing experiences as various students assume the roles of group facilitator and recorder at least once during the semester. The purpose of the group facilitator role is to give the students the opportunity to learn and exercise the skills of a community organizing group leader. The responsibility of the facilitator is to bring his or her group members through the steps of the week's exercise and to analyze the process and their performance. The purpose of the group recorder role is to encourage students to learn minute-taking skills while witnessing group process dynamics in action as a political, strategic process rather than a clinical, administrative function (Mizrahi, 2015). The group recorder's responsibility is to submit a one-page synopsis of his or her group's experience and success with the exercise the following week.

The role-playing aspects of the group offer students the chance to build organizing skills in a supportive environment. The roles of facilitator and recorder require that each student become actively involved with the group's activity rather than wait for these roles to evolve out of the group process. Initial experiences with these roles begins to bolster the confidence of some students who might otherwise not engage in discussion. Assignment of different roles in part ensures that every student's contribution is captured by the group, a fundamental tenet of community organizing practice (Hardina, 2013).

The time spent engaging in discussion and activities in small groups also allows the students to develop their emotional intelligence or the ability to monitor their emotions while cultivating awareness of their peers' emotions. Emotional intelligence promotes students' social and intellectual growth through understanding emotions and eventually using them to access information through self-reflection (Mayer & Salovey, 1997).

The group work/learning circles allow for reciprocal learning and teaching to occur. For some students, this is their first chance to actively participate in their own learning and to value the contribution of peers as well as teachers, becoming what Freire (1970/2000) calls "student–teachers" and "teacher–students" (p. 83). According to Lee (1996), small groups "promote motivation, problem solving, and psychic comfort, [which] contributes to [students'] self-direction and empowerment" (p. 234).

Grading and Course Feedback

Martell applies the general Freirian principle of "guided process" to the grading procedure. In a course such as this one that emphasizes nonhierarchical power sharing, assigning grades is challenging but necessary to remain as a course offering at the university. Martell is very transparent in making the grading process an experience in self and peer evaluation learning. She does this by sharing her rubric with students, which lists all the course assignments and includes a power analysis of race, gender, and class; expectations of how the written papers and presentations should be constructed; and "the habits of mind" taken from Meier (2002, pp. 49–51). The students then apply the rubric to their own body of course work and to that of their peers for each assignment. In addition, the students, teaching assistant, and Martell evaluate the two group assignments (the reading group and the community profile) collectively. At the end of the course, Martell provides a take-home evaluation form in which students assign a letter grade to themselves, their peers, and the instructor and teaching assistant. This activity includes their explanation about the rationale for the grade.

According to the literature on peer assessment in higher education, employing peer feedback enhances student learning (Cartney, 2010; Cassidy, 2006; Topping, Smith, Swanson, & Elliot, 2000) and is viewed as a valuable way to share power in the classroom (Brown & Glasner, 2003; Cartney 2010). This is similar to what we have found in the course. A recommendation we are taking from Cartney (2010), who worked with bachelor's level social work students in a "Social Policy for Social Workers" course, is to highlight the "feedforward impact of formative feedback" (p. 18) by supporting students in better understanding how providing their peers with feedback on assignments and presentations will impact their own learning and also will be a useful skill to develop in their professional lives (Falchikov, 2005; Smythe, 2006; van den Berg, Admiral, & Pilot, 2006a, 2006b).

The final grading and evaluation includes one of multiple opportunities for students to earn extra credit through sharing their knowledge and skills with the class. Students can also attend community marches or political rallies related to the course content to earn extra credit through writing a one-page summary and sharing about their experience with the class. Students who actively participate and take leadership in the cultural celebration at the end of the semester can also earn extra course credit. Students have also created their own ways to earn it through leading the class in writing a collective response to an opinion piece in a local newspaper.

Martell notes that giving students different ways in which to engage in the course subject matter allows them to fully participate in their own learning experiences and challenges them to think creatively about what they are learning from the course. In the rare instance in which there is a discrepancy between

Martell and a student as to final letter grade, Martell initiates a negotiated process in which the student is given a chance to advocate for him- or herself.

An additional, more standardized course evaluation has also been conducted since the inception of the course in 1995. The students complete a pre- and postcourse survey developed by Mizrahi and Martell that is an assessment of their learning and ways they will utilize their learning in the future. Students report at the end of the semester becoming empowered and encouraged to look at themselves and evaluate their own privilege and/or internalized oppression (hooks, 1994; Sue et al., 2007).

As part of the standardized course evaluation, students complete a 12-item activism scale that asks them to identify which civic and organizing activities they have participated in before and during the course semester and in which activities they now plan to engage in the future. Throughout the years, more than 800 students have consistently reported that they anticipate becoming more active in the future and express newfound passion for social justice causes and organizing for social change whether in a paid job or as a volunteer (Mizrahi & Case, 1998). Every year, most students state that this course is the one from which they learned the most during a semester and the one for which they did the most work. Note that as an elective, some students drop out because of the course demands and time commitment. Students have consistently recommended it be a four-credit course or held over two semesters, for which there is agreement by the faculty but not the administration.

Challenges in Applying Freire's Method

In a world that is accustomed to the "banking" method of education, it is perhaps no surprise that applying Freire's pedagogical theory in practice is a challenge. One of the greatest challenges is knowing how to effectively "meet the students where they are," a term essential to social work methodology. According to Horton et al. (1990),

> If you're going to start where they are and they don't change, then there's no point in starting because you're not going anywhere. . . . If you [as the educator] don't have some vision of what ought to be or what they can become, then you have no way of contributing anything to the process. (p. 149)

This challenge was identified by Bartlett (2005), who analyzed a case study of the Sao Paolo popular schools. Bartlett observed several teaching sessions in which facilitators celebrated popular knowledge, the knowledge that students brought to the table, even when the knowledge was "contrary to the aims of the program or simply wrong. I heard students tell folk stories or popular sayings that were fundamentally racist" (pp. 357–358) and were not contradicted by the facilitators. As a result, Bartlett suggests the following to facilitators: "Rather than the emphasis on 'getting along' and valuing students' utterances on principle, students might benefit from a more straightforward discussion of the way unequal power and wealth relations operate in everyday social interaction" (p. 359).

In his practice, Steve Burghardt, a colleague and community organizing professor, confronts the challenge of instructor viewed as expert on a daily basis, noting that "it is much easier to stand in the front of a lecture hall, make jokes and talk at students for a couple of hours than to struggle with others to be honest and strategic" (personal communication, April 11, 2013). However, he sees all the possibilities that teaching using Freire's pedagogical theory can offer, and despite the challenges, he strives to model the theory. He often refers to Freire's quote: "Liberation is thus a childbirth, and a painful one" (Freire, 1970/2000, p. 49). Pedraza (2005) also expressed the difficulty of applying Freire's pedagogical theory in practice, but he found that there was a specific role for teachers to play in their interaction with participants, quoting Freire (as cited in Horton et al., 1990):

> In discussing my practice with the people as an educator, I have to know something more than the people know. . . . "[If we do not have this knowledge] we as popular educators begin to walk in a circle, without the possibility of going beyond the circle, without going beyond man's theory of why we do not go beyond." (p. 99)

Another challenge in applying Freire's theory to the course has been the actual process of creating a democratic classroom. According to Freire (Horton et al., 1990), students arrive at the classroom

> absolutely convinced that the teacher has to give a class to them . . . they come to receive answers for any questions they asked before. This is an obstacle—how to confront a group of students who, in perceiving that you are interested in knowing what they think you know, think that you are not capable. . . . I think that in such a case, the teacher, understanding the situation, would be 50 percent a traditional teacher and 50 percent a democratic teacher in order to begin to challenge the students, and for them to change a little bit too. (p. 160)

Martell reflects that no matter how prepared instructors think they are to teach using this method, they are never prepared enough. She reminds instructors to always have alternatives available for unprepared students and class emergencies. Through her time as the course instructor, Martell notes that students constantly complain about the number and types of assignments and the individual and collective responsibility they must assume; from the students' viewpoint, there is never enough time to cover all the intended material. Students initially experience Martell's classroom environment as disorganized because the students are accustomed to the banking system of education. She and the teaching assistant continue to experience the reality with each new cohort that even after attempting to create an environment in which students understand that they are actually the experts in their experiences, students still view the teacher as the holder of knowledge and do not look to one another enough for answers. In reality, students may not be looking for critical consciousness-raising experiences and often worry about grades and academic performance. Martell notes struggles with supporting students in holistic engagement while respecting demands on their academic, work, and home lives.

By the end of the course, some of the students have more questions than when they started. When asked if they want to become community organizers, some say "No, it's too much work and there are very few victories." Others say that this was the best class ever; they learned a great deal but they cannot make money as a community organizer. Almost all say that they will use what they learned in their personal lives and share the information with family and friends. From the standpoint of the course's philosophy, wherever the students end up, it is ok. Usually, their ending perspectives reflect the challenges they faced during the semester, how much work they did, and the relationships they developed among each other.

CONCLUSIONS AND IMPLICATIONS FOR HOLISTIC ENGAGEMENT

In his speech, "A Critical Understanding of Social Work" (1990), Freire calls on progressive social workers to develop qualities or virtues that he states are nurtured only through practice. These qualities include social workers taking action on what they say needs to be done rather than simply pontificating about social change; social work practitioners "stimulat[ing] a critical curiosity" in themselves and in the people they work with; social work professionals tolerating differences among the social work profession in order to unite against our enemies; social workers being impatiently impatient where change is not seen as impossible in this lifetime; social workers understanding the social, ideological, cultural, political, and historical limits of social work practice; and also understanding what is historically possible (pp. 6–9).

One of the main visions and values of the social work profession is the promotion of social justice and social change (CSWE, 2012; NASW, 2008). We come back to the fundamental question: How do we educate social workers to be progressive social change agents? Beyond social work education, the C.O. course has implications for educators across disciplines looking to foster analytical thinkers and social change agents who can take ownership of their own educational experiences, engage in respectful dialogue in community, learn about themselves, and understand their own emotions.

Freirian and feminist/womanist educational philosophy would behoove social workers to explore processes through which they develop leadership from the people they are serving and authentically share power to work for collective liberation. However, creating anti-oppressive pedagogy takes time, patience, and community. In this chapter, we provided an example of applying Freirian theory as a popular education model employed as a method for educating social workers as agents for progressive social change. The social work profession as a progressive movement acts out of commitment to each other, or love (Freire, 1970, p. 70), and that love has no conditions. "Love will always move us away from domination in all its forms. Love will always challenge us" (hooks, 2003, p. 137). Although the task seems daunting, we are confident that social work education will answer the challenge.

Transforming students' hearts and minds is not an easy task in the face of the daily oppression we all experience. We have to work with the resistance from the students as we are reaffirming and giving them tools to become critical thinkers. It is challenging for students to own their educational process. It is conflicting for them to critique themselves and others. To be allowed to rewrite a paper, to openly support each other, to work in groups, to have a say on their grade and what goes on in the classroom, and to be able to challenge the teacher are transformative experiences.

Martell has learned many lessons that have sustained her throughout the years and continue to serve as her guiding principles of teaching, including the following: What works for one student does not work for another; every generation has to figure it out for themselves with guidance; there will be students who will disagree, get angry, and resist the process; the instructor must suspend judgment and not personalize; and to always do my best with love, joy, and compassion. In her own words,

> dealing with the whole person in the classroom and learning from the experience is what good social work practice is all about. We are constantly growing, learning, and challenging ourselves. We are not only relying on past experiences as activist educators. We are still organizing, training, and learning throughout our lives. My vision of love for all people generates my desire to restructure this society. We need to go beyond the cause at hand and strive to sustain our work for the long haul, creating new leaders, strengthening existing ones, and building sustainable communities that will mobilize millions for peace, economic justice, and to protect all our national resources. Humanity will survive, freedom is ours.

ACKNOWLEDGMENTS

A special thanks to Madeline Perez, PhD, for her ideas and editing. We also acknowledge Christina Danguilan, Cindy Urquidez, and Dieniz Costa for their contributions.

REFERENCES

Abrams, L. S., & Gibson, P. (2007). Teaching notes: Reframing multi-cultural education: Teaching white privilege in the social work curriculum. *Journal of Social Work Education, 43*(1), 147–160.

Bartlett, L. (2005). Dialogue, knowledge, and teacher–student relations: Freirean pedagogy in theory and practice. *Comparative Education Review, 49*(3), 344–364.

Boal, A. (1979). *Theatre of the oppressed.* London: Pluto.

Bobo, K. A., Kendall, J., & Max, S. (2010). *Organizing for social change: Midwest Academy manual for activists* (4th ed.). Santa Ana, CA: Seven Locks Press.

Brown, S., & Glasner, A. (Eds.). (2003). *Assessment matters in higher education: Choosing and using diverse approaches.* Philadelphia, PA: Open University Press.

Brun, C., & Rapp, R. C. (2001). Strengths-based case management: Individuals' perspectives on strengths and the case manager relationship. *Social Work, 46*(3), 278–288.

Burghardt, S. (2013). *Macro practice in social work for the 21st century* (2nd ed.). Thousand Oaks, CA: Sage.

Cannon, L. M. (1990). Fostering positive race, class, and gender dynamics in the classroom. *Women's Studies Quarterly, 18*(1), 126–134.

Cartney, P. (2010). Exploring the use of peer assessment as a vehicle for closing the gap between feedback given and feedback used. *Assessment and Evaluation in Higher Education, 35*(5), 551–564.

Cassidy, S. (2006). Developing employability skills: Peer assessment in higher education. *Education & Training, 48*(7), 508–517.

Champeau, M. (2011). *Each one teach one: We are all educators.* Retrieved from http://humaneeducation.org/blog/2010/08/11/each-one-teach-one-we-are-all-educators.

Choules, K. (2007). Social change education: Context matters. *Adult Education Quarterly, 57*(2), 159–176.

Cohen, B. Z. (1999). Intervention and supervision in strengths-based social work practice. *Families in Society: The Journal of Contemporary Social Services, 80*(5), 460–466.

Cook, K., & Rice, E. (2002). *Social exchange theory: The handbook of social psychology.* New York, NY: Kluwer/Plenum.

Council on Social Work Education. (2008). *Educational policy and accreditation standards.* Retrieved August 21, 2015, from http://www.cswe.org/Accreditation/2008EPASHandbook.aspx.

Crass, C. (2013). *Towards collective liberation: Anti-racist organizing, feminist praxis, and movement building strategy.* Oakland, CA: PM Press.

Early, T. J., & GlenMaye, L. F. (2000). Valuing families: Social work practice with families from a strengths perspective. *Social Work, 45*(2), 118–130.

Falchikov, N. (2005). "Unpacking" peer assessment. In P. Schwartz & G. Webb (Eds.), *Assessment: Case studies, experience and practice from higher education.* New York, NY: Routledge.

Freire, P. (1990). A critical understanding of social work. *Journal of Progressive Psychology, 1*(1), 3–9.

Freire, P. (2000). *Pedagogy of the oppressed* (30th anniversary ed.). New York, NY: Continuum. (Original work published 1970)

Graybeal, C. (2001). Strengths-based social work assessment: Transforming the dominant paradigm. *Families in Society: The Journal of Contemporary Social Services, 82*(3), 233–242.

Gutierrez, L. M., Lewis, E. A., Dessel, A. B., & Spencer, M. (2013). Principles, skills and practice strategies for promoting multicultural communication and collaboration.

In M. W. Weil (Ed.), *Handbook of community practice* (2nd ed., pp. 445–460). Thousand Oaks, CA: Sage.

Hager, R. L. (2012). Paulo Freire: Neglected mentor for social work. *Journal of Progressive Human Services, 23*(2), 159–177.

Hardina, D. (2002). *Analytical skills for community organization practice.* New York, NY: Columbia University Press.

Hardina, D. (2013). *interpersonal skills for community organization practice.* New York, NY: Springer.

Harris, M. (2010). *Gifts of virtue, Alice Walker, and womanist ethics.* New York, NY: Palgrave Macmillan.

hooks, b. (1994). *Teaching to transgress: Education as the practice of freedom.* New York, NY: Routledge.

hooks, b. (2003). *Teaching community.* New York, NY: Routledge.

Horton, M., Freire, P., & Bell, B. (1990). *We make the road by walking.* Philadelphia, PA: Temple University Press.

Huss, E. (2012). *Using images in research, therapy, empowerment and social change.* London, UK: Routledge.

Hyde, C. A. (2008). Feminist social work practice. In T. Mizrahi & L. Davis (Eds.), *Encyclopedia of social work* (20th ed., pp. 216–221). New York, NY: Oxford University Press.

Hyde, C. A. (2012). Challenging ourselves: Critical self-reflection on power and privilege. In M. Minkler (Ed.), *Community organizing and community building for health* (3rd ed., pp. 428–436). New Brunswick, NJ: Rutgers University Press.

Jones, P. (2009). Teaching for change in social work. A discipline-based argument for the use of transformative approaches for teaching and learning. *Journal of Transformative Education, 7*(1), 8–25.

Joseph, B., Lob, S., McLaughlin, P., Mizrahi, T., Peterson, J., Rosenthal, B., & Sugarman, F. (1991). *A framework for feminist organizing: Values, goals, methods, strategies and roles.* New York, NY: Education Center for Community Organizing.

Kadushin, A. (1985). *Supervision in social work* (2nd ed.). New York, NY: Columbia University Press.

Lawler, E. J. (2001). An affect theory of social exchange. *American Journal of Sociology, 107*(2), 1–52.

Lee, J. (1996). The empowerment approach to social work practice. In F. Turner (Ed.), *Social work treatment* (4th ed., pp. 218–249). New York, NY: Free Press.

Mayer, J. D., & Salovey, P. (1997). What is emotional intelligence? In P. Salovey & D. Sluyter (Eds.), *Emotional development and emotional intelligence: Implications for educators* (pp. 3–31). New York, NY: Basic Books.

McDonell, J., Strom-Gottfried, K. J., Burton, D. L., & Yaffe, J. (2006). *Behaviorism, social learning, and exchange theory.* In S. P. Robbins, P. Chatterjee, & E. R. Canda (Eds.), *Contemporary human behavior theory: A critical perspective for social work* (pp. 349–385). New York, NY: Pearson.

Meier, D. (2002). *The power of their ideas: Lessons for America from a small school in Harlem.* New York, NY: Harper.

Miehls, D. (1997). Neurobiology and clinical social work. In J. Brandell (Ed.), *Theory & practice in clinical social work* (pp. 81–98). Thousand Oaks, CA: Sage.

Miller, P. M., Brown, T., & Hopson, R. (2011). Centering love, hope and trust in the community transformative urban leadership informed by Paulo Freire. *Urban Education, 46*(5), 1078–1099.

Mishna, F., & Bogo, M. (2007). Reflective practice in contemporary social work classrooms. *Journal of Social Work Education, 43*(2), 529–541.

Mizrahi, T. (2015). Community organizing principals and practice guidelines. In K. Corcoran & A. R. Roberts (Eds.), *Social workers' desk reference* (3rd ed., pp. 894–906). New York, NY: Oxford University Press.

Mizrahi, T., & Case, A. (1998). *Educating for social change: The impact of an innovative interdisciplinary community organizing course on Hunter students' career and civic pursuits.* unpublished manuscript.

Mizrahi, T., & Dodd, S. J. (2013). Student perspectives on social activism and goals of the social work profession before and after completing a graduate social work program. *Journal of Social Work Education, 49*(4), 580–600.

Mizrahi, T., & Lombe, M. (2006). Perspectives from women organizers: Views on gender, race, class, and sexual orientation. *Journal of Community Practice, 14*(3), 93–118.

Mullaly, R. (2006). *The new structural social work* (3rd ed.). New York, NY: Oxford University Press.

National Association of Social Workers. (2008). *Code of ethics of the National Association of Social Workers.* Retrieved from https://www.socialworkers.org/pubs/code/code.asp.

Pedraza, P. (2005). *Latino education: An agenda for community action research.* Mahwah, NJ: Erlbaum.

Pyles, L. (2013). *Progressive community organizing: Reflecting practice in a globalizing world* (2nd ed.). New York, NY: Routledge.

Reisch, M. (2013a). Social work education & the neo-liberal challenge: The US response to increasing global inequality. *Social Work Education, 32*(6), 217–233.

Reisch, M. (2013b). What is the future of social work? *Critical & Radical Social Work, 1*(1), 67–85.

Reisch, M., & Andrews, J. (2002). *The road not taken: A history of radical social work in the United States.* New York, NY: Routledge.

Rothman, J., & Mizrahi, T. (2014). Balancing micro and macro practice: A challenge for social work. *Social Work, 51*(1), 91–93.

Sakamoto, I., & Pitner, R. O. (2005). Use of critical consciousness in anti-oppressive social work practice: Disentangling power dynamics at personal and structural levels. *British Journal of Social Work, 35*(4), 435–452.

Saleebey, D. (1992). *The strengths perspective in social work practice.* White Plains, NY: Longman.

Samimi, J. C. (2010). Funding America's nonprofits: The nonprofit industrial complex's hold on social justice. *Columbia Social Work Review, 1,* 17–25.

Shepard, B., & Hayduk, R. (Eds.). (2002). *From ACT UP to the WTO: Urban protest and community building in the era of globalization.* New York, NY: Verso.

Sims, D. (2014). The global agenda: Developing international perspectives and critical discourse in UK social work education and practice. *International Social Work, 57*(4), 360–372.

Smythe, D. M. (2006). Research paper assignments that prevent plagiarism. In D. Carless et al. (Eds.), *Assessment supports learning: Learning-oriented assessment in action* (Section 3.1). Hong Kong: Hong Kong University Press.

Specht, H., & Courtney, M. (1994). *Unfaithful angels: How social work has abandoned its mission.* New York, NY: Free Press.

Starhawk. (2002). *Webs of power: Notes from the global uprising.* Gabriola, British Columbia, Canada: New Society Publishers.

Sue, D. W., Capodilupo, C. M., Torino, G. C., Bucceri, J. M., Holder, A. M. B., Nadal, K. L., et al. (2007). Racial microaggressions in everyday life: Implications for clinical practice. *American Psychologist, 62*, 271–286.

The Ten Chairs. (2014, January 1). Retrieved January 1, 2014, from http://www.teachingeconomics.org/content/index.php?topic=tenchairs.

Topping, K. J., Smith, E. F., Swanson, L., & Elliot, A. (2000). Formative peer assessment of academic writing between postgraduate students. *Assessment and Evaluation in Higher Education, 25*(2), 149–169.

Vaid, U. (1995). *Virtual equality: The mainstreaming of gay and lesbian liberation.* New York, NY: Anchor Books.

van den Berg, I., Admiral, W., & Pilot, A. (2006a). Student peer assessment in higher education: Analysis of written and oral peer feedback. *Teaching in Higher Education, 11*(2), 135–147.

van den Berg, I., Admiral, W., and Pilot, A. (2006b). Design principles and outcomes of peer assessment in higher education. *Studies in Higher Education, 45*, 477–501.

West, C. (1994). *Race matters.* New York, NY: Vintage Books.

Wiggins, N. (2011). Critical pedagogy and popular education: Towards a unity of theory and practice. *Studies in the Education of Adults, 43*(1), 34–49.

Williams, A. (1997). On parallel process in social work supervision. *Clinical Social Work Journal, 25*(4), 425–435.

CHAPTER 4

"By the End of the Term, You Will Have Gained Power in the Classroom and I Will Have Lost None"

The Pedagogical Value of Discomfort and Vulnerability in the Teaching of Community Practice

STEVE BURGHARDT

INTRODUCTION

Everyone who becomes a teacher of social work practice is necessarily influenced by the experiences, skill sets, values, and beliefs that shaped her or him in one's work outside the classroom. While adhering to a school's curricular emphases and the inevitable mandates passed down from the Council on Social Work Education, a new practice teacher enters that first classroom brimming with high hopes. My hopes were as heartfelt as they were fundamental: that the primary nuggets of practice wisdom gained through the rocky, uphill road of experience will somehow be imparted through the lectures, discussions, and case studies over the academic term. *Theories from the classics + my practice experience + their fieldwork = praxis! How great is that!?* A new teacher's course on practice will help students get needed skill sets and the critical reflection to use them well in any situation.

If only that were true. The following is the case study of a once young, dedicated community organizer whose lessons as a practitioner and professor have been more of the humbling kind of imparting what did not work rather than illuminating points of activist brilliance. Paradoxically, my own growing capacity to embrace the forms of discomfort such stumbles have created perhaps has made it possible to impart something of value along the way. As the reader will see, the more I embraced my vulnerability, the less I and others in the classroom had to fear; the more my fearful edginess at student disagreement was replaced with respect, the easier it became for them to receive and for me to impart my skills; the less I uncomfortably struggled for power in the classroom, the more authority I could claim—alongside that of my co-learners, the students.

This chapter examines how my community organizing curriculum has evolved from a content-heavy and more theoretical emphasis on models, strategic options, and historical examples to a blend of present-day experience—including dynamics in the classroom that model actual organizing processes, such as the use of power, privilege, the creation of voice, and model building—as well as the needed theory. As such, *my* classroom learning framework consciously engages with a mix of student skepticism, critically reflective questioning, and purposeful discomfort that ends, 14 weeks later, with *our* classroom engaged in lively debate, respectful challenging of ideas, and deeply felt openness to the personal and collective strategic challenges that await us in the 21st century.

The pedagogical approach throughout the term is modeled on two underlying design principles—one drawn from history, the other from theory.[1] Each is operationalized through my own openness to struggle with the students on how difficult it can be, whether organizer or professor, both to truly share power and to engage in the mutual discovery of how co-learning and collective voice enriches rather than diminishes expertise and individualized forms of learning and leading.

The historical principle comes from Gandhi and later updated by the organizational theorist Peter Senge: "Embody the change you seek" (Gandhi, 2002; Senge, Scharmer, Jaworski, & Flowers, 2005). What a noble idea! What organizer or practice professor doesn't aspire to that? *Oh, really? For the organizer*: In the crush of time and limited resources, is that meeting really open to all? Are new people genuinely trained for leadership, or is there just not quite enough time? Are decisions a mutual process of search for agreement or maybe, just maybe, predetermined? *For the professor*: Can a smart student's offering of a reading

---

1. As will become obvious, much of this work builds on that of Paulo Freire, whose theories are written about elsewhere in this book and are not repeated here. His other works that have influenced me greatly include *Pedagogy of Hope* (2000b) and *Education for Critical Consciousness* (1973). bell hooks's writings, especially *Teaching to Transgress* (1994), have also been highly influential. These three books pose a serious, albeit implicit, critique of the limits to "competency-based" educational models because they require efforts toward mastery of *incompletion* rather than additive models of only "positive" growth.

be sent around to her classmates? Who gets the last word on strategic debate? If some students disagree with your preferred model of organizing, is there an implicit and even explicit downgrading of their work? Are those two conservative students given the same respect in the classroom as those progressives who think more like you? *Really?*

The theoretical principle on living your values in all that you do and who you are, drawn from Paulo Freire and reinforced by bell hooks's writings, seems to pour cold water on Gandhi's noble idea. It, too, is presented in the first class as both an organizing and a classroom design principle: "The fundamental problem (for the practitioner seeking co-creation) is this: Initially, for the oppressed, as divided, inauthentic beings, *to be* is *to be like,* and *to be like* is *to be like the oppressor*" (Freire, 2000a, p. 33). In other words, people arrive in a moment of investigation and action, whether in a campaign or a classroom, as historical beings whose primary experience heretofore has been all-too-often as recipients of others' knowledge and direction—followers expected to follow, not lead; students expected to learn from whoever is in front of the room, not from each other. The result, the brilliant Brazilian pedagogue went on, is that the inevitable resistance and fears associated with a new model of learning (or organizing) necessarily require understandable resistance *and* necessary respect from learner and teacher, and likewise from organized and organizer).[2]

And thus by the end of our first 2-hour session, the classroom principles have been elucidated in order to breed personal discomfort and collective struggle. By the end of that session, strategic answers have been replaced by my questions:

- If a teacher or organizer is to embody openness to others' abilities, how does he or she handle their inevitable initial resistance?
- Furthermore, as a teacher or organizer, isn't one supposed to have something to offer that is more strategic or more informed than others?
- After all, one is not hired without skills and strategic smarts. Isn't an organizer supposed to demonstrate those smarts and strategic savvy?
- Likewise, if the goal is co-learning in the classroom or genuine member empowerment in a campaign, what actual value does the teacher or organizer have in the first place if everyone is truly "equal"?
- Couldn't this approach end up as a futile example of democracy in inaction, or verbiage masquerading as education?

This is probably not a typical practice class in social work because only dilemma-filled questions are posed rather than answers given. I offer design

2. This approach has some similarities to problem-based learning pedagogy used in some social work education. (For a review of this approach, see Altshuler & Bosch, 2003). What remains distinctive are the dynamics of power as well as the expressed vulnerabilities of the faculty/leader as part of this particular pedagogical approach.

principles that create unresolved paradox instead of strategic direction. Here I am, an older white man with a bunch of published books, sitting in front of the room discussing some of his limits, not his insights, while he invites often-perplexed students, most of them women and in combination a mosaic of color, gender, and sexuality, to share their own stories. Sometimes that first class ends well, with lots of enthusiasm; more often than not, less so. Years ago, such ambiguity and uncertainty with the potential for student discord would have unnerved me; now I embrace it.[3] This chapter seeks to explicate how such an admittedly challenging approach to learning has had sustained value for all of us who enter that first classroom together. It may also explain, 40 years on, why I still look forward with anticipation to each new class. After all, there's so much more that I'm going to learn.

THEORY CRASHES THE CLASSROOM: ACTIVIST LESSONS, STRATEGIC SMARTS, AND THE LIMITS TO IDEOLOGICAL CERTAINTY

As a young organizer deeply immersed in the social and political movements of the late 1960s and 1970swho had also trained in social work's community practice methods, I brought with me three key lessons from my own work that I hoped to impart to my students. Mixing a lot of theory drawn from the political left and some dawning awareness of what those theories ignored or devalued, my early practice courses had three key, overlapping emphases:

1. *Developing strategies and tactics outside of an historical context made many organizing campaigns mechanistic and less effective.* While in school, I had been impressed with Jack Rothman's typology of organizing variables and the three distinct models (locality development, social planning, and social action) that used such variables (decision-making processes, use of data, use of experts, etc.) in varying ways (Rothman, 2008). Understanding that different models' emphases would lead to different strategic and tactical choices was illuminating and helpful for any budding practitioner. At the same time, my readings on the political left had made clear that the models

---

3. I am well aware—and make sure the issue is woven into discussion in some modest way during that first class—that as a white, male, straight, WASP from New England, issues of my social and racial privilege, power, and position may construct unfair advantages in relationship with others and have given me unearned benefits others do not possess. I am also aware that given these socially constructed dynamics, other faculty will confront a different balancing act between demonstrating substantive smarts and humility in their "embodying the change they seek" in the classroom. Although the balancing act will require a different calibration, I argue the effort nevertheless was worth it, for truly liberating pedagogy that frees us all to grow and learn from each other across our differences is a pressing historic task of the 21st century.

themselves were inevitably influenced by the larger social, political, and economic forces of the historic period in which one lived (Draper, 1990). While Rothman's models were different from each other, a model of locality (community) development from the 1930s had a very different set of tactical choices than those in the 1970s (or the Watergate 1970s from the Reagan 1980s). Although later greatly helped by Robert Fisher's brilliant distillation of organizing history, *Let the People Decide* (Fisher, 1994), from the outside my classes were a cauldron of historical comparison and strategic option, with a disproportionate emphasis on the value of social action over all other method choices.

2. Active in the ideological battles of the political left for many years, I had grown weary if not insightful about the causes of the in-fighting between political groups that made up in ideological ferocity what we lacked in size or influence. As those battles raged, the key insights from an old chestnut of an essay written by Robert Michels in 1905, "The iron law of oligarchy," kept circling inside my head. He had argued that there was an inevitability—an iron law—that as one group seized power over another that it, too, would assert domination, often misusing the same levers of control it had once fought against (Michels, 1959). Having read of the genocidal disasters of Mao and Stalin—both leaders of what were supposed to be socialist revolutions—and been witness to (and, for a brief moment, participated in) petty purges and ruthless infighting against other political factions, I brought to those early classrooms the wounded desire to explore not only the politics of injustice but also the psychology of power. *Classes would explore not only what elites did to the oppressed but also what we did to each other when power was at play and decisions had to be made.*

3. Finally, I had one other, idiosyncratic interest. Maybe it was my proper New England white Anglo-Saxon Protestant (WASP) upbringing, or perhaps having a close relationship with my fraternal twin sister. I could not understand why so many people—political leftist, seasoned social worker, well-published academic—who espoused commitments to the poor and oppressed and thundered at the harshness of the wealthy managed in turn to treat those they worked with like, well, crap. It was as if being on the side of the political angels gave one permission to be mean to a young colleague or political ally. It was seemingly okay to scream at a coworker beneath you on the organizational chart, or loftily dismiss others' ideas with a mix of condescension and scorn. Always musing on what it would take for large numbers of people to join and turn a militant campaign into a social movement, I had an intuitive interest in "the personal is political," and that "personal" included decency toward one another, too. *No matter what else, my classroom, I was sure, would mix the fire and brimstone of political and strategic insights with an engaging personal process of mutual sharing and individual discovery.*

It almost worked. When one is young, passionate, active in poor communities, filled with theory, and has a genuine desire to hear from people throughout the room, it is pretty easy to create an exciting classroom climate. Two things went especially well. First, there was lots of work on strategy and tactics and model building that helped students become increasingly more strategically savvy. Rothman's comparative models, later influenced by Cheryl Hyde's feminist contribution, truly helped students unpack how different models necessarily used the same variables—who made decisions, the value of expertise, etc.—in different ways that led to very distinct forms of organizing (Hyde, 1989; Rothman, 2008). By using role plays and simulations, students began to grasp how tactical choices revealed strategic intent. It was exciting for me and them as they began to "read" others' underlying strategic interests by the choices they made in a campaign or action regardless of what they may have espoused.

Little by little, I also was learning to slow down and provide questions rather than answers in the classroom simulations. It was not easy for me, someone who had thrived on ideological certainty for many years, but over time I began seeing how much more happened on the other side of the room when students grappled with and came to embrace their own answers rather than quickly accepting my own. I still found myself necessarily raising historical context as an important part of their strategic equations—people wanted the 1960s to reappear in the 1980s and 1990s—but ever so slowly I found a few ways to get a piece of classroom ownership away from the front of the room.

The other significant success was to get students to look at themselves and their own strengths and weaknesses as tactics with more or less effectiveness in different organizing situations. Dubbed "tactical self-awareness" (Burghardt, 1982), it was a conscious creation to address issues of power and strategic inflexibility that creep into organizers' lives. An organizer's reinterpretation of the social work profession's "conscious use of self," it also was directly opposed to Saul Alinsky's listing of traits that every organizer had to have—from street smarts to humor, a disciplined mind, and an openness to new issues (Alinsky, 1971). I had eagerly read Alinsky early in my organizing life, and I had been taken aback by his list, for no one I knew, starting with myself, came close to embracing all those talents.

Furthermore, through my own organizing experience I had come to see that I was great at getting a group going but not so good at details later on. Other people hated being in the front of the room but could keep important attendance records and phone trees operational and in order so that necessary follow-up work was not a disaster. While each of us could improve, figuring out whose strengths fit which part of an organizing activity increased the group's flexibility as well as each person's awareness of how he or she contributed and where he or she needed support. (This applies in classrooms as well!) Replacing Alinsky's implicit "great organizer theory of history" through tactical self-awareness (TSA) and the personal insight that "less is more" by allowing for self development and not just community development proved liberating for a number of students. TSA seemed to lessen people's internalized anger and external rigidity as well. As one student said, echoing others, "Allowing myself to be less than perfect freed me to actually work on areas that were hard for me. I spent less time beating myself up and more on celebrating my own 'little victories' of improvement." I was proud of the results. Who knows? If it hadn't been for the subtle, ever-present dynamics of power and rage, fear and trembling—mine as well as students'—wrought by race, those classrooms might have become the islands of strategic decency I had hoped for (Horton, 1997).

The subtle dynamics of power in the classroom evolved slowly, more or less at the edges of my awareness, over a number of years. On the other hand, as detailed later, classroom dynamics of race arrived one spring day in my third or fourth year of teaching and had all the subtlety of a brick thrown through a large, plate glass window. In both cases, I came to see that personal, heartfelt commitments to alter dynamics of power and end racial injustice did not make me any more prepared to transform how I and others dealt with them up close in the classroom.

The issues of power in the classroom perplexed me, leading to a kind of internal discomfort that caused me to seesaw back and forth on how to handle shifting power away from me and toward others. The truth was that I was a popular teacher. Students liked me, gave me strong ratings and wrote engaged, thoughtful papers showing real commitment to organizing and increasing strategic sophistication. The problem was that the more I studied the social psychology of power and its dynamics in the classroom and the more I experienced the struggle for empowerment in organizing among communities conditioned by structural oppression, the more I realized it was impossible for me to *give others power.* Likewise, I had been part of too many campaigns and movements where the actual process of *taking power* had had the seductive effect of people holding that power way too tightly. The hands of power, not its shape, were all that changed.

I was confronted with a painful dilemma. I could be a nice-guy professor and organizer and show students and community people ways where I gave them power—they could decide role plays, set the agenda for a meeting, lead part of it. Given others' initial anxiety about their own authority—Freire's dictum was never far away from my thoughts—almost everybody was happy. However, while this approach was indeed benevolent, it still left me completely in charge: I determined the level of beneficence, not they. Given other, more oppressive experiences in classrooms or communities, few people ever complained as the comparison had the veneer of genuine participation. People had their voice . . . in *my* classroom. Strategically, the best I could hope for was that others would replicate my kind and gentle model themselves. Although students could claim a part of their voice, their full authority was never as great as mine. The iron law lived on, wrapped in the soft glove of weekly participation.[4]

4. These dynamics reminded me of the co-optive mechanisms used by some agencies regarding "participation of the poor"—poor folks got a chance to come inside and

On the other hand, I also knew that if students simply took power that I would be replicating the pernicious zero-sum game fostered by elites for generations. To capitulate to the idea that everyone in the room was exactly alike in what they brought to learning was to deny my own "subjectness." Had I read countless books, studied strategies, and honed tactics for 20 years with no meaning? As much as I wanted students to be engaged with genuine co-learning, I could not accept others "taking" the classroom without a struggle either. Grading papers, following some kind of syllabus, maintaining some coherent approach to learning—those things mattered! But how could I assert my knowledge and experience without replicating forms of domination, especially by WASP men like me?

With too little assertion about the learning, others misuse power. With too much assertion over the learning, I abuse power. Semester by semester, the discomfort quietly grew within me.

There was nothing quiet about race. As a committed organizer working in New York City multiracial coalitions and campaigns since undergraduate school and at the time working in the South Bronx who counted about as many black and brown friends as white ones, I felt that I was well prepared to handle whatever racial issues came up in the classroom. Having read everything from Hamilton and Carmichael's work on Black Power (Ture & Hamilton, 1992) to Gutman's work on slavery and the black family (Gutman, 1977), as well as the works of W. E. B. DuBois and Franklin Frazier (DuBois, 1994; Frazier, 1997), I was pretty confident on the theory side as well.

As an important classroom assignment, I had created different student groups, with members purposely selected randomly to avoid cliques and to stimulate discussion across social lines. Each group was to conduct research together and make presentations on issues of race, gender, and ethnicity, with topics such as gentrification, educational opportunity, and job mobility. I felt well prepared, as these were topics I had studied in graduate school and recently had been involved with in the South Bronx.

What I was not prepared for was the anger, hurt, fear, guilt, and tears that came spilling into the classroom on the first day of presentations. I have never forgotten that scene: Six students who a few weeks earlier had happily formed their workgroup came to the front of the room, grim-faced and silent. A white student had barely begun to speak when eye rolls from two students of color signaled displeasure. Others in the group had their eyes down. A young white woman's eyes teared up; a black student's lower lip began to tremble. It was obvious something was very, very wrong.

People barely got to the content before the emotions poured out. The students of color were angry, frustrated, and hurt; most whites were fearful,

---

"participate," they just could not decide anything. They were always thanked for sharing, however. See Orleck and Gayle (2011).

guilt-ridden, and confused. The former group could not believe how insensitive and ignorant the white students were; the latter were stunned that students of color did not recognize their good intentions and heartfelt commitments. Other students in the class began to emotionally voice similar comments about their own groups. Listening to them all, my response was simple: I wanted to throw up.

Thus emerged what proved to be one of the most pivotal moments of my teaching career: Fighting back the desperate need to retch, *I knew I had to consciously approach whatever happened between these students and my own lack of personal and intellectual reserves to better help them through these uncomfortable dynamics or I was failing to embody the change I sought.* I also knew intuitively that I was embarking on a process of personal and social inquiry that was not going to be "answered" in one class or one term but over many years of reflection (*How could I, deeply committed and actively engaged in racial justice issues, still be so unprepared for others' emotional upheaval? And what did "prepared" look like, since it wasn't about changing the syllabus?*) and action (*What steps could I take in the classroom or community that laid a foundation for dialogue rather than distress among progressive people?*)

THE MIDWIFERY OF LIBERATION IS FOREVER, NOT NINE MONTHS

Freire had written that "the midwifery of liberation is always painful" (Freire, 2000a). My classroom explosion made clear what those intriguing, albeit still-abstract words actually meant. The painful inquiry that I had to embark upon has turned out to be the most liberating process of my life—not just career. This discomforting process forced me to recognize that my commitment to "embodying change" had to be joined to an awareness that "change within others" relating to dynamics of power was a twofold process of mutual de- and co-construction between "teacher–student" and "organizer–organized" that would go on *forever*. I came to see that this dynamic and often paradoxical process had to be examined with *respect* in its original, socially limiting forms so that it could be *challenged* and co-created together for more liberating possibilities later on—in each and every classroom, year after year (Burghardt, 2013). There could be no predetermined approach to how these dynamics would unfold: one year, early in the term; another year, later on in the term. Some students would be excited by the potential for mutual discovery; others were turned off, sometimes permanently. I had to approach each classroom with the "beginner's mind" of complete openness to what might happen, even while aware, paradoxically, that I was using a purposeful pedagogical methodology directed towards co-creation (Epstein, 1999).

CONSTRUCTING THE UPHILL STEPS TOWARD A RESPECTFUL AND CHALLENGING CLASSROOM

Throughout the years, three lessons (listed here and then detailed) emerged through this lifelong process that are the foundation to a *classroom design of emerging co-creation* that I hope can be of benefit to teacher, student, and organizer alike:

- Becoming comfortable with discomfort, both with one's own social and personal identity and with how others might understandably perceive it differently
- Genuinely respecting others' initial reactions and responses to authority, including too much deference to the front of the room and too little toward their peers and themselves
- Combining attention to strategic substance—history matters, discerning how tactical choices reflect different strategic models—with problem-posing questions about power, identity, and process

Becoming comfortable with discomfort, both with one's own social and personal identity and with how others might understandably perceive it differently

That fateful class long ago brought home two elemental lessons in my life. First, no matter one's deep commitments to social and racial justice, a person's own comfort in her or his social and personal identity and how others' perceive the degree of power and privilege one carries with it will greatly influence her or his openness to shifting dynamics in a classroom or community setting. To be concrete, I had to come to terms with my male, straight WASPness in all the multiracial, multicultural settings I was in and neither be embarrassed by my social privilege nor misuse it.

"Coming to terms" with one's identity is not easy. I partially had been aided in undertaking steps toward this humbling affirmation through my own ongoing TSA work (Burghardt, 2013). The ongoing TSA practice of affirming strengths in some situations and limitations in others had given me some personal resilience and the growing capacity to explore the more painful and disconcerting dynamics of race, class, and gender that were at play in class. Perhaps the most disconcerting was the *awareness that situations and contexts that had been safe and affirming for me in my own development often had felt unsafe and threatening for women, people of color, and lesbians and gay men.*[5] That painful class early in my teaching career had brought home that what I assumed was a safe learning

---

5. At the time, attention to transgender issues was all but nonexistent even in progressive circles.

environment in which my identity could thrive and what others needed in that same environment were very, very different.

This insight initially did not breed intellectual or emotional flexibility and comfort. It bred guilt, and guilt can create an overreaction and overcompensation for one's past ignorance that simply replaces one form of marginalization with another. Validating racial unfairness at the expense of white students' own personal stories provided a short-term salve of assuaging my guilty conscience for past sins of omission, but it did nothing in creating a safe learning environment for everyone. The search for "the democratic experience of co-creation" without including every voice in the room was impossible.

For that to happen, I had to fully embrace my own identity while doing the same toward everyone else in the classroom. This was a twofold process: It began by acknowledging and affirming who I was with neither overt pride nor abject deference while affirming others' right to understandably doubt my commitments to their own well-being.

Neither overt pride nor abject deference: It took years to easily and comfortably state my social background in a mixed group. Only as I came to trust myself that I did not misuse my social privilege could I fully embrace my social and personal history and present it comfortably with others.[6] Likewise, I came to expect the inevitable nervous laughter from students when I wove in the obvious but almost never acknowledged whiteness of the teacher in the front of the room. Such nervousness is a reflection of the underlying, unstated dynamics of race, gender, and sexuality that make up almost every classroom experience. By implicitly acknowledging them through affirmation of who I was—neither dwelled on nor denied—I began to set the stage for more inclusion.

Understandable doubt: Coupled with my own affirmation was respect for students' possible doubt of my intent. As such, it affirms their own historical experience—the creation of their own identities—as separate and unique from my own and from each other—which may have included marginalization from people who looked and behaved like me. Whatever initial skepticism, fear, or hope they brought to this classroom as a safe learning experience had nothing to do with me and everything to do with them and all the other classrooms, meetings, and strategy sessions of which they had been a part. Respecting their doubts while affirming my own identity is the initial use of paradox necessary for eventual critical reflection: Don't my social qualities lead to a misuse of privilege? Won't expressing doubts undermine learning? What if the story of my identity conflicts with someone else's?

It is through this initial design of affirmed identity and respect for difference that a safe classroom begins to take shape. The eventual reflection on this early classroom encounter among all of us is designed to remove primary fears that

6. An illuminating example of another faculty member's struggle with discomfort and identity can be found in Wong (2004).

exist in multiracial and multicultural groups: for a person from a marginalized or oppressed group, the fear that to affirm others' stories will ignore the larger forces of historical and systematic oppression; for those from more privileged groups, that acknowledgment of this greater systematic oppression will deny the personal pain and struggle within their own individual stories.

Concretely, there is a "trusting and testing" process that takes place over a number of weeks in class, often woven through other discussions on tactical choices, group formation, and leadership development issues. Because social issues are woven into each session rather than provided in one or two class segments, there is no predetermined moment when difficulties in sharing assumptions about others' identities emerge. Trusting their safety, people from oppressed groups can initially express pent-up anger at straight and/or white students' lack of understanding of why their voices are often muted in classrooms or how exposed they feel when most other classroom discussions focus on clients of color. In turn, white students tend to opt for either overly deferential affirmation of their peers' oppression (which can lead to objectified forms of victimhood) or silent, perplexed upset, fearful that anything they say will be misinterpreted (which can lead to later, unresolved conflict). No longer nauseous, my role is to help students recognize their understandable overreactions, in whatever form they take, as caused by a lack of previous engagement in the sharing of their stories without fear that their own history, whether from oppression or privilege, will be denied.

Instead of the debilitating, seesaw experience of one group having pride of oppressive place over another, this slow, paradoxical acceptance of the "multiple truths" of greater social oppression of some people and the mutual struggle for affirmation for everyone becomes a solid foundation for listening to others' stories, sharing insights, and flexibility in strategic choices that are the hallmarks of democratic experience—including a classroom. And it begins with a teacher's comfort with discomfort and the humbling, affirming acknowledgment of one's own identity.

There of course will be inevitable differences in this process wrought by the distinct social identities of other faculty. There is no question that faculty whose social identifies are from oppressed populations (or at least appear to be) will confront other dynamics in the interpretation and construction of privilege, who is perceived as "smart," degrees of deference (or the lack thereof), etc. However, raising the issues early in the classroom experience rather than waiting for either explosions or misinterpretations later in the term is a way to enrich the learning experience for everyone. No one can escape his or her own midwifery experience toward liberation as one grows through the painful discomfort and humility of discovering how hard and how beautiful becoming a "subject of history" can be. Ongoing dialogue among like-minded faculty on how this plays out in the classroom can be of enormous pedagogical value (Wong, 2009).

Genuinely respecting others' initial reactions and responses to authority, including too much deference to the front of the room and too little toward their peers and themselves

Freire's quotation on "divided, inauthentic beings" (Freire, 2000a, p. 33) and the dilemma it poses for the educator or organizer in how one engages with people to undo these fractures is also woven into the first classroom discussion. This dilemma remains a potent backdrop throughout the term, for I make clear that this term is not simply about "the oppressed" with whom they work but also includes themselves as students. An early dilemma surfaces: As previously successful students throughout their academic careers, how much of their success has led them to internalize principles and practices of the "banking system of education" (Freire, 2000)? As organizers, they obviously intellectually believe in the rights of others to have voice. Does that belief extend to those sitting next to them? Gentle probing and problem-posing during the next few weeks reveals the difference between an internalized belief and an externalized behavior (one can fervently believe in racial or sexual justice and still be uncomfortable around people who carry those identities; people may want "democratic experience" in the classroom but not the added responsibilities that experience requires). Over time, students admit to and reflect on their impatience with those class members who talk a lot, the fact that they never take notes from each other's comments, and their growing consternation that the guy who wrote the textbook they are using is not providing many definitive answers either.

The themes related to deference to formal authority and the tendency to diminish each other's contributions in the classroom lead to important discussions on power: Who has it? Can it be shared? Is it a zero-sum game? Is that iron law of oligarchy inevitable? Having used TSA as an example of "multiple truths"—everyone is good at some things and not so good at others, not "either/or"—these discussions are deepened to explore how to break down that most pernicious of constructions in organizing (and in life)—*binary thought* (Berger & Luckmann, 1966). The task of the strategically effective organizer or educator is to surface the mechanistic and limiting "either/or-ness" in one's thinking so that a truly innovative and supple approach to how one works—and thinks about the work—begins to emerge.[7] For example, some people can come from

---

7. It is important to underscore that this is not the "on the one hand . . . on the other hand" vacillation to take a position but, rather, the strategic and educational reality that the world in which we work and live can hold "multiple and even opposing truths" at the same time that must be taken into account: Some people have had objectively more oppression than others, and many people from privileged backgrounds have their own stories of personal pain and struggle. Both are "true" and will require different yet supportive responses in a classroom or organizing campaign. For example, some racially oppressed groups have strands of homophobia and sexism; as well, there is racism among some sectors of the LGBT community. That said, this takes time: Students or community members must have enough built-up resilience and authentic comfort with each other—a truly safe space shared over

oppressed backgrounds and neither feel nor be oppressed; a child welfare worker may remove a child from her or his home and still be deeply committed to that child; a short-term tactic can be conciliatory in the midst of a long-term strategy of confrontation—and the reverse.

Having explored TSA as an alternative to Alinsky's perfect list of organizer attributes and begun weaving in respectful ways to hear each other's stories about their identities, there will already be concrete examples of "multiple truths" in the classroom. But the real modeling of how difficult it is to break down binary thinking must come from the front of the room. Whereas classic readings define "teachable moments" as those concrete examples of how to show someone what to do or how to correct a problem (Oshry, 2007), in these classrooms "teachable moments" also include the struggle by the teacher to undo one's own preconceived ideas of teaching, what it means to be "smart," and—finally—the fears attached to giving up some of the classroom or organizing action to others with less training.

For it is through awareness of the understandable fear of losing control—of the class, the discussion at hand, the meeting's agenda—that deep-seated and profound notions of power and position surface for almost everyone. It is where the iron law of oligarchy and the possibility of throwing up come together. Only if one remains attuned to her or his own struggle to maintain "multiple truths" of experience, identity, and skills can one comfortably use her or his position of authority—whether teacher or organizer. It means neither succumbing too easily to challenges to your position nor condescendingly ignoring students' or community members' initial and often awkward attempts to gain some control of the learning process. It means sharing that discomforting struggle openly without giving up your hard-earned skill set and strategic smarts. To embody the change you seek, one must embody how difficult it is to change as well.

There will come a time in class—usually somewhere in the middle of the term—when a student or two will challenge the structure of the class: who gets to write on the board, who gets the more comfortable teacher's chair, why the professor still sits in the front. None of these challenges are especially profound or even thought out; they are often masked with wry humor or pop up unexpectedly. But they are indeed important moments of discovery and reflection for the entire class. Students are glad to have me sit somewhere else ... but not comfortable having me next to them. Why? It's great to have others use the board, but does that mean the professor no longer will? The discomfort of teachable moments extends to everyone in the room, for with more authority comes more responsibility. The liberating moment of potential co-creation carries with it the burden of more, not less, to do. The power in democratic experience, whether classroom or meeting hall, is filled with the liberating midwifery of struggle and

---

time—if the "dirty laundry" within oppressed groups is to be aired in a room in which people of other social privileges are present.

discomfort alongside the joy of giving birth to new, unrecognized possibilities of co-creation. Students begin to see that alongside their growing strategic smarts is the need for resilience and tenacity, too. After all, a full life does not mean an easy one.

Combining attention to strategic substance—history matters, discerning strategic purpose within tactical choices takes practice, etc.—with problem-posing questions about power, identity, and process

The unfolding of these classroom dynamics and their application to community organizing would continue to be abstractly academic—or an escape from the "real world"—if they were not grounded in the actual organizing experiences of the students. In turn, those present-day experiences need to be contextualized in the dynamic interplay between model building, tactical choice, and historic context. Therefore, the one, rather long, formal lecture of the term occurs in the second class, in which I consciously contextualize the models of Rothman (2008), Hyde (1989), Smock (2004), and Weil (2012) in the larger political economy—now in the globalized, wired 21st century; at other times, in the Reagan 1980s or the Clinton 1990s. The underlying intent is the same as with the process of the class itself: to capture the dynamic interplay between tactical choices and other, historically determined forces—in this case, the economic forces and political currents of, for example, 2014 compared to 1984 and the ensuing differences in strategic and tactical options wrought by these trends.

Using this global context as backdrop and flowing from a similar approach as case-based learning (Altshuler & Bosch, 2003), each ensuing class draws upon concrete examples of students' experiences in their fieldwork or other organizing activities: their campaigns, meetings, and outreach efforts. Because these actions can often appear to students to be "minor" or inconsequential compared to other, more famous moments in organizing history, situating their work in the dynamic interplay of a larger context helps foster the same flexibility of thought sought in the classroom.[8] Successful outreach in a poor community in 2014 may have smaller numbers than in a previous generation; this does not make it less successful. The interplay between context, strategic models, and tactical choices is thus respected and challenged in ways similar to those applied to the evolving identities of the student organizers and to the shifting dynamics of power and authority in the classroom. The emphasis on the "personal process" begun early on comes full circle: The strategic flexibility of the work and the personal flexibility of the student/organizer are joined in common purpose of mutual discovery—transformation of self and that of of the community become part of the same human prospect (Burghardt, 2013; Pyles, 2013).

8. Although his work does not cover the 21st century, Fisher's *Let the People Decide* (1994) remains extremely helpful for students in understanding these dynamics.

At the same time, the vulnerability one experiences throughout this process of context, strategy, and tactics and the other constructed dynamics between teacher and students is ever-present. By definition, these classrooms are forever changing, not only because 2014 is different from 1994 but also because the social and personal identities of everyone in the room—especially me in relationship to them—are changing over time, too. When I began teaching, I was close to the same age as the students, unpublished, and certainly untested. The dynamics at play sometimes included too much familiarity and too little respect; generations later, I am older than most students' parents and all too often receive too much deference. What has remained constant is the need for me to struggle to co-create a genuine relationship of mutual respect without denying (ever-changing) differences. The vulnerability wrought by having to be forever critically reflective on how these dynamics will play out each new term is paradoxically what sets me free to explore and inquire. For although it is somewhat clear what I expect to teach, I never know what I am going to learn.

CONCLUSION

Effective organizing committed to the transformative process of fundamentally alternating dynamics of power takes patience and persistence if both social justice is to be achieved and the shape of power, not just its hands, is to change as well.[9] The slow, incremental process of problem-posing with others, students' gradual assertion of authority combined with a changing sense of their own identities as "subjects of history," and strategic success in the larger world comes to be experientially understood through our own struggles in the classroom to co-create learning together. Early tensions and discomfort with affirming others' identities without denying one's own give way to the growing capacity to hear others' stories and affirm differences. The awkward embrace of mutual authority in the classroom—from seating arrangements to use of the blackboard and greater responsibility for classroom discussion—is understood as our own classroom midwifery experience—painful and freeing at the same time—and to be expected in the "outside world" as well. Reflecting on this dynamic of embracing mutual authority comes about by weaving many "little things" over time in the classroom that signify a lot. For example, I am humorous about the fact that the last seats filled in the classroom circle are the ones next to me. I joke about first calling on people furthest from me so people will come nearer. Later, when finally sitting somewhere other than the front, I ask people to take note of their discomfort in me sitting next to them. All trivial—except they speak to subtexts of power, authority, deference, and—yes—the safety in the insular, divided world

9. For two complementary approaches to this topic of transformation, see Pyles (2013) and Homan (2010).

of a "banking system" of education (Freire, 2000). Such reflections become a critical component to this pedagogical process. In its place, the conflict-ridden "either/or-ness" of how learning and organizing take place over time is replaced with the mutual affirmation of the overlapping and enriching rhythms embedded in flexible, strategic work, whether classroom or community.

Such transformation, as it begins to occur—first moment by uncomfortable moment, and then, surprisingly, minutes and then hours breathing and acting freely—affects everyone—whether organizer or organized, teacher or student—in our mutual discovery of individual differences and shared similarities. At a pedagogical level, the learning process has expanded the case study approach to one that has begun to reconfigure new ways for students and teachers alike to re-imagine how power itself in the learning/organizing can be transformed. Some will have gained power, others will have lost none. For it is from such transformation, whether in a small classroom or a large community campaign, that the vital lifeblood of powerful social movements springs forth: hope. Undertaken in other classrooms and communities elsewhere, may such hope regenerate its progressive roots across a world parched by its absence.

ACKNOWLEDGMENTS

I thank Pat Beresford, Michael Fabricant, and Loretta Pyles for helpful comments on earlier drafts of this work.

REFERENCES

Alinsky, S. (1971). *Rules for radicals.* New York, NY: Random House.
Altshuler, S. J., & Bosch, L. A. (2003). Problem-based learning in social work education. *Journal of Social Work Education, 2,* 201–215.
Berger, P., & Luckmann, T. (1966). *The social construction of reality.* New York, NY: Anchor Press.
Burghardt, S. (1982). *The other side of organizing.* Cambridge, MA: Schenkman.
Burghardt, S. (2013). *Macro practice in social work for the 21st century: Bridging the micro–macro divide.* Thousand Oaks, CA: Sage.
Draper, H. (1990). *Karl Marx's theory of revolution.* New York, NY: Monthly Review Press.
DuBois, W. E. B. (1994). *The souls of black folks.* New York, NY: Dover Thrift.
Epstein, E. (1999, September). Mindful practice. *Journal of the American Medical Association, 282*(9), 833–839.
Fisher, R. (1994). *Let the people decide.* Boston, MA: Twayne.
Frazier, F. (1997). *Black bourgeoisie: The book that brought the shock of self-revelation to middle-class blacks in America.* New York, NY: Simon & Schuster.
Freire, P. (1973). *Education for critical consciousness.* New York, NY: Seabury Press.
Freire, P. (2000a). *Pedagogy of the oppressed.* New York, NY: Seabury Press.
Freire, P. (2000b). *Pedagogy of hope.* New York, NY: Seabury Press.
Gandhi, M. (2002). *The essential Gandhi.* New York, NY: Vintage Books.

Gutman, H. (1977). *The black family in slavery and freedom, 1750–1925*. New York, NY: Vintage Books.

Homan, M. (2010). *Promoting community change: Making it happen in the real world*. New York, NY: Cengage.

hooks, b. (1994). *Teaching to transgress*. New York, NY: Routledge.

Horton, M. (1997). *The long haul*. New York, NY: Teacher's College Press.

Hyde, C. (1989). A feminist model for macro-practice: Promises and problems. *Administration in Social Work, 13*(3–4), 145–181.

Michels, R. (1959). *Political parties: A sociological study of the oligarchical tendencies of modern democracy*. London, England: Dover.

Orleck, A., & Gayle, L. (2011). *The war on poverty: A new grassroots history, 1964–1980*. Athens, GA: University of Georgia Press.

Oshry, B. (2007). *Seeing systems: Unlocking the mysteries of organizational life* (2nd ed.). San Francisco, CA: Berrett-Kohler.

Pyles, L. (2013). *Progressive community organizing: Reflective practice in a globalizing world*. New York, NY: Routledge.

Rothman, J. (2008). *Strategies of community intervention*. Peosta, IA: Eddie Bowers.

Senge, P., Scharmer, O., Jaworski, J., & Flowers, B. S. (2005). *Presence: An exploration of profound change in people, organizations, and society*. New York, NY: Crown.

Smock, K. (2004). *Democracy in action: Community organizing and urban change*. New York, NY: Columbia University Press.

Ture, K., & Hamilton, C. V. (1992). *Black power: The politics of liberation in America*. New York, NY: Vintage Books.

Weil, M. (Ed.). (2012). *Handbook of community practice*. Thousand oaks, CA: Sage.

Wong, Y. L. (2004). Knowing through discomfort: A mindfulness-based critical social work pedagogy. *Critical Social Work, 5*(1).

CHAPTER 5

Conversation and Dialogue in Social Work Education

BENJAMIN SHEPARD

INTRODUCTION

The path from neighborhood to subway to the re-zoned and rapidly transforming downtown Brooklyn neighborhood where our campus sits can be a precarious one. It is worth contemplating, as it informs the kinds of experiences our students bring into their education as social workers. Just a stone's throw from the Manhattan and Brooklyn Bridges, it connects students' lives, from their homes, to the bus routes and subway rides. It marks a path between the spacial inequalities of the streets through cultural and political histories of the residents of our global city. Some of our students are immigrants; others have been here generations. Our classroom is a microcosm of the city, a living lab stretching from our campus to Bedford Stuyvesant, Fort Green, Gowanus, and the South Bronx, from Wall Street to City Hall, and back to the waterfront, where ships once sailed, factories created jobs and pollution, and today people enjoy riding bikes and playing while contending with the violence that is still part of living here. For many of our students, their lives and life stories are drawn from eastern Europe, the Caribbean, South America, and East Asia. The space around our campus, our students' lives, and their engagement in human services tells a story that is anything but linear. This space also applies to faculty, connecting them with students. After all, faculty end up in the same classroom, the same university, many of the same special inequalities at the same time, with equal access to that often uneven space between classroom, university, and the street. Yet, as a part of a post welfare neoliberal city, we are all impacted by the changes between the campus and community, the city and government, Wall Street and civil society. Through each class, we discuss how this is transpiring, as we share through dialogue.

I teach in the Human Services Department at City Tech, an undergraduate senior college at the City University of New York, where I have taught associate- and baccalaureate-level students for 7 years after a career as a social worker working in harm reduction and AIDS-based settings. Throughout campaigns from Chicago to Atlanta, San Francisco to the South Bronx, Yonkers to the Lower East Side of Manhattan, my activism connected struggles to save community gardens, with efforts to secure housing, nonpolluting transportation, reproductive autonomy, freedom from police abuses, AIDS medications, and global justice, bridging a gap between direct action and direct services, social movements and social programs (Shepard, 2014). Here, seemingly dispersant movements and issues were somehow linked, if only we listened with openness to making connections.

I bring this perspective to the classroom, beginning every class by asking students what brought them to this place in their lives where they would like to take part in efforts to secure a better life for others. I invite them to share their motivations and histories, and I help them to bring these stories into our classroom and their subsequent practice, transforming this experience into lessons for their work. Throughout each class, students are charged to take on the complicated circumstances of urban poverty, organizing, community development, as well as services provision. Here, students are given the opportunity to compare their hopes and desires with the realities of life in the streets of New York's neighborhoods.

Students are charged to become reflective practitioners as described by Schon (1987), connecting doing and thinking, participant observation and engagement, theory and practice (Freire, 2000; Gramsci, 1971). In order to deserve Schon's designation, students are asked to contemplate their lives and history vis-à-vis their chosen profession. Not a static place or a one-time destination, reflective practice is a dynamic, ongoing developmental progression. To get there, students are asked to connect the pulsing work taking place in neighborhoods and communities with their budding development as practitioners. This interplay between the streets and classroom infuses vitality into their practice. This dialogue begins with the individual and the class, connecting self, culture, and other. This analytic third reminds practitioners that culture is always in the room, inviting students to step away from detachment toward engagement as participant observers of their own practice (Sullivan, 1954).

Here, students are asked to make sense of who they are, where they come from, how they are reacting to their clients, and the struggles they encounter. Learning to notice and pay attention to the culture becomes a critical part of the unfolding dialogue. While faculty and student live in story with community, with each other, the aim of each class is to integrate awareness of the interactions between self, culture, and other, building their story as the guiding concept. Students are encouraged to see their story in relationship to others while recognizing that storytelling involves a reciprocal process of empathy and active listening, opening new directions for alternative narratives of their and their clients' lives (Cohler, 1982).

Contemplating the biopsychosocial–spiritual functioning of each client, students must make sense of who their clients are, how they feel about them, and what connects and separates their lives and needs. This holistic perspective charges students with contemplating their whole lives in relationship to their social work education. Sitting in a circle, each class takes shape as a conversation and exercise in reflective practice. This is a pedagogy that engages the whole self, connecting bodies and ideas, awareness of difference, with culture, ambition, jobs, stories about where we come from, and what we aspire to be. At best, each class is a conversation. This chapter explores the concept of dialogue in social work education, in relationship to holistic social work practice, conversation, community engagement, and the ways we connect awareness of our whole lives with our practice.

HUMAN SERVICES AND HOLISTIC SOCIAL WORK EDUCATION

In the introduction to this volume, Pyles and Adam argue that holistic education is an intentional practice necessary to use the whole self to attune into and creatively respond within a dynamic, globalizing social work environment. This pedagogy includes the following four components:

- Presence with the whole self
  - The experiences of the individual's body, mind, heart, and spirit
  - The individual's awareness of and interaction with the historical and current physical, social, and energetic environments
  - How the individual's own experiences and awareness interact with other individuals' experience and awareness
- Whole self-inquiry
  - A lifelong authentic and deliberate learning about all aspects of the whole self
- Empathic connection
  - With whole self presence, intentionally joining with the experience of an other (individual, family, community, and environment) to bear witness to that experience
- Compassionate attention
  - Seeing things as they are with a discerning capacity to suspend action or judgment en route to uninterrupted presence

Holistic engagement brings together ways of connecting the head and heart, the body and mind, drawn together through a reflective contemplation of the whole self in relation to questions about micro and macro social work practice. To do so, students in my classes are engaged in efforts including reflexive reading, answering questions, journaling, listening to music, watching films, working in groups, getting out into the community vis-à-vis internships, community projects such as community gardening, service learning, breathing exercises, mindfulness, and in class tai chi, among other contemplative traditions, aimed at connecting their lives with their practice and the classroom. All of these contribute important pieces to the developing story.

Each class, comprising 20–35 students, begins with students moving the chairs from a linear arrangement of rows facing the front of the classroom into a circle in which these human services students support each other in an exercise in care and conversation. Doing so, we move the classroom so we are all poised to learn from each other instead of simply from the classroom instructor. Students are encouraged to share comments and questions about their lives and education—their internships and subjects of study. Each class begins and meanders in its own way as the conversation leads us to the topic of a given session of study.

After a check in about the good and bad, painful and/or funny parts of their week, we review their field logs and answers for brain teaser questions regarding topics of social work education, as well as aspects of their lives (emotional self, spiritual self, creative self, embodied self, social self, etc.). Some brain teaser questions address topics related to classroom readings, whereas others involve a disposition regarding social work education. For example, early in my field practicum class, I give the students a copy of a sheet of paper with the old saying by Australian Aboriginal Elder Lilla Watson: "If you've come here to help me, you're wasting your time. But if you've come because your liberation is bound up with mine, then let us work together." Students usually have a lot to say in response. Some brain teasers produce big answers; others, such as this one, are the prompts for dialogue and connection. The question seems to give everyone permission to talk about what we need from this work, what brought us here, and the work we still have to do on ourselves as we strive to be healthy, connect with and support others, in collaboration.

As noted in Chapter 1 of this text, bringing aspects of self-inquiry into the classroom encourages student practitioners to ask the simple question: "Who am I in this moment?" In doing so, the practitioner tunes into his or her own feelings, as well as those of others and "the context to gain more clarity and presence, arguably leading to more effective and sustainable practice." Students are not always ready to participate in all of these ways, so I remind them that they have the power to pass if I call on them. However, they are encouraged to participate and expand their perspectives as we explore. Most do so willingly. Others write thoughtful reflection logs or prefer to share their answers with each other in small groups. Some actively engage questions in class. Others find it more difficult.

"Help her out," I remind students, if a student is struggling with an answer. This is not a competition. We all have to help each other. After all, we are involved in a field based on notions of mutual aid and support for social outsiders. We all do well to remember this in each classroom. Check in with the body, we remind each other. "How do you show other students you care about what they are saying?" I ask, engaging students in a conversation about practice, self, and other. Each social work student is charged with developing distinct forms of knowledge, connecting practice wisdom and skills with social work values and ethics, necessary for students to take part in holistic practice. Along the way, students engage the complexity and vibrancy and values that are inherent to this field. Students' views change, evolve, and grow over time as students come to see that social work is not only a profession but also a disposition, a practice akin to art as well as science (Goldstein, 1990). "You are human services students," I remind students. "How can we embody this in the classroom? What do we do if another student is struggling—Do we lend the student a hand to help support his or her own steadying?"

At some point in each class, I remind students that we are working with an educational process that is parallel to clinical supervision. Here, the instructor assesses each student in class as if the student–practitioner was in practice with clients. The way the student sits, talks, listens, and engages is assessed and supported from this vantage point. Supervision is assumed to be a mirror of their practice. If a student is not modeling effective practice in supervision or the classroom, it is assumed that he or she is not doing the same in the field. Conversely, the effective use of active thinking, compassionate engagement, and support for other students here are thought to be reflective of practice skills from the field. Much of this process takes place through conversations and dialogue between self and other about practice in the classroom (Kadushin & Harkness, 2002).

CONVERSATION AND DIALOGUE IN THE HUMAN SERVICES CLASSROOM

Of course, conversation and dialogue do not just happen. People make them happen.

Brazilian educator Paulo Freire (2000) argues that all people bring a problem-solving orientation to their lives. Much of this begins through dialogue in which we take part in a mutual learning relationship (Habermas, 1981). Yet to do so, we must have an equal chance to *enter into* dialogue. This requires a breakdown in the rigid hierarchies between teachers and students, as well as among students. Dialogue cannot take place between those who have no right to speak and those who would deny others the right to do so. It is therefore a foundation of a democratic society and effective social work education. Such a situation extends beyond traditional social work pedagogy, helping us explore misunderstandings and contradictions and barriers and develop possibilities. Attending to basic active listening skills, we must make a concerted effect at hearing each other (Freire, 2000; Habermas, 1981).

"[A] humane collective life," Habermas writes, "depends on vulnerable forms of innovation-bearing, reciprocal and unforcedly egalitarian everyday communication" (as quoted in Smith, 2001). For students, the collective effort of listening, of actively attempting to hear and learn from one another, marks the beginning of holistic engagement, which it is hoped is mirrored with clients. Through these conversations, students reflect on their practice and communities. Such dialogues help us build a community in the classroom and neighborhoods beyond the campus walls (Smith, 2001). As John McKnight (2014) explains, "People who come together to pool their capacities are the real community builders." Through these alternative requirements on students' engagement, holistic engagement really begins, as students connect ideas and people, experiences and understandings.

"EVERYTHING IS RELEVANT": OPENING SPACE

For me, teaching begins by opening a space for ideas, opinions, care, and motivation. This psychodynamic educational approach takes into account student motivation, desire, and intent (Cohler, 1989). To tap in, I allow students to concentrate on areas of their interest, allowing them to grow as scholars and individuals as they direct their own areas of research and scholarship. To make this philosophy real takes interest, empathy, care, and active demonstration of respect for students.

Many of my academic mentors take such an approach. For example, a writing professor, Dr. Barry Sanders, at Pitzer College, respected my interest in writing, helping me cultivate a writer's voice. I had gone to a prep school before this, viewing writing as a drudgery, my papers returned full of red comments after every edit. During a class on world literature, Sanders passed back a paper of mine without an iota of red ink. He noted that I must love writing and would work with me on it. We would fix the typos later, but for now I should just keep on writing. It was the first time anyone had ever suggested I was good at writing—and I have never stopped. That use of a strengths-based approach (Saleebey, 1996) changed my writing and teaching. It taught me to see the whole person, not just a few errors on a page. And if I cannot see that person, I need to look harder at his or her life, as well as the challenges faced in the labyrinth of the modern metropolis. That would be my job as a teacher.

Sanders explains his approach: "You have to love young people to be a great teacher." Care and respect are cornerstones of his approach. "Everybody, rich and poor, majority and minority, incarcerated or on the outside, they want to be respected, they want to be taken seriously, and they want to be loved" (Pitzer Participant, 2005).

Sanders' insight was that everything students bring up is relevant. In a class on Chaucer, we talked sports, the history of laughter, and comedy performances by Lenny Bruce. It was all relevant. Here, the professor taught us to think expansively, connecting ideas and questions, narratives and philosophy into an ever-flowing history of ideas—a vast culture tale in which we all took part in the panorama. Sanders listened with a keen empathy and model of engagement I later recognized as a cornerstone of effective pedagogy (Cohler, 1989).

As a teacher, I combine several of these described educational approaches, with a practical application of a low-threshold practice method aimed at reducing barriers to care and connection, meeting those in the classroom where they are at as people, parents, workers, activists, and, most important, students. Meeting them where they are at means actually respecting and caring to learn what they bring to the table so student and professor can collaborate and make the time spent together productive and meaningful. If education combines these spaces for dialogue and conversation, then learning is usually not far behind (Cohler, 1989; Habermas, 1981).

The steps of cultivating interest and participation from students take countless forms. It begins with a respect for a diverse range of perspectives, providing reading materials from a cross section of subject viewpoints, incorporating differing race, class, and gender points of view when compiling course readings. Yet, it also means listening for the telling silences in the room as well as the boisterous responses. Faced with questions about grief or abuse, the room often goes silent, whereas questions about sexting and pop culture often follow with a fully engaged classwide discussion. Each is telling. In each class, we build on active listening as well as presentation of student ideas and papers, creating a dialogue between educator and student, student and student.

This kind of attunement was the cornerstone of my dissertation advisor Irwin Epstein's (1987) teaching. He was a master of acknowledging student anxiety, addressing needs, and creating spaces for laughter and critical engagement at the same time. A student of Richard Cloward and Robert Merton, he did not care what questions I was asking in my research as long they were framed in thoughtful ways with sound methods (Shepard, 2011). The point was to tap into my own motivation as a student and scholar. Respect for student engagement and concern is a cornerstone of the process. Conversely, I have tried to maintain a similar perspective in each of my classes, as my mentors Irwin Epstein, Bert Cohler, and Barry Sanders did in theirs. I reflect on their lessons in countless ways. At various times, each told me stories of those who impacted them. Bert Cohler recalled his work with Bruno Bettleheim and Heinz Kohut. Irwin Epstein (2005) recalled the positive and negative impacts of his work with Richard Cloward and Robert Merton, recalling the stories of their efforts together. We all need essential others, who help us grow (Galatzer-Levy & Cohler, 1993; Shepard, 2015). Their honest recollections helped demonstrate this, pointing to the importance of self-reflection among educators. The process of learning these strategies impacts cohorts of students generationally.

DIALOGUE AS COMMUNITY ENGAGEMENT

Much of human services education is based on high-impact education practices, including service learning and community projects. Pedagogy encompasses community engagement, group projects, assessment of micro and macro community projects, and engagement in these challenges. Throughout our conversations in the classroom, we consider what is happening in our communities and the significance of such events. When a local high school student, Kimani Gray, was killed by the New York Police Department, we talked about what this meant (Goodman, 2013). Several students pointed out that they had known him and that this practice of aggressive policing that killed him was far too common in their communities. These insights connected their own personal histories with larger policy debates in this global city. Several students became involved in research on stop-and-frisk policing, focusing their semester's work on the ways the city could change this policy. Within a year of this conversation, lawsuits would put an end to the policy, and a new mayor was elected who denounced this practice. Student participation, dialogue, and organizing around the issue were part of the groundswell that put this issue on the agenda for the next mayoral election and led to a change in administration and evolution of this policy. However, the problems with racism and institutional discrimination would not go away. The topic would remain a part of the conversation in classes from field practicum to community organization, community mental health, and health and social welfare policy. Over time, I would see many of these students in the streets at protests just steps from our campus, on the Brooklyn Bridge or downtown, a part of the burgeoning Black Lives Matter movement.

Little of this would be possible without a pedagogy that allowed for getting out of the classroom and working in communities (Shdaimah, Stahl, & Schram, 2011). Many social workers have a limited understanding of notions of what is meant by "person in environment" (Shdaimah et al., 2011). Holistic engagement opens up a space for us to imagine new ways of looking at ideas of individual functioning within the "environment." Here, students are charged with making sense of the ways people help each other, in large ways and small, while supporting their communities. After all, holistic engagement is as much about noticing the day-to-day, moment-by-moment experiences as it is the "outlier" events. As well, students are engaged to contemplate what happens when we cope with events such as Superstorm Sandy, which robbed many students of house and home, taking away electricity or ways of moving through their city. Through service learning around such experiences, students explored new models of environmental social work (Dominelli, 2012; Grey et al., 2013), as well as innovations on holistic social work practice and engagement within the community.

GRIEF, AWARENESS, AND HOLISTIC EDUCATION

For educators involved in holistic engagement, the classroom is a place to bring conversations about our whole selves to bear. But this begins with the faculty members modeling such behavior. A brief story speaks to the point. In was late March 2014. I woke up at 6 a.m. and found several missed calls on my phone, enough to draw my attention. Something was wrong. When I spoke with my younger brother, he explained to me that our father, who by this point was not a young man, had passed away while sleeping in the middle of the night. We both had a good cry, reflected, and got off the phone. By this time, it was 7 a.m. Dad had been sick for years, so the news did not come as a surprise. Still, it is not the stuff that leaves someone ready to teach on a college campus, especially if one is using a didactic pedagogy. A more traditional lecture-based approach asks one to teach with the head in a way that is often removed from our experience of emotion, of the whole self. Holistic engagement, on the other hand, opens a space for a different kind of a conversation involving "the experiences of the individual's body, mind, heart, and spirit." My heart said for me to go teach as my father had done. So I followed that instinct, and it would guide the class session.

Thus, by 11:30 a.m., 4 hours later, I walked into my Field Practicum II class for undergraduate students in internship. Those in the field practicum class are students I have taught for years now. Many are involved in field placements with elderly people in health care settings, youth in schools, and everyone in between. Yet, at one point or another, they all must cope with questions about illness and even death. And to do so effectively, we all have to make sense of our own feelings, history, and responses to death; in other words, we have to handle our own "stuff" (Garfield, 1978; Garfield & Spring, 1995). For us to be effective caregivers and providers, it is important that we have made sense of our own understandings of death (Garfield & Spring, 1995; Shepard, 1997).

So, we all circled up and I told everyone what had happened to my father and that we would have a more reflective class discussion for the next 75 minutes. We talked about how we cope with pain and loss, as well as revel in the people who have been good to us through the years. Some students talked about loved ones who had passed. Others reflected on other kinds of pain they had experienced and the ways they did or did not confront it, or the pain of loss and trauma. There were plenty of issues shared. But more than this, I was different in the classroom, more open, more interested in hearing and being in the listening process while students felt like it was a time for them to be honest and make sense of their lives without judgment, to be better people, better human beings, not just better students. Many talked about those people who had helped them along the way.

I recalled some of the lessons my Dad—a former lawyer, college professor, and ordained minister—brought to my teaching. "Ask students to help each other out if someone is struggling during a discussion," Dad explained after my first day of teaching, starting me down the road toward the use of dialogue as opposed to lectures in the classroom. And so the students and I talked about lessons for coping, including spirituality, social support, and a sense of humor, all of which can be considered part of a framework for meaning creation and struggle, as Viktor Frankl (1963), a survivor of the Holocaust camps, so eloquently described. The ability to connect is one of the skills necessary to survive catastrophes such as AIDS, abuse, or similar struggles. Frankl suggested that those who forged tight bonds had a much better chance of surviving the concentration camps. Yet, Frankl's lessons are relevant for everyone surviving and coping with the inevitable losses and struggles of modern living.

Finishing the class, a few of the students discussed what we had done. Some talked about the use of spirituality as a strength in social work practice. Others spoke directly to me.

"First of all, I would like to start off by saying, I am truly sorry for your loss," noted one student. "Secondly, I pray your father is resting in peace. Lastly, today was truly a touching moment and thank you for showing us that we as human service professionals, doesn't matter rain or shine, we have to endure the reality, digest it, and go on with our life. Thank you for coming today, I hope you will have the time to be with your entire family. Stay strong."

The class turned out to be one of the most powerful days I have ever had as an educator. And much of it was born from bringing the whole self, a different depth and vulnerability, into the classroom and opening up the space for different forms of knowledge creation. A transformative learning environment is one in which we learn from each other (Freire, 2000).

FROM THE DARK WOODS TO OUR OWN STORIES

Throughout most of my classes, I ask students to reflect on their own lives in relation to larger social forces, connecting the dots between their own stories with the narratives of their clients and communities. C. Wright Mills (1959) described such thinking as moving from personal troubles to public problems. Social workers describe such a process as moving from case to cause (Reisch, 1987). This thinking overlaps with core components of holistic social work practice, including presence with the whole self, and the individual's awareness of and interaction with the historical and current physical, social, and energetic environment. (See Chapter 2.)

For many of my classes, the step from individual awareness begins with in-class reflection and poetry. Such writing and cultural work helps make visceral breakthroughs more possible, connecting head and heart (Kahn, 1995). In my field practicum class, required of all undergraduate students, I ask students to read and write a small reaction to the first canto from Dante's *Inferno* (Alighieri, 1954):

Midway in our life's journey, I went astray
From the straight road and woke to find myself
Alone in a dark wood. (p. 28)

This short paragraph is usually enough to spark an inspired conversation about students' lives and struggles. Some students talk about what they did when they found themselves alone in dark woods or lost from their lives. Some describe moments when they lost partners or suffered abuse. Others talk about the need for empathy with others who may have lost their way, increasing their empathy about the feeling of being off track or astray.

Other classes, such as community organization, charge students with exploring the resources in their communities, connecting their own experiences of neighborhood life with larger policy debates and challenges. Along the way, some students find a path from their own feeling of being lost toward a closer engagement with the community. At least this was the case for a student who recently took community organization. The first assignment in the community charges students with going out to attend a meeting in their community and report back on the meeting. Sometimes students go to tenant meetings in their buildings or Occupy events (Writers for the 99%, 2011). Usually, they attend a community board meeting, as one student, Stephanie Samuals (2014) did, in between struggling with her own health issues. Here, she describes a meeting she attended in Brownsville, her own Brooklyn neighborhood:

Up until September 2013, I have to admit that it was not a community which I would say I was proud to claim. It's dirty, and aside from learning what it means to grow up struggling and always looking over your shoulder hoping you were not going to be the victim of the next violent attack, or a case of "wrong place, wrong time," I couldn't really see what it has to offer anyone. It's what any urban society would call a ghetto. I don't mean to sound shallow, but to me, Brownsville was like the halfway house. It was the place you stop in to get your life together until you can do bigger better things. Well, boy was I wrong. On this particular Tuesday evening of September 24, 2013, I attended my first Brownsville Community Board Meeting. I went there with no intention of learning anything; it was just a class assignment I had to get done. As I sat there, I looked around and saw that the community knew and recognized each other. It seemed clear they realized how important the meeting was. The place was packed and people were even standing because the place ran out of seats. (p. 73)

There, Samuels saw a world of ideas, debates, and stories take shape in front of her eyes. In short, she found a community in which she could take part. She described what she took away:

> The Community Board meeting opened my eyes to things in a way that I never thought about before. I realized that Brownsville is a diamond mine. You don't just find a few diamonds here and there hidden around the neighborhood. They're everywhere—you don't really even have to look. At this meeting, there were so many educated people. These people included parents, teachers, retired people, business people, and even other college students. I didn't realize that so many people took such an active role in the attempt to live in and create a better Brooklyn. Until I attended this Community Board meeting, I think that though I lived in Brownsville, I was just like any other outsider looking in. And as the chairperson, Mrs. Bettie Kollock-Wallace, closed on that night I will now end by saying "Peace Out."
>
> Stephanie Samuels, 1987–2014 (p. 73)

The bitter irony of this hopeful narrative is that Stephanie Samuels would only live for a few months after that community board meeting, the report of which was posthumously published in the school literary journal with her family's permission. But the community board assignment created a new narrative for her, offering a way out of a lonely space, perhaps a dark wood, into a welcoming community.

CONCLUSION

Education is fundamentally about relationships, reflection, and power (Freire, 2000; Gramsci, 1971; Rofes, 2005). Throughout this chapter, I have explored the ways that I bring holistic engagement into the classroom. In so doing, the chapter considers the ways holistic engagement helps support a dialogue that transforms understandings of power, education, and knowledge. Here, students are invited to bring parts of their experiences to bear in a process that supports reflection in action, as well as notions of engagement in ideas larger than themselves. Holistic engagement helps students connect an awareness of their own experiences with larger social forces and stories from the streets and the classroom. In this endeavor, everyone can and should be a student, learning from each other, as we all take a part. Holistic engagement reminds us that in every person there is something we can learn; in this, we can all be pupils.

REFERENCES

Alighieri, D. (1954). *The inferno* (J. Ciardi, Trans.). New York, NY. Mentor Books.

Cohler, B. (1982). Personal narrative and the life course. In P. Baltes & O. G. Brim (Eds.), *Life span development and behavior* (Vol. 4, pp. 205–241). New York, NY: Academic Press.

Cohler, B. (1989). Psychoanalysis and education, III: Motive, meaning, and self. In K. Field, B. Cohler, & G. Wood (Eds.), *Learning and education: Psychodynamic perspectives* (pp. 3–83). New York, NY: International Universities Press.

Dominelli, L. (2012). *Green social work: From the environmental crisis to environmental justice.* Cambridge, England: Polity Press.

Epstein, I. (1987). Pedagogy of the perturbed: Teaching research to the reluctants. *Journal of Teaching in Social Work, 1*(1), 71–89.

Epstein, I. (2005). Following in the footnotes of giants: Citation analysis and its discontents. *Social Work in Health Care, 41*(3–4), 93–101.

Frankl, V. (1963). *Man's search for meaning: An introduction to logotherapy.* New York, NY: Pocketbooks.

Freire, P. (2000). *Pedagogy of the oppressed: Thirtieth anniversary edition.* New York, NY: Bloomsbury.

Galatzer-Levy, R., & Cohler, B. (1993). *The essential other: A developmental psychology of the self.* New York, NY: Basic Books.

Garfield, C. (Ed.). (1978). *Psychological care and the dying patient.* New York, NY: McGraw-Hill.

Garfield, C., & Spring, C. (1995). *Sometimes my heart goes numb.* San Francisco, CA: Jossey-Bass.

Goldstein, H. (1990, January). Knowledge base in the social work practice: Theory, wisdom, analogue, or art?" *Families in Society, 71,* 32–43.

Goodman, D. (2013, March 13). Anger in East Flatbush persists over teenager's killing by the police. *New York Times.* Retrieved from http://www.nytimes.com/2013/03/14/nyregion/teenager-killed-by-new-york-police-was-shot-7-times.html?pagewanted=all&_r=0.

Gramsci, A. (1971). *Selections from the prison notebooks.* New York, NY: International Publishers.

Habermas, J. (1981). *Theory of communicative action.* Boston, MA: Beacon Press.

Kadushin, A., & Harkness, D. (2002). *Supervision in social work* (4th ed.). New York, NY: Columbia University Press.

Kahn, S. (1995). Community organization. In R. L. Edwards (Ed.), *Encyclopedia of social work* (19th ed., Vol. 1, pp. 569–576). Washington, DC: NASW Press.

Mills, C. W. (1959). *The sociological imagination.* New York, NY: Oxford University Press.

Pitzer Participant. (2005). *Interview with Barry Sanders* (Vol. 4, p. 15).

Reisch, M. (1987). From cause to case and back again: The reemergence of advocacy in social work. *Urban and Social Change Review, 19,* 20–24.

Rofes, E. (2005). *A radical rethinking of sexuality and schooling: Status quo or status queer.* Lanham, MD: Rowman & Littlefield.

Saleebey, D. (1996). *The strengths perspective in social work practice.* New York, NY: Longman.

Samuels, S. (2014). Brownsville. *City Tech Writer, 9,* 73.

Schon, D. (1987). *Educating the reflective practitioner.* San Francisco, CA: Jossey-Bass.

Shdaimah, C. S., Stahl, R. W., & Schram, S. S. (2011). *Change research: A case study on collaboration between social workers and advocates.* New York, NY: Columbia University Press.

Shepard, B. (1997). *White nights and ascending shadows: An oral history of the San Francisco AIDS pandemic*. London, England: Cassell.

Shepard, B. (2011). *Play, creativity and social movements*. New York, NY: Routledge.

Shepard, B. (2014). *Community projects as social activism: From direct action to direct services*. Thousand Oaks, CA: Sage.

Shepard, B. (2015). *Rebel friendships: "Outsider" networks and social movements*. New York, NY: Palgrave Macmillan.

Smith, M. K. (2001). Dialogue and conversation. *Encyclopaedia of Informal Education*. Retrieved February 2014 from http://infed.org/mobi/dialogue-and-conversation.

Sullivan, H. S. (1954). *The psychiatric interview*. New York, NY: Norton.

Writers for the 99%. (2011). *Occupying Wall Street: The inside story of the action that changed America*. New York, NY: OR Books.

CHAPTER 6

A Deliberate Pedagogy

Introducing the Hidden Curriculum, Social
Pedagogy, and the Common Third

METTE CHRISTIANSEN

INTRODUCTION

"I don't know how you do it! I'm so overwhelmed." I am in between classes the first semester as a student in my Master of Social Work (MSW) program and I am thoroughly discouraged and close to tears. I cannot keep up with the work required, and I am watching my peers, who all seemingly have no issues keeping up. They participate actively in classes and respond articulately to questions from the professor. When I ask my peers how on earth they do it, the essence of their answers surprises me: They just pretend when there is work that they do not get to. "You mean to say that you fake it in class?" I ask. "Yes . . . , you have to! There is no way you can possibly do all that work," they reply. I am further startled during a break in another class. We are chatting outside, and there is a general discontent with the way the professor is teaching the material. This professor has asked all of us to hand in an index card at the end of each class providing her with feedback on her teaching. When I hear my peers' concerns, I suggest that they just write these concerns on the index card so the professor can address them in class. They respond, "Oh, no, I'd never write something like that! I want a good grade!" I marvel at other students asking the professor how long the assigned papers are supposed to be. I think "Are you kidding me?!? This is graduate school!" I cannot believe that adult students act so immaturely, lack such independence, and behave as if they cannot think for themselves. I find myself judging these students and feel even more alienated in the educational program in which I am enrolled.

CULTURE SHOCK IN CONTEXT

At this time in the early 1990s, I had been in the United States 3 years and had decided to stay. I needed American credentials because few people understood or recognized my Danish degree and profession. I had a social pedagogical degree and had practiced as a social pedagogue for several years in Denmark before coming to the United States. Social pedagogy is the main human services profession throughout Europe, and social pedagogues (also called social educators) are employed in agencies that provide services across the life span (Cameron, 2004, 2013; Hatton, 2013; Storø, 2013). Social pedagogues work in a variety of settings, including residential child welfare facilities, domestic violence shelters, criminal justice settings, centers supporting people with a variety of disabilities, shelters for homeless people, and day care and after school programs for children and youth. They work hands-on with people providing direct services, including support in activities of daily living, counseling, and advocacy. Throughout Europe, social pedagogy is a recognized profession with degree requirements, state authorized examinations, and a long history of union affiliations. In the United States, however, working hands-on as direct support staff is not recognized as a profession and therefore the respect and compensation are minimal. I came to the United States as part of a program whose mission it was to introduce social pedagogy to residential agency practitioners and administrators as a way to promote professionalization of direct support staff. When looking for credentials in the United States, an MSW seemed the closest to my educational background in Denmark. I therefore found myself at an American university in a graduate program studying social work. Having worked 3 years as a direct support worker in a residential treatment facility for children and youth, I honestly thought that I had had my fill of cultural differences and culture shock. But now I was in this professional, academic setting asking myself, "Why are these adult students behaving as if they cannot think for themselves?" The educational environment seemed so distinctly different from the one in which I was socialized in Denmark. No one faked it or asked questions about the length of a paper. If someone felt overwhelmed, it was discussed among peers and professors. We did not worry about our grades (or at least not to the point of not speaking up), and we were seldom graded. As a matter of fact, when asked by one of my students about grading during a study trip I conduced in Denmark, the dean of the college from which I graduated answered, "Oh, we don't grade students! That would get in the way of learning!" (P. Harrit, personal communication, 1999). Instead, we were provided with written and verbal feedback from both peers and professors.

My judgmental attitude lessened as I began to learn more about the lives of my American peers and about the circumstances under which they studied. There was a new mother and Child Protective Services worker, who worked 40+ hours a week while she also went to school full-time. There was a single mother driving 4 hours back and forth to classes every week because she could not afford the private university closer to home. They were people who had so much on their plates that I got overwhelmed just listening to them. I wondered, "How do my peers do it?" I heard some of them try to negotiate with professors and advisors as they navigated through the educational process. I also heard some of the responses from the faculty and program administrators: "You better get used to it. This is how the real world works!" I then began to wonder if there was a connection between the stressors of the educational process and the social welfare practices I had observed. For example, I heard a case worker at the Department of Social Services tell a mother that it was the mother's problem that the Department of Social Services closed at 5 p.m. and that she had to find a way to get there on time while also holding a job and attending required substance abuse treatment and parenting classes—all without a car in a rural upstate county. Another example involved a youth who I was working with as a direct support staff in a residential child welfare program. She was aging out and when I approached the social worker to plan for her discharge, he immediately wrote "reunification." When I reminded him that this youth could not go home to her mother due to the abuse that she had encountered and that we needed to explore alternatives, he stated, "Well, I always just write reunification. That's what they [the administrators] want us to do." These observations made me wonder about the impact and role of professional socialization in the educational process. Was there a parallel between what happened in the educational process and what I witnessed in the work I was part of? What would make an otherwise bright social worker disregard the needs of the youth so quickly or a case worker appear to lack empathy for a mother who was trying to do what was required of her? I began to ask myself about how the way we are educated influences the way we practice. What do we know about the professional socialization of social workers in MSW programs? And what is *really* going on in these programs? I shared my observations with a colleague, a sociologist and dean of a social pedagogical college in Denmark. She stated, "Mette, there is a term for what you are describing: It is called the 'hidden curriculum.'" (M. Lieberkind, personal communication, 1997). Really? It had a name? I began to explore the concept and examined the social work literature. There was nothing about the hidden curriculum. My sociologist colleague suggested looking at the fields of sociology and education. In these two fields, I found what I was looking for: literature and research on professional socialization and the hidden curriculum.

Since the exchange with my Danish colleague and my initial research, the social work community has expanded the discussion of professional socialization and conceptualized curriculum as something beyond the explicit (Bogo & Wayne, 2013; Council of Social Work Education (CSWE), 2008; Grady, Powers, Despard, & Naylor, 2011; Miller, 2013; Quinn & Barth, 2014). My aim in this chapter is to discuss professional socialization of social workers through the lens of the hidden curriculum. I then present the European social pedagogical profession and, specifically, the Danish model of education for social pedagogues.

The social pedagogical model has served as inspiration for the Concentration in Human Services (CHS) within the Department of Sociology, a bachelor's program at the State University of New York (SUNY) at New Paltz (Jacobs, 1995; Lamanna, 1992). The CHS provides a case study for deliberate pedagogy and also includes the concept and practice of the Common Third. It is my hope that the introduction of educational programs similar to social work will provide models that will inspire social work educators. Specifically, the pedagogy in the CHS is reflective of the parallel processes that can be cultivated in the student–faculty and service participant–social worker relations. The CHS also addresses the empathetic connections that are paramount to social work practice, and it does so via engaged activities that are integral to the educational process. The CHS attempts to provide opportunities for transformation of both student and faculty in the educational process, not merely transmission of knowledge from faculty to student.

PROFESSIONAL SOCIALIZATION
AND THE HIDDEN CURRICULUM

Social workers are expected to facilitate opportunities to increase social and economic justice, uphold human rights, and eliminate poverty (CSWE, 2008). These charges assume that social workers leave the educational institution with tools to facilitate change and tools to create opportunities for the people with whom they work. They are supposed to do so by using "critical thinking augmented by creativity and curiosity" (CSWE, 2008, p. 4). It is consequently anticipated that social work students become socialized into the profession as social change agents. Webb (1988) states that becoming a social worker happens "via the various formal and informal socialization experiences that comprise social work education" (p. 40). Twenty years after Webb used the terms formal and informal, the Educational Policy and Accreditation Standards developed by CSWE introduced the explicit and implicit curriculum as features of an integrated curriculum design. The explicit curriculum includes formal educational structures, whereas the implicit curriculum mainly refers to the educational environment. The implicit curriculum is supposed to be reflected in, among others, commitment to diversity, fair and transparent policies, culture of interaction, and priorities in the educational environment (CSWE, 2008). However, research on the impact of social work education on the professional socialization of social work students has been lacking, and the research that has been done is inconclusive and, at times, contradictory. Some studies claim a positive impact, some negative, others no impact, and some posit that there is a disjunction between the mission of social work—facilitate change and increase quality of life—and the orientation toward preserving the status quo—keeping practices as they are. The lack of empirical knowledge leaves the social work profession vulnerable to assumptions about how its practitioners are prepared (Barretti, 2004; D'Aprix, Dunlap, Able, & Edwards, 2004; Frans & Moran, 1993; Landau, 1999; Leichtentritt, Davidson-Arad, & Wozner, 2002; Miller, 2013; Moran, 1989; O'Connor & Dalgleish, 1986; Pike, 1996; Weiss, Gal, & Cnaan, 2004). Students are supposedly "transformed into the type of persons social work practitioners are expected to be" (Loseke & Cahill, 1986, p. 247). But do social work students really become change agents? Kivel (2007) refers to social services workers, who stay within the strict confines of already existing agency practices, as buffers and survival workers. They do exactly what is required in order to ensure that people survive as opposed to become change agents addressing structures that can change the life circumstances of people. Kivel challenges human services practitioners to be more than buffers. It is possible to educate human services professionals who will challenge the status quo, meaning the "this is what we always do, get used to it because this is the way it is!" mentality, so that practices become respectful of the rights of people, not just the needs of systems (Ife, 2008; Kivel, 2007). Given what is known about the hidden curriculum from the fields of sociology and education, the hidden curriculum lens can uncover educational practices that might counteract the mission of social work and therefore point us toward practices congruent with the purposes of the profession.

Jackson (1968/1990) coined the term "hidden curriculum" when he observed the behaviors of children in kindergarten (K)–12 public schools. Through classroom observations, Jackson identified features of classroom life that were inherent in the social relations of schooling, such as learning to wait quietly and exercising restraint, cooperating, keeping busy, showing allegiance to the teacher and peers, and being neat and punctual. According to Jackson, students learn to conform, be docile, and to reproduce the status quo. The existence of a hidden curriculum, however, is not limited to K–12 education; it is also present in colleges and universities (Bergenhenegouwen, 1987; Gair & Mullins, 2001; Margolis & Romero, 1998). The hidden curriculum is the unstated norms and non-academic, but educationally significant, consequences of schooling that are not made explicit. It is the business-as-usual, tacit ways that schools compel students to comply with dominant practices. In other words, the hidden curriculum consists of the invisible and taken-for-granted processes in education.

Kaufman (2005) supports this idea by presenting the concept of an "unmarked" category: "The unmarked represents the unnoticed and taken-for-granted elements of our social world that are often neglected by researchers as they focus on more marked [e.g., deviation-related] phenomena" (p. 247). In order to examine and uncover the dynamics of the socialization process, we must challenge and explore the taken-for-granted assumptions about everyday experiences and illuminate the invisible or unmarked—the hidden.

The hidden curriculum in social work education might very well be what Barretti (2004) refers to when she points to the "unintentional socialization" (p. 277) and the "unofficial socializing agents and varied conditions that may be complementary, contradictory, or irrelevant to the official definition [of sociali-zation]" (p. 279). Barretti remains silent as to what might underlie the "uninten-tional socialization," but Miller (2013) has begun the process of exploring the "intended and unintended consequences" (p. 369) of the professional socializa-tion that might occur within social work educational programs. What are these "unofficial socializing agents"? Are they the taken-for-granted or invisible forces that, because they are "unmarked," have not gained the interest of social work researchers and educators? According to Bowles and Gintis (1976), these forces must be examined because it is the *form* of socialization rather than the *content* of the formal curriculum that becomes the vehicle for preparing students for their corresponding places in the workforce.

SOCIAL WORK EDUCATION AND THE HIDDEN CURRICULUM

One form, to stay with the terminology used by Bowles and Gintis (1976), that influences socialization is the physical environment—the brick and mortar (Apple & King, 1983; Gair & Mullins, 2001). It is the unmarked and taken-for-granted frame in which education takes place. After discussing the physical envi-ronment, I present aspects of the hidden curriculum as these pertain to students and faculty.

The Physical Environment and the Hidden Curriculum

The context that influences professional socialization is not limited to the direct student–educator relationship. The physical environment also factors in (Bogo & Wayne, 2013; Costello, 2001). The architecture and physical environment act as socializing factors, and the way an educational institution is structured reflects the agenda of that institution (Gair & Mullins, 2001; Martin, 1983; Snyder, 1971). I remember entering the educational institution where my MSW program was located and remember sitting in classrooms confined to a chair while learn-ing about how to work with people who were oppressed, marginalized, and often difficult to reach due to their previous experiences with the human services sys-tem. As I literally became increasingly uncomfortable (3 hours is a long time in a hard chair), my thoughts returned to the social pedagogical colleges with which I was familiar from Denmark. Most educational institutions for social peda-gogues in Denmark have few classrooms because there is little emphasis on lec-turing as a teaching and learning modality. There is ample space for group work; in some instances, there are designated rooms for student group projects. At the college from which I graduated, we all worked in groups, and each group had its own room for the semester. At the colleges, there are also a variety of workshop rooms and equipment for creative learning opportunities and projects, such as music, arts, physical movement, drama, and ceramics. The moment we entered as students, it was clear that we were expected to be creative, to move around, to use artistic tools and instruments, and to work together.

Entering a traditional school of social work in the United States communicates a different agenda than a school of social pedagogy in Denmark. The traditional university setting in the United States reflects an agenda of limitation. You can be creative, but practice within the classroom. You can dance and build, but do so within the classroom. You will sit in rows or, at best, in circles or around tables that can be moved. The restriction of the classrooms parallels the restriction of the office: the typical site of social work practice—a site distinctly different from the lived realities of the very people with whom social workers interact. The current physical environment limits the pedagogical choices of faculty; what goes on has to fit in a classroom full of chairs and tables and within a predetermined amount of time (Gair & Mullins, 2001; Ife, 2008). These restrictions may force faculty to abandon or limit more innovative pedagogical strategies that could prepare students for new and different approaches. The physical settings of educational programs send messages to students that are indicators of a hidden curriculum. The CSWE's (2008) Educational Policy and Accreditation Standards (EPAS) clearly articulate that programs are expected to promote innovation and creativity. However, most settings have traditional classrooms that leave few opportunities for creativity.

Students and the Hidden Curriculum

Until recently, there was little focus on social work students' perception of their educational experiences (Grady et al., 2011; Miller, 2013; O'Connor & Dalgleish, 1986; Schreiber, 1989). Schreiber, in her study on the influence of peer groups in social work education, found that peer groups had a buffer effect and mediated the bewildering process of professional education in the large bureaucratic structure. With the support of peer groups, students learned to conceal their failures and manipulate their educational experiences, including ignoring or modifying what they experienced as the faculty's authoritative approaches. This practice is exactly what I observed when I began my graduate studies, and I still see evidence of these strategies in my daily work with current students and alumni who stay in touch. Students share how they are overwhelmed and must prioritize what to focus on while at the same time feeling that they have to appear as if they are on top of everything. In the literature, terms such as gamesmanship (Barbour, 1985; Snyder, 1971), survival and resiliency (Barretti, 2004; Gair & Mullins, 2001; Schreiber, 1989; Snyder, 1971), and even "unibluff" (i.e., university bluff; Bergenhenegouwen, 1987) repeatedly appear indicating the strategies students develop to counter what they perceive as the authoritative stressors put on them by the educational processes and structures. The term survival stands out here. Students literally use the term "survival" to describe how they feel during their studies. As mentioned previously, Kivel (2007) notes that human services practitioners, including social workers, end up as survival workers, as buffers, as opposed to social change agents working *with* service participants to create changes that will go beyond mere survival and actual increase people's quality of life.

Snyder (1971) describes two orientations that students take on. The two orientations are seen in instrumental students and expressive students. Instrumental students are pragmatic. They seek utility and higher grades to further their future career or life plans. Expressive students, on the other hand, look for how what they learn is congruent with their values and how knowing themselves, their capacities, and limitations fit into their future goals. Instrumental students often deny or are unaware of the dissonance between the formal and the informal curriculum, whereas the expressive students struggle with integrating the two curricula, whether they are conscious about these two curricula or not. Depending on their orientations, some students might experience the presence of a hidden curriculum, whereas others might not. In discussing students in general, Snyder posits that a lack of recognition of the hidden curriculum results in students not being able to change when they are faced with new and unfamiliar situations. Roche et al. (1999) and O'Connor and Dalgleish (1986) claim that social work students are not given tools or the opportunity to develop approaches needed in order to facilitate social change. What is achieved instead is a mastery of selective negligence—that is, the ability to select exactly what the faculty is perceived to want and no more (Snyder, 1971). I use the term perceived because many faculty members are trying to cultivate learning environments that can be models for empowering practices, but many students do not experience or possibly distrust the intention of faculty. In the aforementioned example about the students not writing honest feedback on the index cards to the professor, I know that the professor welcomed the feedback—even the less than good feedback. How do I know that? Because I wrote this kind of honest, and often negative, feedback, and the professor and I often spent time after class to discuss my critique. As an educator myself, I have tried many different approaches to build an environment in which students can feel safe to provide honest feedback. An example on the lighter side is pointing out to students that they do not have to start each paper reflecting on assigned readings with "I found these readings to be very interesting. . . ." I often encourage students who disagree with a reading or with me to share the disagreement in class. The intent is that students can do well in class even if we disagree and also if students risk voicing this disagreement.

Students' socialization has begun very early on—long before entering the MSW program. This anticipatory socialization (Bronstein & Abramson, 2003; Miller, 2013; Zeichner & Gore, 1990) comes through very strongly. During a student-selected group project in one of my classes (discussed later), Kathy, who had always been a straight A student, became very distraught. She became stressed because she had to rely on her peers for both the group process and the product. I verbally reassured her that she did not have to worry. This project would receive a very good grade given how all the groups sincerely struggled with learning the skills required of the project. Despite my good intentions and reassurance, Kathy clearly became increasingly stressed. I approached the group, and we discussed what the group could do in order to lessen Kathy's stress and reassure her that the grade was not something to worry about. After her peers' direct involvement, Kathy finally began to trust that she could focus on the learning process and not the grade. It became an important learning moment for me, however. Regardless of my good intentions, students still feel vulnerable and feel an incredible pressure to perform—a pressure that can result in breaking down or "bluffing." Roche et al. (1999) and Snyder (1971) note that students experience the amount of work and its encroachment of it on the rest of their lives as overwhelming. The educational process has thereby been turned into a game of "bluffing" in which professors are to believe that the students are doing everything required of them.

Some students do resist—that is, develop strategies that, in this case, are meant to buffer oppressive forces (Margolis & Romero, 1998, 2001; Shor, 1996). Resistance can be proactive in that students take actions to create change. Resistance can also be passive as a strategy of survival. Students' agency—their action—is evident, but with different outcomes and consequences. Students calculate their resistance because of the risk of what might be termed reprisal: blaming the victim, cooling out, and silencing. Blaming the victim refers to "social interactions that socialize students to define themselves as the problem, rather than exploring the structural causes for their experiences within the institution" (Margolis & Romero, 1998, p. 13). Cooling out results from the dynamics that force students, who would otherwise protest, to lower their expectations for their educational experience—a point also made by Shor (1996). Cooling out is closely related to silencing, in which students are socialized to not question the experienced dynamics and practices: "Breaking the silence is a violation of the unspoken rules of the hidden curriculum" (Margolis & Romero, 1998, p. 21). When students do break the silence and address structural issues, faculty might take the critique personally, resulting in an exclusion of the students (albeit not in an official form). Kathy clearly believed that she risked negative consequences if she did not adhere to a specific set of expectations as a student. As a student in the CHS, there are structures in place to (attempt to) address these specific challenges. These structures are addressed later in the chapter. Being socialized to espouse the characteristics outlined previously (e.g., inability to change, being silenced, or cooled out) flies in the face of the mission of social work. Social work students consequently risk graduating without the tools or impetus to fulfill the purpose of the profession.

Faculty and the Hidden Curriculum

Social work students must experience feeling empowered in their educational socialization process in order for them to become empowered practitioners—practitioners who themselves will facilitate empowerment in their work with service participants. Social work faculty are charged with the task of ensuring an environment that is conducive to such a socializing experience (Franz & Moran, 1993; Huff & McNown Johnson, 1998). Many educators utilize pedagogical paradigms that are congruent with this notion of socialization, and they develop strategies that more closely mirror the practices that they hope students will implement once they enter the field of social work (Burstow, 1991; Coates, 1994; Finn & Jacobson, 2003; Graham, 1997; Ife, 2008; Neuman & Blundo, 2000; Pearson, 1998; Roche et al., 1999). This book offers examples of such paradigms and strategies.

The foundation of most of the more congruent paradigms is critical pedagogy based on the work of Paulo Freire (1993). Critical pedagogy focuses on transformation throughout the educational process as opposed to transmission. It not only allows but also consciously facilitates student empowerment and resistance. In collaboration with educators, students become knowledge creators and mobilizers (Freire, 1993; Ife, 2008; Weick, 1993). Rather than reproducing the status quo, students and educators prepare for the future, a yet unknown future, in which transmitted knowledge at best might ensure a status quo and at worst hinder the changes needed to facilitate social justice and equality (Brookfield, 1995; Giroux, 1983b; Shor, 1996).

Selective negligence in students has a parallel in the faculty practice. The term "publish or perish" is well-known in academia (Brookfield, 1995; Gair & Mullins, 2001; Snyder, 1971), and faculty are often rewarded for their research productivity first and for their teaching record second. In addition to the emphasis placed on research as opposed to teaching, the research endeavor can be an isolating experience in which collaboration may not be encouraged (Brookfield, 1995). To be fully recognized, faculty members have to produce journal articles and books, preferably as sole or first authors. Importantly, faculty have internalized the unilateral authority of teachers as normal. As a first step toward becoming an effective and reflective educator, faculty need to become aware of their own socialization as teachers (Shor, 1996; Zeichner & Gore, 1990). Brookfield posits that the best learners often make the worse teachers because they have not been struggling with dissonance throughout their own educational process and therefore have not reflected on their role as educators. Educational programs are often thought of as learning places for students, not for teachers. However, the realities of students and faculty have many parallels, and both are "prisoners in the same box" (Snyder, 1971, p. 155). Students and faculty are not passive recipients; they are capable of producing and mediating circumstances (Giroux, 1983a). By critically reflecting on the processes within education, teachers recognize that what happens in the classroom "changes the world" (Brookfield, 1995, p. 266). "[T]he ways they treat students increase or dampen students' sense of agency. Being aware that classrooms mirror the structures and inequalities of the wider society, they make a deliberate attempt to work democratically" (Brookfield, 1995, p. 266). The education of social pedagogues and the CHS provide examples of such deliberate pedagogy.

DELIBERATE PEDAGOGY: INTRODUCING SOCIAL PEDAGOGY AND THE COMMON THIRD WITHIN THE CONCENTRATION IN HUMAN SERVICES

Social Pedagogy

The social pedagogical profession has a more than 100-year-old tradition in Europe, and although the professionals have different titles depending on the country in which they are educated, there are many theoretical and practice similarities. For example, social pedagogy is the main human services profession for people working directly with or in the life space of children, youth, families, and communities facing a variety of challenges (Cameron, 2013; Wood & Long, 1991). These challenges include abuse, neglect, interpersonal violence, disability, addiction, and poverty. The social pedagogical education ranges from 3½ to 7 years depending on the country, but most social pedagogues have a bachelor's degree. The profession draws from the fields of theoretical and applied pedagogy; sociology; psychology; social policy; law; cultural studies; criminology; communication; and applied activity subjects such as drama, movement, textile, woodwork, nature, ceramics, music, and sports (Cameron, 2004, 2013; Giesecke, 1992; Gottesman, 1994; Harrit, 1999; Hatton, 2013; Smith, 2009a; Storø, 2013). The applied activity subjects are often referred to as animation in France and Italy and in some countries in South America. The use of drama, for example, is inspired by the work of Augusto Boal and his *Theatre of the Oppressed* (1979)—discussed elsewhere in this book. Paulo Freire's critical pedagogy is seen in the way activities are used to increase opportunities for conscientization (Smith, 2009b).

In the Nordic countries, especially Denmark, the term *Det Fælles Tredje*, literally meaning the Common Third, is used. The Common Third is the deliberately planned activity that is used to build relationship between the service participant(s) and worker(s), to build competence, and to create small successes from which growth and change can occur (Hatton, 2013; Storø, 2013). Field education internships, the doing and implementation of social pedagogy, are an integral component of the educational process. In Denmark, for example, there are three internships, and they constitute more than one-third of the education. They are block placements where students spend 32 hours a week working side by side with educated pedagogues while they receive extensive supervision (International Committee of the Rectors' Conference (INCORE), 2002). A social pedagogue is focused on the whole person, and responsibilities include support in activities of daily living, family work, and service coordination—both hands-on work and counseling. This model differs from especially the child welfare and disability field in the United States, in which social workers are responsible for the counseling and service coordination and paraprofessionals (without specific educational requirements) are responsible for the hands-on tasks. I remember feeling as if half my job was taken away from me when I came to the United States and was told to "not talk about treatment-related issues" with families because I was only the direct support staff, not the social worker.

Social pedagogy derives from different traditions, including German progressive education, the Danish folk high school movement, and John Dewey's educational philosophy. The most significant influence has been Paulo Freire's critical pedagogy with its focus on a transformative, reciprocal, and egalitarian educational process (Hatton, 2013; Smith, 2009a; Storø, 2013). According to INCORE (2002), the key elements of the education are democracy, equality, and dialogue, all of which are congruent with a Freirian approach. Cameron (2004) claims that social pedagogy is a professional field that crosses the social work/education divide, and according to her, it is social education that integrates the Heart, Head, and Hand combination.

Cameron (2004) presents several themes based on her research in different European countries. One is the expectation that service participants play active parts in decision-making processes. This facilitation of self-determination is evident already in early childhood settings. Second, relationships are the main vehicle for growth and change; relationships often include physical contact and intimacy. The focus on close physical contact is in stark contrast to what students are told to do in social work education in the United States. For the past two decades, former students have told me that social work professors tell them to never touch and show physical affection for anyone with whom they work. Students assume that it is because of the risk of abuse allegations. The social pedagogical focus on relationships, and sometimes close emotional ones, is connected to the Heart aspect of social pedagogy. It refers to the ability and willingness to give of oneself without expecting that the service participant necessarily reciprocate. It also requires strategies for self-care and, as a Danish service participant stated, "a good pedagogue was one who had a 'professional heart'" (Cameron, 2004, p. 145). The Head refers to the use of the theoretical foundations of social pedagogy and the pedagogues' ability to integrate and use these theories in their work: "A central tenet of a pedagogic approach is to reject universal solutions and accept a multiplicity of possible perspectives, depending on personal circumstances" (Cameron, 2004, p. 145). Social pedagogy is not prescriptive, and responses such as "Well, it depends" and "We talk about it" are standard in cross-cultural exchanges when my American students ask Danish pedagogues,

"So, what do you do here when . . .?" The ongoing dialogue between worker and service participant has been referred to as reflexive pedagogy. The success of this dialogue, this interaction, is related to the relationship and rapport that have been established through the Heart–Head combination. The tool used to develop and cultivate this relationship is reflected in the Hand, which is Cameron's term for the Common Third.

The Concentration in Human Services

Social pedagogy as a profession does not exist in the United States. However, the CHS in the Department of Sociology at SUNY New Paltz is inspired by European social pedagogy and was specifically modeled after Danish social pedagogy. Human services agency directors in the Hudson Valley in New York state were introduced to social pedagogy in the 1980s. With the goal of improving the quality of services and professionalizing the direct support staff, they initiated the CHS in 1992 (Jacobs, 1995; Lamanna, 1992). Although not a CSWE accredited social work program, the CHS shares many similarities with social work education. The CHS has a liberal arts foundation, and students obtain a Bachelor of Arts degree in sociology with required courses that correspond with courses required in Bachelor of Social Work programs. Many of the required readings come from social work literature, and since its inception, most of the faculty members have been social workers. The CHS can therefore serve as an inspiration for social work education, and it provides an excellent case study example in a text on holistic engagement.

In line with social pedagogical programs in Europe, the educational philosophy of the CHS is based on Paulo Freire's critical pedagogy and both inductive and deductive approaches are used as students explore their education and practices through several lenses, the most prominent of which is an international human rights lens. The CHS is a 60-credit program in the students' junior and senior years leading to a Sociology degree with a CHS. In addition to being provided with a solid sociological base, students are immersed in a comprehensive educational program with deliberately developed components both inside and outside the classroom setting. Some of the main deliberate components are a cohort format with consecutive course work, field education courses, and a focus on the Common Third via Arts and Recreation course requirements.

The first main feature is the cohort. After the introductory course, students enter the CHS cohort and stay together for three semesters while they take three consecutive human services theory and practice courses and three field education courses. Students are therefore in classes together nearly 6 hours a week. The human services theory and field classes are purposefully scheduled back-to-back, which allows for flexibility of time, including opportunity for co-teaching and extended time for field trips, guest speakers, or special projects. The cohort structure also provides a laboratory for group dynamics and practice. Rather than just reading about group dynamics and teamwork, students live it as they practice their human services skills.

Another example of using the cohort format as a laboratory is the student selected themes component. During the fall of their senior year, the students identify topics that they want to focus on in their capstone course. Although they, of course, have to compromise and cannot focus on endless topics, students consistently express that they appreciate that they get to choose their own topics. Before, during, and after the process of deciding—and when the capstone course is evaluated—discussions take place about how students really know how to identify what they need to know more about and also how to go about it. They are learning a format that they can bring with them into the field. This process is both explicit and implicit because it is brought to the forefront of the discussions that students can identify what they need to learn and now have experienced one way of going about obtaining knowledge and skills about topics that they identify as essential. They are not just receptacles of the knowledge that the faculty members decide they must have transmitted to them. A theme that now, based on student feedback, has been instituted originally came from a student selected theme process. Several years ago, a cohort of students decided that they wanted to "get their hands dirty" and they wanted to learn about program development and grant writing. The CHS students now work closely with nonprofit organizations and their grant writers writing real grants. Students express a deep sense of empowerment knowing that they are part of a student selected theme, they do the actual work, and, when grants are awarded, they see the real benefit to the service participants and organizations involved. And, of course, the students leave the CHS with skills that are quite impressive at the undergraduate level.

The second main feature in the CHS is the field education course. Students meet with the faculty, and together they decide which sites will provide the best learning opportunities. Students are not placed but, rather, are active participants in the decision-making process. When students are in their internships, they meet weekly with peers and faculty for group supervision and support. They have one-on-one supervision throughout the semester with the faculty, who also visit students at their site for a three-way meeting with the agency field supervisor. This format is deliberately developed to role model a participatory process in which supervision is a reciprocal process with students providing and receiving supervision from peers as well as having supervision meetings with both faculty and field supervisors. It is a democratic model and different from the hierarchical model that is common in some social work programs. In many social work programs, students are placed into the field education sites without significant input, and they are not part of a planned, ongoing support or supervision process with peers and faculty in the program. Peer support and supervision can seem coincidental as opposed to deliberately integrated into the curriculum.

The last main feature of the CHS is the Common Third. The Common Third is integrated into most components of the CHS, and students are introduced to the concept from the very beginning. Loris Malaguzzi's famous poem, "The Hundred Languages of Children," is shared in the first class, pointing out that providing one kind of approach is "stealing the 99," as the famous Italian pedagogue wrote. The prevailing focus on verbal therapies done in office settings as the main modality in social work education is severely limiting. The CHS attempts to balance the focus on verbal approaches with Common Third activities. For most of my career before entering academia, I worked with people who were either nonverbal (due to autism) or socially marginalized (due to addiction and mental health issues). For both groups, verbal approaches were problematic. For the latter group, I represented "the system"—a system that they believed had let them down. One man in the halfway house in which I worked refused to talk with me, so I joined him in the garden. After gardening side by side for a while, he began to share, and some of the best "verbal therapy sessions" I have ever been a part of occurred while literally resting my arms on a shovel. I needed alternative or holistic tools to reach most of the people I worked with and the Common Thirds, in this case gardening, became the vehicle to do so—to establish relationships. Verbal therapy in an office setting could not have accomplished such an outcome.

In order to provide students with knowledge and skills to plan and implement Common Third activities in their internships and later at their work sites, they are required to take two courses in Arts and Recreation. Being located within a traditional university system, the CHS does not have its own workshop rooms, studios, or auditorium as is seen in European programs, but students have access to related courses at the college. In addition to traditional college courses such as piano, photography, film making, ceramics, dance, or sculpture, the CHS, in collaboration with the School of Education, offers two Expressive Arts courses. These courses introduce students to a variety of expressive arts media, including Boal's (1979) *Theatre of the Oppressed*. Students *do* these arts, practice them, and bring them into the field to be implemented at their field sites. Students use music and tie-dye, sports, and games, and they also use daily activities as Common Thirds. For example, Adam did his internship at a residence for adult men with intellectual disabilities. Very quickly, he learned that several of the men were interested in fish and fish tanks. Rather than a one-shot Common Third, Adam chose to do his required Common Third as a process. He discussed what kinds of fish the men were interested in, explored them on the Internet, made a wish list, obtained funds, and then began buying what they needed to get their fish tank. At the end of the semester, the men had their tank and felt a tremendous sense of pride, and Adam had had endless opportunities to establish relationships and do counseling sessions—in the living room, around the dining room table, while in the car driving to the shop, while putting together the tank, and so on. Darlene did her internship at a daytime homeless shelter. The people at the shelter were some of the most marginalized people imaginable. One of her Common Thirds consequently focused on facilitating a sense of inclusion, intimacy, and feeling of self-worth. She set up a table with water, soap, lotion, and nail polish in the living room. When I visited, she was putting lotion of the hands of a homeless man. Behind him was a line of men and women waiting for their turn. Darlene and the man hardly spoke, but the intimacy and closeness were some of the most beautiful human services work I have ever seen. The man beamed when he was done, and Darlene had clearly made a special connection with him—one without judgment, one of compassion and of respect for him as a person. I cannot think of a better base from which to continue providing services.

In addition to the Common Thirds required in the field education internships, students also work in icebreaker groups in their first Human Services course. They implement these icebreakers for the purpose of bonding as a group and also to develop a repertoire to be used in their practice. Social pedagogues are life space workers, much as the original settlement workers were in the United States (Reid, 1981; Smith, 2009a; Specht & Courtney, 1994; Toseland & Rivas, 1995). In the CHS, students are socialized to be life space workers as well. Students are expected to meet people where they are—figuratively and literally. Storø (2013) notes that in order to implement Common Thirds, workers must move from the office to the playground, to the football field or to the computer, if that is where the service participants are. A Common Third is an activity that takes place between worker and participant, and it connects them. It is a consciously guided interaction, and it is planned, implemented, and evaluated by the human services generalist(s) in collaboration with the service participant(s). It is a "shoulder-to-shoulder" experience as opposed to a "face-to-face" experience. Both Hatton (2013) and Husen (1996) call the Common Third a subject-to-subject experience. Common Thirds must have a high communicative content; the activity has to promote and develop communicative competencies—for example, social relations, understanding, empathy, cooperation, and collaboration. When successful, the Common Third develops self-esteem, strengthens identity, and builds solidarity (Hatton, 2013; Madsen, 1993). CHS students and faculty discuss Common Thirds in classes and during individual supervision. In addition, students work closely with service participants and agency field supervisors to develop Common Thirds that accomplish the previously stated purposes.

The Common Third also has another dimension. Storø (2013) and Husen (1996) discuss how Common Thirds can be used to give people a break from intervention, from the intensity of the "work" that continuously is taking place. Storø expresses it as a deliberate focus on the object as something outside the subject—to give the therapeutic relation and work a rest. This is a powerful concept when social work practice in the United States is considered. Social workers practice in relatively short time intervals and with focused goals in mind. The interventions are therefore intense and direct, "face-to-face," so to speak, as opposed to the "shoulder-to-shoulder" approach (Madsen, 1993). Service participants and social workers in the United States are often not given the option of a break, or a rest, as Storø suggests is needed. The use of the Common Third can provide such a rest from human services work. An example that comes to mind is cooking a meal with a family and just *being with* the family without a formal intervention. Hatton (2013) and Smith (2009a) claim that the use of the Common Third provides opportunities to work holistically with children and adults, and Cameron (2004) specifically states that the Hand is "necessary as a *medium* to the development of the relationship between workers and young people as a means of encouraging small, achievable successes" (p. 146). The service participant might not be able to be reunited with his mother or control his anger right away as an immediate result of the intervention, but through a Common Third, something that is very concrete, he can experience a sense of success. The concept of the Common Third and the subject-to-subject relationship are reflected in the deliberate pedagogy employed in the CHS. For example, students and faculty participate in an initial ropes course or rock climbing field day. The purpose of this field day is to build cohesion in the newly formed cohort but also to get out of the classroom and experience each other in a different setting (Storø, 2013). It is a powerful message when students see their professors struggle up a climbing wall or being petrified hanging from a tree during a high ropes course exercise. Students also get to experience a different side of each other. It is not unusual to see more quiet students literally speed up trees while outspoken students stand hesitantly on the ground watching. The purpose of employing Common Thirds also includes developing empathy. Professionals often expect service participants to leave their comfort zone. Professionals need to explore their own comfort zones as well. In the CHS, students and faculty create personal lifeline projects that they share with each other. The lifelines are very powerful, and students always come prepared to the class sharing how they were deeply impacted creating these lines. Many have also implemented lifelines at their field site.

Another kind of Common Third is the field trips that are part of all human services theory and practice courses in the CHS. In addition to the explicit purpose of augmenting the topics covered in the course, the field trips also have implicit purposes. Storø (2013) articulates it well by stating that trips provide an opportunity to get away from the everyday tasks and, as students and faculty experience in the CHS, provide the participants opportunities to get to know each other better and see different sides of each other. Riding in a vehicle provides an excellent opportunity to talk and share. Explicitly, it can also be a powerful learning experience. Sitting in the General Assembly at the United Nations knowing that the topic of women's rights was discussed there yesterday by nearly 200 country representatives is very different from reading about it for class. In addition, students have expressed that they truly "get" what the purposes of human rights and the United Nations are because they were physically there. In other words, the explicit and implicit curriculum becomes uncovered when processing it with the students.

Group work is integral to the CHS. Initially, students are assigned groups that they have to stay in the first semester for the purpose of developing relationships and creating a comfort zone. As the educational process moves along, students get to choose their own groups and, interestingly, students have sometimes requested assignment of groups if they believed that the group dynamics warranted such directions. Such requests have been made when a cohort has had members who appeared to be marginalized and some students then ended up in the "leftover" group. Another example is to explicitly assign students to groups. One cohort recently had a group of students who remained very quiet despite my efforts to draw them out. Another group of students in the same cohort talked excessively, again without significant change in behavior despite my intervention. I then decided to assign the quiet students in one group and the talkative students in another during group work. Initially, I did not point it out, but when the quiet students began to talk in their group and the talkative students had to be quiet to let the others contribute, I pointed out the dynamics. The students, of course, had immediately caught on. The cohort is a laboratory, and both students and faculty can use it as illustrated here. The cohort members, including the two assigned faculty members, get to know each other well. Both faculty members teach theory courses and also teach and supervise students in the field education courses. Building close relationships while also maintaining professional boundaries are integral components of the CHS. At times, conflicts arise around relationships and boundaries, but these struggles are part of the living laboratory. The dialogue and processing are ongoing in the 2-year process and, as Cameron (2004) states, "a pedagogue is not expected to like everyone, however, a pedagogue has to be prepared and willing to 'use the self to gain access to [the young person's] way of thinking and feeling'" (p. 145). This is true in the CHS as well. The relationships between the students are significant. To follow the students from their initial meeting and first internship to a graduating cohort is powerful. They guide and encourage each other weekly as they struggle with dynamics at their internships, and they support each other when they are exhausted during their senior thesis process. This support is explicit in that it is part of the syllabus with classes set aside for peer feedback and guidance in the process. But it is also implicit in that students develop their own means of support. Since the advent of Facebook, cohorts have had a Facebook group where they share and support each other. The faculty is purposefully not part of the Facebook groups but does join when the cohort graduates. All cohorts have experienced loss when, for example, loved ones have passed away. And all cohorts have experienced special happy moments, such as when students have gotten married, had babies, traveled abroad, and have been offered jobs at their internship sites.

The students truly are able to use the cohort as a support or, if not experienced as a support due to problematic group dynamics, then at least as an example of how to deal with conflict. It is clear to both students and faculty that what develops is a synergy. This kind of synergy cannot be accomplished by simply implementing powerful exercises in discrete courses. It is a process that requires time and investment.

A final example of preparation for the future by means of exploring alternative and holistic approaches and systems is through the international focus in all the courses. The CHS in itself provides an international perspective due to being modeled after a Danish social pedagogical program. The structure of the CHS is distinct, and students repeatedly share how their peers in other programs are "envious because they don't get to go on field trips and rock climb" or establish the same kind of close connections to peers and faculty. Integrated in the CHS is also an ongoing introduction to human services models from different countries. Study abroad courses have been a part of the CHS since its inception; indeed, the program began due to a study trip to Denmark. International Social Welfare study trips take place every summer, rotating between Denmark, Italy, and South Africa. In previous years, faculty have also conducted trips to Germany and Spain. Not all students have the means or interest in participating, but the international influence is a constant presence. Three observations from the 2014 study trip to Denmark stand out. Students were amazed by the fact that the leisure center for young adults with disabilities has a massage therapist come to give massage to both services participants and staff as part of the self-care that is taken for granted in the agency. At a shelter for women sex workers, the students saw the massage room used to help the women connect with their bodies in a healthy way. Students also got to experience a drug consumption room and meet a man who had just injected drugs—in a safe, supportive, and respectful harm-reduction environment. Finally, every student made a note of how the 1- to 2-year-olds in the day-care center were given opportunity to be independent. They got up and down from the table themselves; poured their own drinks into regular glasses, not sippy cups; and went to the playground to choose their outdoor toys. The staff were present to support, but only if needed. The socialization to self-directedness begins early.

These study trips are intended to introduce students to different models—and to not take them for granted. The trips also function as learning tools and inspiration for the faculty. They provide, in very concrete ways, examples for faculty members to share in their teaching, but they also more subtly give faculty tools when they explore interventions with students in field education supervision—be it in class or individually. As a result of these study trips, faculty has the experiences to pose questions such as the following: What would it look like if everyone had access to universal health care, as in Denmark? How could you help facilitate prevention initiatives in a resource deprived community, as in South Africa's townships?

The CHS provides the students with opportunities to experiment with different solutions and do so as a group and as individuals. Students get to test hypotheses and are prepared to face a complex and yet unknown future in which they will be challenged to come up with new and innovative approaches to address a diversity of needs.

CONCLUSION

In this chapter, I introduced social pedagogy as a profession and the CHS as an educational model that can serve as an inspiration to social workers and social work educators. Given the fact that research on professional socialization is inconclusive, it is essential that educators develop deliberate content and pedagogical approaches to prepare social work students for the challenges they face upon graduation. The CSWE, with its EPAS, has presented educators with very clear expectations to the content of the education—the explicit curriculum. The inclusion of the implicit curriculum in the EPAS is what I term a beginning discussion of the hidden curriculum; this chapter on the hidden curriculum expands the concept of the implicit curriculum. I believe that Bowles and Gintis (1976) are correct when they posit that it is the form of socialization rather than the content of the formal curriculum that becomes the vehicle for inculcating the dispositions and skills expected for their corresponding places in the workforce. Educators must consequently become aware of the dynamics of a hidden curriculum and the subsequent socializing agents so that they can act accordingly.

How educators treat students and what they actually *do* with students have consequences in terms of parallel processes: Student–educator interactions mirror service participant–social worker interactions. By implementing a Freirian approach, educators and students can create an educational process together that is transformative as opposed to merely transmission of content. I do not mean to imply that it is easy to go against the currents of the traditional educational system and structures. Educators face real challenges in terms of their own and their students' anticipatory socialization. They also face limitations in time and space, and possibly most important, many educators and students have limited exposure to alternative educational models such as the ones presented in this chapter.

This chapter presented several pedagogical approaches and modalities, such as the structure and main features of the CHS and the Common Third. These examples are part of holistic engagement. They enrich the learning environment for students and educators and challenge both to get out of their comfort zones and expand their knowledge of alternative ways of approaching education. As when working with service participants, *doing* can be a vehicle to move outside the comfort zone and experiment with new ways of approaching the challenges we all face in the process of preparing the next generation of *both* social workers and social work educators. As Claire Cameron (2004) observes about social pedagogical practice, "[T]he social relations of everyday living are seen as sources for individual, joint, and group reflections, growth, and change" (p. 149). And the social relations are well captured through *doing* the Common Third.

REFERENCES

Apple, M., & King, N. (1983). What do school teach? In H. Giroux & D. Purpel (Eds.), *The hidden curriculum and moral education: Deception or discovery?* (pp. 82–99). Berkeley, CA: McCutchan.

Barbour, R. S. (1985). Dealing with transsituational demands of professional socialization. *Sociological Review, 3,* 495–531.

Barretti, M. (2004, Spring–Summer). What do we know about the professional socialization of our students? *Journal of Social Work Education, 40*(2), 255–283.

Bergenhenegouwen, G. (1987). Hidden curriculum in the university. *Higher Education,* 16(2), 535–543.

Boal, A. (1979). *Theatre of the oppressed.* London: Pluto.

Bogo, M., & Wayne, J. (2013). The implicit curriculum in social work education: The culture of human interchange. *Journal of Teaching in Social Work, 33,* 2–14.

Bowles, S., & Gintis, H. (1976). *Schooling in capitalist America: Educational reform and the contradictions of economic life.* New York, NY: Basic Books.

Bronstein, L. R., & Abramson, J. S. (2003, July–September). Understanding socialization of teachers and social workers: Groundwork for collaboration in the schools. *Families in Society, 84*(3), 323–330.

Brookfield, S. (1995). *Becoming a critically reflective teacher.* San Francisco, CA: Jossey-Bass.

Burstow, B. (1991, Spring–Summer). Freirian codifications and social work education. *Journal of Social Work Education, 27*(2), 196–207.

Cameron, C. (2004, August). Social pedagogy and care: Danish and German practice in young people's residential care. *Journal of Social Work, 4*(2), 133–151.

Cameron, C. (2013). Cross-national understanding of the purpose of professional–child relationships: Towards a social pedagogical approach. *International Journal of Social Pedagogy, 2*(1), 3–16.

Coates, J. (1994). Education for social transformation. *Journal for Teaching Social Work,* 10(1–2), 1–17.

Costello, C. Y. (2001). Schooled by the classroom. The (re)production of social stratification in professional school settings. In E. Margolis (Ed.), *The hidden curriculum in higher education* (pp. 43–59). New York, NY: Routledge.

Council of Social Work Education. (2008). *Educational policy and accreditation standards.* Washington, DC: Author. Retrieved June 5, 2008, from http://www.cswe.org/NR/rdonlyres/2A81732E-1776-4175-AC42-65974E96BE66/0/2008EducationalPolicyandAccreditationStandards.pdf.

D'Aprix, A. S., Dunlap, K. M., Able, E., & Edwards, R. L. (2004, June). Goodness of fit: Career goals of MSW students and the aims of the social work profession in the United States. *Social Work Education, 23*(3), 265–280.

Finn, J. L., & Jacobson, M. (2003, Winter). Just practice: Steps towards a new social work paradigm. *Journal of Social Work Education, 39*(1), 57–78.

Frans, D. J., & Moran, J. R. (1993). Social work education's impact on students' humanistic values and personal empowerment. *Arete, 18*(1), 1–11.

Freire, P. (1993). *Pedagogy of the oppressed* (Rev. ed.). New York, NY: Continuum.

Gair, M., & Mullins, G. (2001). Hiding in plain sight. In E. Margolis (Ed.), *The hidden curriculum in higher education* (pp. 21–41). New York, NY: Routledge.

Giesecke, H. (1992). *Indføring i pædagogik* (3rd ed.). København, Denmark: Nyt Nordisk Forlag.

Giroux, H. (1983a). *Theory and resistance in education: A pedagogy for the opposition.* New York, NY: Bergin & Garvey.

Giroux, H. (1983b). Critical theory and rationality in citizenship education. In H. Giroux & D. Purpel (Eds.), *The hidden curriculum and moral education: Deception or discovery?* (pp. 321–360). Berkeley, CA: McCutchan.

Gottesman, M. (Ed.). (1994). *Recent changes and new trends in extrafamilial child care: An international perspective.* London, England: Whiting & Birch.

Grady, M. D., Powers, J., Despard, M., & Naylor, S. (2011, Fall). Measuring the implicit curriculum: Initial development and results of an MSW survey. *Journal of Social Work Education, 47*(3), 463–487.

Graham, M. A. (1997). Empowering social work faculty: Alternative paradigms for teaching and learning. *Journal for Teaching Social Work, 15*(1–2), 33–45.

Harrit, P. (1999, June 12). Presentation at Skovtofte Social Pedagogical College. [Peter Harrit is the retired Dean of Skovtofte Social Pedagogical College in Denmark.]

Hatton, K. (2013). *Social pedagogy in the UK: Theory and practice.* Dorset, England: Russell House.

Huff, M. T., & McNown Johnson, M. (1998, Fall). Empowering students in a graduate-level social work course. *Journal of Social Work Education, 34*(3), 375–385.

Husen, M. (1996). The common third—About community and value in the pedagogical work. In B. Pécseli (Ed.), *Culture & Pedagogy* (pp. 218–232). København, Denmark: Hanz Reitzels Forlag. [In German]

Ife, J. (2008). *Human rights and social work: Towards a rights-based practice* (Rev. ed.). Port Melbourne, Australia: Cambridge University Press.

International Committee of the Rectors' Conference (INCORE). (2002). *Presentation of the Danish social educator programme. The professional bachelor degree: Bachelor in Social Education* (2nd ed.). København K, Denmark: Author.

Jackson, P. W. (1990). *Life in classrooms.* New York, NY: Teachers College Press. (Original work published 1968)

Jacobs, H. (1995). A new development in the education of direct care practitioners. *Journal of Child and Youth Care, 10,* 37–53.

Kaufman, P. (2005, June). Middle-class social reproduction: The activation and negotiation of structural advantages. *Sociological Forum, 20*(2), 245–270.

Kivel, P. (2007). Social service or social change? In INCITE! Women of Color Against Violence (Ed.), *The revolution will not be funded: Beyond the non-profit industrial complex* (pp. 129–149). Cambridge, MA: South End Press.

Lamanna, P. G. (1992, Fall). A new program for direct care practice. *Brandeis Review,* 32–35.

Landau, R. (1999). Professional socialization, ethical judgment, and decision-making orientation in social work. *Journal of Social Services Research, 25*(4), 57–76.

Leichtentritt, R. D., Davidson-Arad, B., & Wozner, Y. (2002). The social work mission and its implementation in the socialization process: First- and second-year students' perspectives. *Social Work Education, 21*(6), 671–683.

Lieberkind, M. (1997). Personal conversation. [Margot Lieberkind is Dean of Gentofte Social Pedagogical College in Denmark.]

Loseke, D. R., & Cahill, S. E. (1986). Actors in search of a character: Student social workers' quest for professional identity. *Symbolic Interaction, 9,* 245–258.

Margolis, E., & Romero, M. (2001). *The Hidden curriculum: Reproduction in Education, a reappraisal.* London: Falmer Press.

Madsen, B. (1993). *Socialpædagogik og samfundsforvandling: En grundbog.* København, Denmark: Munksgaard. Socialpædagogisk Bibliotek.

Margolis, E., & Romero, M. (1998, Spring). "The department is very male, very white, and very conservative": The functioning of the hidden curriculum in graduate sociology departments. *Harvard Educational Review, 68*(1), 1–32.

Martin, J. (1983). What should we do with a hidden curriculum when we find one? In H. Giroux & D. Purpel (Eds.), *The hidden curriculum and moral education: Deception or discovery?* (pp. 122–140). Berkeley, CA: McCutchan.

Miller, S. E. (2013). Professional socialization: A bridge between the explicit and implicit curricula. *Journal of Social Work Education, 49,* 368–386.

Moran, J. R. (1989). Social work education and students' humanistic attitudes. *Journal of Social Work Education, 25,* 13–19.

Neuman, K., & Blundo, R. (2000). Curricular philosophy and social work education: A constructivist perspective. *Journal of Teaching in Social Work, 20*(1–2), 19–38.

O'Connor, I., & Dalgleish, L. (1986). The impact of social work education: A personal construct reconceptualization. *Journal of Social Work Education, 22,* 6–30.

Pearson, P. G. (1998, Fall). The educational orientations of graduate social work faculty. *Journal of Social Work Education, 34*(3), 427–436.

Pike, C. K. (1996). Development and initial validation of the social work values inventory. *Research on Social Work Practice, 6,* 337–352.

Quinn, A., & Barth, A. M. (2014). Operationalizing the implicit curriculum in MSW distance education programs. *Journal of Social Work Education, 50,* 34–47.

Reid, K. E. (1981). *From character building to social treatment: The history of the use of groups in social work.* Westport, CT: Greenwood.

Roche, S. E., Dewees, M., Trailweaver, R., Alexander, S., Cuddy, C., & Handy, M. (1999). *Contesting boundaries in social work education: A liberatory approach to cooperative learning and teaching.* Alexandria, VA: Council on Social Work Education.

Schreiber, M. S. (1989). Student peer group: A key aspect of professional socialization in graduate social work education. *Jewish Social Work Forum, 25,* 33–42.

Shor, I. (1996). *When students have power: Negotiating authority in a critical pedagogy.* Chicago, IL: University of Chicago Press.

Smith, M. K. (2009a). Social pedagogy. In *The encyclopaedia of informal education.* Retrieved May 19, 2014, from http://infed.org/mobi/social-pedagogy-the-development-of-theory-and-practice.

Smith, M. K. (2009b). Animateurs, animation and fostering learning and change. In *The encyclopaedia of informal education.* Retrieved May 19, 2014, from http://www.infed.org/mobi/animateurs-animation-learning-and-change.

Snyder, B. R. (1971). *The hidden curriculum.* Cambridge, MA: MIT Press.

Specht, H., & Courtney, M. (1994). *Unfaithful angles: How social work has abandoned its mission.* New York, NY: Free Press.

Storø, J. (2013). *Practical social pedagogy: Theories, values and tools for working with children and young people.* Bristol, England: Policy Press.

Toseland, R. W., & Rivas, R. F. (1995). *An introduction to group work practice* (2nd ed., pp. 47–67). Needham Heights, MA: Macmillan.

Webb, N. B. (1988). The role of the field instructor in the socialization of students. *Social Casework, 69*(1), 35–40.

Weick, A. (1993). Reconstructing social work education. *Journal of Teaching in Social Work, 8*(1–2), 11–30.

Weiss, I., Gal, J., & Cnaan, R. A. (2004). Social work education as professional socialization: A study of the impact of social work education upon students' professional preferences. *Journal of Social Service Research, 31*(1), 13–31.

Wood, M. M., & Long, N. J. (1991). *Life space intervention: Talking with children and youth in crisis.* Austin, TX: PRO-ED.

Zeichner, K. M., & Gore, J. M. (1990). Teacher socialization. In W. R. Houston, R. Hawsam, & J. Sikula (Eds.), *Handbook of research on teacher education* (pp. 329–348). New York, NY: Macmillan.

PART III

Theater, Arts, and the Human Spirit

CHAPTER 7

Mimesis

A Theory for Holistic Engagement

PHILLIP DYBICZ

INTRODUCTION

As social work educators, we seek to promote within our students the acquisition of knowledge on the human condition and the application of this knowledge to facilitate positive change within the life situation of clients with whom they will work. Concerning this knowledge acquisition, there are two types of knowledge of the human condition to consider: objective knowledge (derived from scientific study) and subjective knowledge (derived from humanistic inquiry). A holistic view of what it means to be human needs to include both types. Thus, to holistically engage students in their endeavor at social work knowledge acquisition and application, they must be introduced to both objective and subjective knowledge of the human condition.

It is quite apparent that scientific, objective knowledge is well ensconced in our professional body of knowledge. Since the inception of the profession in the early 20th century, scientific inquiry was seen as the means to build a social work body of knowledge (Dybicz, 2006; Trattner, 1998). It has been only relatively recently (since the 1980s) that postmodern inquiry has yielded subjective knowledge as a contribution to our professional body of knowledge (Applegate, 2000). This imbalance between the overall contribution of both to our social work body of knowledge makes it possible and quite easy to solely present objective knowledge to students as the means to inform practice. Yet to do so carries with it some important limitations, as Rubin and Babbie's (1997) own statement in their text on research methods clearly reveals:

> To summarize, the kind of understanding we seek as we analyze social work research data inevitably involves a deterministic model of human behavior. In looking for the reasons why people are the way they are and do the things they do, we implicitly assume that their characteristics and actions are determined by forces and factors operating on them. (p. 23)

A deterministic model of human behavior offered by scientific investigation is woefully inadequate to capture the full measure of the human condition. This deterministic understanding of the human condition arises because Science views humans as creatures of nature (e.g., we are classified as mammals and belong to the animal kingdom). Thus, we can take scientific models that describe the workings of nature (e.g., an ecological system) and apply them to the human condition (person-in-environment). When comparing human beings to other animals, this scientific view depicts us as being different in *degree* (e.g., use of reason and intellect in attempts at adaptation—which higher functioning animals employ to a limited extent). This difference in degree is why we can take the ecological model and apply it to describe human interaction and also why we can take Pavlov's observations on dogs or Skinner's observations on pigeons and apply them to human behavior. But such an approach only yields half a picture on the human condition.

As human beings, there are many ways in which we are different in *kind* from animals. People base their actions on such things as the following: values and beliefs we hold, the spirituality we embrace, use of imagination on how one's self or environment could be different, the meaning-making we apply to our experiences, one's purpose in life, a desire to make the world a better place, and so on. This is the area encompassed by subjective knowledge.

If educators are to holistically engage students in their acquisition of knowledge, both of these aspects to being human (differences in degree and kind from animals) need to be informed by theory that guides practice. As the name implies, the *huma*nities seek to explain the various qualities that make us uniquely human. For example, one mental quality that makes us uniquely human is our imagination. Whereas all creatures interact with their environment, humans are unique in their ability to imagine how things could be different, that rather than simply adapting to one's present environment, one can envision a new environment and work toward achieving it (e.g., Martin Luther King Jr.'s "I Have a Dream" speech).

Social constructionism (Berger & Luckmann, 1966) and phenomenology (Gadamer, 1999) are two such postmodern theories that speak to this dynamic: They envision human beings as being more than just embedded in an environment; rather, we operate within a world—a world created by our meaning-making ability. Such a view holds much promise in understanding the workings of social work ideas such as resilience and empowerment—qualities that allow an individual to alleviate or overcome the oppressive forces acting against her or him. *A Dictionary of Social Work and Social Care* (Harris & White, 2012) defines *resilience* as "an individual's capacity to cope with stress and adversity" and defines *empowerment* as "the processes through which people who lack power become more powerful." Uniquely human qualities such as hope and the ability to imagine a better future have a large role to play in fostering resilience and empowerment. Beyond the scientific understanding of simply noting that hope and imagination foster resilient and empowering acts, postmodern theories of meaning-making offer the promise of understanding the dynamics of *how* these qualities are effectively employed to create acts of resilience and empowerment; how hope and imagination influence one's interpretation of events that allow one to weather blows of misfortune or oppression and to find a better path to influence one's situation for the better.

Science excels at uncovering truths based within objective knowledge concerning reality; postmodern investigation uncovers truths based within subjective knowledge. Subjective truths move beyond the mere empirical description of reality by offering explanatory power to the meaning attributed to this reality. This involves the examination within a social context of the value judgments that arise from culture and negotiation within the public sphere. Thus, for example, the process of being pregnant and carrying the baby to term is something captured by scientific, objective knowledge and can be applied to all pregnant women. Yet the meaning a woman or society attributes to her pregnancy can fall anywhere within the range of blissful to dreadful. The fact that there are so many subjective valuations that can be placed upon one's situation, all potentially equally valid, offers the opportunity for the social worker and client to collaboratively find a way to embrace the meaning that is most life affirming for the client—hope and imagination play important roles in bringing this life-affirming meaning to fruition.

To continue previous the example, when making a valuation of one's pregnancy, a woman uses observed events in her life that act as evidence for this valuation. This is not a scientific process. Rather, the selecting and ordering of which events are important to include in this valuation is a process of meaning-making through the use of linguistic construction or rhetoric: She is creating a "story" or narrative of her experience. Although rhetoric as commonly used has a negative connotation, it is used here to capture the process of the ordering of events into a persuasive depiction of reality. In the social work literature, much has been written about how social constructionism informs this process (Geraghty, 2012; Keddell, 2011; Parton, 2003; Witkin, 2011). To a lesser extent, there have been writings on how in this vein to apply phenomenology to social work (DePue, Finch, & Nation, 2014; Kowalski, 2010; McCormick, 2011). Both of these theories are worthy of note and have much to offer with regard to informing holistic engagement in the acquisition and application of knowledge.

Phenomenology (Gadamer, 1999) argues that in addition to interacting with our environment, we as human beings attribute meaning to our acts and that which we act upon. Furthermore, this meaning is not something apart from the reality of our interaction but, rather, forms an integral part of it. Consequently, this opens the door for multiple realities to exist. To illustrate, let's take the example of a man who is living his life as an openly gay man. As was the case with the example of a woman's pregnancy discussed previously, the scientific understanding of what comprises gay sexual relations never changes; however, the meaning society attributes to it can create a multitude of realities. Thus, in ancient Greece and Rome, such acts were considered the norm and a sign of virility for the penetrating male (Hubbard, 2003), whereas in Colonial times in America, such acts were viewed as reprehensible—the result of giving in to the temptations of sin (Godbeer, 2002). In our modern times, although one can find both individuals who support the right of a man to live an openly gay life and those who do not, most individuals do not understand this behavior as "a man pursuing a gay lifestyle" but, rather, as "he *is* gay": These sexual interactions come to form a core part of this person's identity in a way that was not the case in Colonial America or Ancient Greece. These three examples illustrate how three different "worlds" are created around the same scientific understanding of the behavior.

Social constructionism (Berger & Luckmann, 1966)—as a theory explaining how this meaning is constructed—offers the promise of guiding efforts to assist clients in confronting problematic societal constructions of reality. Rather than accepting the dominant societal construction as a steadfast reality, the client can counter by constructing alternative, life-affirming realities of his or her situation in the public sphere. Arising from hope and imagination, the construction of these alternative realities represents a form of resilience and empowerment in action.

Although social constructionism and phenomenology have been widely discussed, this chapter is devoted to elaborating upon a postmodern theory that has received less attention in the social work literature: the theory of mimesis. Mimesis offers a theory of causality based on humans' meaning-making ability. Although it has much to offer in guiding social work practice (Dybicz, 2010), the same principles can be used to inform pedagogy in social work education by guiding the educator in attuning to students' meaning-making around delivered content (attributing importance and relevance), student motivation, and student engagement as a member of the profession.

THE ROLE OF IMAGINATION AND IDENTITY IN MIMESIS

Mimesis was first elaborated as a theory by Aristotle (c. 335 B.C./1996) in his work *Poetics*. Aristotle builds his theory of mimesis on a few fundamental premises about being human. The first premise is that human beings possess imagination: We are able to imagine possibilities of what can be, and we are able to project these possibilities into a future where they will occur. Pedagogically, we can help cultivate students' imagination so that they have not only an understanding of what social work is—via their practicum experience—but also a greater understanding as to what social work could be, thus contributing to the evolution and growth of our profession through innovation. The second premise is that human beings possess a sense of identity: We view ourselves as possessing various qualities and place a positive value on some (e.g., courage, intelligence, and kindness) while placing a negative value on others (e.g. procrastination, bluntness, and weakness). As educators, this would direct us to consider not only how social work values guide practice but also how they contribute to one's identity as a social worker. Lastly, there is the premise that human beings possess free will. Hence, the student—by his or her actions as a social worker—will be actively crafting his or her professional identity.

Upon these three premises, Aristotle offers the following theory in regard to human behavior: Each of us has an image of who we are (i.e., one's identity), as well as an image of who we would like to be in the future; this image of who we would like to be provides a guiding light for our free will, and thus we engage in behaviors in our present that seek to move us toward meeting the image of who we would like to be in the future. Consequently, this theory directs us as educators to the importance of helping students articulate their dream of what it means to be a social worker as a means to promote their future development as social workers. In addition, having a clearly articulated dream of what it means to be a social worker can help individuals visualize how things should be when they find themselves, for example, in an unsupportive work environment—directing them away from feelings of hopelessness that can lead to burnout.

I often use the following exercise to illustrate the concept of mimesis to students: "Let's use theory to explain a present action on your part—attendance in class today. If we seek to explain your behavior scientifically, it is a result of outside factors and forces acting upon you" (e.g., a reflection of attempts to adapt to the environment—one needs a job to function comfortably in society, and attending class positions you to do so once you graduate). "Using mimesis to explain your behavior yields the following. You have a dream of becoming a social worker, a dream that arose from your personal value system—that is, you place a high value on what a social worker is and does. It is this dream of who you would like to be that motivates your present behavior to attend class today." Note that both theoretical explanations are equally valid; each speaks to a different area of motivation behind human action. As educators, continuing with the example of student attendance, it behooves us to consider more than simply creating attendance and participation policies to motivate students in these areas; we must also consciously and actively make the case to students concerning the relevance of the content being presented—how it moves them closer to their dream of becoming a good social worker.

When applying mimesis to the educational situation, one turns one's attention to the future and to concerns regarding identity: Understanding a student's dreams and goals takes on great importance because these represent the image of who the student would like to be. As described in greater detail later, the broad steps to this process are the following: collecting information from the student on how the problematic behavior has impacted his or her identity (i.e., "who I am"); helping the student articulate and develop possibilities of "who I can be" that are life affirming; and kindling the student's spirit into initiating action based on this future, life-affirming image through the introduction of hope.

This ability to kindle the human spirit speaks powerfully to issues of resiliency and empowerment. Resiliency can be seen as one's ability to stay true to one's life-affirming image *despite* the many forces and factors acting upon oneself in a contradictory manner. Empowerment can be seen as the ability to marshal the inner and outer resources to promote change that moves one toward this life-affirming image *despite* the many forces and factors acting upon oneself in a contradictory manner. When applying mimesis pedagogically to social work education, it speaks to the issue of kindling each student's spirit toward learning the content that we teach. Making the case for the relevance of the information being taught—via an anecdote based on experience, the examination of a case study, or a classroom exercise applying the information—allows students to connect this information to their preferred image of the type of social worker they would like to be. Thus, beyond merely an exercise in skill acquisition, this approach to learning fuels the student's process of becoming, of attaining the image of who he or she would like to be—a good social worker. Whereas kindling a student's spirit toward learning can be seen as a common goal of any educator, mimesis as a theory offers insight into the mechanisms on how this can be accomplished.

The literal translation of mimesis is "imitation." As Davis (1992) notes, "All human action is always an imitation of action—Achilles is living up to his own image of himself . . . like all brave men, he wants 'to die like Achilles" (i.e., courageously) (p. xviii). Yet, as elaborated by Golden (1992), each human action has a deeper level of understanding that is revealed via the context in which the action is placed: a narrative. This speaks to the notion that one's lived experiences are not simply isolated parcels of memory; rather, one uses these experiences as "evidence" toward commenting on an aspect of one's identity. This is accomplished by stringing together various experiences to form a narrative—a narrative that is organized by a plot (e.g., one's trials and tribulations surrounding a life problem). The plot acts as a controlling force within the structure of narrative. When one is crafting one's story concerning a particular life issue, the plot determines which experiences are relevant to include in one's narrative and which experiences are irrelevant and omitted.

From this controlled structure arises a theme. Whereas the plot controls the ordering of events in the narrative, the theme directly speaks to the identity of the actor: It is composed of various human qualities (e.g., courage, perseverance, and intelligence) that are universal among all cultures (e.g., all cultures have a concept of courage) but that get their expression in this instance via the particular actions taken by the actor in the narrative. Thus, within mimesis, one is defined by one's actions. A universal theme (e.g., courageous warrior) combines with the plot of the narrative (e.g., standing one's ground in battle) to establish a "script" that the actor uses to guide future actions. This is how one's present and future actions get influenced by the image of who one would like to be (e.g., courageous warrior). Thus, the role of the social worker or educator is to help the client or student to articulate these images of "who I am" and "who I would like to be."

When one's life experiences contain problematic events, the sparking of one's imagination is needed to consider new possibilities of arranging these problematic events with other, more positive, life experiences in order to create a life-affirming narrative. This preferred identity and the realistic appraisal one derives from it in terms of "who I can be" serve as the motivating factors of present and future actions; when one's preferred identity—currently obscured by problematic events—is suddenly presented as realistically attainable, hope fans a kindling of the human spirit to strive and achieve it.

In summary, mimesis states that human action—the process on which we seek to promote change in students—arises from efforts to maintain or achieve one's preferred identity. This formulation does not account for all human action because we are prone to act on instinct and conditioning as well; rather, mimesis speaks to action that is guided by free will and the human spirit pursuing this preferred identity. Postmodern thought further argues that human identity is constructed via the creation of narrative when attempting to understand one's life experiences. This narrative yields subjective truths that formulate this identity (Bruner, 1990; Gergen, 1991). Being subjective truth, the articulation of one's identity is open to a number of potentially equally valid formulations. Thus, the task of the educator becomes that of assisting the student to articulate a life-affirming identity as it relates to his or her dream of becoming a social worker—one that will tap into the student's heart, mind, and spirit to guide positive change.

An Extended Example

Let's take as an example a student who is struggling and experiencing problems at an internship or in the classroom, resulting in a remedial staffing to address student shortcomings in this area. The student who has been called to the staffing has been using a well-established script to understand a particular aspect of his or her life experiences (e.g., one's performance at school and practicum serve to define one's identity in the area of competence). A problem arises and the student is no longer functioning adequately in this area, causing a reappraisal of this aspect of identity. This well-established script (e.g., "Good/competent future social workers do not struggle with academics or practicum experiences") is now acting in a dispiriting and disempowering manner: It yields an image of the client as dysfunctional or broken.

Students experiencing problematic issues within a program are often "stuck" in this now disempowering narrative; in effect, they are experiencing the equivalent of a writer's block in that they are unable to configure these recent events into a life-affirming narrative (and thus in need of having their imagination sparked to consider other possibilities). The identity arising from this disempowering narrative often runs counter to values that the student holds dear (e.g., being good, competent, and smart), thus pitting one's heart against oneself. As further problematic life experiences are added to this disempowering narrative—without any change in the script—the burden on one's spirit grows increasingly heavier, sapping hope for change.

Conversely, the educator can attempt to engage the student's imagination to create a new script, a different understanding of the current life struggles. Note that this is not an exercise in trying to put a positive spin on a student's problematic life events (e.g., stating, "Whatever kills you makes you stronger" or "This presents an opportunity for growth"). Doing so can serve to delegitimize the real pain and frustration that the student is experiencing. The key events that comprise a student's current life struggle (i.e., the reason he or she is seeking help) will remain in the newly configured narrative. It is to the events selected that will surround these key events where attention is turned, a process Ricoeur (1984–1988) describes as emplotment—the creation of a new plot. Rather than concentrating on the dysfunctional effects arising from the current life struggle (and tracing them to various forces acting on the student), the educator helps the student examine how he or she has already responded to the challenges created by the problem.

This is known as exploring for exceptions in solution-focused therapy (De Jong & Berg, 2008), exploring for unique outcomes in narrative therapy (White & Epston, 1990), and the elaboration of strengths and successes in the strengths perspective (Saleebey, 2006). Saleebey captures the essence of this process in the following quote elaborating the strengths perspective:

> In a sense, what is happening at this point is the writing of a better "text." Reframing is a part of this; not the reframing of so many family therapies, but adding to the picture already painted, brush strokes that depict capacity and ingenuity, and that provide a different coloration to the substance of one's life. (p. 89)

By taking the problematic events (i.e., the picture already painted) and surrounding it with events illustrating strengths and successes (i.e., brush strokes depicting capacity), a different and empowering narrative with a new script is crafted. This new script becomes life affirming as it aligns with client values and thus emboldens the heart to action. The life-affirming identity arising from the theme—an identity that is seen as realistically attainable by the client—kindles hope that it is within the student's grasp, thus further guiding actions to support this new narrative.

An approach guided by mimesis attempts to engage the student's imagination to construct a new script concerning the student's missteps. The problematic behavior is still examined, but rather than investigating possible causes, attention is devoted to exploring its effects—especially as they relate to obstructing the attainment of various client goals and dreams (e.g., obtaining a degree, obtaining a fulfilling job, and making a difference in clients' lives). The student's goals and dreams become the defining source of the student's identity in this newly configured narrative, with the problematic behavior taking on the role as a barrier to those dreams. According to this new script, acceptance that the behavior is problematic and needs to change is indicative of the student's preferred identity (e.g., "good student" or "competent social worker") being covered over and hidden from the world by the problematic behavior. To construct this new, empowering narrative, the student is directed toward the conscious selection and consideration of events that support the plot of this newly envisioned narrative: student strengths and successes in moving toward these stated goals (hence reinforcing the proposition that these goals reflect the student's preferred identity—and providing evidence of its attainability). Included in this selection are events in which the student was successful in fully or partially keeping the problematic behavior from arising.

The goal for educators and student alike with such a staffing is to improve the student's performance. However, when adopting a problem-solving approach in the staffing as the means to achieve this goal, this staffing comes across as punitive in the eyes of the student. Working under a script akin to "good/competent future social workers do not struggle with academics or practicum experiences," the student perceives such a staffing as providing the rhetorical evidence that she or he is a substandard student/future social worker. The student may express some resistance at such a meeting as her or his means of resisting this negative image that faculty—through their problem-solving approach—are inadvertently trying to place on the student according to the previously mentioned script.

Using mimesis to apply a strengths-based, solution-focused approach yields a quite different result. The goal of improving student performance remains the same, as does the recognition of problematic behaviors. However, instead of faculty telling the student what type of social worker she must be, time is given to the student to express her image of the type of social worker that she would like to become. Building on this image, faculty contribute to the process by suggesting additional qualities that the student may not have yet expressed (e.g., the ability to critically reflect on one's practice as a means to improve one's professional use

of self). Next, both the student and faculty mine for student strengths and successes that contribute rhetorical evidence to this preferred image of the social
worker she would like to be. The problematic behavior is then addressed. By
placing it within this already established narrative framework of strengths and
successes, the problematic behavior no longer takes center stage in terms of identifying the student but, rather, takes on the role of an obstacle interfering with
the ability of others (and the student) to see the preferred image of the student
established by the student's strengths and successes.

A new narrative is thus configured, yielding a different script emphasizing various positive qualities already present in the student. Within this newly
configured narrative, the causes behind the problematic behavior are not given
importance; rather, the student's response to the problematic behavior is given
importance. This can yield a script such as "good/competent future practitioners
use supervision (i.e., the staffing in this instance) as a means to critically reflect
and grow in the professional use of self." At this point, guided by this new script,
a bit of reframing and normalizing needs to take place concerning the staffing.
Normalizing can take the form of emphasizing that at some point all social workers face challenges regarding their practice. The staffing can then be reframed as
a very structured supervision and as a practice run for avoiding burnout through
applying appropriate critical reflection followed by corrective action. Thus, by
giving careful attention to both subjective knowledge (e.g., the student's life-
affirming narrative) and objective knowledge (observable student behaviors)
when helping the student to process the learning experience presented by the
staffing, faculty are engaging the learning situation holistically.

THE ROLE OF HOPE IN MIMESIS

As illustrated previously, imagination plays a key role concerning the social construction of an alternate reality and preferred identity. However, in addition to
imagining such alternative realities, one must act according to them to make
them so—this is where hope comes in. It serves to spark a kindling of the human
spirit to take action. Continuing with the extended example presented previously,
in order to keep this newly configured narrative active, the student's present and
future actions must continue to contribute to it; thus, the student must continue
to supply examples of his or her resilience in the face of the problem. This is where
the importance of hope comes into play as it serves to highly motivate the student to do this because these actions serve to reinforce the life-affirming identity arising from this narrative—and it is this process that produces the desired
change that is sought. Hope provides assurances that this new articulation of
one's preferred identity is attainable, thus prompting the student to base actions
on it. Without hope, and the promise of possible attainment, no action will be
taken to correct the situation. In addition, through the introduction of various

services (i.e., recommendations for corrective action that arise from the staffing) to this newly configured narrative, student participation in these services acts to support his or her life-affirming identity, as it contributes to the plot of "my ability to use common social work tools (i.e., supervision and critical reflection) in which to overcome the problem and advance my goals" as opposed to the plot of "only those who are dysfunctional need services designed to help them combat the problem."

One can easily see how this process reflects the metaphor of author–editor used to describe the client–social worker relationship by postmodern practitioners: The student is acting in the role of narrator through the conscious selection of already lived events to include in the counternarrative while seeking to author present and future events to further contribute to this counternarrative. The educator listens to this counterstory and provides feedback and advice on exploring various possibilities to make the counternarrative more life affirming and more believable. As the author and narrator of the story, the client has the final say regarding the direction and elaboration of this counternarrative (i.e., how to incorporate the results of the staffing into the counternarrative). As such, this new direction and elaboration of events in the form of a counternarrative must "ring true" to the client as this new narrative unfolds. The process of "listening" to the emerging counternarrative is captured by Ricoeur's (1984–1988) elaboration of mimesis as *refiguration*. Refiguration speaks to the process involved in receiving such a narrative (i.e., acting as audience member). Recall that the creation of narratives is our method for understanding our life experiences in a coherent manner. Hence, the narratives that we create need to "make sense" for this understanding to take place.

Now, also as noted previously, this effort at "making sense" of one's life experiences is not a scientific endeavor: that of uncovering objective knowledge of action–reaction mechanisms. Rather, one is seeking a subjective truth of one's identity (an image of who I am and who I want to be), which acts as the source of one's actions. Both objective and subjective truths rely on evidence to maintain their claim as true. Objective truths (sometimes referred to as scientific facts) rely on careful observation as the means to achieve this. Subjective truths (sometimes referred to as poetic truths) rely on a rhetoric of believability—which is captured by the term *verisimilitude* (Bruner, 1990), meaning "lifelike" and "plausible" (i.e., that the rhetoric "makes sense"). Verisimilitude captures the notion of poetic truth well in that a truth claiming to be plausible does not eliminate the notion that other equally plausible claims may be made.

Within mimesis, the selection of events and their organization within a plot act as "evidence" for the subjective claim one is making about one's identity. The following anecdote may serve as illustration. I pass by a music store and see a guitar in the window. This sparks my imagination, and I start to have images of being a rock star (who I would like to be). I begin taking actions based on this image: I purchase the guitar and sign up for guitar lessons. However, I find myself struggling to master the simplest of chords, and in testing my acuity, the guitar teacher tells me that I am partially tone deaf. I share my heartfelt dream with family and friends who know me well, none of whom express confidence in my ability. In addition, I try writing a few songs and playing them in a public arena, but those who listen respond with little enthusiasm. These experiences of failure produce events that run counter to my narrative of becoming a rock star, thus detracting from its verisimilitude. As these experiences add up, they begin to sap hope that my goal is attainable, and eventually the rhetorical evidence running counter to my narrative of becoming a rock star gets so strong that I no longer find the narrative to be believable and hence stop basing my actions on it. I no longer see qualities within myself (who I am) that will enable me to attain the image of being a rock star (who I would like to be). Lastly, possessing a measure of resilience, I take these same experiences and, with the help of my parents' encouragement in considering other possibilities in interpreting these actions, I craft a counternarrative with them that is life affirming—for example, an image of myself as "someone who is not afraid to take risks to follow my passions." Within this new narrative, my epic failures at learning to play the guitar serve as positive examples that support the narrative—the greater my failure illustrating the greater the risk I am willing to take.

There are a number of points concerning *refiguration* that we can take from this anecdote. First, the most important audience member to one's narrative is ultimately oneself. As the actor in one's story, when it no longer possesses verisimilitude in one's view, one no longer bases one's future actions on it. Thus, verisimilitude of a narrative leads to action. Second, although imagination is the productive source for identity features that guide one's actions, one lives and acts in one's world. Life experiences—as events, the building blocks of narrative—occur when one acts within one's world, not within one's imagination. Hence, there is a social component to achieving verisimilitude wherein others act as audience members and play a part as well in contributing to the verisimilitude of the narrative. The previous anecdote illustrates three such ways in which this occurs. One such way is via the value judgments of others with whom I interact in the pursuit of my dream (e.g., playing my songs in a public arena). Another is via the value judgments of family and friends who know me well; because these individuals know "who I am" better than most people, their value judgments will carry a heavier weight. Lastly, there are the value judgments of experts in the area where my narrative is situated (e.g., the guitar teacher); these individuals know about the attainability of the image of "who I would like to be" better than most people and thus their value judgments will carry more weight than that of the average person.

Applying this concept of refiguration to social work education and the previous extended example yields the following insights. Faculty act as experts in the field and thus exert a strong influence in the construction of the student's identity as social worker. This occurs wherever interaction takes place (e.g., staffing, classroom, and evaluation of assignments). Thus, faculty can play a major role in assisting a student trying to construct a counternarrative. The practicum site acts as a public forum for the demonstration of the student's skills and, thus, is another potent source from which to draw support for a counternarrative. Finally, classmates may serve as knowledgeable friends in supporting the construction of a life-affirming identity.

Although I used the scenario of a student staffing to illustrate the various dynamics of mimesis at work, the application of mimetic principles can be applied to minor crisis in confidence as well. For example, one technique that I use as an educator in practice classes is to have the students break up into groups of three (client, social worker, and observer) in order to practice the various skills that we are covering in class. The task of the observer is to provide feedback on the student's performance of the skills (with directions to emphasize the various skills the student did well). Then we reconvene as a class, and in processing the various skills, I ask students who were in the role of client or observer to relate examples of the student acting as social worker who performed the skill particularly well. The experience for students in hearing their classmates speak well of their ability provides a positive event in which to configure within their narrative concerning their potential to be a good/competent social worker. This then helps them to overcome any self-doubts in their ability and thus be more willing to try the skills in their practicum.

CONCLUSION

There is no doubt that scientific inquiry has vastly contributed to the social work body of knowledge. It is due to this fact that for educators it can be quite easy to fool oneself into thinking that this scientific contribution of knowledge represents the sum total of social work knowledge and thus teach accordingly. Yet similar to a body builder who only develops one's arm and chest muscles while ignoring development of one's leg muscles, such an approach to teaching achieves a disproportional result. A more balanced approach to the social work body of knowledge via accessing both the objective knowledge of scientific inquiry and the subjective knowledge of postmodern inquiry offers a way to holistically engage students in their acquisition and application of said knowledge. As these students enter practice, their ability to employ both scientific and postmodern forms of inquiry offers them the knowledge base and capability to engage holistically with clients.

This chapter elaborated mimesis as a theory to inform postmodern inquiry that has applicability to both the teaching and the helping situation. As stated previously, both social constructionism and phenomenology are theories that also direct postmodern inquiry in the creation of subjective knowledge. When combined with the objective knowledge of scientific inquiry, learning

experiences can be created in which concepts such as resilience and empowerment take on a deeper meaning for students and get woven into their personal
narratives—thereby making them more effective social workers.

REFERENCES

Applegate, J. (2000). Theory as story: A postmodern tale. *Clinical Social Work Journal, 58,*
   141–153.
Aristotle. (1996). *Poetics* (M. Heath, Trans.). London: Penguin. (Original work published
   c. 335 b.c.)
Berger, P. L., & Luckmann, T. (1966). *The social construction of reality: A treatise in the sociol-
   ogy of knowledge.* Garden City, NY: Anchor Books.
Bruner, J. (1990). *Acts of meaning: Four lectures on mind and culture.* Harvard, MA: Harvard
   University Press.
Davis, M. (1992). *Aristotle's poetic's: The poetry of philosophy.* Lanham, MD: Rowman &
   Littlefield.
De Jong, P., & Berg, I. K. (2008). *Interviewing for solutions* (3rd ed.). Belmont, CA: Thomson
   Brooks/Cole.
DePue, M. K., Finch, A. J., & Nation, M. (2014). The bottoming-out experience and the
   turning point: A phenomenology of the cognitive shift from drinker to nondrinker.
   Journal of Addictions & Offender Counseling, 35, 38–56.
Dybicz, P. (2010). Mimesis: Linking postmodern theory to human behavior. *Journal of
   Social Work Education, 46,* 341–355.
Dybicz, P. (2006). *A genealogy of the good: An examination of the discourse on social wel-
   fare from poor laws to strengths perspective* (Doctoral Dissertation). Retrieved from
   Proquest.
Gadamer, H. G. (1999). *Truth and method* (2nd ed.). (J. Weinsheimer & D. G. Marshall
   Trans.). New York: The Continuum Publishing Company. (Original work
   published 1960).
Geraghty, K. (2012). Ethics education from a social constructionist view. *Journal of Social
   Work Values and Ethics, 9,* 1–52.
Gergen, K. (1991). *The saturated self: Dilemmas of identity in contemporary life.* New York,
   NY: Basic Books.
Godbeer, R. (2002). *Sexual revolution in early America.* Baltimore, MD: Johns Hopkins
   University Press.
Golden, L. (1992). *Aristotle on tragic and comic mimesis* (American Classical Studies, No.
   29). Atlanta, GA: Scholars Press.
Harris, J., & White, V. (2013). *A dictionary of social work and social care.* New York,
   NY: Oxford University Press.
Hubbard, T. (2003). *Homosexuality in Greece and Rome: A sourcebook of basic documents.*
   Berkeley, CA: University of California Press.
Keddell, E. (2011). A constructionist approach to the use of arts-based materials in social
   work education: Making connections between art and life. *Journal of Teaching in
   Social Work, 31,* 400–414.
Kowalski, R. (2010). The phenomenology of development. *Journal of Comparative Social
   Welfare, 26,* 153–164.
McCormick, M. (2011). The lived body: The essential dimension in social work practice.
   Qualitative Social Work, 10, 66–85.

Parton, N. (2003). Rethinking professional practice: The contributions of social constructionism and the feminist "ethics of care." *British Journal of Social Work, 33*, 1–16.

Ricoeur, P. (1984–1988). *Time and narrative* (Vols. 1–3). Chicago, IL: University of Chicago Press.

Rubin, A., & Babbie, E. (1997). *Research methods for social work* (3rd ed.). New York, NY: Brooks/Cole.

Saleebey, D. (2006). The strengths approach to practice. In D. Saleebey (Ed.), *The strengths perspective in social work practice* (4th ed., pp. 77–92). Boston, MA: Pearson/Allyn & Bacon.

Trattner, W. I. (1998). *From poor law to welfare state: a history of social welfare in America* (6th ed.). New York: The Free Press.

White, M., & Epston, D. (1990). *Narrative means to therapeutic ends.* New York, NY: Norton.

Witkin, S. L. (Ed.). (2011). *Social construction and social work practice: Interpretations and innovations.* New York, NY: Columbia University Press.

CHAPTER 8

Improvisation

A Practice for Praxis

UTA M. WALTER

INTRODUCTION

"All professional practice," writes practice researcher Donald Schön (1987), "requires an art of problem framing, an art of implementation, and an art of improvisation—all necessary to mediate the use in practice of applied science and technique" (p. 13). The notion of improvisation as part of practice in the field or in education, however, is only sparsely present in social work literature to date, even though it stands to reason that improvisations in the "indeterminate zones" (Schön, 1995, p. 28) of professional social work practice are indeed ubiquitous. Where improvisation is mentioned, it most often refers to the uncertainties of direct practice with clients (Blom, 2009; Graybeal, 2007; Madsen, 2011; Perlinski, Blom, & Moren, 2012; Seligson, 2004). Harold Goldstein (1998) points to improvisation in practice when he argues that the social worker can be thought of as a "performing artist" who will "move beyond the constraints of method and technique and respond imaginatively and creatively to the impromptu, unrehearsed nature of the special human relationship" (p. 247). Similarly, Seligson (2004), herself a social work practitioner and an actress, finds that both activities need the mastery of basic skills, intuitive knowledge of when to let go, self-knowledge in service of an other, and an ability to act spontaneously by being in the moment. Beyond this, however, authors rarely explain or expand on the concept of improvisation.

The same is true for literature on social work education, in which improvisation is even less frequently referenced. Given that role plays or similar activities have long been part of the educational repertoire in classes that focus on counseling skills or group work (Hargreaves & Hadlow, 1997; Petracchi & Collins, 2006), this overall lack of attention to and representation of improvised activity in social work education is somewhat surprising. It likely results from a discourse around professionalism that remains steeped in a technical–rational paradigm (Schön, 1987). Current pressures of neoliberal market ideology dovetail with a technical–rational view and increasingly cast the purpose of education—and much of social work practice—as making people "fit for the market." For instance, recent publications on "role-play" in social work education highlight the use of so-called "standardized clients"—that is, persons trained to display certain symptom clusters to enhance future clinicians' diagnostic recognition and interviewing skills (Logie, Bogo, Regehr, & Regehr, 2013). Just as practice turns its focus toward securing measurable and typically predefined "outcomes," education is at risk of being reduced to "training marketable competencies" in students (Giroux, 2011; Reisch, 2013; Scanlon & Saleebey, 2005).

In this atmosphere, improvised activity is rendered largely invisible. After all, improvisation denotes proceeding without preplanning or preparation. Associated largely with the arts, including jazz music, dance, or theater, improvisation invokes associations of uncertainty, irrationality, even frivolity, altogether unbecoming of a scientific profession. Where the status of "scientific profession" is equated with rationality and controlled practices, the idea of improvisation as not only a frequent but also perhaps a valuable part of professional practice in the field and the classroom seems anathema.

The concept of improvisation, however, offers complex ideas for theory and practice in social work. As a heuristic to reimagine professional practices, improvisation has already found its way into the literature of various professional fields, including therapy, organization science, and education. And theorists from diverse fields, such as sociology, psychology, performance studies, or anthropology, have invoked improvisation as a common feature in social and cultural life that deserves further attention (Carlson, 1996; Holland, Lachicotte, Skinner, & Cain, 1998; Rosaldo, 1993). In social work education, improvisation can add what Saleebey (1989) called a "mimetic view" to the profession's analytic tradition. This orientation "requires one to know and do with a kind of spontaneity and simultaneity, and to grasp the world-as-whole rather than according to subject vs. object dichotomies" (Saleebey, 1989, p. 558).

This chapter casts improvisation as part of a heuristic for an epistemology of practice that bridges traditional dichotomies such as art–science, mind–body, or thinking–doing. To this end, I conceive of teaching as improvised performance and introduce principles and exercises of theater improvisation whose lexicon proves useful for communicating improvisational skills and attitudes. My own ongoing practice of these principles, on stage and off, continues to influence my approach to teaching, and some theater games and exercises have found their way into my classrooms. These transpositions between the world of theater and social work education have been exciting and generative, and they continuously bring forth tensions and ambivalences. Most important, I currently wonder how improvisation in social work may need to be similar to and different from improvisation in other contexts if we seek to arrive at a critical and creative practice within and without the classroom.

IMPROVISATION—MORE THAN MAKING DO

So what exactly is "improvisation"? In its casual use, the term improvisation typically refers to "making do," "getting by," or points to a "doing whatever" attitude in which no rules or structures seem to apply. Improvisation, however, is far more than getting oneself more or less elegantly out of a tight spot. A closer look into social and performance theories, as well as into improvised theater, reveals improvisation as a complex and structured phenomenon that opens spaces for creativity and resistance.

Improvisation is part of a long tradition of thought about the power of "mimesis" in that it is not just a mental activity but rests in part on physical (re-)enactment. Physical spaces, postures, gestures, bodily tensions, and sensations are all important ingredients of mimetic knowledge (Gebauer & Wulf, 2003). Akin to what Schön (1995) called practitioners' "knowledge-in-action," mimetic knowledge frequently escapes verbal explanations. As a form of embodied knowledge, it goes beyond rational analysis or mere technique but is developed and held in the physical doing (Gebauer & Wulf, 2003). Current neurobiological research has come to support the idea that some knowledge resides outside conscious cognitive processing, is difficult to describe, and yet influences everyday actions and decisions (Wilson, 2002). In fact, emotions, bodily sensations, and high-level cognition are interwoven in what Immordino-Yang and Damasio (2007) termed "emotional thought." Hence, physicality and emotions are essential ingredients in all learning and decision-making processes (Immordino-Yang & Damasio, 2007), and learning occurs more easily, faster, and is more likely to translate outside of the classroom if positive emotions are connected to content and process (Hüther, n.d.; Immordino-Yang & Damasio, 2007).

Like the larger concepts of performance and mimesis, improvisation has no singular meaning or definition. In general, improvisation is a process characterized by unplanned, creative, and spontaneous reflexivity, as well as moment-to-moment decision-making in continuous reaction to the social context (Janesick, 2000; Johnstone, 1981, 1999; Sawyer, 1992; Spolin, 1999). Moreover, it is associated with playfulness and fun, frequently experienced in close collaboration with others.

Stephen Nachmanovitch (1990) provides a fundamental characterization of improvisation in his book *Free Play—Improvisation in Life and Art,* in which he explores various artistic improvisations. To him, the improvisatory process involves setting free an existing creative capacity in a "play space" that is similar to the mythical Greek *temenos*, a sacred, magic, and safe place in which extraordinary things can occur. Like childhood play, the ability to improvise in the temenos is not limited to those with special talent but, rather, is a creative force inherent in all human beings. Hence, improvising is "not a matter of making the material come, but of unblocking the obstacles to its natural flow" (Nachmanovitch, 1990, p. 10). The main obstacles to improvising are fears, such as the fear of being seen as foolish or incompetent or the fear of actually being foolish or incompetent. Expert teachers of improvisational theater therefore foster an atmosphere in which learners are encouraged to "make mistakes and stay happy." Mistakes are viewed as creative and valuable moments that are not only inevitable but also inspiring for learning processes and thus should be joyfully embraced rather than avoided, hidden, or denied (Walter, 2006). They are, in Nachmovitch's words, "a grain of sand around which we can make a pearl" (p. 89).

Another central feature of improvisation is its emphasis on collaborative practice. Out of such collaboration, ideas emerge that are more than a compromise or the mere sum of ideas provided by individual participants. Rather, the process ideally dissolves dichotomies of self and other, and it unites performers into one big "self-organizing whole" (Nachmanovitch, 1990, p. 101). The practice of paradoxes such as "collective individuality" is essential to improvisation, much like practicing "rehearsed spontaneity" or "anxious confidence" (Mirvis, 1998). As a collaborative enterprise, it centrally focuses on dialogue in word and deed to build a team in which all members are leaders and supporters.

A third feature of improvisation is its use of limitations to inspire and transcend what is given. Improvisations creatively utilize existing resources and structures to address new conditions and problems in a process also known as "bricolage" (Nachmanovitch, 1990). As such, they are reliant on what is given while at the same time seek to go beyond. Contrary to popular belief, improvising is therefore not breaking with forms and limitations just to be "free" but, rather, using those forms and limitations as "the very means to transcend ourselves" (Nachmanovitch, 1990, p. 84). In other words, improvisation thrives on the power of limits, and it uses structure to inspire rather than stunt spontaneity. Thus, far beyond "making do" or "doing whatever," improvising well means doing the unexpected and extraordinary with what is present—building on existing ideas but re-performing them not as mere copy but, at its best, as a transformation.

Performance theorists in particular use the concept of improvisation to describe the dynamic tension between innovation and repetition that is inherent in all mimetic approaches (Gebauer & Wulf, 2003). For Bourdieu, for instance, improvisations are impromptu actions that occur when past ways of acting ("habitus") are met by circumstances and conditions for which there is no set response (Holland et al., 1998). The resulting improvisations are "openings by which change comes about from generation to generation" (Holland et al., 1998, p. 16). Therefore, playful improvisational practices hold resistive and liberatory potential (Holland et al., 1998; Shepard, Bogad, & Duncombe, 2008) that may result in re-performances that generate alternative readings and subvert the original in what Jackson (2000) called a process of "re-formance."

Attend, Accept, Advance

A look toward theater improvisation provides additional insights into the principles and processes involved in the "how to" of improvisational practices. Although it has older roots in the Commedia dell' Arte tradition of the Renaissance, modern improvisational theater began to form in the United States in the 1930s and 1940s and a decade later in England mainly to help actors be more real, connected, and relaxed on stage. Two major figures in the development of improvisational exercises are Viola Spolin (1999), who is considered the mother of improvisational theater in the United States, and Keith Johnstone (1981, 1999), who began his work in England, later moved to Canada, and is perhaps best known for "Theatresports," a mock competitive format in which two teams of improvisers challenge each other, in good humor, to win points for short theatrical scenes and games. Spolin incidentally was first introduced to the use of games and storytelling at Chicago's Hull House in the 1920s, where she trained to become a settlement worker.

Learning improvisational theater (or, for short, improv or impro[1]) today typically means being introduced to some version of three interdependent core activities. Through games and exercises, theater improvisers practice how to attend, accept, and advance. Much like the principles of holistic engagement outlined in Chapter 1, *attending* means paying attention to everything that happens, to intended and unintended actions, words, and emotions of fellow players, to one's own feelings and behaviors, and to the physical environment including elements that are imaginary and merely mimed. Although this is the most basic of tasks for improvisers, it is already a challenge because this kind of attention requires relaxed and alert awareness of broadened perception rather than zooming in on anything in particular. Several authors have likened this kind of attention to practices of meditation and Zen mindfulness (Madson, 2005; Taibbi, 2009).

Accepting extends attending and asks an improviser to be invested in what is already given and support fellow players. It is akin to a willingness to say "yes" to what has been offered in words, deeds, or emotions. In improv, everything, be it intended or unintended, is considered an "offer," a gift, to be recognized and treated as such. Hence, improv students learn how every offer can be used and

---

1. In North America, the term "improv" is common, whereas in other areas of the world, "impro" is more typical. Although some discussions in the field link different styles of improvisation to each term, I do not make such distinctions here and simply opt for "improv."

built upon by virtue of how the offer is accepted. The impact of saying "yes" to offers can be experienced by first learning the effects of its opposite, called "blocking," meaning to say "no" to offers by denying or contradicting someone else's reality. Rejecting or ignoring offers physically, verbally, or emotionally is at the heart of blocking, and it is a familiar activity. In life, blocking offers often keeps us safe, but it also hinders building collaborative relations and stunts chances of discovering and developing anything new together. As Johnstone (1981) stated, "There are people who prefer to say 'Yes,' and there are people who prefer to say 'No.' Those who say 'Yes' are rewarded by the adventures they have. Those who say 'No' are rewarded by the safety they attain" (p. 92). In theater improv, adventures are the preferred direction, and thus a willingness to take risks by saying yes to offers, to trust fellow players, and to make one's partner rather than oneself look good is paramount.

The third component essential to good theater improv is to *advance* or build on existing offers by adding something to further the scene or story. Together, accepting and advancing are often subsumed in the cardinal improv rule of saying *"Yes, and . . . ."* Rather than inventing entirely new ideas in an attempt to be clever or original, improvisers advance by using what happened before to inspire the next action. In other words, in improvisation, meaning, order, and form emerge through a retrospective approach in which improvisers must be willing and able to move forward while looking back, all the while leading and following in this effort. Results of a qualitative inquiry with professional theater improvisers (Walter, 2006) have led me to distinguish two kinds of advancing: moving forward the relationship between characters and moving forward the story.

The idea of *advancing relationships* between characters centers on being changed in response to the other. Allowing oneself to be changed requires a willingness to be vulnerable because it means leaving a perhaps familiar or otherwise comfortable position in service of the other. Johnstone's "status games" are staple exercises that bring into focus how relationships are enacted and enhanced through the changes in position of bodies and the use of space and language. Exemplifying Watzlawick, Beavin, and Jackson's (1967) axiomatic "you cannot not communicate," status exercises highlight how verbal and non-verbal actions inadvertently communicate relational dynamics and impressions of hierarchies. Because the stage functions like a magnifying glass, observers of status exercises become aware how quickly we read bodily positions through cultural frames in terms of "high" or "low" (dominant or less dominant) relational status in interactions. At the same time, those who play characters on stage experience how physicality inspires them to react and relate. Imagine, for instance, a person sitting stiffly at the edge of a chair, with all limbs tightly tucked to the body. This image immediately invites interpretations and projections of "anxiety" from the audience and frequently evokes similar emotions and thoughts in the player. Add to this scene a second character, who stands firmly grounded, occasionally looking at the seated figure with an extended gaze.

Without a word being spoken, a status relationship between the two emerges both in the minds of onlookers and in those who inhabit the bodies.

At the same time, this type of relational status differs from social status in that it is far more fluid. Small changes can quickly alter the relational status that appeared so clear a moment ago: The person in the chair comfortably leans back, holds the gaze of the other, raises a single eyebrow, and suddenly the person who stood with such clear dominance is lowered in relational status. Social and relational status may even be contradictory. Observing a person with low social status ("servant") act "high status" in his or her interaction with a social superior ("master") is not just the material of classic comedy; studying and playing it also highlights the agency in relational status behaviors that can subvert social status.

Advancing story means moving forward the narrative if and when longer scenes or stories are improvised (not all improv involves narrative). To this end, improvisers learn basic structures of storytelling, including the role of genres or other culturally established styles. Understanding and constructing improvised stories is a complex enterprise in that jointly improvising a story means that players serve simultaneously as co-authors, co-directors, and co-actors by "yes, and-ing" each other's offers.

Improvisation in Professional Fields

Many of the features outlined previously re-appear in the professional literature that invokes improvisation as a heuristic for practice. In therapeutic practices, for instance, sociodrama, psychodrama, social therapy, and music or drama therapy have incorporated improvisational activities as instruments for assessment or intervention with clients (Emunah & Blatner, 1994; Moreno, 1987; Newman & Holzman, 1996; Wiener, 1994). The work of Brazilian activist Augusto Boal (1985, 1992, 1995), which is rooted in Paulo Freire's (1989) *Pedagogy of the Oppressed*, uses theatrical improvisation for both educational and therapeutic practices. Aside from its use as a therapeutic tool, improvisation has also been described as central in the therapeutic process itself in that it focuses the practitioner on the moment-to-moment unfolding of intersubjective experiences, on not-knowing, instead of a false sense of certainty provided by models or schools of thought (Keeney, 1991; Ringstrom, 2001). In the words of Irving Yalom (1989),

[T]he capacity to tolerate uncertainty is a prerequisite for the profession. Though the public may believe that therapists guide patients systematically and sure-handedly through predictable stages of therapy to a foreknown goal, such is rarely the case: Instead . . . therapists frequently wobble, improvise, and grope for direction. The powerful temptation to achieve certainty through embracing an ideological school and a tight therapeutic system is treacherous: Such belief may block the uncertain and spontaneous encounter necessary for effective therapy. (p. 13)

In organization sciences, authors have drawn similar parallels between improvisation and processes of decision-making, achievement, creativity, and product innovation (Barrett, 1998; Crossan, 1998; Mirvis, 1998; Weick, 1998). Insisting that organizations and environments are largely unpredictable, Crossan, Lane, and White (1996) describe improvisation as a "potential link between the need to plan for the predictable and the ability to respond simultaneously to the unpredictable" (p. 21). Weick (1998) suggests that taking improvisation seriously may enable organization theorists to

> do more with the simultaneous presence of seeming opposites in organizations than simply label them as paradoxes. There is currently an abundance of conceptual dichotomies that tempt analysts to choose between things like control and innovation, exploitation and exploration, routine and non-routine. . . . Improvisation is a mixture of the pre-composed and the spontaneous, just as organizational action mixes together some proportion of control with innovation. . . . A routine becomes something both repetitious and novel. (p. 551)

For the field of education, several authors put forth the idea of teaching as performance replete with improvisation. Embedded in a performance or social constructionist paradigm, improvisation is not merely a metaphoric descriptor but bespeaks a view of pedagogy as collaboratively evolving knowledge. Less concerned with identification and categorization of the known and more with the unidentified unpredictabilities inside and outside the classroom, educational improvisation means to engage in spontaneous and open-ended activities that develop from raw ideas, activities that respond to change and express transformation, and that develop according to interpretation by participants (Fusco, 2000; Sawyer, 2004a, 2004b). As a "theatrical event," teaching is viewed as an activity in which "cultural knowledge is performed in the 'how' rather than in the abstract ideas of its content, replete with stable and uncertain aspects, improvised and planned actions" (Shem-Tov, 2011, p. 105). Teaching thus conceived is not a technical but a hermeneutic activity, requiring those involved in education to be creative rather than prescriptive and to look for meaning rather than truth.

Authors who suggest the improvisation analog for teaching share a vision of education as an activity that seeks to remove obstacles to playful learning and stresses the collaborative nature. In contrast to what Freire (1989) called the traditional "banking model," according to which the teacher "deposits" his or her knowledge in students' heads, education is seen as an activity geared to "draw out" (as derived from the Latin *e-ducere*) rather than "stuff in." As such, education must "tap into the close relationship between play and exploration; there must be permission to explore and express. There must be validation of the exploratory spirit, which by definition takes us out of the tried, the tested, and the homogenous" (Nachmanovitch, 1990, p. 118). Just as in theater improvisations, "in true discussion, the topic and the flow of the class emerge from teacher and students together; the outcome is unpredictable" (Sawyer, 2004a, p. 13).

Such a form of dialogic learning requires teachers to step outside of comfort zones, in which they "know better" at all times or aim for predetermined answers, and instead face their own fears of uncertainty in a joint discovery process (Borko & Livingston, 1989). This does not mean abdicating the knowledge teachers hold but, rather, integrating it flexibly and staying open to learning something new in the process. Authors suggest that exposing teachers to improvisation concepts and exercises might help them overcome fears of "losing control" of classroom process or contents. It might make them better leaders of classroom discussions, who know how to respond flexibly to spontaneous developments in the classroom and to reflectively integrate the scripts of curricula with the improvised practices in teaching (Sawyer, 2004a, 2004b; Shem-Tov, 2011).

At the same time, any given context frames improvisation through external and internal elements (Zaunbrecher, 2011). The physical spaces we inhabit, the lights and sounds, the number of people present, the silent and expressed expectations, and so on all provide structures and limits to improvised actions. For educational settings, these frames result in what Sawyer (2004a) has referred to as "disciplined improvisation," meaning that "teachers locally improvise within an overall global structure" (p. 16). Just as the term "discipline" holds various shades of meaning, improvisations that are "disciplined" by the context of education point us to questions about how such restrictions may be wanted or unwanted; how limits are imposed externally or internalized, conscious or perhaps unconscious; and how they are embedded in larger discourse.

The fact that current literature on social work education rarely references improvisation is likely itself a result of such discursive and institutionalized self-disciplining that foregrounds technical–rational ideas of "professionalism" and "competency-focused education." Only few authors explicitly refer to improvisational aspects in the learning or teaching of social work (Feldman, Barron, Holliman, Karliner, & Walter, 2009; Todd, 2012), and none expand on the concept to include its mimetic and critical potential.

IMPROVISATION IN THE SOCIAL WORK CLASSROOM: FROM PRACTICE TO PRAXIS

Improvisation offers social work education a collaborative and playful approach that pushes for more holistic pedagogical practices and takes education beyond utilitarian "competency training." Todd (2012), for instance, describes how she altered her use of "standardized clients" as role-play partners to train future clinicians to find the "correct" diagnosis. Not surprisingly perhaps, she initially observed students' focus on outcome rather than process in which "getting it right" was the main concern. In order to foreground elements of uncertainty in practice including unconscious and emotional knowledge, as well as the unpredictability of relational encounters, Todd then introduced improvisational theater exercises. As a result, she found the focus of the class shifting from concern about self-mastery to attention to the relationship. Todd concludes that improvisation

> facilitates the development of skills that are central to social work yet difficult to bring into the classroom through other pedagogical approaches. They are those aspects of social work practice that are difficult to quantify. Improvisation works against the certainty and overdetermined pedagogical practice. (p. 312)

Further extending these insights, I believe that improvisation in social work education is best served when it explicitly integrates critical pedagogy. Consistent with literature on improvisation in education, critical pedagogy calls for dialogical learning, in which students' perspectives are encouraged and have room (Giroux, 2004, 2011). But drawing on critical theories, including those put forth by the Frankfurt School, Antonio Gramsci, and Paolo Freire, critical pedagogy also seeks to analyze and alter the sociopolitical dynamics, power structures, and ideologies that infuse our thinking of what is "common sense" or "normal." Arguing for a critical pedagogy in social work, Saleebey and Scanlon (2005) define it as an "educational practice that links theory and action, social thought and social change" into a "union referred to as 'praxis' " (p. 4). Ideally, it culminates in activities based on jointly developed critical awareness (Saleebey & Scanlon, 2005). In current classrooms, creating this critical awareness is too often limited to cognitive processes and excludes much of the richness of mimetic knowledge. Therefore, the use of improvisational games and exercises expands critical pedagogy to be more inclusive of embodied knowledge production and in turn benefits from critical analysis so as to not lose its transformative sociopolitical potential.

The following are examples of my efforts to teach from an improvisational mindset and use games or exercises from theater improv as a part of a critical pedagogical concept. My own practice of improvisational theater has undoubtedly made me more comfortable with the discomfort of uncertainty in the classroom. But to be clear, creating an atmosphere of nonjudgment, of playfulness and risk-taking, remains no easy feat in the existing structures of academic learning. Students and teachers are equally socialized to a form of learning that has little in common with the sacred temenos of free play. It takes creative and resistive acts to fashion nonjudgmental spaces where "performance" denotes not playful learning but "being up to snuff." Altering traditional performances of "teacher" and "student," and turning, or returning, classrooms into spaces in which we play together to explore the unknown, is a communal improvisational effort.

Setting the Stage: Safe to Be Uncomfortable

Understanding the crucial role of the temenos, I set out to use improv games in hope of facilitating a safe space. The notion of social work classrooms as "safe spaces" has been explored by Holley and Steiner (2005), who found that students most often associated an instructor's nonjudgmental attitude with feeling safe. Then again, what do we mean by "safe space"?

Fook and Askeland (2007) nicely troubled a simplistic view of "safe space" in the social work classroom when they pointed out how social work improvisations may be inadvertently "disciplined" through the internalized frames of curriculum, habitus, or conventions. Considering the challenges of critical reflection in classroom discussions, the authors found "clinical" tendencies in social work education that may lead educators and students to believe that "safe" means "comfortable" and keep them from the discomfort of challenging ideas. Not only do notions of "professional objectivity" discourage discussion of anything that is considered "subjective" but also therapeutic habits in social work may hamper critical "why" questions of oneself or others because they might be considered judgmental, intrusive, too personal, or otherwise inappropriate. The increasingly bureaucratic–technical focus of work routines and an "argument culture," in which only one side can be right, heightens anxieties about having it done "right" (according to protocol). Therefore, it becomes all the more important—although difficult—to critically inquire into ambivalences, ambiguities, or uncertainties (Fook & Askeland, 2007).

To this end, social work education as an improvisational activity requires creating a "safe (enough) space" that must not be mistaken for "feeling comfortable" at all times. Quite the opposite: The space is safe to take risks, to "play" in ways that challenge, push, and disturb the ostensibly "common-sense" practices in which we engage and which we encounter. Hence, the temenos is ideally a space making it safe to be challenged, to be vulnerable, to be changed, and to be uncomfortable for students and teachers each in their own ways.

Because this space is created not by declaration but in the continuous experience and exchange of those who are present, I am not the only person in the room making a space safe enough. I discuss with students what this means to them as we go over the syllabus, in which one section explicitly asks students to help make seminars a place to "think out loud," to try things out, and be constructive in the giving and receiving of feedback. But more important, before I enter into this discussion, I typically invite students to play games that provide an opportunity to explore what I am trying to communicate in a joint experience and model a combination of risk-taking and playfulness, openness and critical thinking.

The Clown Bow

In order to integrate the improv principle of "making mistakes and staying happy," I often begin classes, especially early in the semester, with icebreaker games and exercises designed to foster teamwork, communication, spontaneity, and, most of all, fun.[2] These games and exercises require students to stand up or move, thus physically altering the typical student position of sitting behind a desk. Rather than just watching, I participate in activities, physically moving into the circle of learners, which makes me an equal player—or at least a somewhat more equal player.

To further combat the fear of making mistakes and instead promote the idea of failing happily, I choose games and exercises in which everyone, including myself, will look silly or fail. After the exercises, or during breaks between rounds, I engage students in reflections on what is happening, in their heads and in the group, when, for instance, the object of the game is to "throw an invisible 'hot potato' to someone else and make a sound with it." Of course, different things happen: There is immediate amusement and laughter for some; other students will identify a sense of embarrassment, getting flustered or stressed because they focus on "doing it right" and feel very unhappy when they think they did it wrong. Some discover that they tried to follow "rules" that no one established, such as "I thought I had to come up with a new sound that nobody had done before." I then introduce the "clown bow"—the boisterous, happy, and proud raising of the arms after "failing" or when feeling embarrassed accompanied by a loud call of "whoo-hoo!"[3] and a big bow, which is cheered and applauded by the group. Taking the "clown bow," to not shrink in shame but make themselves physically and emotionally big, to proudly accept the cheers of their peers when feeling stupid, can be a liberating experience for students and invite future risk-taking. It helps students to recognize their fears, and it offers a way to make them public so as to fashion new meaning around the notion of "mistakes" and "failure" in the classroom and beyond. This meaning is expanded when I invite students to discuss how fears of making mistakes impact their learning and how the institutions into which we have been socialized play a role in this. Thus, these ostensibly silly games open opportunities to experience, discover, discuss, and alter how we negotiate our internal and external social worlds that are at the heart of social work theory and practice.

Sometimes I hear students employ the "whoo-hoo" in small group exercises during the course of a semester, or even beyond, and I quietly hope that it indeed serves as an embodied reminder of the nonjudgmental attitude that is essential

---

2. For a compilation of games and exercises used in improvisational theater training, see http://www.improvencyclopedia.org.

3. For the "whoo-hoo," I am indebted to the unstoppable Laura Derry of San Francisco's BATS Improv Theatre Company.

to explorative learning processes and to the co-creation of a safe space in which "being right" is far less interesting than being challenged and surprised by one's discoveries.

Yes and . . . No!

Part of my own improvisational teaching stance is the effort to say "yes, and . . ." to the offers my students make and allow myself to be altered in response to their ideas and actions. This includes changing the use of improv-based activities and leading and following in the course of discussions to see where we end up. For instance, in the first session of an undergraduate class on counseling, I asked students to get into groups of four or five, brainstorm for 3 minutes, and then improvise a 30-second scene that depicts a counseling session in which they do "everything wrong." Initially, I designed this exercise to help students work in groups quickly, be spontaneous, have fun, and lose their fear of being in front of the class. It was meant as merely a warm-up. But students quickly expanded on this purpose. Based on their observations of what was "wrong" in the counseling scenes, we engaged in conversations about what they thought was "right." Discussions soon turned to another valuable aspect, namely questioning the idea that one can judge things as being simply "wrong" or "right" without attention to context. Is the use of vernacular or dialect really always wrong in counseling, or isn't it at times useful for connecting with clients? Where does the idea of "professional language" come from? How do we come to our ideas of what is or is not "professional"? Saying "Yes, and . . . !" to students' curiosities and encouraging them to think out loud allowed the class to co-produce knowledge that dissolved a simplistic binary right–wrong coding and instead opened space for ambiguity. In the process, students expanded my own awareness how "yes, and . . ." is not identical to simple agreement but that one can also accept and advance by saying "yes, and . . . no!" I now allow far more time for discussing the complexities of the "do everything wrong" exercise, occasionally prompting students to question simple dichotomies of right–wrong or to re-enact the same "wrong" behavior in a context that makes it seem "right."

Identity Improvisations

Students in the same counseling class provided another example for a critically enriched improvisation when they invented the idea of separating the role from the player: All students in this class improvise counseling situations either in a live role play or in a videotaped version, making themselves remarkably vulnerable to the gaze and judgment of others who are asked to provide reflective feedback to presenters. One group of players presented their videotaped scenes and pointed out that they had discovered it was helpful for them to speak of themselves not as "I" or by their real names but, instead, in the third person and in their role as, for instance, "the counselor" and "the client." The rest of the class immediately followed suit and also referred in their feedback to those who had shared their work in the third person. Accepting the idea created a space in which students could keep down fears of being personally judged, which in turn allowed them to make themselves vulnerable and look critically upon the roles they co-created. Eventually, they began to question how the improvised roles reproduced stereotypes of "clients" and "professionals" alike. Students discussed how they came to hold these stereotypes; how they inadvertently invoked them verbally and physically; and how they could challenge themselves to alter their own performances of gender, socioeconomic status, etc. Since then, I have gratefully shared this idea of linguistically separating "player" from "role" with all subsequent counseling classes, many of which have incorporated it. And the question of how students think they came up with their characterizations has also become part of my repertoire.

Sculpted Words

An exercise I have borrowed from Augusto Boal's *Theatre of the Oppressed* (1985, 1992) is the idea of sculpting words. I first introduced it spontaneously when students in a practice class were unsure to what extent language use made a difference in the construction of social realities. In a discussion about the question why we speak of "professional distance" but not of "professional closeness" and how this makes a difference in our image of "professionals" and "clients," I asked students to stand in a circle facing outward. Silently, students sculpted their bodies into positions that—to them—reflected "professional distance." After all students found their image and got to look at others' sculptures, they repeated the exercise sculpting "professional closeness." The ensuing discussion was much enriched by people's observations of self and others. The kinesthetic experience of holding a posture or facial expression stimulated perceptions and thoughts, as did the impression of looking upon others' sculptures. In their ability to reference bodily sensations, students linked emotion to cognition in ways that let them discover new dimensions of the power of words.

Status Games

Another exercise in which the body provides critical information is based on Keith Johnstone's (1981, 1999) status games, which occasionally find their way into my classrooms. I share the ideas behind the concept of relational status and ask three students to play a simple improvised scene, such as a job interview or a family waiting for a teenager to return home late. Unknown to the audience, each person is assigned a number between 1 and 3. Whoever has been assigned the number 1 is trying to be dominant or high status, the person assigned the number 3 holds the lowest relational status, and the person assigned number 2 is somewhere in between. After a brief scene, I ask the audience to judge, based on what they observed, who is "on top," "in the middle," or "on the bottom" of the relational hierarchy. I often repeat the same scene with the same players, this time having them choose a number themselves and not sharing it with each other. The ensuing scene frequently looks quite different from the first, especially if two persons happen to be fighting for the same position. Aside from the amusement in the room, students quickly begin to realize that relational status is always in flux and not independent of the observer. Minor adjustments in reaction to one another can alter the impression of status in an instance. In addition, students enacting the roles often begin to reflect how they may prefer playing a particular status. Not unlike Virginia Satir's (1972) idea that people have preferred ways of dealing with threats to self-worth by acting as a "computer," "distractor," "blamer," or "accommodator," students recognize that some bodily postures, voice, or speech habits are more familiar than others, and they discover that playing and observing "status" are gendered activities.

CONCLUSION

Improvisation holds a rich promise not only for direct use with and by students to learn practice-related skills but also for an educational stance that resists the technological and ideological closing of social work education in favor of spaces for dialogic, playful, and critical explorations. As part of a holistic approach to education, it expands Goldstein's (2001) emphasis on the necessity of experiential learning and can combine modes of learning including Kolb's (1984) concrete experiences, reflective observation, abstract conceptualization, and active experimentation. Learning how to improvise through the use of theater games creates opportunities for students and educators alike to experience the uncertainty and creative potential of collaborative activities in the classroom. Knowledge and exercises borrowed from improvisational theater grant structures for "planned serendipity" in which improvising can be taught (Mirvis, 1998). Such experiential learning inextricably weaves together doing and knowing (Bruner, 1996) that is also consistent with current neurobiological insights.

As part of a critical education approach, improvisation can inform a move from practice to critical praxis within and outside of classrooms by quite literally incorporating critical analysis and reflection. Critical reflection as part of improvisation is not just "in the individual head"; rather, the body provides inspiration and holds residues heretofore unnoticed. Similarly, material surroundings, as well as the interactive and intersubjective construction of social realities, become tangible in the group process of improvised activities. Improvisation as an educational concept can thus help create a space in which social work students and educators engage in experiences that are simultaneously fun and serious, creative and critical, analytic and mimetic, as well as collaborative and transformational.

REFERENCES

Barrett, F. (1998). Creativity and improvisation in jazz and organizations: Implications for organizational learning. *Organizational Science, 9*(5), 605–622.
Blom, B. (2009). Knowing or un-knowing? That is the question in the era of evidence-based social work practice. *Journal of Social Work, 9*(2), 158–177.
Boal, A. (1985). *Theatre of the oppressed.* New York, NY: Theatre Communications Group.
Boal, A. (1992). *Games for actors and non-actors.* New York, NY: Routledge.
Boal, A. (1995). *Rainbow of desire.* New York, NY: Routledge.
Borko, H., & Livingston, C. (1989). Cognition and improvisation: Differences in mathematics instruction by expert and novice teachers. *American Educational Research Journal, 26*(4), 473–498.
Bruner, J. (1996). *The culture of education.* Cambridge, MA: Harvard University Press.
Carlson, M. (1996). *Performance—A critical introduction.* New York, NY: Routledge.
Crossan, M. M. (1998). Improvisation in action. *Organization Science, 9*(5), 593–599.
Crossan, M. M., Lane, H. W., & White, R. E. (1996). The improvising organization: Where planning meets opportunity. *Organizational Dynamics, 24*(Spring), 20–35.
Emunah, R., & Blatner, A. (1994). *Acting for real: Drama therapy process, technique, and performance.* New York, NY: Brunner/Mazel.
Feldman, N., Barron, M., Holliman, D. C., Karliner, S., & Walter, U. M. (2009). Playful postmodernism: Building with diversity in the postmodern classroom. *Journal of Teaching in Social Work, 29*(2), 119–133.
Fook, J., & Askeland, G. A. (2007). Challenges of critical reflection: "Nothing ventured, nothing gained." *Social Work Education, 26*(5), 520–533.
Freire, P. (1989). *Pedagogy of the oppressed.* New York, NY: Continuum.
Fusco, D. (2000). The role of performance in teacher education. *Teacher Education Quarterly, 7*(4), 89–105.
Gebauer, G., & Wulf, C. (2003). *Mimetische Weltzugänge.* Stuttgart, Germany: Kohlhammer.
Giroux, H. (2004). Critical pedagogy and the postmodern/modern divide. *Teacher Education Quarterly, 31*(1), 31–47.
Giroux, H. (2011). *On critical pedagogy.* New York, NY: Continuum.
Goldstein, H. (2001). *Experiential learning: A foundation for social work education and practice.* Alexandria, VA: Council on Social Work Education.
Goldstein, H. (1998). Education for ethical dilemmas in social work practice. *Families in Society, 79*(3), 241–253.
Graybeal, C. T. (2007). Evidence for the art of social work. *Families in Society, 88*(4), 513–523.
Hargreaves, R., & Hadlow, J. (1997). Role-play in social work education: Process and framework for a constructive and focused approach. *Social Work Education, 16*(3), 61–73.
Holland, D., Lachicotte, W., Skinner, D., & Cain, C. (1998). *Identity and agency in cultural worlds.* Cambridge, MA: Harvard University Press.
Holley, L. C., & Steiner, S. (2005). Safe space: Student perspectives on classroom environment. *Journal of Social Work Education, 41*(1), 49–64.

Hüther, G. (n.d.). *Learning enthusiastically*. Retrieved July 30, 2014, from http://www. gerald-huether.de/populaer/english/learning-enthusiastically/index.php.

Immordino-Yang, M. H., & Damasio, A. R. (2007). We feel, therefore we learn: The relevance of affective and social neuroscience to education. *Mind, Brain and Education, 1*(1), 3–10.

Jackson, S. (2000). *Lines of activity: Performance, historiography, Hull-House domesticity*. Ann Arbor, MI: University of Michigan Press.

Janesick, J. V. (2000). The choreography of qualitative research design: Minuets, improvisations, and crystallization. In N. K. Denzin & Y. S. Lincoln (Eds.), *Handbook of qualitative research* (2nd ed., pp. 379–400). Thousand Oaks, CA: Sage.

Johnstone, K. (1981). *Impro—Improvisation and the theatre*. New York, NY: Routledge.

Johnstone, K. (1999). *Impro for storytellers*. New York, NY: Routledge.

Keeney, B. P. (1991). *Improvisational therapy*. New York, NY: Guilford.

Kolb, D. A. (1984). *Experiential learning: Experience as the source of learning and development*. Englewood Cliffs, NJ: Prentice Hall.

Logie, C., Bogo, M., Regehr, C., & Regehr, G. (2013). A critical appraisal of the use of standardized client simulations in social work education. *Journal of Social Work Education, 49*(1), 66–80.

Madsen, W. C. (2011). Collaborative helping maps: A tool to guide thinking and action in family-centered services. *Family Process, 50*(4), 529–543.

Madson, P. R. (2005). *Improv wisdom*. New York, NY: Harmony/Bell Tower.

Mirvis, P. (1998). Practice improvisation. *Organization Science, 9*(5), 586–592.

Moreno, J. L. (1987). *The essential Moreno: Writings on psychodrama, group method, and spontaneity*. New York, NY: Springer.

Nachmanovitch, S. (1990). *Free play—Improvisation in life and art*. New York, NY: Tarcher/ Putnam.

Newman, F., & Holzman, L. (1996). *Unscientific psychology: A cultural-performatory approach to understanding human life*. Westport, CT: Praeger.

Perlinski, M., Blom, B., & Moren, S. (2012). Getting a sense of the client: Working methods in the personal social services in Sweden. *Journal of Social Work, 13*(5), 508–532.

Petracchi, H. E., & Collins, K. S. (2006). Utilizing actors to simulate clients in social work student role plays. *Journal of Teaching in Social Work, 26*(1–2), 223–233.

Reisch, M. (2013). Social work education and the neo-liberal challenge: The US response to increasing global inequality. *Social Work Education, 32*(6), 715–733.

Ringstrom, P. (2001). Cultivating the improvisational in psychoanalytic treatment. *Psychoanalytic Dialogues, 11*(5), 727–754.

Rosaldo, R. (1993). *Culture and truth*. Boston, MA: Beacon.

Saleebey, D. (1989, November). The estrangement of knowing and doing. *Social Casework*, 556–563.

Saleebey, D., & Scanlon, E. (2005). Is a critical pedagogy for the profession of social work possible? *Journal of Teaching in Social Work, 25*(3–4), 1–18.

Satir, V. (1972). *Peoplemaking*. Palo Alto, CA: Science and Behavior Books.

Sawyer, R. K. (1992). Improvisational creativity: An analysis of jazz performance. *Creativity Research Journal, 5*(3), 253–263.

Sawyer, R. K. (2004a). Creative teaching: Collaborative discussion as disciplined improvisation. *Educational Researcher, 33*(2), 12–20.

Sawyer, R. K. (2004b). Improvised lessons: Collaborative discussion in the constructivist classroom. *Teaching Education, 15*(2), 189–201.

Schön, D. (1987). *Educating the reflective practitioner*. San Francisco, CA: Jossey-Bass.

Schön, D. (1995). Knowing-in-action: The new scholarship requires a new epistemology. *Change, 27*(6), 27–34.

Seligson, L. V. (2004). Beyond technique: Performance and the art of social work practice. *Families in Society, 85*(4), 531–537.

Shem-Tov, N. (2011). Improvisational teaching as mode of knowing. *Journal of Aesthetic Education, 45*(3), 103–113.

Shepard, B., Bogad, L. M., & Duncombe, S. (2008). Performing vs. the insurmountable: Theatrics, activism, and social movements. *Liminalities: A Journal of Performance Studies, 4*(3), 1–30.

Spolin, V. (1999). *Improvisation for the theater* (3rd ed.). Evanston, IL: Northwestern University Press.

Taibbi, R. (2009). The Tao of improv—Embracing life on the edge. *Psychotherapy Networker, 33*(1). Retrieved January 10, 2012, from http://www.bobtaibbi.com/page7/page8/page8.html.

Todd, S. (2012). Practicing in the uncertain: Reworking standardized clients as improv theatre. *Social Work Education, 31*(3), 302–315.

Walter, U. M. (2006). *Into the third space—Social work as improvised performance.* Doctoral dissertation, University of Kansas, Lawrence, KS.

Watzlawick, P., Beavin, J., & Jackson, D. (1967). *Pragmatics of human communication.* New York, NY: Norton.

Weick, K. E. (1998). Improvisation as a mindset for organizational analysis. *Organization Science, 9*(5), 543–555.

Wiener, D. J. (1994). *Rehearsals for growth.* New York, NY: Norton.

Wilson, T. D. (2002). *Strangers to ourselves.* Cambridge, MA: Belknap.

Yalom, I. D. (1989). *Love's executioner and other tales of psychotherapy.* New York, NY: Basic Books.

Zaunbrecher, N. J. (2011). The elements of improvisation: Structural tools for spontaneous theatre. *Theatre Topics, 21*(1), 49–60.

CHAPTER 9

Teaching to the Holistic Self

A Case Study of a Critical
Social Work Classroom

JULIANA SVISTOVA, LARA BOWEN,
AND MEERA BHAT

For the things we have to learn before we can do them, we learn by doing them.
Aristotle

Learning takes place through action, but it is driven by emotion.
Zull (2011, p. 54)

INTRODUCTION

Threaded throughout this book is a growing consensus on the need for applied, participatory, and holistic approaches to educating social workers and other helping professionals. Positioned uniquely on the educator–student spectrum, we seek to contribute to this book by presenting a lesson plan on the practice of critical social work wherein students' cognitive and emotional selves are embraced and invited to the stage. We begin with describing pedagogy and theater of the oppressed as content that can be covered and methods that can be used in social work classrooms. As we do so, we offer our reflections on the possibilities of such classroom experiences to enact transformation of learning (and, by extension, social work practice), making a connection to the recent advances in the neuroscience of learning. Through our synthesis of literature on neuroscience, practice, pedagogy, and social change and our own learning and teaching experiences, we begin to visualize the process of holistic learning as we see it.

Social Work Education in the 21st Century

Higher education institutions (as primary educational sites of professional social workers) arguably hinder transformative learning opportunities for the change agents soon-to-be. Operating in the context of increasing financial constraints and relying more heavily on a neoliberal efficiency model (Reisch & Jarman-Rohde, 2000), universities often seek to achieve measurable results (predominantly equated to the quantity of knowledge transmitted and regurgitated) quickly and cheaply. Such quantitative outcomes (Reisch, 2013), however, through "a rote, assembly-line approach" (hooks, 1994, p. 13) arguably produce like-minded automatons rather than progressive critical thinkers and culturally versed practitioners. In this chapter, we seek to make a case for critical holistic education as an antidote for the assembly-line production of helping professionals. We argue that teaching to the holistic self, although neuroscientifically and pedagogically valid, is not always structurally viable.

In this regard, at the beginning of the 21st century, Reisch and Jarman-Rohde (2000) started the discussion about how globalization, technology, demographic changes, and the changing nature of social services and American universities would affect social work education. The central question of their discussion was whether social work schools are "educating students *for* the changing practice environment or to *change* the changing practice environment" (italics in original, p. 210).

Later, Reisch (2013) problematized the influence of neoliberalism on social work education and the profession itself. Regarding educational content, he criticized its digression from social justice, emphasis on "individual rather than structural transformation" (p. 718), "reliance on practice theories and methods that emphasize equilibrium rather than change" (p. 719), promotion of evidence-based practice, and preference for quantitative research methods. Reisch critically appraised measurable "quantitative 'outcomes' as indicators of students' performance," the micro/macro divide, and the depoliticized learning experiences of aspiring social workers (p. 716). Following Reisch, we further argue that linear, one-dimensional theories of, and hence prescriptive technical solutions for, complex problems teach social work students to fit into and reproduce the established social order turning/co-opting them into agents of social control.

As doctoral students, we certainly have experienced firsthand the prevailing positivist ideation, depoliticized learning, and the lack of attention to human interaction, processes, and empowering outcomes. In our educational experiences, the intuitive and emotional lives of students have been undervalued. Having qualitatively oriented mindsets, through our required doctoral coursework, we have often felt like misfits while being immersed into the exclusively positivist research agenda. We felt deprived of an in-depth discussion of what counts as knowledge, evidence, and knowing. As agents of our own fate, we had to seek such opportunities elsewhere. Being trained by older faculty members who themselves were trained in a strictly quantitative school of thought may partially explain our experience.

Reisch (2013) proposed that "questioning assumptions, reawakening curiosity, sitting in uncertainty and deconstructing discourse" serve as "exercises in liberation" in the classroom that can be "transferred into student's practice techniques" and action toward social change (p. 724). Similarly, we argue that creating opportunities for praxis, or practical application of theoretical learning, can serve as a vehicle to integrate fractured feelings and thoughts that a social work student may face when approaching complex problems. The inherent and ever-growing complexity of social problems that prospective social workers are charged to solve calls for comprehensive, interdisciplinary, and innovative thinking as well as practice skills. We argue that alternative approaches to pedagogy and multisensory learning through dialogue, participation, and practical application of theory allow teaching to these skills and to the development of a holistic self. In this chapter, we understand the holistic self of the learners as a balance of cognitive–rational and emotional–creative ways of learning and knowing. When simple processing and storing of information is paired with instant creative application, we believe that a learner's cognitive–emotional well-being is stimulated and enhanced (Zull, 2011).

We also argue that experiencing a distant, rational interaction in the classroom, it is not easy to replicate compassionate attention and build empathetic connections (both constructs developed in this text) with clients when out in the world of practice. We argue that the traditional social work education system leaves the initiative of cultivating compassionate attention and empathetic connection to the student or the educator. Conceiving of learning as the process of co-construction, educators must not forget, however, that instructional methods and classroom environment leave imprints on, and model real-world interactions for, the learners. Yet current typical social work classroom experiences offer limited opportunities for exploration of student emotional selves and provide minimal exposure to the real-world interactions.

The Neuroscience of Learning

The recent advances in the neuroscience of learning support our argument that the reception and instant application of information result in sustainable learning. The key premise of the neuroscience of learning, according to Zull (2011), is that effective teaching and sustainable learning happen when learners' cognitive and emotional (brain) selves are integrated. He argues that a teaching approach that stimulates cognition through choices, decisions, predictions, and actions creates a feeling of satisfaction and joy through accomplishment, progress, and ownership. There exists an emotional, rewarding power of learners' success that can be explained neuroscientifically as immediate pleasure through dopamine releases. Zull explains that such joyful learning experiences help repress the fearful part of the brain—amygdala—that is often stimulated by the test-driven approach of "assembly-line education." In such a model, it is important to regurgitate the information fed by the instructor rather than the student's own interpretation of it. The fear stems from the anxiety to give the absolutely correct answers and the fear of interpretation. In addition, the neuroscience of learning proposes that the way the brain physically processes information explains why the information that is simply heard is not registered and is forgotten by the learner. We suggest that the audiences' attention spans are also low in this manner of education. In contrast, integration, reflection, and action (also known as problem-solving) transform learning processes from mere "injection" of information into one's brain to "cementing" knowledge into one's mind (Zull, 2011). In other words, ownership of learning happens through curiosity, figuring out, and interpretation (not concretization).[1] The neurobiology of learning (Zull, 2011) also suggests that such "imprints" of classroom experiences, positive or negative, can be traced in the neural wiring and neuroplasticity of the learners' brains. Hence, in addition to educational philosophers such as Freire and Boal, neuropsychology supports the thesis of this chapter that the well-being of learners in the all-round and positive emotional stimulations of the mind.

In this chapter, we seek to contribute to this book and the general literature on social work education in two keys ways: (1) to provide an example of practical applications of critical pedagogy and theater of the oppressed (Boal, 1979) as content and method in social work classrooms and (2) to theorize their potential to promote holistic learning experiences. We present an example of a lesson plan that covers the material about, and applies the techniques of, pedagogy and theater of the oppressed. We offer our reflections on the process and potential outcomes of this learning experience that we think exemplifies teaching to the holistic self.

OUR POSITIONALITY

We believe that we provide a fresh perspective because we are not only social work educators but also students. The previous section is our shared perspective as we perform our roles as social work students. Speaking from the role of the emerging social work educator, we heretofore are not yet tenure process haunted, de-ideated, and de-politicized by the neoliberal operation and ideation of our university. Our pedagogue selves are in full agreement with our student selves.

---

1. Concretization refers to rote learning in which a set of information is repeated again and again so as to memorize it rather than integrating, interpreting, or reflecting on it.

We believe that these "nots" allow us to speak our minds freely, critically, and reflectively.

We believe that we also bring in a blend of social work training and work experience from India, Latvia, and the United States in rather contrasting welfare, academic, and political systems. My (Juliana Svistova) educational and professional experiences in Latvia can be described as going through the motions surrounded by the remnants of the Soviet machine. Educationally, I went through a typical Soviet pedagogical approach of content memorizing and regurgitation with all-knowing teachers in a position of authority. Professionally, I worked as a social worker in a social service agency. I was essentially a bureaucrat with some power who abided by the prescribed laws and disciplined the poor and fragile segment of society. A fairly new profession (approximately 15 years old) at a time, social work was borrowing from the US, UK, and Scandinavian schools of social work and social welfare thought. The profession was rapidly developing as it was attempting to break through the profoundly imprinted practices of the Soviet (welfare) system. The word "empowerment" was unheard of because the Latvian or Russian equivalent of this word had not been created (I am not sure it exists today either).

In contrast, my (Meera Bhat) social work educational experience in India is from a feminist, hands-on program in which one-third of the undergraduate program constituted intensive fieldwork, sometimes in an agency or sometimes one-on-one with a supervisor in a community. Classes were very often held under trees, on rooftops, in community settings, or on hikes depending on both the students' and teacher's comfort and needs. There was an assertive focus, particularly in the early semesters, on observation, journaling, and group reflection. Grading was mostly through assignments that compelled students to question themselves, their values, and the systems around them, including their teachers and theories. This could result in new definitions or the development of manuals on specific topics.

INTRODUCING CRITICAL PEDAGOGY AND THEATER OF THE OPPRESSED

We suggest that the pedagogic method of Paulo Freire and theatrical processes promoted by Augusto Boal offer a means to bridge the emotional and cognitive selves of the learner by offering an opportunity to reflect on and integrate course content. Their approaches, we believe, invoke emotions and provide tools to maximize self-awareness that conventional cognitive approaches to teaching cannot offer. Their approaches stimulate learning by doing and allow students to quickly grasp often paradoxical ideas that require cognitive comprehension and empathetic connection. We also argue that pedagogy and theater of the oppressed (Boal, 1979) can serve dual roles as a pedagogic approach and a set of practice skills to develop for aspiring social work and other helping professionals.

Critical Pedagogy as Method and Content

Critical pedagogy, or pedagogy of the oppressed, pioneered by Paulo Freire, is a grassroots pedagogic strategy for adult education. Conceived during Freire's work with peasants in Brazil, it is founded on a premise that education of the marginalized and poor populations has to begin with consciousness-raising about their daily life situations. Here, we discuss its dual role as both a pedagogic approach that can be applied to and content (e.g., a method of community practice) that can be taught in a social work classroom.

As an instructional approach, critical pedagogy is learner-centered. Freire rejected the roles of all-knowing teacher and ignorant students in favor of a learning process as a shared practice between them. He believed that teacher and student are capable of dialogue and of problematizing together (Freire, 1974, 2000; Gadotti & Torres, 2009). This standpoint of Freire functions as a mantra in our classrooms as well.

Furthermore, Freire (1974) was in opposition to a "banking" education, a kind of traditional approach to education in which the student is viewed as an empty account to deposit information into by the knowledge-holding teacher. Alternatively, critical pedagogy asserts that the teacher's job is not to transmit or inject information but, rather, to engage and to challenge students, ensuring that the voices of everyone are fully involved (Gadotti & Torres, 2009; Kollins & Hansman, 2005). We also reject a simple injection of knowledge and seek to create space for a two-way transaction and mutual learning process with our students.

In addition, "banking" education rarely works for adults who are enriched with prior experiences. This experiential baggage needs to be accounted for, and built on, in the education process (Freire, 1974, 2000). Therefore, critical pedagogy builds on the experiences of the learner, helps people assert their rights, encourages questioning, enhances resistance to authority and confrontation, and increases feelings of empowerment (Freire, 1974). We value this important characteristic of adult learners and seek to incorporate it in our own instruction as a component of continued holistic development of learners' selves.

According to Freire (1974, 2000), "critical consciousness" emerges as a result of such a learning process, which means that learners become aware of oppressive structures and their own abilities to participate in the creation of knowledge and change. Consequently, their perspectives of themselves and their worlds change. Furthermore, by means of critical education, the students acquire tools to resist oppression and exploitation and learn to challenge existing and permeable structures of domination. Through the use of these tools, social transformation, participation, and social mobilization ensue (Gadotti & Torres, 2009; Kollins & Hansman, 2005). Critical consciousness or awareness is a central component of the kind of pedagogy that we advocate for in the social work classrooms. We believe that holistic selves of learners emerge from the awareness of their inner selves and their relationships with the world.

Primarily understood as a philosophy of education, Freire's critical education approach is also widely applied as a method of community practice intended to raise consciousness and mobilize people to resist unjust social conditions. While working primarily with people struggling with poverty and illiteracy in Brazil, Freire began drawing connections between education and socioeconomic development. He approached development from the perspective of a political and pedagogical scholar–activist trying to revive the question of ethics in education and its implication for citizenship building (Gadotti & Torres, 2009; Kollins & Hansman, 2005). Therefore, critical education as community practice is by, and with, the people, wherein people are understood as engaged citizens who come to know themselves, understand how social reality functions, and proceed with transforming it (Freire, 1974). Pedagogy of the oppressed relies on assumptions that unofficial, community knowledge is more valuable than outside "expert" knowledge as a resource for problem-solving at the individual and societal level.

Critical Pedagogy in Social Work Education

Given our own focus on Freire's use of critical analysis and dialogue in higher education classrooms, we inquired into the literature across disciplines that describes previous experiences using images, dialogue, and reflection. Some of the examples to date include the use of illustrations from school textbooks to deconstruct teachings of religion (Badanelli, 2012); guided imagery to challenge students' preconceived ideas about heterosexism and heterophobia (Henderson & Murdock, 2012); fine arts images to emancipate students as spectators (Lewis, 2011); discourse analysis to evaluate classroom interaction (Hjelm, 2013); and dialogue and reflection to deconstruct power, privilege, and silence in the classroom (Ochoa & Pineda, 2008).

In relation to social work education, although there is an abundant discussion about Freire's fit with, and contribution to, social work as a discipline, scant literature exists on the practical application of his methodology in the social work classroom. However, we found one example of critical pedagogy at play. This example of training aspiring therapists is discussed in depth next.

Nylund and Tilsen (2006) describe their experience applying critical pedagogy in the family therapy classroom. Terming it a "postmodern approach," they implicate attendance to, and development of, students' reflexivity and awareness of sociopolitical issues. They describe activities and assignments that, according to them, foster critical thinking and flatten hierarchy between student and teacher. One of the activities includes deconstruction of what students know, or what the authors call "unteaching" thinking, wherein students are invited to consider the impact of their own family of origin on their ideas, values, and responses. Another assignment engages students in critiquing theory. Authors provide readings that critique theories and a list of questions to guide such critical appraisal with an objective to reveal that theories are socially constructed and project certain positionalities. They also provide students with options to learn "alone or in group, live or online, and through visual, auditory, and kinesthetic channels" (p. 30).

Nylund and Tilsen (2006) suggest that through their own openness to being vulnerable and "touched and transformed" as teacher–learners, the hierarchy gap between them and students shrinks (p. 26). Their approach to grading and assessment further facilitates power flattening. Specifically, they encourage students to generate their own assessment criteria—for example, expressed through the voice of the clients that they serve. They also use peer reviews and feedback. This whole approach, they suggest, creates a "postmodern spirit" in the classroom that "encourages knowledge and knowledge-making" (p. 30). In other words, such an approach exemplifies the essence of critical education by mapping a two-way transaction between teachers and learners instead of traditional one-way authoritative evaluation of learning.

Theater of the Oppressed as Method and Content

Augusto Boal applied Freire's concepts of pedagogical oppression in the educational system to illuminate the oppressive nature of theater. He compared the classroom experience to the theater experience as methods of indoctrination and drew parallels between the function of the teacher to the function of the actor on stage and the role of the students to the role of the audience (i.e., both as passive recipients). It warrants comment, relative to social work education, the irony of teaching content that values interaction, empowerment, and social justice when it is delivered in a traditional "banking" format.

Boal conceptualized traditional theater as a weapon wielded as a mechanism of tyranny to influence the poor through dramatizations of plays selected, funded, and produced by the aristocracy (Boal, 1979). He rebelled by producing alternative formats that disarmed traditional theater by eliminating the barriers between the audience and the actors, thus inviting an interactional experience; descriptions of these interactive theater formats can be found in his book titled *Theatre of the Oppressed* (1979)—an homage to Freire's (1974) *Pedagogy of the Oppressed*. Whereas Boal translated Freire's critical perspective of education as it applied to theater, we reciprocate by presenting applications of Theatre of the Oppressed (TO) in social work education.

Boal is an important historical figure to be included in the social work curriculum because he was an example of a social change agent who utilized theater as a participatory method for community organizing and empowerment. He was critical of the social injustices perpetuated by traditional theater and yet was able to transform theater for the people and harness its power to provide a voice for people who are poor and an arena for dialogue. It would be valuable for social work students to understand the political nature of theater (and, more broadly, media), to recognize its potential to be used for social control by those in authority, as well as how to reclaim its power for social change by those who are marginalized and oppressed. We offer Boal's critique of theater as a metaphor of what is currently happening in social work education. To provide a more egalitarian model of learning, we suggest that instructors holistically engage their students by simultaneously teaching about and learning from Boal's methods, delivering both content and context for critical social work pedagogy.

His work was visionary in that many of his ideas are echoed in contemporary fields of research, such as communications and neuroscience. For example, Boal (1979) made the assertion that audience members of ancient Greek tragedies were manipulated to identify and empathize with the protagonist so profoundly that they were brought to a state of catharsis that served as a compelling lesson or warning to behave and conform to the social norms or else suffer the consequences experienced by the tragic hero on stage. This emotional response from audiences can be explained by the recent discovery of "mirror neurons" in the science of brain mapping that demonstrates empathy is an innate neurological reaction within the brain of the observer that resonates with the neurons firing in the brain of the observed (Watson & Greenburg, 2009).

Empathy is a foundational skill required for social workers to engage clients and build rapport for enhancing the therapeutic alliance and clinical outcomes (Watson & Greenburg, 2009). Teaching this skill set poses challenges that traditional hierarchical pedagogy fails to address fully. Among them is the skill to identify and express empathy effectively to the client while avoiding the danger of unbridled empathy and undefined boundaries in the therapeutic relationship, rendering it ineffectual and unsustainable. The inability to manage their own emotional responses can result in vicarious traumatization, empathic distress, and professional exhaustion for social workers (Grant, 2014), as well as poor outcomes for the client. By engaging students to interact using a theatrical format in the classroom, students are given the opportunity to master empathic emotional responses with the support of their peers and feedback from the instructor.

In Boal's analysis, the original goal of theater to create an empathic response and promote an experience of catharsis has recently evolved to also include an effort by playwrights such as Bertolt Brecht to raise the audience's critical consciousness (Boal, 1979). This is done by dramatizing subject matter that is not only emotionally engrossing but also arouses cognitive processes through provocative ideas that may conflict with the audience members' preexisting beliefs. Although an effort to stimulate thoughtful interaction from audience members shows progress toward a more egalitarian appreciation for them, Boal viewed it as a passive experience and therefore still oppressive. The relatively recent focus on critical thinking in social work pedagogy (Gambrill & Gibbs, 2009), although progressive, still conspicuously lacks the action required for liberation, as per Boal.

Boal's review of the purpose of theater culminates in a detailed account of his involvement with the People's Theatre and the Arena Theatre of Peru that were both designed to engage audiences to participate beyond passive experiences of empathy and critical observation and to inspire them into *action*. The intention was to liberate the hearts, minds, and bodies of the audience and engage them in a transformational experience. The theatrical events, as outlined by Boal (1979), provide a forum to explore (1) feelings about the situation that increase awareness of internalized oppression; (2) new ideas and thoughts about the topic to illuminate latent themes or conflicts; and (3) an opportunity to practice alternative active approaches to a problem through audience involvement, thus increasing self-efficacy (Sood, 2002).

Boal's theatrical practices are a good fit for a holistic approach to social work education because empathy, catharsis, critical consciousness, and social action are all concepts central to social work. For example, intentional use of TO strategies in social work education can instruct social work students how to increase empathy skills while also creating an environment for critical reflection, self-regulation of emotions, and social action—in other words, an applied method of consientization, a la Freire.

TO in Social Work Education

Improvisational and scripted role plays have been marginally incorporated into social work education to demonstrate social work practice skills in the classroom (Moss, 2000; Todd, 2012; Walker, 2003). Role playing, especially with peers, has been associated with increased self-efficacy (Bosse et al., 2012; Rogers & King, 2012) and empathy (Bosse et al., 2012). Not only can role playing offer an arena to develop counseling and communication skills but also there is utility for social work students to learn improvisational acting skills to help them manage the unpredictability of interviews with clients (Todd, 2012).

Despite the positive learning outcomes that role play and improvisation have demonstrated in students, we believe that these methods are underutilized within the context of social work education. We argue that role play and improvisation within a TO format will offer a better fit for implementation by social work instructors because this format is designed to holistically engage participants *with the explicit intent* for social change. Also, using Boal's methods will offer an historical and global context to the challenges inherent in the work of a social change agent.

The following activities are just a couple of suggestions of how TO can be applied within the typical social work curriculum. We hope to catalyze thinking about how TO may be useful for students and how they may be adapted further. Detailed descriptions of warm-ups and the format for each of the following theater activities can be found in the chapter titled "Experiments of the People's Theatre of Peru" in Boal's (1979) *Theatre of the Oppressed*. After implementing any of the following TO activities, it is important to allow time for the students to practice whole self-inquiry by journaling or large group discussion, for example, to provide an opportunity for praxis and transformation. This will solidify learning by allowing the students to reflect and process thoughts and feelings stimulated by the activities and to consider the applications for social work practice.

OUR CLASSROOM EXPERIENCE

I (Juliana Svistova) was the instructor of a community and organizational theory undergraduate social work course during the fall semester of 2012. I invited Lara Bowen and Meera Bhat to be guest teachers in a class introducing community practice. Together we designed a lesson plan, "Critical Social Work and Its Global Origins and Practice: Pedagogy and Theater of the Oppressed." This lesson plan targets the development and practice of critical thinking and diversity in practice as core Council on Social Work Education (CSWE) Educational Policy and Accreditation Standards (EPAS) social work competencies. Specifically, it promotes critical thinking, creativity, curiosity, and the demonstration of effective and collaborative communication by students. The lesson plan outlines a multisensory teaching model whereby the students receive the content as well as get to implicate it for themselves directly. The class consists of two parts and usually takes approximately 3 hours.

The lesson plan provides an overview of the origins of critical social work and the approaches of Freire and Boal, incorporating classroom activities exemplifying their techniques. For instance, the students practice the SHOWED questioning technique, a mnemonic for the following: What do you See here? What is really Happening? How does this relate to Our lives? Why does this problem or strength exist? How can we become Empowered? What can we Do about it? (Wang, Morrel-Samuels, Hutchison, Bell, & Pestronk, 2004). The technique was applied to the images from the Hampton Institute (a historically black university founded to provide education to freed men and later Native Americans) to explore one's personal perceptions about diversity in relation to others. In addition, the students participate in a small group activity that demonstrates Boal's Image Theatre to depict and explore the power structure of relationships and provide an opportunity for reflection on the influence of personal bias in practice.

We began the class by introducing Paulo Freire and his pedagogic and activist work with illiterate peasants in Brazil. The key concepts that we discussed included the "culture of silence," "critical consciousness," the oppressed person as object acted upon, "banking education," dialogic reflection, and praxis. We intended to provide language and a theoretical basis for our further whole-group discussion. We explained that the underlying principle of changing reality, according to Freire, lies in the ways we think and that no one can sit still once they face the challenge, understand it, and recognize the possibilities of response. To explain this process, the first author used an analogy of a fish breaking through the trapping, oppressive system of the fish tank (awareness), joining other small fish in a critical dialogue and further uniting forces to stand up against a big fish (social change). The key reading materials that will help students, as well as the reader of this text, in preparation for the class are those by Freire (1974, 2000).

Furthermore, we provided an example of images that Freire used to encourage social analyses. We used two images of hunters (taken from Freire, 2000, pp. 66, 68) that Freire used to frame and guide the deconstruction of nature and culture. Here, we explained that nature is out of the control of humans; culture, on the other hand, was constructed by people and therefore can be undone and recreated.

Furthermore, the SHOWED technique, a questioning strategy, is introduced. The students are further invited to practice the application of this technique of deconstruction. For this specific lesson plan, we used the images from the Hampton Institute by Benjamin Johnston (1966) depicting the transformation of Native Americans from arrival at the Hampton Institute to graduation. During the activity, the teacher took on a role of a facilitator of the discussion generated by the students. Students were invited to critically appraise the images and voluntarily share their thoughts and reactions with the rest of the group. The nature of the activity and the setup created a heated and emotional discussion, cultivated critical thinking, curiosity, and predictions; and promoted exploration of diversity issues. As a facilitator of the activity, I (JS) sought to create a safe environment, inclusive of all perspectives, and to foster reciprocal learning with an ultimate goal of consciousness-raising. I did not give out answers but, rather, probed for deeper inquiry and critical assessment of the visuals in connection to prior knowledge, backgrounds, and experiences of the learners. Lindsey (1995), Johnston (1966), and Armstrong and Ludlow (1874) can assist the reader in their preparation for this whole-group activity. This part of the class lasts approximately 1½ hours.

After the break, we lectured on Augusto Boal as an activist in the 1960s and his role in starting an international movement that used conventions traditionally associated with theater in the service of social change. We reviewed the ways he transformed theater as a way to facilitate social action and provided definitions of Image Theatre, Newspaper Theatre, Invisible Theatre, Forum Theatre, and Legislative Theatre as outlined by Boal (1979). Then, we showed a clip of an interview from "Democracy Now!" of Boal describing an instance of Invisible Theatre about Brazilian social policy addressing hunger and starvation that was staged at a restaurant.

After providing the content, we transitioned by introducing how some of Boal's techniques can be used for holistic engagement in community practice. We demonstrated this by inviting the class to participate in Boal's preliminary stages of transforming the spectator into the actor: knowing the body, making the body expressive, and using theater as a language to communicate (Boal, 1979). We began with some simple warm-ups to engage the students' physical body. Then, to engage their imagination and help them to express themselves through movement, we used the "what if" technique used to teach acting (Stanislavski, 1987): While the students moved around the room, we directed them by asking questions such as "How would you behave if you were late? Or, if you were expecting the one you love? Or, if you just got some great news? etc."

After the warm-ups, we explained how to use Image Theatre (Boal, 1979) to communicate a story using the actors' bodies. We guided them to tell stories with themes that were relevant to the student social worker experience. We did this by dividing the class into small groups to share with each other about their experiences as interns in their field placements and the challenges that emerge in the process of developing a professional identity. Students first discussed the developmental tasks required to manage paradoxical feelings and experiences while transitioning from student to practitioner and the tension between competing aspects within the role of intern. They addressed questions that they had in common, such as the following: "What can I do when I observe people experiencing marginalization or bias?" Have I felt, seen, or heard bias or discrimination within the context of my internship or field placement?" "How do I cope with my role as learner in my placement?" and "How do I resolve feelings of having to prove competence but also cope with the vulnerability of not knowing?"

The groups were then instructed how to use their bodies to create Image Theatre (Boal, 1979) to represent an experience that they had shared in the small group discussion about their field placements. Image Theatre can be especially useful to highlight contradictory roles or expectations that students may be experiencing. It is a nonverbal way to communicate complexities of internal as well as external conflicts, influences, and power struggles in professional and personal relationships. Students use their bodies to create a sculpture that represents the power dynamics by using spacing and positioning to depict alliances or differences in relationships. The image they create can be representative in either a realistic or an abstract way, but it needs to tell a story. Each student participates in the story by posing in ways that symbolize different elements within the characters and/or in the themes of the story. The activity concluded with a large group discussion to reflect on the images portrayed and what they were communicating.

Lessons Learned From the Classroom

From the critical pedagogic perspective, it is common practice to solicit student feedback on a class-to-class basis in order to evaluate teacher performance and course content (Nylund &Tilsen, 2006). Asking students to assess what helped them learn and what could have been done differently, we sought to incorporate student suggestions to improve class content, the learning experience, and our own teaching. Feedback was collected through short written anonymous forms that were submitted at the end of class. We used the feedback that students provided to gauge students' level of comfort engaging in these activities and the overall utility of such classroom experience. Here, we present some valuable lessons learned from students' feedback and some observations and reflections from the overall classroom experience made by us.

Our experience shows that students are enthusiastic and enjoy multimedia and multisensory models, an interactive style of teaching, and hands-on application of the content. The following are quotes extracted from student feedback: "I liked how we were asked to connect what we learned to our real life experiences"; "It was uncomfortable, but I liked stepping out of my comfort zone"; and "I think visuals, group activities, and role play are very helpful to learning. It's just as important as reading because some people learn better with 'hands on.'"

However, we were also reminded that our own excitement and perhaps romanticized notions of our pedagogic approach and techniques will not always coincide with those of our students. For example, a few students were not comfortable with "acting." For this classroom experience to be truly free and joyful, instead of threatening and controlling, we advise asking if everyone is comfortable to participate or, as an alternative, inviting only volunteers to present their sculptures so that students do not feel forced. Also, thinking through how to divide students into groups for the Image Theatre activity may help lessen the discomfort. For instance, being in a familiar group of people or having similar field placement groups may help students engage in activities more comfortably. There are certainly advantages of working with a small group: The experience is more meaningful because participants are able to reflect and engage with themselves much better with a little bit of direction. We also learned that students are accustomed to gathering content rather than experiencing a class and that we needed to provide more information about the Hampton Institute. Hence, it is important to strike a good balance between the content we provided and the method we used.

We observed that students are desperate for correct answers and will seek more information, particularly in the critical analysis of the images. They also tend to jump into interpreting rather than simply observing/seeing the sculptures. This dynamic made us realize that we need to invite students to observe recurrent patterns and reflect on them together. For example, one such theme in our classroom that came up was the note-taker role of the social worker in almost every image. This was followed by an intense discussion on the potential reason for such a pattern to occur. Due to the value-laden content and diversity of experiences as well as perspectives driving the discussion, emotions arise and "hot moments" ensue (Harlap, 2014). Hot moments occur when emotions get involved and the objective discussion becomes personal. As an instructor, one needs to be prepared for such tensions and be able to acknowledge and incorporate them. Also, our experience shows that the discussion tends to remove the spotlight from the students' self-inquiry as a soon-to-be social worker to the topic of discussion. With this in mind, in both activities it is important to keep the focus on student selves and their self-awareness development.

DISCUSSION

We believe that in the scholarly social work literature discussing Freire's influence on education, the analytic lens tends to fall onto his philosophy of pedagogy, whereas the method or the mechanism of putting such a philosophy in practice is rarely explicated and exemplified. To this end, we believe that Freire's critical literacy and use of images for deconstructive inquiry (Freire, 2000) is particularly overlooked. We find these activities to be powerful for the purposes of exploring self in relation to others and building critical inquiry and appraisal skills. Similarly, although role-play and improvisation techniques have been previously used with social work students (Moss, 2000; Todd, 2012; Walker, 2003), we found no existing literature applying formats associated with *Theatre of the Oppressed* (i.e., Newspaper, Image, or Forum Theatre) in social work education, although it does exist in the social work practice literature (Pyles, 2009). Based on our experience, however, we view these methods as excellent tools for decoding "existential situations" (Freire, 2000), increasing awareness, and generating dialogue in a social work classroom.

Echoing Freire (1974, 2000) and bell hooks (1994), Zull (2011) draws from neuropsychology to further suggest that implementation of an instructional approach that is the agenda of this chapter is challenging in today's "organized education" system wherein students are kept without control of their own and under control of others. Most social work programs are extremely structured; classify content as well as students into micro or macro; and are limited by resources, marketability (of the course and students), and policy even if they support the use of alternate approaches. Much like the welfare system, the system assumes more importance than the people and purpose for which it has been built. Such restrictive conditions and dogmatic thinking deprive students of the freedom and joy of learning (hooks, 1994; Zull, 2011). Zull accentuates the importance of transformative, joyful learning experiences by stating that they are related to the brain's plasticity. This means that learning that is rooted in positive emotions can alter people's emotional functions such as curiosity, optimism, and focus (Zull, 2011).

Based on our conceptualization of, reflection on, and student feedback for this classroom experience, in Figure 9.1 we lay out a visual map of transformative learning. The figure depicts a process of teaching to the holistic self that begins with a specific teaching philosophy and style. In our example, the creation of the classroom setting is informed by critical pedagogy of Paulo Freire that centers learners as knowledgeable actors and emphasizes reflexive learning. Such a process incorporates interactive and participatory activities in the classroom (e.g., the SHOWED questioning technique or Image Theatre) with an underlying pedagogic logic to tie content and method, to generate dialogue, and to foster analysis and reflection. A composite of such a pedagogic strategy is treating "hot moments" (a heated discussion when a clash of ideas occurs), emotions, creativity, empathic connections, and our physical bodies as valid ways of knowing and learning. We suggest that through such teaching, a holistic self of the learner is staged and transformation of self, knowledge, power, and professional practice may occur.

Not only is this nontraditional approach transformative but also, we argue, it results in more sustainable knowledge and skill development. It is more sustainable because knowledge development is meaningful to the learner and his or her context, promotes analysis rather than recall, and integrates the cognitive and emotional journeys of the learner. Specifically, we draw from the neuroscience of

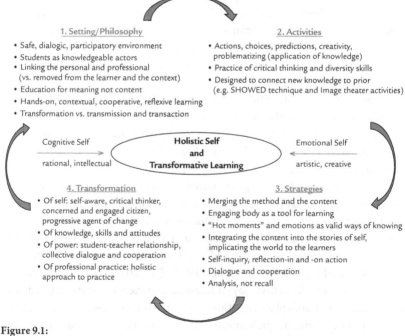

Figure 9.1:
Teaching to the Holistic Self.

learning and speculate that an approach to teaching that requires application of knowledge by taking actions and making decisions will result in better learning. Because the knowledge is sought by the students rather than being imparted, the students are engaged in seeking and applying it to what they already know and perhaps problem-solving issues important in their life or work context. Freire's and Boal's techniques can harness the elusive neuroscience of learning while neuroplasticity can change the way people are programmed to act. Hence, the physiological effect of challenge, ownership, creativity, and satisfaction of learners on their learning process and outcomes can be achieved and sustained.

CONCLUSION

In this chapter, we sought to make the connection between Boal's and Freire's work and recent advances in the neuroscience of learning. We explored how the use of conventions and processes traditionally associated with theater may be incorporated into social work education as a method of teaching to the whole self—that is, integrating the cognitive and emotional journey. We described Freire's questioning technique and Boal's Image Theatre that capitalize on the use of all the senses to stimulate learning by doing and maximizing self-awareness. In doing so, we suggested that these activities or teaching techniques offer a method for students to quickly grasp relevant and often paradoxical ideas that conventional cognitive approaches to teaching often struggle with.

Teaching to the holistic self by using these methods, we seek to indulge and untangle both the intellectual/cognitive self and the artistic/creative self of the learners. It seems to be a rather complete effort because it does not shy away from exploring emotions to bridge the personal and professional connection. This alternative pedagogy will serve as a catalyst for students to develop skills of self-awareness, empathy, concern, and critical thinking and to edge closer to become progressive agents of change.

Having discussed our theoretical foundation, experience, and positionality, we leave the reader with some food for thought as we ask ourselves the following: How do we ensure that students learn holistically to take on the role of the social change agent rather than the agent of social control? Shall we embrace our role as artists of teaching? What action can we take in creating a space for holistic pedagogy within the contemporary culture of academe?

REFERENCES

Armstrong, M. F., & Ludlow, H. W. (1874). *Hampton and its students. By two of its teachers, Mrs. M. F. Armstrong and Helen W. Ludlow. With fifty cabin and plantation songs.* New York, NY: Putnam's Sons.

Badanelli, A. M. (2012). Representing two worlds: Illustrations in Spanish textbooks for the teaching of religion and object lessons (1900–1970). *Journal of the History of Education Society, 41*(3), 303–338.

Boal, A. (1979). *Theatre of the oppressed.* New York, NY: Theatre Communications Group.

Bosse, H., Schultz, J., Nickel, M., Lutz, T., Möltner, A., Jünger, J., & Nikendei, C. (2012). The effect of using standardized patients or peer role play on ratings of undergraduate communication training: A randomized controlled trial. *Patient Education & Counseling, 87*(3), 300–306.

Freire, P. (1974). *Pedagogy of the oppressed.* New York, NY: Seabury Press.

Freire, P. (2000). *Education for critical consciousness.* New York, NY: Continuum.

Gadotti, M., & Torres, C. (2009). Paulo Freire: Education for development. *Development & Change, 40*(6), 1255–1267. doi:10.1111/j.1467-7660.2009.01606.x

Gambrill, E., & Gibbs, L. (2009). *Critical thinking for helping professionals: A skills-based workbook* (3rd ed.). New York, NY: Oxford University Press.

Grant, L. (2014). Hearts and minds: Aspects of empathy and wellbeing in social work students. *Social Work Education, 33*(3), 338–352.

Harlap, Y. (2014). Preparing university educators for hot moments: Theater for educational development about difference, power and privilege. *Teaching in Higher Education, 19*(3), 217–228.

Henderson, A. C., & Murdock, J. L. (2012). Getting students beyond ideologies: Using heterosexist guided imagery in the classroom. *Innovative Higher Education, 37,* 185–198.

Hjelm, T. (2013). Empowering discourse: Discourse analysis as method and practice in the sociology classroom. *Teaching in Higher Education, 18*(8), 871–882.

hooks, b. (1994). *Teaching to transgress: Education as the practice of freedom.* New York, NY: Routledge.

Johnston, F. B. (1966). *The Hampton album; 44 photographs from an album of Hampton Institute.* New York, NY: Museum of Modern Art.

Kollins, J. M., & Hansman, K. A. (2005). The role of women in popular education in Bolivia: A case study of the *Oficina Juridica para la Mujer. Journal of Adult Basic Education, 15*(1), 3–20.

Lewis, T. E. (2011). The future of image in critical pedagogy. *Studies in Philosophy and Education, 30,* 37–51.

Lindsey, D. (1995). *Indians at Hampton Institute, 1877–1923.* Urbana, IL: University of Illinois Press.

Moss, B. (2000). The use of large-group role-play techniques in social work education. *Social Work Education, 19*(5), 471–483. doi:10.1080/026154700435995

Nylund, D., & Tilsen, J. (2006). Pedagogy and praxis: Postmodern spirit in the classroom. *Journal of Systemic Therapies, 25*(4), 21–31.

Ochoa, G. L., & Pineda, D. (2008). Deconstructing power, privilege, and silence in the classroom. *Radical History Review, 102,* 45–62.

Pyles, L. (2009). *Progressive community organizing: Reflective practice in a globalizing world* (2nd ed.). New York, NY: Routledge Taylor & Francis.

Reisch, M. (2013). Social work education and the neoliberal challenge: The US response to increasing global inequality. *Social Work Education: The International Journal, 32*(6), 715–733.

Reisch, M., & Jarman-Rohde, L. (2000). The future of social work in the United States: Implications for field education. *Journal of Social Work Education, 36*(2), 201–214.

Rogers, E. R., & King, S. R. (2012). The influence of a patient-counseling course on the communication apprehension, outcome expectations, and self-efficacy of first year pharmacy students. *American Journal of Pharmaceutical Education, 76*(8), 1–7.

Sood, S. (2002). Audience involvement and entertainment-education. *Communication Theory, 12*(2), 153–172.

Stanislavski, C. (1987). *An actor prepares.* New York, NY: Theatre Arts Books.

Todd, S. (2012). Practicing in the uncertain: Reworking standardized clients as improv theatre. *Social Work Education, 31*(3), 302–315. doi:10.1080/02615479.2011.557427

Walker, U. (2003). Toward a third space: Improvisation and professionalism in social work. *Families in Society: The Journal of Contemporary Human Services, 84*(3), 17–322.

Wang, C., Morrel-Samuels, S., Hutchison, P., Bell, L., & Pestronk, R. (2004). Flint Photovoice: Community building among youths, adults and policymakers. *American Journal of Public Health, 94*(6), 911–913.

Watson, J., & Greenberg, L. (2009). Empathic resonance: A neuroscience perspective. In J. Decety & W. Ickes (Eds.), *The social neuroscience of empathy* (pp. 125–137). Cambridge, MA: MIT Press.

Zull, J. (2011). *From brain to mind: Using neuroscience to guide change in education.* Sterling, VA: Stylus.

PART IV

Mindfulness and Integrative Social Work

CHAPTER 10

There Is a Path. You Are on It.
It Does Lead Somewhere.

DAVID PETTIE

INTRODUCTION

After I dispensed with the necessities of housekeeping at the beginning of our first meeting, I asked the class to indulge me in a brief exercise. "Imagine you haven't met the teacher for this class yet and you're waiting for him to arrive. I'm going to re-enter the room and introduce myself. It won't take long. You just need to observe and give me your impressions."

Out in the hallway, I pulled out a shirttail, loosened my tie, messed up my hair, and rolled one sleeve higher than the other. I then stuffed all my paper materials under one arm, clutched my briefcase awkwardly in the other, and opened the door. I trudged across in front of them to the lectern and dumped my belongings on top of it. A few stray items cascaded to the floor. I paused, sighed, ambled over to the black board, wearily wrote my name, broke the chalk, sighed, reloaded, and listlessly added the name of the course underneath. I returned to the lectern, leaned heavily onto it with my elbows, and, stifling a belch, looked toward the class. I told them I was asked to teach this at the last minute—which meant we were stuck with each other.

I cut the scene and tidied myself to a ripple of laughter, then asked for what they had noticed. I wanted descriptive data first and then an evaluative judgment. This was my way of introducing the concept of contracting as a key component of working with individuals and groups. In most new relationships, both parties carry in two essential questions: Who are you? and How is this going to work? These questions get answered through the establishment of agreements and expectations. Some aspects of the contract get formulated explicitly, others implicitly.

We examined the impersonation exercise for aspects of contracting. They agreed that the process had begun as soon as the instructor had entered the room. My plan was to use the impersonation to introduce contracting as a concept while simultaneously beginning to contract with the class regarding what kind of teacher I would be and how we would proceed. This happened in the earliest days of my teaching career in 1998.

Although this plan ostensibly served the course and students, its primary effect was to ease me into the unfamiliar role of classroom teacher. I had facilitated hundreds of hours of training and education for mental health professionals, but teaching a college class seemed more formal and sophisticated. This was about being an expert—an authority on everything in the text. Just standing in front of the class and being myself was not going to cut it. That was too frightening. In order to soothe myself and ease my way into this unfamiliar territory, I borrowed from the familiarity of my acting and theater background. I knew I could not simultaneously enjoy the role of apathetic teacher and remain frightened at the same time. By committing to this strategy, enjoyment would trump fear—at least temporarily. And it worked. By creating a role within a role, I discovered I could hide out behind a character and avoid being myself. This clever capacity to hide out is something I have struggled to unlearn as I attempted over many years to recover the person of the teacher and integrate more of my whole self into the role. What follows is a synopsis of that process.

My sloppy professor role first debuted at a community college. I hung onto him for several years thereafter and took him with me to my current setting. He continued to make appearances during the first few years I taught the course under examination in this chapter. Micro Practice in Social Work II is the second part of a sequence for first-year students in the Master of Social Work (MSW) program. However, my course is taught in the summer to incoming advanced standing students as a bridge between their Bachelor of Social Work program and the second year of the MSW curriculum, which they begin in the fall.

The master syllabus charged me with fulfilling 11 course objectives, such as "Students will demonstrate the ability to evaluate the effectiveness of practice interventions." Additional directives call for a demonstration of knowledge and skills that are "accurate, clear, systematic, and comprehensive" covering treatment models, assessment, interventions, outcomes, goals, minorities, middle and ending phases, individuals, groups families, theories, ethical implications, social justice, oppression, advocacy, case management, community resources, use of self, evaluation of practice, and intervention effectiveness. Additional mandated infusions were expanded over time, including human diversity, critical thinking, global perspectives, and an evidence base for all of it. This syllabus listed 35 book chapters and 15 articles as required reading, in addition to a theory presentation, case analysis, group analysis, and case conference assignment. The master syllabus was 5 pages long, and my own final version eventually topped out at 12 pages once I listed the assignments, grading system, and numerous policies in granular detail.

While teaching as an adjunct, my primary, full-time job at the school is Assistant Director of Field Education, wherein I develop and troubleshoot internships for MSW students. I also facilitate ongoing seminars to train first-time field instructors in supervision of interns. Upon arrival in the job, I asked permission to sit in on some classes to see what students were learning preparatory to field. I expected they were learning practice skills in class, but this was my presumption. Through PowerPoint presentations, they were learning the names and purposes of skills, but the pace was brisk and permitted little more. I wondered, "Perhaps the depth is being delivered in advanced electives?" I confessed my perplexity to a senior faculty confidant. Her outburst of laughter startled me: "Haven't you heard the saying 'a mile wide and an inch deep'—that's the social work curriculum" (Padgett, 2008).

INFLUENCES

I spent the next several years making modifications to the class all the while in subordination to the strong influences cited next. I refer to them as the *forces of sameness, safety, and security.* They were eventually offset by the countervailing *forces of wholeness and vitality,* which are identified thereafter. These forces represent a combination of both objective and subjective realities that I grappled with as I taught the course. Thus, the following content is a retrospective teaching journal of these key themes, or forces. The writing style reflects the dialectic between the internal and external dimensions of the course revision process.

Content Coverage. There were numerous course objectives, each hatching subcategories and spawning derivative progeny of their own . . . all besprinkled with ideas such as Diversity, Critical Thinking, Global Perspectives, and an Evidence Base. Also, there was the integration of chapters and articles . . . I had my work cut out for me.

Pace. With the first class devoted to icebreakers, syllabus review, and general housekeeping, there are 11 meetings left. Skill-building activities, videos, and guest speakers further reduce the time for unspooling content.

Student Satisfaction. Early on, I developed a customized class evaluation to target feedback beyond the generic evaluation our school offers students. They complete this customized version during the last class. We discuss their input, and I include questions I have about the course that accumulated throughout the semester.

Fidelity to Master Syllabus.   Too much drift between different sections of the same course running simultaneously may prompt comparison by students and trigger complaints.

Privilege and Responsibility.   The academy bestows a tremendous privilege, responsibility, and trust on the adjunct instructor. There is a reverence befitting such trust that applies itself when making decisions. It resulted in me being too careful and cautious for too long regarding creative innovation.

Critical Self-Talk.   "You are not a researcher. You are not a scholar. You are not from the academy but from the streets of practice. Your membership is provisional and as with any social worker in a host setting, you serve at the pleasure of your host." Much of this one-down status narrative was my own mental doing, but I diluted it, in part, by reminding myself that I could bring things to the classroom that research-oriented faculty do not (see Powell, 2003).

In retrospect, I have come to think of this part of my path as the genuflecting phase, a disguised form of fear-based teaching. Although the previously mentioned forces held me confined during the first few years, I slowly began taking creative license. Over the years that followed, I continued building a strong case to overhaul my class. I had attended teacher workshops, read, talked to colleagues, and made incremental changes that reinforced my inclinations. One of these changes occurred in 2012 and is synopsized in the next section. I cannot recall the linear progression, but key contributors to this momentum appear later. These are the forces of *wholeness* and *vitality*.

By the Numbers.   I taped a pie diagram, bar graph, and stratified pyramid side by side on the wall over my worktable in my office. They reinforced one another, stating the same thing about how students learn. Each pie slice, bar, and pyramid layer included percentages of learning efficiency by method. Reading and writing were the least effective for retention and proficiency. More successful were modes of learning that mobilize more of the learner's faculties (hearing, watching, and doing). Even though I knew it was true from my own experience that learning becomes deeper and more durable, I felt bolstered by the numbers and wanted to display them. If experience really is the best teacher, perhaps this is why (see Kolb, 1984). I began using this insight as a discussion trigger while training supervisors and teaching classes. "What's the difference between a thought and an experience?" I would ask. Students reliably agreed that an experience mobilizes more of the whole person than a thought.

Learning Styles.   If, in fact, the majority of our students learn best by watching and doing, how then do we explain the tsunami of reading and writing required in most courses? I suspect that the dominant student learning styles (watching and doing) are not aligned with those of the academics (reading and writing–publishing) who teach them. This hypothesis would help explain the dissonance and its persistence.

Seminar as Laboratory. During the past 13 years, I have taught a seminar on supervision to first-time field instructors. I pilot tested methods in this seminar throughout the years and then transferred successes to the classroom with MSW students. There was a content-driven syllabus, but I set up structured inquiries starting with a probing question that led to reflection and problem-solving based on insight. We utilized the collective experience assembled in the room to co-create our own best practices and then compare them with what the experts said. I continuously culled content in favor of depth and discussion. Facilitating this process was fulfilling and well received by the participants. Attendance increased enough to necessitate adding an additional section of this seminar.

Permission From Afar. During this period, I stumbled onto a column by David Locher (2004) in *The Chronicle of Higher Education* called "When Teaching Less Is More." Locher spoke of his early days covering as much material as possible at a breakneck speed, gradually making incremental changes to the course but longing for something more radical. Having forgotten his notes one day, he had to wing the entire 3-hour class. Without a list of names, dates, and details, he spent the entire 3 hours discussing the day's topics in general terms, focusing more intently on ramifications for the student's lives. He stated, "Afterward, three students told me it was the best class period they ever attended. I realized what made the class exceptional was the depth of discussion, not the number of details presented" (p. 1).

What stood out was that Locher reinterpreted his responsibility as a teacher, giving himself permission to cut content in exchange for depth, and instead of leaping, he was pushed off the ledge by necessity. The discoveries followed. The experienced instructor had suspected that something was missing and yet suspicion alone was insufficient to propel a transformation. He needed evidence. As for me, I was past suspicion and well into conviction, while still stockpiling evidence. I needed something else. I needed fellowship and support. Locher's disclosure was a start, knowing I was not alone in my longing for depth and animation.

Art Class Syllabus. One year, I decided to cash in on my tuition remission as an adjunct instructor and take a class in the Art Department. I located my preference, received permission to audit, and picked up the syllabus at our first meeting. It was a one pager. In fact, it was less than a full page. I wondered, what allowed this syllabus to be so different? A different field, a different culture? Different standards? An advanced elective? A seminar? I taped this up on my wall beside the pie, bars, pyramid, and a copy of David Locher's (2004) story.

A 1-Page Syllabus Versus 12 Pages.   I have spent 30 years off and on defending social work against its public reputation as a half-baked profession. Its struggles both internal and external for legitimacy are well-known, scratching and struggling for a place at the table with medicine and law. Could a profession have self-esteem issues and be prone to overcompensate? Might my own profession have just as bad a case of physics envy as other softer sciences? Try as social work researchers might, they cannot produce the mathematical precision to measure up.

Practice Roots.   We are all creatures of our culture. As a creature of practice, now embedded in the academy, it became clear that the course, as inherited, did not work. It needed more emphasis on proficiency and the person of the learner/practitioner. This insight became a driver for me to adapt. If I think of conflict as growth trying to happen, the tension between these two lists becomes significant. The first list is filled with constraints representing a "safety first" position. The second list represents a fueling up for escape velocity.

THE COURSE BY 2012

By 2012, the course had undergone substantial revisions. Via successive approximation, these revisions served to deepen the learners' reflections, reinforce the connection between inner life and external outcomes, and strengthen skill proficiency with regard to both learners and clients. One illustration of this process appears next.

Professional Identity Development

As I listened to hundreds of students in class and field, themes, patterns, and principles began to emerge. Beginning social workers embark on an internal process as well as an external journey that requires an integration of professional and personal selves (Loseke & Cahill, 1986). The process of developing a professional identity involves developmental tasks, obstacles, and milestones (Deal, 2002), and there is an ongoing evolution despite long stretches of relative stability. When these tasks, obstacles, challenges, and crises are encountered, workers often respond in one of four ways. They struggle and muddle through privately, seek input, bolt, or burn out.

A parallel exists between the contracting phase of practice with clients and the fundamental questions that underlie the psychological and emotional life of the social worker. Essentially the client wants to know from the practitioner, "Who are you and how is this going to work?" Similarly, the new professional enters an identification process asking of the profession, "What is this?" and "Where do I fit in?"

When I introduce the topic of professional identity in class, I start by writing a phrase on the board—"Fake it 'til you make it." There is usually plenty of smiling and nodding. We talk about what this means, and they quickly connect it to field. I suggest it may be a solution strategy and invite them to consider the problem with which it helps. Ultimately, two needs collide within the learner: the desire to prove competence to oneself and to one's supervisor and coping with the vulnerability of not knowing (what is happening or what to do about it) (see Rodgers, 2002).

I draw two characters on the board facing one another. The client on one side is producing a great deal of information extemporaneously while the new social worker, on the other side, frantically checks and rechecks her mental file for some way of helping. But the client is not giving her X, Y, or Z from class. So now what? To gain perspective on the predicament, I ask students to consider the same question from a different angle: If a classmate asked you, "How can I be doing so well in class and struggling so much in field?" what factors might explain this? On reflection, students begin to recognize that two different skill sets make for success—one for success in class and another for field. We clarify each of the items and I add a few. Ultimately, the list looks similar to the one shown in Box 10.1.

The students and I review these lists, discuss their implications, and acknowledge that they are not mutually exclusive. We examine "The Vulnerability of Not Knowing" and "The Desire to Prove Competence." Because managing the balance between these two needs is a beginning developmental task, we then proceed to examine self-soothing as the primary skill for this. Students are invited to share their methods for self-soothing and their levels of satisfaction with their approach. I sometimes point out that my sloppy professor character was itself partly a solution strategy that reduced my anxiety by substituting acting expertise for scholastic expertise.

We cover two additional developmental tasks—Agency Sort and Population Sort. In exploring the issue of Agency Sort, the students are answering the following questions: "Where do I fit in?" and "Who am I working with?" By interning at an agency, students receive an extended snapshot of one place that some social workers would call home. Can they imagine themselves working there? Is it too big or too small, too fast or slow, too loose or too tight? What is the organizational culture and climate? We share lists of personal criteria that are beginning to form—criteria they will need to guide themselves through the job market after graduation. Some items are negotiable, and others are non-negotiable.

Next, we explore the task of Population Sort. What type of client or client group seems to easily elicit my compassion? Some professionals continue to explore this by changing jobs, whereas others seem clear from the beginning. Should one be ready and willing to work with all types of clients? Is this necessary or even realistic? I assign an exercise that helps students get in touch with their biases and preferences. They discuss the outcome in pairs first, then with the larger group.

Box 10.1
DIFFERENT DEMANDS FOR THRIVING AND SURVIVING

Academic Success	*Field/Internship Success*
Time Management	Self-Soothing
Note Taking	Spontaneity
Writing Ability	Improvisation
Critical Thinking	Adaptability
Analysis	Acceptance of Learner Role
Organization	Confidence
Study Skills	Establish and Maintain Boundaries
Reading Comprehension	Role Transitioning
Test Taking	• Detective
	• Enforcer
	• Salesperson

Now in the home stretch of this unit, we address the Myth of Cruise Control. Many beginners assume that 10 or 15 years in the field will result in having all questions resolved. However, the process of identity development remains ongoing despite stretches of relative equilibrium and stasis. We review the transition from direct practice to supervision or administration noting the challenges and fresh tasks. Students watch a videotaped interview of a social worker who candidly discusses his decision to give up agency work for private practice. The students identify developmental concepts and cite evidence for their applicability. Finally, we divide into small groups to review the following mid-career position statement:

MID-CAREER POSITION SUMMARY

Right now I've plateaued. I realize I'm not going to become Social Worker of the Year on a national level, or any other for that matter. I have my work-life in perspective . . . meaning . . . it fulfills a function in my overall life. It allows me to earn a living—it's honorable work and I'm aware of its limitations. I don't expect it to meet all my needs for which I have other outlets outside of work. I know exactly where I stand in the organizational food chain, and I could stay here as long as I like. I've been in this job long enough to know what it takes and recognize all the themes that recycle in various disguises. I do the job well enough to satisfy myself and have found ways to compensate for my shortcomings.

No one is complaining about me. I conserve time and energy by fending off unwanted extra assignments and avoiding nuisance "opportunities." At the same time, I would welcome the right opportunity . . . something hard to define but I'd know it if I saw it.

I ask each group to "compose a single sentence that summarizes your group's descriptive assessment and then an evaluative judgment of the above statement." This generates a lively discussion between younger and older students. Evaluative judgments often break down according to age. Younger students often characterize the statement as Surrender, Resignation, Defeat, and Burnout. Older students are often more sympathetic, selecting characteristics such as Realism, Balance, Acceptance, and Contentment. After considerable discussion, a compromise may emerge. Some younger students will concede that "hanging out," be it geographically, in a relationship, or in a job is not, in and of itself, concerning. Older students often come to acknowledge that the description lacks joy.

Cloaked in the mystique of subjective experience, these aspects of identity formation remain largely invisible and elusive. My goal is to assist students in becoming more conscious and deliberate about their developmental processes. I want them to begin to see that there is a path, they are on it, and it does lead somewhere (see Loseke & Cahill, 1986).

INFLUENCES REVISITED

Shortly before the 2012 class, the first in a series of events occurred that would encourage the transition of my course and provide practical assistance. The State University of New York Community Mindfulness Retreat was one of them. There were several highlights and takeaways from the event. Heinz-Dieter Meyer, a colleague from the School of Education, read aloud an entry from his teaching journal. I was encouraged to hear a senior scholar of 20 years acknowledge his inner life and its connection with student learning. Walking to class one day, he reported having felt that the students had been unresponsive in the previous class and worried that today the class dynamic might ruin a discussion of his favorite author. "I decided *not* to respond to their lack of interest by flying into a frenzy of enthusiasm about how great this author was. I did not want to be the only moving part in the engine that was my class." He made a snap decision to listen rather than talk, to discover what would happen rather than push an agenda. "So I started class with a few seconds of silence, followed by a deep breath, and a soft 'be here now.'" Things went very well. Since then, he has employed more listening and had the experience quite often. He believes his initial response was based on seeing himself as the main source of knowledge in the class. His listening response comes from seeing the class as a community of learners. "The best response is to *breathe*. As the students see you relax, they'll relax too."

Overall, the retreat was exciting, frightening, and empowering . . . a bit like a coming out party. There was nothing clandestine about the gathering, and yet several other attendees agreed that a felt sense of vulnerability came with revealing this side of themselves within a university setting. The wall, so closely guarded, between objectivity and subjectivity was beginning to be acknowledged as a more permeable membrane. Might this also serve as a declaration of amnesty for subjective experience long exiled by the pledge of allegiance to science? I came away with the intention to apply my long-term study and practice of mindfulness in the service of student learning.

I also discovered that there is a national group called Association for Contemplative Mind in Higher Education (ACMHE) and subsequently attended its fall 2012 conference. There, I listened to Harold Roth, a Religious Studies faculty at Brown University, speak of the trials and triumphs he experienced while establishing a contemplative studies initiative within the department, leading to the first university concentration offered in this subject in the country. He admitted that some of the fiercest opposition came from within his own Religious Studies Department. The difficult road to legitimacy for Religious Studies had been uphill all the way. Perhaps its status, partial and fragile, as with social work, required protection from threats both internal and external. Another soft science with self-esteem issues?

The conference offered me a potential affinity group, brain trust, and clearinghouse of resources—not an unusual outcome for a professional conference. Yet there was something unique about this one. It was the people and the atmosphere. I have often experienced academic conferences as competitive and alienating. Here, however, people seemed present, self-aware, approachable, and attentive. I had excellent conversations with researchers, therapists, and high school teachers.

There may be fewer obstacles to bringing mindfulness practices into professional degree programs where skills training is the norm. Greater barriers may exist where the focus is purely on academic goals with no precedent for valuing emotional intelligence or self-awareness. Academics with their own mindfulness practice may be drawn to the ACMHE conference and also well represented in professional programs hospitable to the introduction of these practices.

However, within the landscape of any given professional program, receptivity may vary. I realize now that the same dynamic tension between positions within myself is also reflected in the culture of my work organization. Throughout the process, my navigation of resistance has required courage, support, and persistence.

A long incubation period led up to 2013 during which dozens of incremental changes occurred. Also, the forces of sameness, safety, and security (reviewed later) became diluted and offset by the arrival of other noteworthy influences.

Content Coverage. Over time, I gradually traded out theoretical content and replaced it with practice skills, principles, and time for reflection.

Pace. This became more elastic. Occasionally, we could park and dig deeper. To permit this, I would forego some or all of the content that did not have a corresponding assignment.

Evidence Base. I was pleased if what I chose to include came with a substantial quantitative evidence base.

Fidelity. At times, there was a sensation of space walking from the mother ship that was the master syllabus. I remained tethered by a thin meandering line of reasoning back to the original course objectives. On closer inspection, the new content and methods could be categorized three ways related to course objectives: (1) completely aligned, as with "self-awareness" and "use of self"; (2) aligned, given an expanded definition of terms such as "assessment"; and (3) unaligned. I presumed this fell within the acceptable range of what academic deans call "drift."

Student Satisfaction. Except for 2 years during which they flatlined, student evaluations nudged upward each year.

Privilege and Responsibility. Faint traces of privilege remained, a shadow of its former potency. Somehow, when I was not looking, the pendulum of my responsibility as a teacher had swung from the master syllabus to the students.

Self-Talk. The imposter syndrome occasionally lurked, but it had faded considerably. My orientation toward induction, intuition, and subjective experience as valid evidence, and co-creating with students, though ever present, had now been integrated more fully into both my identity and my functionality as instructor.

2013 UPDATE 1: MINDFULNESS

My next revision aimed to encourage reflection both inside and outside the class-room, to mobilize more of the person of the learner, and to introduce even more practice skills applicable to clients. The first change was designed to better engage the students by devoting more attention to the place of mindfulness in social work. The folder holding my notes on this was labeled "Mindfulness Justification," revealing the sense of vulnerability I carried with me. Recent research supported the hypothesis that meditation can result in enduring beneficial changes in brain function outside the meditative state, especially in areas of emotional processing. I consolidated a related reading list for distribution and identified links for fur-ther information (see Desbordes et al., 2012; Massachusetts General Hospital, 2012; McCarthy, 2012; Raffone, Tagini, & Srinivasan, 2010; Tang et al., 2012; Zelazo & Lyons, 2012).

Mindfulness practice is a skill or activity that increases one's capacity for being present in the here and now. Again, we are talking about the intersection of the role and person, sometimes referred to as "the person of the practitioner." To further justify the use of mindfulness in the classroom, I invoked the term "use of self," a well-established arena of aptitude and self-awareness, as an umbrella under which mindfulness could be neatly placed. Mindfulness practice can benefit the clinician's inner life while enhancing direct work with clients. It may improve skills for self-soothing, tolerance of ambiguity, spontaneity, improvisation, and permit deep attunement to the client (Hart, 2008; Shapiro, Brown, & Astin, 2008). One is more present and free from distraction, including worrying about what to do next. Deep attunement with full presence actually increases the likelihood that something will come to us by creating a quiet space inviting our spontaneity and improvisation. This might result in reaching for latent emotional content or simply allowing the pain that has just been revealed without rushing to fix it. "How do I calm down and stay open to be present even if I don't know what to do?" Many students admit they do too much of the talking with clients. They think, "I must be doing something because words are coming out of my mouth." I remind students that the WAIT acronym works well here: *Why am I talking?*

What changes in our lived experience as we build our capacity for mindfulness? The progression often reported by students, teachers, and therapists is synopsized next. Initially, an activating event triggers a strong emotional response within us. Before we know it, we become completely fused with our emotional experience. It is the only thing that is real or true (Walser & Westrup, 2006).

Early in the practice, an event may trigger the same emotional response. We are still reactive, yet there is a hint of awareness present. "Here I go again." This is the embryo of our observer. With continued practice, our emotional response may still surface as our first inclination, but our observer consciousness shows up sooner and stronger, creating space for the possibility of a different choice (Spiegler & Guevremont, 2010).

Eventually, the entire dynamic and ratio shifts. The number of things that trigger us decreases, as does their potency. We may still get triggered, but our response will take place within a larger expanded observer consciousness. I finish by adding the following: "Mindfulness makes you a better practitioner with clients; at the same time, it makes you a better person."

From here, I proceed to the experiential portion. We take an experiential dip with a meditation practice by entering the shallow end and remaining ankle deep. I distribute an instruction sheet adapted from Cher Huber, talk about posture, reassure them that intrusive thoughts are normal, and scale back expectation. We sit for just 2 minutes with the following instructions:

- Feel your body breathing. Feel the air enter your body, fill your body, and leave your body.
- Thoughts will arise and pass away. Feelings will arise and pass away. You may hear sounds, smell odors, see sights, feel sensations. Just notice them, resisting nothing, holding onto nothing, allowing everything to be as it is.

- Just sit—not trying to accomplish anything, not trying to change anything, especially yourself. Breathe in and breathe out.

I carefully ring the bells I brought from home. As the tone of the bells begins to fade, I think, "How long is it going to take before these things stop ringing and I can put them down?" "You're no master." "You forgot to say a bunch of stuff." "Don't lose track of time." "Open your eyes to catch cheaters." "Don't forget to say *blah blah blah.*" "You're not even meditating yourself."

Such inner talk is a normal occurrence during meditation, perhaps interspersed with brief periods of spaciousness and calmness. I picked up the bells again but unintentionally clanked them into each other ahead of schedule, making a clumsy sound. I almost exclaimed, "That's not it!" but simply rang them again in a pleasing tone. I sat still a moment or two and looked slowly around the room. I sensed calmness and neutral indifference besprinkled with impatience and restlessness. I encouraged them to try the exercise on their own, and I explained that we would be doing the practice at the beginning of every class and build to 5 minutes' duration. I explained that it could help center us and clear out our mental pallets.

It was a very entry-level experience for them and for myself. An extended version would have required me to have more confidence and conviction. I also would have had to sideline other topics I had lovingly customized just to make room. I also wondered: Were social workers supposed to become certified meditation trainers and then come back to teach mindfulness? Were meditation masters supposed to get MSWs so they could teach social work? Some colleagues had imported an expert to conduct the meditation. I had been studying and practicing mindfulness for more than 20 years but not teaching it. Some of my hesitancy was an expression of ambivalence. My own connection to meditation was deeply spiritual, and I was not sure if I should or could convincingly promote a version of mindfulness carefully sterilized for secular consumption in the West. Yet I had jumped in . . . ankle deep.

At the end of the semester, on my customized class evaluation, mindfulness ranked third out of 10 in educational value. Thus, the effort seems sufficiently successful to keep, and I will probably expand it in future years.

2013 UPDATE 2: PSYCHODRAMA

What is the difference between a thought and an experience? As with mindfulness and reflection, psychodramatic interventions mobilize more of the whole person. When students in psychodrama training are stumped and lapse into excessive talking, the director will declare, "On your feet! Let's figure this out!"

I introduced one psychodramatic warm-up technique each week for the first half of the course, progressing from relatively simple exercises to ones demanding more facilitation and participation. Thereafter, each student chose one of the techniques to demonstrate with classmates' participation. Each student facilitator identified the types of client roles we were to play, generally corresponding to the facilitator's internship placement. With 20 students in the class to cover five psychodrama exercises, everyone had a chance to see four different interpretations of the same technique. Each student completed a summary sheet in preparation for the in-class demo and also submitted a follow-up reflection aided by feedback notes from class members (Mingun & Fortune, 2013).

An activity known as "the spectrogram" is one of the action method warm-up techniques from psychodrama that I demonstrated. Its purpose is to establish and reinforce contracting, warm-up/deinhibitize, and allow assessment. An imaginary continuum is established across the room, with position statements at opposite ends—for example, "I'm satisfied with the supervision at my internship" on one end and "I'm unsatisfied with the supervision at my internship" at the opposite end. Class members choose to stand somewhere along the line, sometimes consulting with their neighbors to refine their exact placement. Some facilitators prefer to disqualify the center location. With smaller groups, members can report on why they are where they are. If the group is large, a student can explain his or her choice to a neighbor, or the instructor can ask for sharing from a sample of participants. Another variation is to hinge the line in the center, having one side swing around to face the other so that those on opposite sides of an issue can discuss their diverging views.

The level of demand between questions should be progressively increased. Two types of questions work best. One requires them to locate themselves in comparison to other members. "Line up, without talking, by order of birthday throughout the year." "How long have you been coming to this program?" The other type simply asks each member to reflect on how he or she feels in relation to the end points. "Do you prefer a supervisor who stays nearby or keeps his or her distance?" "When trying new things, do you tend to wade into the shallow end of the pool or jump into the deep end?"[1]

---

1. As a teacher, I have long been perplexed by silent students. I had difficulty identifying with them, and they seemed to make my job more difficult. Over the years, I have extended a variety of invitations to help quiet students find and own their professional voice. There are quiet members in every group, and psychodrama trainings are no exception. By the luck of the draw (or maybe not), a few years ago I was put in a small workgroup with the two quietest trainees. Both seemed to work very hard at invisibility. They each did profound work over the next 3 days with a very skilled director. By age 9 years, one had caught enough flak from teachers in school to keep her mother coming for conferences. Her intentions were laudable, even beyond her years, but it was her behavior that caused static. Her takeaway? Being myself is not okay. Escape was more literal for the other. To avoid a perpetually angry mother, she took to climbing trees for hours on end and also reconstructed for us a hideout she maintained in the crawlspace between walls in her house. I have never looked at quiet members quite the same since.

Following any psychodrama exercise, students debrief on three questions: What? So what? Now what? Although originally found in treatment settings, I have been able to apply this debrief approach to good effect in the classroom. In order to answer the first question, group members chime in simply to describe the task completed. The second question asks members about how the activity was relevant to their own work or learning. The final question invites members to consider how they can apply what they learned outside this setting. I ask students to think of a continuum that would fit a group at their internship, such as the many gradients of sobriety. Other questions could apply to all groups and provide the leader useful information as part of a process intervention. "How safe do you feel in this group? How safe would you like to feel?" "Do you think other members have problems similar to yours?" "Do you prefer a group leader who is quite active or participates less often?" Such questions can provide an opportunity for re-contracting and a focus for deeper work.

The typical size of this class is 25 students. I subdivide them into groups of 5 that remain together for the semester. They collaborate on activities and assignments from a team-based learning perspective. I plan to put more emphasis in the future on students sharing their experience of mindfulness practices with one another in small groups and pairs. I expect this combination of format and content to amplify safety and trust within the small groups and increase the cohesiveness of the class overall. Sacrificing safety for anonymity is often the trade-off when working with larger classes. In such cases, the motivation level of the participant is important. Although I have had positive experiences attending large gatherings centered on learning contemplative practices, these participants represent a self-selected group with background with the topic or keen curiosity.

PRESENT REFLECTIONS

According to our school's course evaluation instrument, all categories of my 2013 course improved in relation to the 2012 course from 3% to 33%. The following categories received the highest upgrades: "Was receptive to student's ideas and viewpoints" (+27%) and "Communicated course content in ways you understood" (+33%). By normalizing the anxiety interns feel in their new role of practitioner and the critical need for self-soothing, the person of the practitioner has become a legitimate subject for learning and development. As beginning workers, they experience the acute vulnerability inherent in grappling with a new role.

Simultaneously, my own vulnerability as an instructor comes from introducing new approaches and revealing more sides to the person of the instructor. Increased vulnerability and the challenge of self-soothing are part of a parallel process that I share with the students. We are both traveling a path toward greater authenticity whereby inner functioning is reflected in outer functioning. Their inner development will be reflected in their ability to remain open and tuned in to their clients. My inner development and authenticity will be reflected in the course design and my ability to remain open and attuned to my students.

Indeed, I believe that students long for the relational embodiment of course content. Such animation serves not as a model of perfection but, rather, as an accessible reference point for their own progress and development. In a professional school, this constitutes legitimate course content equivalent to the ostensible curriculum (see Fox, 2011). This year, my mindfulness content is expanded; it includes an assignment geared toward this content, and it is taught by a more confident instructor. Before class, I often challenge myself with a personal slogan: How slow can you go? During class, I remind myself to breathe deeply. Sometimes facing the white board I hear a small voice inside reminding me that I do not have to write so fast.

Heinz Meyer and David Locher both had transformative experiences when they freed themselves to be more fully present with students. By subordinating content and becoming more relational, the educational experience became more meaningful for all parties (Rodgers & Raider-Roth, 2006). It seems to be a development process with no end in sight.

Mirabai Bush (2010) believes that synthetic (i.e., holistic) thinking (Barbezat & Bush, 2013) is key to a new way of teaching, learning, and knowing that both complements and challenges critical thinking and the scientific method. We may be turning a corner in academic history whereby the dualistic tradition that "alienates body from mind, emotion from intellect, humans from nature and art from science" is in need of balance and completion from a contemplative understanding that emphasizes wholeness, unity, and integration (Bush, 2010, p. 3). As Arthur Zajonc (2006) states, "Our conventional epistemology hands us a dangerous counterfeit in truth's place, one that may pass for truth, but is in fact partial and impoverished" (p. 1744) (see also Bugental, 1987). Furthermore, Tobin Hart says that the contemplative teacher invites students to the *inside* of the subject matter (Bush, 2010). This sentiment is echoed by Zajonc (2006), who speaks of inwardly assuming the shape and meaning of the contemplative object—inhabiting it not as a spy but as a lover.

I find the contemplative movement in higher education very encouraging as a social work instructor. By reuniting more integrative and holistic ways of knowing with traditional scientific methods, we have the opportunity to create pedagogies that are more versatile and complete and encourage the development of responsive and reflective social workers. By making a place at the table for experience, creativity, imagination, and intuition, we have the possibility, as Shelagh Larkin (2010) says, of "bringing life and livelihood back together" (p. 453).

REFERENCES

Barbezat, D. P., & Bush, M. (2013). *Contemplative practices in higher education: Powerful methods to transform teaching and learning.* New York, NY: Wiley.

Bugental, J. F. (1987). *The art of the psychotherapist.* New York, NY: Norton.

Bush, M. (2010). *Contemplative higher education in contemporary America.* Retrieved from http://www.contemplativemind.org.

Deal, K. H. (2002). Modifying field instructors' supervisory approach using stage models of student development. *Journal of Teaching in Social Work, 22,* 121–137.

Desbordes, G., Negi, L. T., Pace, T. W., Wallace, B. A., Raison, C. L., & Schwartz, E. L. (2012). Effects of mindful-attention and compassion meditation training on amygdala response to emotional stimuli in an ordinary, non-meditative state. *Frontiers in Human Neuroscience, 6,* 292.

Fox, R. (2011). *The use of self: The essence of professional education.* Chicago, IL: Lyceum.

Hart, T. (2008). Interiority and education: Exploring the neurophenomenology of contemplation and its potential role in learning. *Journal of Transformative Education, 6*(4), 235–250.

Kolb, D. A. (1984). Experiential learning: Experience as the source of learning and development. Englewood Cliffs, NJ: Prentice-Hall.

Larkin, S. (2010). Spiritually sensitive professional development of self: A curricular module for field education. *Social Work & Christianity, 37*(4), 446–466.

Locher, D. (2004). When teaching less is more. *Teaching Professor, 18*(9), 2.

Loseke, D. R., & Cahill, S. E. (1986). Actors in search of a character: Student social workers' quest for professional identity. *Symbolic Interaction, 9*(2), 245–258.

Massachusetts General Hospital. (2012, December 12). *Meditation appears to produce enduring changes in emotional processing in the brain.* Boston, MA: Author. Retrieved March 4, 2013, from http://www.massgeneral.org/about/pressrelease.aspx?id=1520.

McCarthy, A. (2012, November 13). *Meditating measurably changes the brain even when not actively meditating.* Retrieved March 4, 2013, from http://preventdisease.com.

Mingun, L., & Fortune, A. E. (2013). Do we need more "doing" activities or "thinking" activities in the field practicum? *Journal of Social Work Education, 49*(4), 646–660.

Padgett, D. K. (2008). Qualitative research. In *Encyclopedia of social work* (Vol. 1, A–C, p. 485). New York, NY: Oxford University Press.

Powell, W. (2003, October). Doing it, artfully. *Families in Society,* 457–462.

Raffone, A., Tagini, A., & Srinivasan, N. (2010). Mindfulness and the cognitive neuroscience of attention and awareness. *Zygon: Journal of Religion & Science, 45*(3), 627–646.

Rodgers, C. (2002). Defining reflection: Another look at John Dewey and reflective thinking. *Teachers College Record, 104*(4), 842.

Rodgers, C. R., & Raider-Roth, M. B. (2006). Presence in teaching. *Teachers & Teaching, 12*(3), 265–287.

Shapiro, S. L., Brown, K. W., & Astin, A. A. (2008). *Toward the integration of meditation into higher education: A review of research.* The Center for Contemplative Mind in Society. Retrieved from http://www.contemplativemind.org/admin/wp-content/uploads/2012/09/MedandHigherEd.pdf.unamuno

Spiegler, M., & Guevremont, D. (2010). *Contemporary behavior therapy* (Rev./expanded ed.). Belmont, CA: Wadsworth.

Tang, Y., Yang, L., Leve, L. D., & Harold, G. T. (2012). Improving executive function and its neurobiological mechanisms through a mindfulness-based intervention: Advances within the field of developmental neuroscience. *Child Development Perspectives, 6*(4), 361–366.

Walser, R. D., & Westrup, D. (2006). Supervising trainees in acceptance and commit-
ment therapy for treatment of posttraumatic stress disorder. *International Journal of
Behavioral Consultation & Therapy, 2*(1), 12–16.
Zajonc, A. (2006). Love and knowledge: Recovering the heart of learning through contem-
plation. *Teachers College Record, 108*(9), 1742–1759.
Zelazo, P., & Lyons, K. E. (2012). The potential benefits of mindfulness training in early
childhood: A developmental social cognitive neuroscience perspective. *Child
Development Perspectives, 6*(2), 154–160.

CHAPTER 11

Is Mindfulness Value Free?

Tiptoeing Through the Mindfield of Mindfulness

ROBYN LYNN, JO MENSINGA, BETH TINNING,
AND KELLY LUNDMAN

INTRODUCTION

Mindfulness is increasingly being integrated into human service workers' professional practice on the basis that, as an approach, it is part of all spiritual traditions
and can be practiced in a secular context without the values of those traditions
(Hick, 2009). Over time, mindfulness has evolved from its traditional roots in
Buddhism and been integrated as a secularized practice into modern therapeutic and social change interventions (Bishop et al., 2004; Didonna, 2009; Hick,
2009; Kabat-Zinn, 2003; Langer, 1989; Segal, Williams, & Teasdale, 2002). This
professional secularization has been supported by scientific research on the benefits of mindfulness-based therapeutic interventions for improving attention and
emotional regulation processes and contributing to self-care in clients (Shapiro
& Applegate, 2000; Shapiro & Carlson, 2009; Siegel, 2010). Many of these interventions also require the practitioner to be authentic, skillful, and accomplished
in the meditation or mindfulness practices that they use in their intervention
process.

Social workers have relatively recently begun to describe the ways in which
they are using mindfulness as an intervention in practice and in social work education (Hick, 2009; Lynn, 2010). Most of this literature focuses on the apparent
success of mindfulness in practice. The emphasis is primarily on its value for self-
care for practitioners (Berceli & Napoli, 2006; Minor & Carlson, 2006), as an
intervention technique for social work (Birnbaum, 2005; Birnbaum & Birnbaum,
2004; Brandon, 1976; Coholic, 2005; Hick, 2009; Hick & Furlotte, 2009; Kane,

2006; Lee, Ng, Leung, & Chan, 2009; Turner, 2009), or as a contemplative practice (Sheridan, 2004; Sherman & Siporin, 2008).

There has also been a larger focus on the mind–body–spirit connection (Birnbaum & Birnbaum, 2008), as well as consideration of how mindfulness might be used in relation to social justice (Hick & Furlotte, 2009). Whereas Hick and Furlotte identify tensions and similarities between the basic beliefs of mindfulness and social justice, Birnbaum and Birnabaum argue that it reflects "ontological and epistemological shifts among social workers, as a group, both in the field and in academia" (Birnbaum & Birnbaum, 2008, p. 88). The paradigmatic shift identified by Birnbaum and Birnbaum is in relation to the use of holistic and transpersonal theories in social work that emphasize the practice of mindfulness to expand consciousness, self-observation, and knowledge of the world. They show how these approaches relate to the central values of social work. Hick and Furlotte also show that there is a convergence between mindfulness and social justice "around the ideas of social relations, dialectics, consciousness, and self-reflection or reflectivity" (p. 5). However, they also note tensions between critical social science theory and mindfulness around the notion of theory and human nature. For example, in relation to human nature, social justice approaches in social work have their roots in a critical theory conception of human nature. From this perspective, "social structures determine social behaviour [and it is the] differential access to wealth and power [that] is the cause of social problems" (Hick & Furlotte, 2009, p. 12). In contrast, a mindfulness approach would see "humans as naturally generous, kind, and caring. Social relations based on material wealth are incompatible with human nature" (p. 12). At the core of these tensions may be a different view of nondualism between mindfulness and social justice approaches (Hick & Furlotte, 2009).

Most accounts in the literature draw on modern accepted definitions of mindfulness and appear to fail to examine whether mindfulness in its secularized form is value free. In addition, there is very little recognition of the confusion that exists in the current literature about the meaning of mindfulness, the implication of separating mindfulness from its spiritual and traditional bases, and the ethical implications for social workers and their practice. A student-initiated inquiry about the application of mindfulness in practice was made by Kelly after she participated in a Mindfulness-Based Relapse Prevention (MBRP) workshop during her final year of her Bachelor of Social Work field placement.

The workshop Kelly attended presented MBRP as a secular intervention that is value free despite its roots in Buddhism. It was assumed that participants would experience it as a technique rather than as something that may have overtones/memories or an explicit link to ideas of spirit for participants. However, the presenter did define mindfulness in specifically Buddhist terms, as an insight-oriented approach that reveals how the mind creates suffering, according to the four Noble Truths. There was no other information provided in the workshop about the origins of mindfulness.

As a Christian, Kelly drew links with ideas of spirit and identified MBRP as having a set of unarticulated Buddhist values and beliefs, in its use of mindfulness, that are not necessarily congruent with other spiritual and cultural values and beliefs. For example, her understanding of suffering is based on Christian doctrines. She considered this understanding to be irreconcilable with the Buddhist explanation. This took her on a path of wondering if mindfulness indeed can be "mindful" practice without an explicit acknowledgment and inclusion of a discussion of the contemplative tradition from which it has emerged. This included questions about how authenticity and integrity are maintained when we "take" ideas in part or in whole—while leaving parts behind. Kelly's response and experience at this point in the workshop are described by the following excerpt from her journal:

> He then urged our group "to put aside all your thoughts and all your beliefs. Suspend your beliefs for now so that you can benefit from this activity. You don't need any beliefs for this activity."
>
> I can't speak for the others, but put my beliefs aside? Not likely! And what about the teacher's own beliefs? Isn't this "authentic" practice based on a set of beliefs, including adherence to such doctrines as the four Noble Truths? I certainly agree that we can stop actively thinking about our beliefs, but we are still nonetheless influenced by them. If he were to put aside these stated beliefs wouldn't his own practice be robbed of its inherent meaning? Hasn't he become the only person in the room privileged by the prerogative to maintain his own beliefs, simply because they are the right ones?

She took the position that Vipassana meditation when used in a therapeutic regime is not value free and put forward the idea that using mindfulness without contextualizing the origins of the practice with the client is potentially problematic for social workers.

Kelly's reflections prompted her field liaison (Beth) to critically reflect on her own views and, with Kelly's permission, she shared Kelly's journal entry with other staff (Robyn and Jo). In our individual reading of her entry, we had critical reactions to her reflections but found that her struggles also resonated with our attempts as educators to introduce contemplative practices into the curriculum and our pedagogy. Our journeys included students who we failed to engage with mindfulness, others who embraced it enthusiastically, and questions about trying to incorporate other forms of knowledge and understanding into education and practice: "Is something lost in the development of secular mindfulness applications?" "Am I authentic enough to facilitate mindfulness practice in the classroom?" "Who can practice this?" "Who should teach this?" "Can it be taught by anybody?" "Do I have to be a practitioner of a certain set of values in order to teach it?" "Should I expect all students to participate in these practices?" We asked ourselves, Do we need to think about this or not? Is it value free or not? Some informal conversations between Robyn, Beth, and Jo prompted the beginning of a structured critically reflective dialogue between us that sought to further explore and respond to Kelly's reflections around her position that mindfulness is not value free.

We want to share what emerged from this dialogue given the growing attention being given in the literature by social work practitioners and educators to mindfulness interventions and its introduction into social work pedagogy. Although there is a growing acceptance of the use of mindfulness and meditation in biopsychosocial therapies and social work, a more thorough evaluation of the interventions and their role in pedagogy is required, not just in terms of apparent success but also in terms of intellectual rigor, ethics, and values. Central to this is a consideration of the differences between mindfulness as a tool and mindfulness as an ideology or way of being that needs to explicitly define the boundaries between the different forms. In this chapter, we present aspects of our dialogue that explored the question, "Is mindfulness 'value free' and what are the implications of this?" The themes that became central for us in addressing this question were the response of social work to the introduction of other ways of "knowing" (ontology and epistemology); mindfulness as a natural, spiritual, and cultural process; and cultural colonization or convergence. Here, we summarize Kelly's reflections. We then provide an overview of our approach, share our reflections on aspects of Kelly's response, and discuss the implications of this for social work education.

A SUMMARY OF KELLY'S REFLECTIONS
FROM HER FIELD PLACEMENT JOURNAL

Kelly's reflections in her field placement journal entry were prompted by her experiences of a MBRP workshop while in her field placement. These experiences generated a number of questions for her, which can be summarized into five areas for thought. First, can "mindfulness" practices (or, indeed, meditation or awareness) be separated from their spiritual origins and traditions? Second, is the use of "mindfulness" that does not explicitly acknowledge the historical spiritual foundations of the practice inappropriate or even unethical for social work? Third, what are the implications of using (1) "spirit-less" mindfulness that is separated from any spiritual tradition and defined as secular in nature and (2) "spirit"-infused mindfulness underpinned by a spiritual ideology? Kelly's fourth area for thought concerns how social workers can respectfully and authentically introduce work that allows for "spirit" into practice. Her final question expanded on the use of "spirit" in social work practice. Kelly asked why there appeared to be less sensitivity required of professionals when using Buddhist traditions in mindfulness practice when, in contrast, Christian and other formal spiritual traditions' practices are used sparingly or with great care in the secular arena of social work. Her reflections on these questions were primarily concerned with the cultural differences embedded in the mindfulness practice to which she was introduced and the more specific issues of diversity, authenticity, openness, and transparency.

In reflecting on these questions, Kelly briefly described how the universal concept of meditation is specifically expressed in a range of religious or philosophical contexts. She sought out examples of people she knew who regularly meditate and asked their opinions about the assumption that meditation is a secular practice. These people came from diverse backgrounds, and she gave examples of three people she spoke to who told her they meditate as a spiritual practice, grounded in their particular religious or philosophical worldview.

On the basis of this diversity, she now believes that social work needs to recognize and acknowledge the implications of this diversity in its possible use of meditation practices. This acknowledgment of the diversity of meditative practices was absent at the training workshop Kelly attended. She explored the discomfort she experienced as a Christian asked to engage in a practice that was specifically defined in Buddhist terms and its incompatibility with her Christian beliefs. This included conflict for her between the Buddhist explanation of suffering and the Christian doctrines of suffering. As such, she had to decide if she was going to participate in what she experienced as overtly Buddhist meditation exercises. She decided to follow the practical instructions of the practices while personally retaining her own Christian understanding and explanation of the concept. In participating in the practice, she decided to include her Christian practice of acknowledging the arising thoughts and sensations as sacred and God-given before gently returning to the breath.

In reflections, she questioned who has the capacity to construct a model of therapeutic meditation based on ancient religious practices. For example, she raised the question of whether she as a non-Muslim could construct a model of therapeutic meditation based on ancient Islamic meditation practices and whether such a construction would be widely believed as morally, intellectually, and professionally bankrupt; contravening many ethical principles; and grossly lacking in any kind of legitimacy, credibility, and cultural or religious sensitivity. The basis of condemnation was the unspoken expectation for "authenticity" in the workshop in terms of expecting the social work practitioner using MBRP to also regularly engage in his or her own Vipassana practice and its associated beliefs. Given her Christian background, Kelly viewed herself as ill-equipped, unsuited, and unwilling to guide anyone in the practices from religions other than her own. Thus, she questioned why Vipassana meditation was being specifically taught to practitioners to use as a tool with clients. The expectation of "authenticity" in the application of these techniques with clients did not sit comfortably with Kelly. In the workshop, the use and integration of meditative practice was justified based on the assertion that "Buddhism is not a religion."

For Kelly, this assertion did not sit well. As a Christian, Kelly would not choose to use or teach a Vipassana intervention because this would conflict with her personal worldview and therefore, as she noted, *would lack the authenticity expected* with clients because she would not be prepared to regularly undertake this form of meditation practice or follow associated beliefs. She concluded that she was only able to credibly use meditation as a decontextualized skills set or to use a personally compatible form of Christian meditation (i.e., authentically Christian) that ascribes thoughts and sensations as sacred and God given. However, from her perspective, this meant that it would only be logically suitable for Christian clients, or for those open and willing to engage with Christian beliefs. The subsequent question that arose was the following: "Is such a practice, even with willing clients, appropriate and professional in the largely secular domain of the helping professions and, specifically, within nonreligious agencies?"

Kelly noted that in her experience, meditation, prayer, or other tools based on explicitly Christian ideas are often deemed inappropriate to include in her work, unless there has been a sensitive and careful negotiation with an individual client. She posited that the same would be true if a colleague actively used meditation, prayers, or tools from, for example, the Islamic tradition. Why should it not be the case then, Kelly argued, for the introduction of authentic Buddhist and Hindu meditations to also be questioned? For some time, social work in Australia has been avidly secular—so much so that many people, she believes, are terrified of the thought of bringing a Christian tradition into practice—but somehow there has been very little question of or curiosity about why there is not the same fear about bringing in a practice based on the Buddhist tradition.

She concluded that the less problematic option is the decontextualized approach of reaching into a toolbox and pulling out "generic" meditation techniques that are free from all religious or philosophical affiliations. However, to Kelly, this did not do away with a further concern about the ethical responsibilities a worker should have to disclose the origins and rationales of meditation interventions or mindfulness activities, particularly in the context of clients with impaired capacities. In the decontextualized situation that she observed, clients were asked to *suspend all their beliefs*. At the same time, the practice they were being asked to engage in was based on a particular set of beliefs. In asking this of others, Kelly saw the teacher's own beliefs being privileged for no other reason than, at that time, being presented as the "right" beliefs. Where is the authenticity in this? Kelly asked. Although Kelly recognizes the implementation of mindfulness and meditation as a decontextualized skill set as a positive move toward holistic practice that brings some benefits to the individual, meditation to her has personal meaning, and this meaning is inextricably woven into the spiritual framework from which she lives and practices. Hence, for her, "mindfulness" is not as culturally or spiritually neutral as it claims to be.

OUR APPROACH

In a series of four critically reflective conversations, Robyn, Beth, and Jo explored the questions Kelly raised. Initially, the group met to plan their approach and determine how we would share our response to Kelly's reflections. The conversations were shaped by our own autobiographies, Kelly's perceptions, others' experiences, and the literature. Through this formative process, we hoped to identify aspects of social work and our own teaching that would improve students' knowledge and practice (Brookfield, 1995). Prior to our first discussion, each of us read Kelly's journal entry and identified what we thought were the themes in her entry. At the first meeting, we tentatively identified the overall theme and question for our discussion. The subsequent meetings provided a space to share our reflections and critically challenge each other on our responses to the different themes in the entry.

The following section of this chapter expands on three areas that emerged when we considered the context of mindfulness in human services professional education. The first was the challenges that present when "new ways of knowing" are introduced into social work and human services education. We argue that the dominance of a particular shared social construction of knowledge and the creation of shared culture and meaning within social work has created barriers for exploring the place of "spirit" in social work education and practice due to the difference in their worldviews. The second area that emerged continued the theme of the challenge of introducing "new" perspectives. Interestingly, this "new" perspective is not necessarily considered "new" in other disciplines. They include the role of biological and physiological responses to the practice of mediation and mindfulness practice in their curricula. Jo, whose PhD studies have focused on the mind–body link in social work practice, expands this discussion further, challenging the idea that "mindfulness" is purely linked to spirit traditions. The third area that emerged was, perhaps ironically, the importance of considering the context of the mindfulness practice and the way it is included (or not) in social work education in Australia today. We debated the argument that perhaps an a-spiritual application of mindfulness practice is a form of cultural colonization, arguing that instead it could be seen as a positive influence on Western traditions in the helping professions by Eastern knowledge and practice.

INTRODUCING OTHER WAYS OF KNOWING INTO THE SOCIAL WORK PROFESSION

During our conversations, we agreed that the profession of social work has a particular way of knowing reality and that it is that way of knowing reality that has also contributed to Kelly's questions about the use of mindfulness in her practice. This view of reality can be traced back to the development of the Western tradition of science. It encompasses a particular set of values that creates a materialist–positivist view that has fostered a humanist and modernist para-digm within social work despite social work's religious origins. This paradigm subscribes to an ethos that, until recently, includes a taboo on teaching anything related to religion and spirituality unless it is secularized and evidenced through empirical science (Stewart, 2009).

In the Australian context, there has been an emphasis on social justice and anti-oppression in social work practice and education (Chenoweth & McAuliffe, 2012; Connolly & Harms, 2012; Healy, 2005). Consequently, anything that appears or has been used as a means of oppression—for example, gender, disa-bility, and religion—needs to be deconstructed and engaged with in a particu-lar way. Within this cultural lens, "suffering" comes from societal structures of power and oppression. This is unlike the Buddhist view of suffering that is ulti-mately connected to the mind and the root delusions of attachment, desire, and ignorance. This view is at odds with a social justice analysis in social work and a Christian value base in Kelly's case.

Kelly, like each of the authors, has been educated in and practiced in this par-adigm of social work that includes a culture of professionalism, empiricism, and evidence-based practice (Rice, 2002). Yet some of us are also influenced by crit-ical and postmodern ideas that step back from the notion of "evidence," profes-sionalism, and a right/wrong dualism. However, even within the large majority of these approaches, the spiritual and ecological have been absent (Coates, 2003), and knowledge from other "ways of knowing" has not been readily accepted (Cameron & McDermott, 2007; Mensinga, 2011).

From our own experiences, the introduction of new ideas into social work is done with extreme care and fear by the educator (as evidenced in the struggle to incorporate spirituality into social work practice and education) or there is an open embrace of the current flavor of the month. In Kelly's case, at that point in her edu-cation, she had had little exposure to this secular application of mindfulness. The paradigm in which she had been educated meant that mindfulness was for Kelly not just a function but also an intervention with values added to it—her own per-sonal values and the values of the profession. Her experience highlights that the application of mindfulness can generate ethical tensions and conflicts with the social work values of social justice and anti-oppression. In addition, her experience points to the need for education and practice to provide a means for the student, practitioner, and educator to identify and navigate the tensions that the different paradigms create.

THE DIFFERENT WAYS IN WHICH MINDFULNESS IS UNDERSTOOD, WRITTEN ABOUT, AND PRACTICED

Kelly's reflections and our own dialogue highlighted that there are different ways in which mindfulness can be understood, written about, and practiced. In our conversations, we explored the concept of mindfulness in three ways: as a spiritual practice, as a natural process, and as a cultural process.

Mindfulness as a Spiritual Practice

As Kelly identified, there is a diversity of religious and spiritual understanding and writing on mindfulness that carry with them specific beliefs and values. In these religious and spiritual traditions, "contemplatives have studied the mind that observes phenomena and that does the investigating" (Wallace, 2008, p. xvii) for a long time. Like Kelly, we also acknowledged that mindfulness is not new in the contemplative traditions of the West. Contemplation in the West had its beginnings with the mystical brotherhoods of the eastern Mediterranean such as the Pythagoreans and the Essenes, of which Jesus Christ was a member of the latter. For the Christian contemplatives, concentration of the mind on a single word was a pathway to union with God. However, we also recognized that contemplation is rare in Protestantism but is still practiced as extended prayer and meditation in orders of the Roman Catholic faith. In addition to these traditions, there is also evidence of a rich literature on mediative practices in the Sufi and Taoist traditions (Wallace, 2008).

Although there is a tendency to think of science as secular and divorced from religion and the spiritual, Wallace's (2008) description of the development of science shows its roots in Christian thought and its eventual replacement of religion

> as the final authority on reality. Even so, scientific thinking never completely divested itself of ideas derived from Christian theology. They were too deeply embedded. As a consequence, the prevailing *popular* view of science in the West is based on the discoveries achieved by the scientific method, but infused with a hidden Christian view of nature. (p. 10)

The philosophy of scientific materialism is based on the principles of objectivism, metaphysical realism, the closure principle, universalism, and physical reductionism. This is an interpretation of science that is still followed by many scientists today (Wallace, 2008) and underpins the current scientific study and understandings of mindfulness. Clearly, from a "spiritual perspective," mindfulness is not "value free," but nor is that the case from an empirical or scientific view of mindfulness. However, this dominant view of reality when focused on the material is identified as secular in nature, separate from religion and value free.

Mindfulness as a Natural Process

In recent years, these scientific principles and inquiry methods have focused on the material phenomena of the mind in which mindfulness is viewed as a chemical process and the function of being aware and fully conscious—a part of what makes us human (Wallace, 2008). To date, an increasing number of studies in the neuroscientific sector demonstrate that participating in mindfulness practices brings about "changes in gray matter concentration in brain regions involved in learning and memory processes, emotion regulation, self-referential processing, and perspective taking" (Holzel et al., 2011, p. 36). Most, if not all, of these studies describe these changes in positive terms, such as an increase in attention and greater emotional regulation. Although these achievements may be outcomes that most individuals wish to attain, the means of achieving these outcomes are not necessarily value free.

In a study by Eileen Luders and colleagues (2012), long-term meditators were found to have a larger cortical folding in the insula—the "hub for autonomic, affective, and cognitive integration" (p. 5). Although there is still conjecture about what this actually means, the authors note that "meditators are known to be masters in introspection and awareness, as well as emotional control and self-regulation, so the findings make sense that the longer someone has meditated, the higher the degree of folding in the insula" (p. 1). From this perspective, mindfulness can be identified as a natural, if not necessary, process, particularly for the purposes of developing the self-reflective capacities of social work students. Is it therefore secular in nature and something akin to eating or bathing?

In addition to the work of neuroscience and its development of our understanding of its effects on the brain, there has been increasing interest in and development of mindfulness-based applications since the late 1990s in clinical psychology, cognitive therapy, education, law, business, and leadership (Mark, Williams, & Kabat-Zinn, 2011). Each of these disciplines is making a particular contribution to mindfulness as a secular practice and process that is natural. Medicine and health were forerunners in recognizing the benefits of mindfulness and developing mindfulness-based programs for use with clients. Psychology has focused on defining mindfulness, the establishment of its traits, and the development of therapies that are mindfulness based. Social work has drawn on the work of these other disciplines and emphasized its application with individuals, groups, and communities. Education, law, and business have also focused on its application for learning, for justice, and for developing leadership.

Wallace (2011) suggests that these developments in mindfulness have a materialist base and are limited by a scientific tradition that has no scientific definition of consciousness, objective means of detecting consciousness, and an ignorance about this mental phenomena. Wallace is highly critical of the methodology used to study the mind and mindfulness, and he argues the need to integrate contemplative methodology that would involve professionally training contemplative scientists who undertake collaborative research with psychologists, neuroscientists, health and medicine, and physicists—"a potential revolution in the physical and mind sciences" (p. 21). Still others suggest that there is already a convergence taking place between "Western empirical science, and that of the empiricism of the meditative or consciousness disciplines [particularly Buddhist forms of meditation] and their attendant frameworks, developed over millennia" (Mark et al., 2011, p. 4). In a 2011 special edition of *Contemporary Buddhism*, Mark et al. identified a number of questions that they believe are important to reflect on at this point in the convergence of the two traditions—questions not unlike those being asked by the authors of this chapter. These included the following:

> Are there intrinsic dangers that need to be kept in mind? Is there the potential for something priceless to be lost through secular applications of aspects of a larger culture which has a long and venerable, dare we say sacred tradition of its own? What are the potential negative effects of the confluence of these different epistemologies at this point in time? Do we need to be concerned that young professionals might be increasingly drawn to mindfulness . . . because it may be perceived as a fashionable field in which to work rather than from a motivation more associated with its intrinsic essence and transformative potential? Can it be exploited or misappropriated in ways that might lead to harm of some kind, either by omission or commission? Might there even be elements of bereavement and loss on the part of some, mixed in with the exhilaration of any apparent "success," as often happens when success comes rapidly and unexpectedly. (p. 4)

In response to these questions, authors (Bodhi, 2011; Grossman & Van Dam, 2011) identified the need for caution as these two "ways of knowing" converge as well as the challenges that arise in bringing the different contemplative traditions into a secular context (Batchelor, 2011; Maex, 2011). Perhaps the question is not so much "Is mindfulness value free?" Rather, the inquiry is concerned with the ethical issues that arise in the convergence of traditions and how these should be addressed.

Mindfulness as a Cultural Process—A Japanese Tea Ceremony

> Imagine that Krisna was serving Arjuna tea in a cup. The tea is the love, it is the juice, the real message. The cup, of course, is the container. You need the cup in order to serve the scalding hot tea; having it without a cup just does not work. It could be a paper cup or a fancy porcelain cup, whatever serves as the vehicle for delivering the tea will do. Arjuna is fascinated by the container, thinking that the cup is what is important, but Krisna tells him "taste the tea, Arjuna! Don't worry about the cup." The direct experience of whatever is being presented (in this case the tea) is what is of import. (Freeman, 2010, p. 132)

Although the three of us agreed on the importance of the experience of meditation, we noted that how we would, and tended to, introduce the practice to

students, clients, and/or clients in the sector largely reflected our personal preferences, experiences, and the context in which we found ourselves. In fact, during
one conversation, we likened our machinations about the different formats in
which meditation could or should be presented to a discussion about how we preferred to consume our tea. Not wishing to diminish Kelly's concerns about her
experience of learning this form of mindfulness, like Krisna in the previous story,
we generally believed that for us the tea (meditation) itself was probably more
important than the container in which it was presented. However, noting that
tea can be consumed in a paper cup as a source of sustenance as well as assume
traditional importance as in a Japanese tea ceremony, we also admitted that each
of us had a preference for a particular vessel to drink tea from depending on such
things as our need, time of day, and context for having "that cup of tea."

Kabat Zinn (2003) notes that "there is nothing particularly Buddhist about
[mindfulness]" (p. 145). This may be true within a Western scientific context and
for Krisna in the Indian myth described previously, but as social scientists with
a strong social justice agenda, we also acknowledge that people's needs and cultural context impact their experience. We recognize that this raises other problematic dilemmas, such as where and how mindfulness is presented and used.

ISSUES PERTAINING TO CULTURAL
COLONIZATION OR CONVERGENCE

Kelly's experience raised two questions for her about the adoption and adaptation of mindfulness in a Western context. First, she asked, Is the adoption and
adaptation of mindfulness colonization of an ancient tradition and is that process watering down its authenticity? Second, she asked, Can anyone construct his
or her own model of therapeutic meditation based on ancient religious practice?

Kelly's questions seemed to assume the takeover of a knowledge base, and she
associates this with dispossession, imposition of one culture on another, oppression, and injustice—all significant concepts in her social work education and
worthy of critical analysis. Her analysis of these questions included concerns
about cultural appropriation, fragmentation, and representation of the Buddhist
belief systems as a generic meditation brand that has been commodified within
a globalized world. We asked if these issues would be of interest or concern for a
psychologist or if there is something particular to social work that generates such
questions. In the social work context, colonization is something to be resisted,
critiqued, and opposed, and the dominant culture is immediately assumed as the
colonizer. And yet is this so? Is this knowledge transfer process more complex
and dialectical in nature in this case?

As we examined Kelly's questions more closely, we thought it was important
to ask, Who is the colonizer? Cultural appropriation and colonization may be one
interpretation as mindfulness is "lifted from its traditional setting in Buddhist

doctrine and faith and transplanted in a secularized culture bent on pragmatic results" (Bodhi, 2011, p. 35). Bodhi cautions that

> there is a real danger that scientists who investigate traditional Eastern contemplative practices might be swayed by materialistic premises to explain their efficacy reductively, on the exclusive basis of neurophysiology . . . and that the contemplative challenge might be reduced to a matter of gaining skill in certain techniques. (p. 35)

However, he also argues for balance and refers to a statement made by the Buddha prior to his death that he interprets "to mean that we can let anyone take from the Dhamma [teachings] whatever they find useful even if it is for secular purposes" (p. 36).

In contrast, other authors would suggest that Buddhism and its adaptation could be described as Eastern colonization. Although not the essence of his overall argument, Mark Singleton (2010) does allude to the idea that the introduction of yoga and its acceptance into the West could be interpreted as an Indian colonization of the West. Mindfulness meditation could also be seen to be a bit like that in its journey into the West through Buddhism and its acceptance in the West.

Conversely, as discussed previously, a number of authors identify that there is an epistemological and cultural convergence occurring—a coming together of the different worldviews of empirical Western science and contemplative disciplines (Mark et al., 2011; Wallace, 2009) that is generating a paradigm shift. Vohra-Gupta, Russell, and Lo (2007) describe the development of Eastern spiritual practice in the Western context in the United States as emerging from immigration policies that increased the diversity of the population. They describe how the first official presentations of meditation by two Buddhist scholars at the World Parliament of Religions in Chicago in the late 19th century received a positive reception. This encouraged some Buddhist teachers to migrate to the United States in the early 20th century to open meditation practice centers. Also during the 20th century, there were cultural and social shifts occurring among the populations of Baby Boomers and Generation X in relation to religion that helped meditation to take root in the United States.

This convergence or adaptation of ancient religious practice has occurred throughout history. Many of "the great contemplative traditions that emerged from India . . . later spread to Southeast Asia, Tibet, China, Mongolia, Central Asia, and Japan" (Wallace, 2008, p. 136). In each country, these traditions were influenced in form and practice by the culture to which they had spread. "Terminology and emphasis have always changed over time as the Dharma entered new cultures, and this is happening once again in our era" (Mark et al., 2011, p. 14). In the Australian context, there have been Aboriginal and Torres Strait Islander adaptations of the practices of Christianity into their cultural context. Likewise, the Christianity practiced today is not the same as that practiced in ancient Rome or Greece but, rather, it has adapted as cultures have evolved. On a lighter level, we do not question the adoption of the coffee culture in Australia. Coffee came to Australia through other cultures, but it has been adapted with a culture around this that is different than in America and in England. Do these adaptations water down the authenticity of any of these practices?

Adaptation is not foreign to social work, which is a profession that has adapted practice in a number of ways. Social work practitioners adapt—they go and sit under a tree if that is what is appropriate for Aboriginal Australians. Social workers engaged in good practice are always interested in and adapting to where the client is at and the value base of the client. If the difficulty is with incorporating spiritual practices and values, then there is also a precedent in social work. As discussed previously, much of the knowledge in Western disciplines including social work is underpinned by Christian values and worldview. With the secularization of social work and a distancing from its spiritual origins (Rice, 2002), through humanism and modernity, these Christian roots no longer seem to be of concern. For example, we fail to acknowledge that psychoanalysis originates from a Jewish culture (Klein, 1987), and yet it is a practice that converged with social work and is freely used with people other than Jews without question. Strangely, however, when it comes to the use of other spiritual practices, ethical dilemmas about authenticity, client self-determination, and openness and transparency are raised.

IMPLICATIONS FOR THE DEVELOPMENT OF MINDFULNESS IN SOCIAL WORK EDUCATION

We began this chapter with the question, Is mindfulness value free and what are the implications of this for social work education? Kelly's experience indicated that mindfulness is not value free. Her response to her experience was guided in part by her own spiritual orientation and the social work culture and values she engaged with in her education. It was her Christian orientation and social work education that generated some of the ethical issues that arose for her. In her reflections, she sought to give attention to the broad principles and values of the Australian Association of Social Workers' Code of Ethics, particularly knowing the context of the client in order to start where he or she is at, addressing cultural competence, and critically reflecting on issues of power. Kelly's initial response in this regard to the presenter may have been hampered by the convergence of multiple value systems (Christian/social work education). However, Kelly was also a participant in this instance, and the workshop provided little opportunity for an exploration of different values and beliefs.

Kelly's entry also indicated that there was no specific educational experience that prepared her for making her decision. This highlights the need for students to have the opportunity in their education to develop their understanding of the mind–body–spirit connection, engage with religion and spirituality, and experience the place of the contemplative in practice. Without this, they are left with little to guide them in their response to the emerging use of mindfulness in practice. Crucial to this is the development of a contemplative pedagogy in social work education that is inclusive and socially just.

We argue that the process of knowledge transfer and development of a "middle way" is complex. Our reflections explore three areas of Kelly's experience: introducing "other ways of knowing" into the social work profession; mindfulness as a spiritual, secular/natural, or cultural practice; and the process of adoption and adaptation of mindfulness. These areas highlight potential cultural and ethical challenges in the integration of mindfulness into social work pedagogy and curriculum.

When introducing new ideas such as mindfulness into social work, we also argue that although mindfulness has been shown to be a natural process that can be cultivated, its translation and evolution into a Western context is also intrinsically connected with the task of marrying different worldviews and cultures that shape and influence the research, evidence, and practice interventions that emerge. The task is no different for social work that also has its own worldviews and culture. There is a need to recognize that social work culture and values and the historical and religious contexts of students' lives impact their adoption and integration of mindfulness as a "way of knowing," practice or intervention. Kelly's story highlights that social work's commitment to inclusivity and social justice must recognize the diversity of meditative practices and student experience that exists in relation to mindfulness. Responding to this diversity requires the educator to have an understanding of the history of the development of mindfulness, its place in different religious traditions, its definition, and a willingness to remain curious and open to students' experience of mindfulness and thus the challenges this creates in the classroom for the student and the educator.

A necessary implication of this is that we urge educators to take a reflective and self-critical approach that "questions how knowledge is generated" and "how relations of power operate" (D'Cruz, Gillingham, & Melendez, 2007, p. 75) in the pedagogy of mindfulness. This requires social work to attend to the different sources about mindfulness, the disjunctures and synergies that exist in its current development, and ask questions of both the traditional/contemplative and the scientific methodology being used to describe mindfulness. The natural/scientific but not spiritual or religious discourse may well speak to the needs of many and serve to distance social work from the realm of religion. Equally, however, Kelly's experience indicates that it can also fail and oppress others. This suggests the need to more closely examine the way in which the current discourse about mindfulness in social work excludes and denies the experience of some students. Rather, educators need to be curious and open to facilitating students' own experiences of mindfulness in the historical and religious contexts of their lives.

In understanding and including this experience of difference and the different emotional experiences of students, it is important to "meet the students where they are at," "remaining nonjudgmental and respectful of the way students adopt the practices and using teaching methodologies and context relevant to the group" (Duerr et al. (2003) and Hassed (2007) as quoted in Lynn, 2010, p. 299). This may require more time to prepare the education culture for the group. As part of this process, it is important to make clear the definition of mindfulness being utilized and the purpose of teaching mindfulness or using it as a pedagogy. From an ethical perspective, it is important to take care to assume that the mindfulness practices/pedagogy may not necessarily be acceptable for all students in the room and may be potentially damaging for some. This highlights the need to provide an environment in which students feel safe to explore any discomfort they may be experiencing with the practice being used, to prepare students for the challenges they may encounter, and to draw on forms of the practice and processes that include the context of the student.

The issue of how mindfulness has been adapted and adopted in the Western context draws attention to larger ethical questions about the appropriation and commodification of knowledge from other cultures and whether there is a larger cultural loss, of which we are not fully aware, that is created in its secular adaptation and application. It is imperative that a social worker concerned with social justice ask questions about whose interest is served in a discourse of mindfulness that is value free and separated from history and tradition. In the case of mindfulness, we argue that the knowledge transfer process is more complex and dialectical in nature than simply one of dispossession and colonization. The implication of this is that the epistemological and cultural convergence occurring in this process provides an opportunity for social work to challenge its own epistemology and ontology and enrich the story of social work.

Such questions have implications in relation to authenticity. Although social work is highly familiar with adaptation, it is also selective in where it raises concerns about authenticity, client self-determination, openness, and transparency. We are not suggesting that these are not important ethical considerations in the use of mindfulness in social work but, rather, that social work needs to be more consistent in its deconstruction and adoption of Western therapies. As educators, we need to help students develop a critical consciousness and examine more closely the conditions under which different practices are questioned. Equally, educators need a reflective and self-critical approach to their own use of mindfulness in the classroom in relation to authenticity, student self-determination, openness, and transparency.

In the specific context of social work field education, Kelly's experience highlights the need for opportunities for students to discuss such experiences with their field educator and at integration sessions. This may involve the field education unit identifying how best to support and resource field educators for this task. The liaison person could also discuss the students' experience in relation to their own issues. Preparation sessions prior to placement could make more explicit the need to examine ethical dilemmas recognizing that in a multicultural society different ways of working may emerge. This may highlight for students that they may be exposed to different values in the workplace whether they are secular or religiously based.

CONCLUSION

As advocates for the inclusion of mindfulness in social work pedagogy and curriculum, we believe it is necessary to create learning spaces where mindfulness and social work practice are experienced as inclusive and socially just. In our commitment to this, we consider it important to open up discussion around some of the historical, cultural, and ethical elements within the current discourse about mindfulness in social work education in order to become more responsible about the knowledge that informs our pedagogy and curriculum. In advocating for critical reflection on the "mindfulness is value free" discourse evident in social work, we do not wish to negate the potential merits in recognizing the scientific basis of mindfulness and its inclusion into curriculum. We hope our dialogue encourages a heightened critical awareness of the complexity and multiplicity of student experiences of mindfulness in social work education, the influence of the social work culture and values, and the issue of power in this process. As educators, we need to consider whether the conditions that separate mindfulness from religion and its philosophical roots are helpful or oppressive and for whom. In addition, educators need to be aware of how the preferred "mindfulness is value free" discourse is shaped by social work knowledge and culture and how the historical contexts of our own lives are involved in this process. The challenge for social work education lies in the use of pedagogy and the implementation of curriculum that encompasses the multiplicity and complexity of mindfulness in social work.

REFERENCES

Batchelor, M. (2011). Meditation and mindfulness. *Contemporary Buddhism*, 12(1), 157–164.

Berceli, D., & Napoli, M. (2006). A proposal for a mindfulness-based trauma prevention program for social work professionals. *Complementary Health Practice Review*, 11, 153–165.

Birnbaum, L. (2005). Connecting to inner guidance: Mindfulness meditation and transformation of professional self-concept in social work students. *Critical Social Work*, 6, 2 [online]. Retrieved September 19, 2008, from http://www.criticalsocialwork.com.

Birnbaum, L., & Birnbaum, A. (2004). In search of inner wisdom: Guided mindfulness meditation in the context of suicide. *Scientific World Journal*, 4, 216–227.

Birnbaum, L., & Birnbaum, A. (2008). Mindful social work: From theory to practice. *Journal of Religion and Spirituality in Social Work: Social Thought*, 27(1–2), 87–104.

Bishop, S. R., Lau, M., Shapiro, S., Carlson, L., Anderson, N. D., Carmondy, J., ... Devins, G. (2004). Mindfulness: A proposed operational definition. *Clinical Psychology: Science and Practice, 11*(3), 230–241.

Bodhi, B. (2011). What does mindfulness really mean? A canonical perspective. *Contemporary Buddhism, 12*(1), 19–39.

Brandon, D. (1976). *Zen and the art of helping*. London, England: Routledge & Kegan Paul.

Brookfield, S. (1995). *Becoming a critically reflective teacher*. San Francisco, CA: Jossey-Bass.

Cameron, N., & McDermott, F. (2007). *Social work & the body*. Basingstoke, England: Palgrave Macmillan.

Chenoweth, L., & McAuliffe, D. (2012). *The road to social work and human service practice* (3rd ed.). South Melbourne, Victoria, Australia: Cengage Learning.

Coates, J. (2003). *Ecology and social work: Toward a new paradigm*. Halifax, Nova Scotia, Canada: Fernwood.

Coholic, D. (2005). The helpfulness of spiritually influenced group work in developing self-awareness and self-esteem: A preliminary investigation. *The Scientific World Journal, 5*, 789–802.

Connolly, M., & Harms, L. (2012). *Social work from theory to practice*. New York, NY: Cambridge University Press.

D'Cruz, H., Gillingham, P., & Melendez, S. (2007). Reflexivity, its meanings and relevance for social work: A critical review of the literature. *British Journal of Social Work, 37*(1), 73–90.

Freeman, R. (2010). *The mirror of yoga: Awakening the intelligence of body and mind*. Boston, MA: Shambhala.

Grossman, P., & Van Dam, N. T. (2011). Mindfulness, by any other name . . .: Trials and tribulations of *SATI* in western psychology and science. *Contemporary Buddhism, 12*(1), 219–239.

Healy, K. (2005). *Social work theories in context: Creating frameworks for practice*. Basingstoke, England: Palgrave Macmillan.

Hick, S. F. (2009). *Mindfulness and social work*. Chicago, IL: Lyceum.

Hick, S. F., & Furlotte, C. (2009). Mindfulness and social justice approaches: Bridging the mind and society in social work practice. *Canadian Social Work, 26*(1), 5–25.

Holzel, B. K., Carmody, J., Vangel, M., Congleton, C., Yerramsetti, S. M., Gard, T., & Lazar, S. W. (2011). Mindfulness practice leads to increases in regional brain gray matter density. *Psychiatry Research: Neuroimaging, 191*(1), 36–43.

Kabat-Zinn, J. (2003). Mindfulness-based interventions in context: Past, present, and future. *American Psychological Association, 10*, 144–156.

Kane, K. E. (2006). The phenomenology of meditation for female survivors of intimate partner violence. *Violence Against Women, 12*, 501–518.

Klein, D. B. (1987). *Jewish origins of the psychoanalytic movement*. Chicago, IL: University of Chicago Press.

Langer, E. J. (1989). *Mindfulness*. Cambridge, MA: Da Capo Press.

Lee, M., Ng, S., Leung, P., & Chan, C. (2009). *Integrative body–mind–spirit social work: An empirically based approach to assessment and treatment*. New York, NY: Oxford University Press.

Luders, E., Kurth, F., Mayer, E., Toga, A., Narr, K., & Gaser, C. (2012). The unique brain anatomy of meditation practitioners: Alterations in cortical gyrification. *Frontiers in Human Neuroscience, 6*, 34.

Lynn, R. (2010). Mindfulness in social work education. *Social Work Education, 29*(3), 289–304.

Maex, E. (2011). The Buddhist roots of mindfulness training: A practitioners view. *Contemporary Buddhism, 12*(1), 165–175.

Mark, J., Williams, G., & Kabat-Zinn, J. (2011). Mindfulness: Diverse perspectives on its meaning, origins, and multiple applications at the intersection of science and dharma. *Contemporary Buddhism, 12*(1), 1–17.

Mensinga, J. (2011). The feeling of being a social worker: Including yoga as an embodied practice in social work education. *Social Work Education, 30*(6), 650–662

Minor, H. G., & Carlson, L. E. (2006). Evaluation of a mindfulness-based stress reduction (MBSR) program for caregivers of children with chronic conditions. *Social Work in Health Care, 43*(1), 91–109.

Rice, S. (2002). Magic happens: Revisiting the spirituality and social work debate. *Australian Social Work, 55*(4), 303–312.

Segal, Z. V., Williams, J. M. G., & Teasdale, J. D. (2002). *Mindfulness-based cognitive therapy for depression: A new approach for preventing relapse.* New York, NY: Guilford.

Shapiro, J. R., & Applegate, J. S. (2000). Cognitive neuroscience, neurobiology and affect regulation: Implications for clinical social work. *Clinical Social Work Journal, 28*(1), 9–21.

Shapiro, S. L., & Carlson, L. E. (2009). *The art and science of mindfulness: Integrating mindfulness into psychology and the helping professions.* Washington, DC: American Psychological Association.

Sheridan, M. (2004). Predicting the use of spiritually-derived interventions in social work practice: A survey of practitioners. *Journal of Religion & Spirituality in Social Work, 23*(4), 5025.

Sherman, E., & Siporin, M. (2008). Contemporary theory and practice for social work. *Journal of Religion & Spirituality in Social Work, 27*(3), 259–274.

Siegel, D. J. (2010). *Mindsight: The new science of personal transformation.* New York, NY: Bantam.

Singleton, M. (2010). *Yoga body: The origins of modern posture practice.* New York, NY: Oxford University Press.

Stewart, C. (2009). The inevitable conflict between religious and social work values. *Journal of Religion and Spirituality in Social Work, 28*(1–2), 35–47.

Turner, K. (2009). Mindfulness: The present moment in clinical social work. *Clinical Social Work Journal, 37*(2), 95–103.

Vohra-Gupta, S., Russell, A., & Lo, E. (2007). Meditation. *Journal of Religion and Spirituality in Social Work, 26*(2), 49–61.

Wallace, B. A. (2008). *Embracing mind: The common ground of science and spirituality.* Boston, MA: Shambala.

Wallace, B. A. (2009). *Mind in the balance: Meditation in science, Buddhism, and Christianity.* Boston, MA: Shambala.

Wallace, B. A. (2011, November). *Conscious universe: Where Buddhism and physics converge.* Public lecture, Sydney, Australia.

CHAPTER 12

Promoting Integrative Mind–Body–Spirit Practice to Advance Holistic Social Work Education

SALOME RAHEIM AND JACK J. LU

INTRODUCTION

Integrative mind–body–spirit (IMBS) social work is a practice approach that draws upon indigenous, Eastern, and Western perspectives with the aim of restoring harmony, balance, and connectedness within and between multiple systems levels, including individual mind–body–spirit, family, group, organization, and community (Lee, Ng, Leung, & Chan, 2009). To accomplish the goals of an IMBS approach, practitioners may engage in a combination of conventional micro and macro social work interventions, along with modalities that have relatively recently been incorporated into helping professions in the West, including acupuncture, family constellations, meditation, reiki, and yoga. Holistic social work education requires incorporating an IMBS approach in the teaching–learning process, as well as content about IMBS practice and related modalities.

IMBS practice is distinct from integrated practice, which is the common conceptualization of holistic social work. The profession has long acknowledged the importance of an integrated, biopsychosocial orientation, which addresses the biological, cognitive, affective, behavioral, social, cultural, economic, and environmental influences on the human experience (Earls & Korr, 2013; Goldstein, 2008; Hollis, 1964; Turner, 1974). The pioneering scholarship of Canda (1988,

1998, 1999) and Canda and Furman (2010) expanded the conceptualization of integrated or holistic social work to include spirituality as an essential area of focus. Canda (1999) defines spirituality as "the search for a sense of life purpose, meaning, and morally fulfilling relationships between oneself, other people, the universe, and the ultimate ground of reality, however one understands it" (p. 12). Despite this expanded holistic view, Western conceptualizations of the human experience, including a mechanistic view of the body, Cartesian mind and body dualism, and the dominant role of humans over the natural world, make integrated social work practice and IMBS social work practice paradigmatically different.

Findings from research in affective neuroscience (Siegel, Fosha, & Solomon, 2010), epigenetics (Curley, Jensen, Mashoodh, & Champagne, 2011), psychosocial genomics (Garland & Howard, 2009; Rossi, 2002a, 2002b), psychoneuroimmunology (Irwin, 2008), and spirituality and health (Williams & Sternthal, 2007) reflect more intricate and dynamic relationships between the biopsychosocial–spiritual dimensions of the human experience than previously understood. Epigenetics and psychosocial genomics studies have shown that genetic expression is influenced by our psychological and social experiences (Garland & Howard, 2009). Lee, Cohen, Edgar, Laizner, and Gagnon (2006) found that meaning-making as a spiritual intervention among cancer patients had positive psychological outcomes. Other studies have linked meaning-making with positive changes in immunity among men with HIV (Bower, Kemeny, Taylor, & Fahey, 1998; Taylor, Kemeny, Reed, Bower, & Gruenewald, 2000) and women who experienced the death of a close relative (Bower, Kemeny, Taylor, & Fahey, 2003). The IMBS approach affirms the complexities of these relationships, employs interventions that use the power of the mind and of the body in the change process, and acknowledges the importance of spiritual growth for positive outcomes on micro and macro levels (Lee et al., 2009).

The IMBS perspective also emphasizes the dynamic of connectedness differently than integrated practice. Beyond physical, psychological, and emotional levels, this connectedness is understood to occur on the energetic level. Everything in the universe is understood to exist within a broader field of energy or information field. This understanding of connectedness is supported by two concepts in quantum physics known as quantum entanglement and nonlocality. When a pair of photons respond in ways that the behavior of one is influenced by the behavior of another, they are entangled. Quantum experiments have repeatedly shown that when entangled particles are separated and have no perceivable connection, "whatever is done to one photon immediately, without time delay and no matter the distance separating them, affects the other entangled photon" (Ives & Jonas, 2011, pp. 139–140; Ursin et al., 2007). If these principles operate on the non-quantum level, people can be connected and influence each other at a distance without any observable means of doing so, as demonstrated by studies on intercessory prayer (Schwartz & Dossey, 2010).

The concept of quantum entanglement or nonlocal connection supports the importance of the IMBS practice focus on restoring harmony, balance, and awareness of connectedness between the individual and other individuals, significant groups, organizations, community, and cosmos (Lee et al., 2009) and is at odds with the common conceptualizations of separateness, individuality, and independent action of individuals. In this way, the philosophical framework of IMBS practice views the physical and social world in a fundamentally different way than contemporary social work. Consequently, IMBS practice represents a paradigm shift for the profession and thus a significant challenge for social work education.

Social work education has yet to comprehensively and systematically explore the underlying principles of IMBS practice, despite the growing body of research that supports the effectiveness of many mind–body–spirit interventions (National Center for Complementary and Integrative Health, 2014). According to the National Center for Complementary and Integrative Health, 40% of the US population, or 125.5 million people, are using mind–body–spirit modalities to support their health and well-being. Clearly, this area of practice is growing faster than US social work education has kept pace. Social workers are engaged in providing IMBS modalities, although few graduate social work education programs offer this content (Raheim & Lu, 2014). If trends among social work educators are similar to those of the US population, a significant percentage of these educators are engaged in IMBS practices to support their health and well-being as well. What, then, accounts for the limited inclusion of IMBS practice and related modalities in social work education? How can this inclusion be facilitated? This chapter explores these questions and describes a course designed to explore IMBS practice and the factors that may account for its minimal presence in social work education.

We (the authors) have found that critical pedagogy and narrative practice offer invaluable theoretical frameworks and conceptual tools for understanding and overcoming the barriers to exploring IMBS practice and facilitating our development as holistic social work educators. In this chapter, we present a Master of Social Work (MSW) elective course we designed that uses critical pedagogy to analyze the sociopolitical–economic forces that have promoted Western-oriented, biomedical approaches to well-being while constraining the IMBS approach and practices. The chapter also provides an analysis of the forces that have inhibited and facilitated our sense of agency to use an IMBS approach in the teaching–learning process and to teach IMBS content in social work education contexts. After presenting the conceptual frameworks of narrative practice and critical pedagogy, we use these concepts to analyze the influences that have inhibited and facilitated our engagement in teaching IMBS content on our journey to becoming holistic social work educators. The chapter examines the impact on the authors of developing and teaching an MSW IMBS course and concludes with implications for advancing holistic social work education.

THEORETICAL FRAMEWORKS: CRITICAL
PEDAGOGY AND NARRATIVE PRACTICE THEORY

Critical pedagogy provides important conceptual tools for understanding the approach we took in designing the IMBS course discussed in this chapter, as well as the liberatory impact the course had on us as the instructors. Advanced by Brazilian educator and philosopher Paulo Freire (2000), critical pedagogy is an approach to education that aims to engage teachers and learners in their own liberation from oppressive systems. Critical pedagogy theory contends that conventional education uses a banking model, which treats students as repositories for knowledge to be gained in the learning process and fosters a passive approach to the world. Freire argued that the banking model of education is often used as a tool of oppression. By contrast, critical pedagogy uses a problem-posing model, which actively engages teachers and learners in analyzing and understanding their world, their role in it, and their ability to change it. Freire posited that the problem-posing approach to education has a mobilizing effect that supports people in understanding the power dynamics that affect their lives and working toward their liberation from oppressive forces. A central component of critical pedagogy is praxis, which is an iterative, transformational process of critical reflection and action (Freire, 2000). Through praxis, individuals and societies are transformed.

Our analysis uses narrative practice theory as a conceptual tool to explore our developmental process of becoming holistic social work educators. The underlying principles of this postmodern theory are that realities are socially constructed through language and are organized through narrative. Reflecting these principles, narrative practice theory rejects the concept of "knowledge" and uses the term "knowledges" to acknowledge that there are no essential truths (Freedman & Combs, 1996).

The groundbreaking work of White and Epston (1990) outlined the basic concepts of narrative practice theory:

- People's narratives (i.e., personal stories) shape their lives and identities.
- People's lives are multistoried, and they have multiple identities.
- People experience problems in their lives, but the person is not the problem.
- When people experience problems or limitations, there is an accompanying dominant narrative that supports a problem-saturated identity while marginalizing other identities.
- People can address problems and limitations by re-storying (also called re-authoring) their lives, which requires developing a thick and rich narrative that supports a preferred identity.

This theory supports critical analysis because it recognizes that the stories of individuals are influenced by broader cultural and societal narratives. Some of these broader narratives promote the dominance of particular social groups and institutions while marginalizing and subjugating others (White, 2002). Germane to this chapter are two dominant cultural narratives. One is the narrative of bio-medicine, which asserts that it is the most effective and credible approach to maintaining or restoring health and well-being. The other is the cultural narra-tive of Western science that asserts that knowledge is singular and discoverable only through use of the scientific method, thereby discounting all other ways of knowing and knowledges derived through other means.

The re-storying or re-authoring concept in narrative practice theory is par-ticularly relevant to our analysis. Re-storying creates an alternative narrative to the problem-saturated story that reinforces a problem-saturated, disem-powered identity. This is accomplished by several processes. Externalizing locates problems that people are experiencing outside of themselves and is an essential component of re-storying. For example, an internalized perspec-tive would have me ask of myself (Salome Raheim), "Why don't you have the courage to discuss your IMBS practices in professional settings?" By contrast, an externalized perspective asks, "What forces are operating that are intimi-dating you?" These forces are viewed as active agents that are influencing my thoughts and behaviors. After locating the problem outside of the person, re-authoring conversations link people with their knowledges, skills, abili-ties, and values to support development of an empowering story that shapes a preferred identity. These re-authoring conversations develop "alternative sto-rylines of people's lives [which] are thickened and more deeply rooted in his-tory" (White, 2005, p. 12). Equally essential to re-storying is a process called re-membering conversations, which assists people to recall and identify con-nections with others who might play important roles in their preferred story and identity (White, 2005):

> Re-membering conversations are not about passive recollection, but about purpo-sive engagements with the significant figures of one's history, and with the identities of one's present life who are significant or potentially significant. These figures and identities do not have to be directly known in order to be identified as significant to persons' lives. (p. 12)

Re-authoring using externalizing and re-membering processes assist people to create preferred identities that mitigate the negative and limiting effects of problem-saturated narratives, including the marginalization and subjugation of hegemonic cultural narratives, such as the superiority of biomedically based health care systems and the inferiority of others (Snow, 1998).

Using concepts from narrative practice and critical pedagogy, this chapter analyzes and interprets our experiences of becoming holistic social work educa-tors in the cultural context of higher education. Our combined experiences illus-trate that societal, institutional, and cultural forces may constrain, while others promote, social work educators' perceptions of agency and ability to engage in holistic social work education.

ON BECOMING HOLISTIC SOCIAL WORK EDUCATORS

Contemporary social work education in the United States is situated within the dominant power arrangements of higher education, which legitimizes particular ways of knowing while marginalizing others. In the physical and social sciences, logic and the Western scientific methods are held as the primary credible and legitimate way to develop knowledge. Intuition, spiritual insight, and other ways of knowing have been ridiculed and disparaged (Davis-Floyd, 2003; Inhorn, 1994). However, constructivist inquiry (Rodwell, 1998), feminist research methodologies such as standpoint research (Harding, 2004; Swigonski, 1994), and indigenous research methodologies (Smith, 1999) have challenged positivistic research and gained legitimacy in the social sciences. Nevertheless, in many corners of the academy, knowledges derived from the scientific method's guiding principles of objectivism, reductionism, positivism, and determinism are held in higher regard than historical, cultural, and indigenous knowledges.

The dominance of Western ways of knowing is a consequence of European countries' systematic colonization of indigenous peoples of Africa, the Americas, Asia, Australia, and New Zealand. The ways of knowing of the colonial powers and Western knowledges were imposed as universal, supplanting the knowledges of the colonized (Smith, 1999). This subjugation is reflected in the cultural narrative of biomedicine as the only credible approach to health care. In this narrative, "health care practices that are not considered scientific are not trustworthy and the path to acceptance demands 'scientific research'" (Cassidy, 2011, p. 43). As Snow (1998) explains, "In this way, biomedicine is seen as somehow more true than alternative systems could possibly be" (p. 115). Fundamental concepts of holistic practice and related modalities have been influenced by or emerged from cultural groups that have been colonized and/or enslaved by European powers and whites in the United States. These concepts and practices that have not passed the litmus test of Western scientific research are devalued in the education of health professionals in the academy, which ignores the social and cultural nature of biomedicine. "[T]he form health care takes is first and fundamentally a matter of sociocultural interpretation. . . . The 'truth' that guides any health care system is relative and is learned" (Cassidy, 2011, p. 42).

In my experience (SR), the dominance of Western knowledges of health and mental health and the subjugation of other knowledges has led to cautiousness among some social workers and social work educators in revealing their support for IMBS conceptualizations of well-being. I have witnessed and heard accounts of the suggestion of the possible effectiveness of such approaches being met with derisive statements, such as "How could any intelligent, well-educated person believe in that nonsense?" or "That's not scientific; that's just superstition."

SALOME'S STORY

The prevailing worldview in my African American family of origin supported holism and connectedness. My northern Virginia-born grandmother and my sole caretaker from infancy believed in the connectedness of mind, body, and spirit, as well as the human connection to the nonphysical world. She accepted intuition, dreams, and spirit communication as legitimate ways of knowing, and experience was always given more credibility than what was written in books. She believed that if people had only read about something but had not experienced it, then they did not really know it. What they had was "only book learnin'," she would say, "They don't really know what they're talking about."

The education I received from elementary through graduate school taught me that "modern ways" based on Western science and derived from use of the scientific method were superior to all others and that my grandmother's practices and ways of knowing lacked legitimacy in dominant culture. By comparison, her prayers for insight and healing, homemade honey and onion cough syrup, and our daily doses of cod liver oil were inferior practices. Although this dominant narrative undermined my confidence in my cultural knowledges, it was inconsistent with my experiences as a young adult. I began to gain verifiable information through precognitive dreams, which had not been derived from objective observation and that defied rational explanation. For example, I had dreams of events I had never witnessed, such as seeing a bright light moving in the sky that illuminated the dark alley behind our house. A few nights later while awake, I saw a police helicopter with a bright light searching the area. I had never seen this occur in my neighborhood before that night. To understand these experiences, I began to study ways of knowing and healing that were unsanctioned by my Western education and professional social work preparation. I learned meditation, methods for sharpening my intuitive knowing, and several forms of energy medicine, including reiki. These knowledges became critical components for maintaining my well-being.

In the 1980s and during my first tenure track position at a Midwestern research university, I received very clear messages from mentors and other senior faculty that spirituality, healing practices, and ways of knowing that were not sanctioned by Western science were not welcomed into discussion, even as areas of study. As an untenured professor and woman of color in a predominantly white institution, I felt vulnerable. The legacy of slavery's persistent narrative of inferiority of African Americans creates perpetual concerns about maintaining credibility, particularly in predominantly white institutions. The combination of dominance of the scientific paradigm and dominant narrative of inferiority of African Americans made higher education an unsafe space for me to explore IMBS practices as an educator and researcher.

For more than 30 years, I continued to study and use these knowledges and practices, but they remained separate from my academic and professional life. Although I wanted to integrate these knowledges, my life reflected a dualism, similar to Du Bois' (1897) concept of double consciousness, along with the compartmentalization and absence of holism that is characteristic of Western education (Smith, 2005). The dominant discourse and operations of power in the academy had me living a disconnected life, which is not uncommon for people of color and women in higher education (Gregory, 1999; Wiegman, 2002; Jones, 2001).

After moving to a new region of the country and beginning my current position as dean and professor, the desire to bring IMBS to social work education continued. To deepen my knowledge of IMBS practice, I began graduate study in IMBS health and healing at a progressive institution of higher education. This program used the cohort model, which enabled me to interact frequently with colleagues who shared similar interests. Opportunities for learning and conversation in this supportive context created re-membering experiences, which helped me to thicken and more richly describe the narrative of my preferred identity as a holistic, IMBS educator.

My most powerful re-membering experience occurred during this graduate program. I regained an appreciation for my grandmother's knowledges and skills as a healer and made the connection between my engagement in IMBS practices and my cultural heritage. I had a new context for understanding myself that strengthened and further legitimized my sense of identity. Rather than seeing myself as an IMBS educator on the margins of academia, I was developing a more powerful self-perception that placed me in the context of my ancestral lineage. I began to see myself as continuing a tradition of healing ways, like my grandmother and her mother before her. I shared this new perspective in an international conference presentation (Raheim, 2013), which further supported my preferred identity. As narrative practice theory asserts, having others witness the re-storying of one's identity is strengthening and liberating. My voice was no longer silenced.

Finally, working with Jack Lu, the the co-author of this chapter, was an important re-membering experience. When we met, he had been an IMBS practitioner for many years and was enrolling in the school's doctoral program. Subsequently, we codesigned and cotaught the graduate course discussed in this chapter. The impact of designing and teaching this course is discussed later in this chapter.

JACK'S STORY

Born in Taiwan and raised in the United States, I (JJL) have a liminal role in society as an Asian American. Upon arrival to this country, my family was encouraged to discard my Chinese given name, Ren, and replace it with an American one. Immigrants who are eager to assimilate frequently choose names for their children from the host country (Gerhards & Hans, 2009; Sue & Telles, 2007), so I became Jack. Acculturation to US society was important to my parents, and my learning of traditional Chinese practices was scant, such as learning to prepare meals. Although I recall my mother's practice of the Buddhist tradition, participation in unique rituals that reflected Chinese culture was rare. I was never formally instructed in Buddhist practices, such as meditation or other mind–body–spirit practices. My witness of my mother's practices was odd to me as a child; I recall thinking that her practice was unique to her generation, but mine was different. This divide reinforced a foundation for the cutoff I experienced from my cultural heritage.

The public education I received in US schools further disconnected me from my cultural roots, such as practicing US rituals (e.g., the Pledge of Allegiance) and the lack of awareness or support of Chinese culture (e.g., use of chopsticks). The value of the US culture appeared high, whereas the Chinese culture remained silent and, therefore, nonexistent. These experiences led me to question any indigenous knowledges learned from my family.

Engaging in martial arts study as a young adult served as a significant re-membering process. My martial arts teacher was predominantly Chinese and helped me to embrace my racial–ethnic and cultural roots through this mind–body–spirit practice, which included meditation. The values I learned through marital arts reconnected me with the values I learned from my parents and their ethnic roots—respect for oneself and others, discipline, honesty, sensitivity, compassion, and solidarity and connectedness of the family system. This re-membering experience supported a strong sense of cultural identity and served as the personal foundation for the social work practice and the IMBS modalities I would later explore.

In contrast to my co-author's journey, during my more than 10-year career as a clinical social worker, I have experienced a supportive environment that nurtured development of a thick and rich story of my identity as an IMBS practitioner and holistic educator. As a first-year MSW intern at an inpatient substance addictions program, my supervisor supported me in using the meditative practices that I had learned during my earlier martial arts training when facilitating clinical treatment groups. We discovered that these practices were helpful in group facilitation and supported clients in managing stress and reducing cravings to substances. Although my supervisor was not trained in meditation, he was open to my use of this practice. During my second-year MSW internship in a hospital behavioral health unit, I observed a senior-level clinician use mindfulness practices with his treatment group. Encouraged by my observations, I enrolled in workshops to learn how to integrate mindfulness practices in my clinical work.

Subsequently employed as a psychiatric social worker by the hospital where I completed my second MSW internship, I attended mindfulness workshops with senior staff and cofacilitated treatment groups with them using these techniques. A senior staff member introduced me to Family Constellations, a phenomenological practice that facilitates healing intergenerational wounds within a family or social system (Cohen, 2006), and encouraged me to attend workshops to learn this modality. Family Constellations addressed the intergenerational, energetic influences on healing, such as historical traumas, that my previous clinical training did not include. My supervisor enthusiastically supported these professional development activities. Senior staff and I conducted mindfulness and Family Constellations training for other therapists at the hospital.

Beyond my experience as a staff member providing services at this hospital, a close mentor encouraged me to invest in my spiritual development by inviting open discussion of spiritual issues as part of analyzing cases during supervisory sessions. In this context, she also discussed her own spiritual development as relevant to concrete tools in her clinical practice. We discussed practice theory, interventions, research, spirituality, and spiritual principles as part of an integrated whole.

My role as a social work educator in a higher education setting began in 2011 as doctoral student instructing MSW students. I quickly understood that mindful awareness and recognition of the energy fields in which interactions are taking place are as necessary in the classroom as in the clinical context. Using techniques and principles from my mindfulness practice became essential to creating a productive learning environment. In my recent role as instructor with MSW students, holistic engagement was a natural outgrowth of my years of personal practice, clinical teaching, and clinical work involving Family Constellations facilitation and mindfulness practice. Engaging in codesigning the IMBS course discussed in this chapter felt like the next logical step in my professional development. As a doctoral student, I have experienced overwhelming support for my interests in IMBS teaching, research, and practice. Recognizing my co-author's experience, I am particularly grateful for this support. My doctoral experiences have strengthened the narrative of my preferred identity as a holistic social work educator.

A COURSE ON IMBS SOCIAL WORK PRACTICE

We designed an elective, 3-credit MSW course currently titled "Integrative Mind–Body–Spirit Social Work." Despite both of our extensive experiences and long histories with IMBS modalities as practitioners and clients, this course was the first venture either of us had made into teaching content related to IMBS practice in a higher education setting.

During this 14-week course, we engage with students as co-learners in a critical examination of the philosophical, theoretical, and cultural foundations of the IMBS and biomedical paradigms; the sociopolitical–economic forces that have enabled the dominance of the biomedical paradigm; and those that have promoted and constrained IMBS approaches to health and healing in the United States. During this examination, we situate Abraham Flexner's historic 1915 speech, during which he concluded that social work was not yet a profession, in the broader context of the publication of his earlier 1910 report on North American medical education (Flexner, 1910). This report promoted the scientific method as the only legitimate approach to knowledge generation and played a pivotal role in advancing the current biomedical approach to health care.

We analyze the juxtaposition of Flexner's aim to improve medical education, which was sorely in need of reform, "with a general political one in order to promote modern biomedical and reductionist strategies in medical and psychiatric education" (Stahnisch & Verhoef, 2012, p. 4). As we study the consequences of the Flexner Report on medical education, we identify ways that it promoted the rise to dominance of the biomedical paradigm, with the aid of subsequent aggressive legislative advocacy that privileged this approach to health care and restricted or prevented the practice of other approaches (Micozzi, 2011). The consequence for medical education was the closure of medical schools that did not use allopathic methods (Barkin, Fuentes-Afflick, Brosco, &Tuchman, 2010; Stahnisch & Verhoef, 2012; Wheatley, 1989), including schools of homeopathy and naturopathy. An additional outcome of the report was "closure of five out of seven predominantly black medical schools. Also noteworthy . . . was Flexner's utilitarian argument that black physicians should serve as sanitarians and hygienists for black communities in villages and plantations" (Sullivan & Mittman, 2010, p. 246). Six of seven women's medical schools also closed. These school closures combined with discriminatory medical school admission policies that excluded most African Americans and women resulted in "modern medicine" becoming an overwhelmingly white male profession (Sullivan & Mittman, 2010).

Flexner's (1915) admonition that professions "derive their raw material from science" (p. 576) and the undoing of medical schools throughout the nation set the stage for social work education to embrace the scientific method as the only valid way of knowing and the biomedical paradigm as the only credible approach to medicine. Considering Flexner's well-known 1915 speech through this broader contextual lens, we invite students to critically examine how social work education has been recruited by the current dominant narrative to view biomedicine as "mainstream" and legitimate while marginalizing approaches that have emerged from indigenous and/or culturally grounded ways of knowing as "complementary and alternative" or trivializing, dismissing, and/or discrediting them.

In the course, we explore Ayurveda (i.e., a system of traditional Indian medicine), Traditional Chinese Medicine, and the National Indian Child Welfare Association's relational worldview model (Cross, 2013) to gain perspective on conceptualizations of health and healing that are rooted in cultural knowledges and paradigms that differ from the biomedical disease-oriented model. The course explores several types of IMBS modalities, including meditation, body movement and manipulation, and energy therapies. See Raheim and Lu (2014) for a detailed discussion of course content and outcomes.

We use several means to promote praxis, critical pedagogy's methodology of ongoing critical reflection and action (Freire, 2000). Reading assignments, didactic presentations, IMBS guest speakers–practitioners, active classroom discussion, personal reflection journals, and other written assignments encourage exploration of the power dynamics that perpetuate dominance and perceptions of legitimacy of biomedicine while subjugating and undermining the credibility of the IMBS approach and related modalities. We examine how these dynamics influence our (instructors' and students') personal perceptions and choices, including our sense of freedom to discuss and explore IMBS modalities in professional and academic settings.

The course combines critical reflection with action, as students are invited to participate in experiential learning in the classroom that promotes greater awareness of the mind, body, and spirit, as well as the connection between these aspects of being. We encourage students to use these techniques for their self-care during the semester and write journal reflections. Although the course introduces a variety of mind–body–spirit techniques, mindfulness is used consistently for experiential learning (Raheim & Lu, 2014):

> Held during the late afternoon, each class session began with a brief mindfulness exercise led by one of the instructors to assist students to be fully present and enhance their ability to release the stresses and concerns of the day, as well as provide experiential learning of mindfulness. These exercises generally began by inviting students to become still, notice their body, focus on their breathing, and notice thoughts that emerged without attachment or judgment. Variations were introduced, such as mindfully eating a raisin, which is used in MBSR [mindfulness-based stress reduction] training. After each exercise, students were invited to reflect on their experience in a brief discussion. (p. 292)

During the reflections that follow these exercises, most students express appreciation for the moments of stillness and the opportunity to mentally and physically slow their pace. Some students note that they experience difficulty with being still, whereas others report easily quieting their minds. As the semester progresses, students often report looking forward to the beginning of class and using these exercises in their self-care practice. As instructors, we feel grateful that students find these techniques useful, both inside and outside of the classroom. I (SR) am delighted to finally incorporate IMBS practice into the classroom after 30 years of feeling constrained from doing so.

Writing assignments ask students to analyze the perceived benefit of their self-care activities and compare and contrast these approaches to maintaining well-being with biomedical approaches they had experienced. Students are also invited to identify their level of comfort with revealing their use of these practices with those not in the class (e.g., family, friends, and coworkers) and reflect on the source(s) of their discomfort, if any.

A final paper further promotes critical reflection. Focused on an IMBS modality of the student's choice, this assignment requires students to examine the philosophical, metaphysical, and/or scientific foundations of the practice, including evidence of its efficacy; determine its acceptance within the biomedical health care systems and among insurance providers; identify the proponents and opponents of the practice; explore power and privilege dynamics that affect availability and accessibility to this practice; and analyze ways that the practice is consistent or in conflict with the student's personal conceptual framework and beliefs about how to maintain or achieve health and wellness.

Our commitment to critical pedagogy requires creating a safe, collaborative learning environment and engaging as co-learners with students and each other. Acknowledging and respecting the knowledges that all of us bring to the learning experience are vital. Before the course began, we developed several strategies to create this quality of learning environment that we implement throughout the course. First, we model for students our respect for each other's knowledges and experience as co-instructors by expressing the importance of the unique perspective that the other brings to the class (e.g., Lu as a licensed clinical social worker with many years of experience with mindfulness and Family Constellations facilitation and Raheim as an IMBS practitioner at a local healing center with many years of experience with energy healing, meditation, and yoga). We made a conscious decision regarding how to address each other in class and selected first names to resist the hierarchical relationship that our institutional roles and titles would have constructed (e.g., dean/professor vs. doctoral student/instructor). For similar reasons, we invite students to call us by our first names as well. To convey respect for students' knowledges, we frequently ask them to share their prior and ongoing personal and practice experiences as related to topics being discussed in class.

We are deliberate in maintaining an accepting, nonjudgmental stance when responding to students' descriptions of their experiences, as well as their opinions about various modalities. When students make generalizations that are judgmental or disdainful of specific practice approaches, we use these opportunities to remind students that social work values require that critical analysis be done with respect and without oversimplification. These types of judgmental comments usually focus on biomedicine (e.g., "Allopathic doctors just want your money. They don't really want to help you get well."). Although some didactic teaching methods are used, content presented is consistently framed as information for further exploration and critical analysis versus "knowledge" to be added to the data bank.

Finally, we meet as a teaching team before and after each class to share self-reflections, observations of each other's presentations and interactions during class, and other classroom dynamics. We discuss moments when each of us may have been less effective in our teaching efforts than we would have preferred or disclosed less about our IMBS practices and experiences than might have been useful. Our analysis of these sessions gives us opportunities to reflect on how we can be more effective and open in the classroom. We also share observations about lack of engagement of particular students and strategize about how to more effectively invite their participation. This ongoing focus on our individual and collective praxis is a valuable process for assessing our teaching effectiveness and strengthening our ability to maintain a safe, collaborative learning environment. These discussions also serve as re-membering conversations that support our identities as holistic, IMBS social work educators.

Participating in the design and implementation of the course is supporting our development as holistic educators. Prior to designing the course, we had only casually examined the sociopolitical–economic forces that advanced the dominant paradigm of biomedicine and constrained IMBS practice. Critically analyzing the history of biomedicine and the tactics it has used to discredit and undermine competing approaches to healing made clear how it became the dominant approach to health care and positioned other approaches as not credible.

These explorations helped me (SR) to develop a critical analysis of how my voice had been silenced on matters related to IMBS practice in social work education. My new critical understanding, my discovery of a growing body of literature that validated IMBS practices, and teaching with a co-instructor who uses IMBS approaches in his practice have helped me to move to a more empowered identity. The experience has enabled me to develop a critical consciousness and sense of agency that further supports my development as a holistic, IMBS educator.

As an experienced IMBS practitioner and clinical trainer, developing an identity as a holistic social work educator has been an easier journey for me (JJL) than for my co-author. Developing my professional identity in an environment and time period that is far more accepting than my co-author's experience is essential to recognize. Although my current doctoral education includes strong ideology from a post-positivist paradigm, there are also strong faculty and mentors who support my growth and development within critical and participatory frameworks, which spawned from a paradigm of social constructionism. Although there is much to be done, my path continues to bring new awareness and experience in developing my knowledge about IMBS.

IMPLICATIONS

The analysis of our experiences discussed in this chapter illuminates ways that societal, institutional, and other cultural forces may support the development of an identity as a holistic, IMBS educator, whereas other forces can constrain perceptions of agency and marginalize this preferred identity. We examined the use of critical pedagogy and the role of narrative practice approaches to support overcoming barriers to inclusion of IMBS practice and advance holistic social work education. In this section, we discuss implications of this analysis for advancing IMBS practice in social work education.

As discussed in this chapter, social work educators who desire to integrate IMBS practice into their teaching may perceive themselves as constrained from doing so. This perception may be accompanied by a sense of vulnerability, particularly among faculty of color, women, faculty who are untenured, and others with marginalized social identities. Initiatives to engage faculty in critical reflection on the dominant narratives and systems of power that operate to influence and subjugate their preferred identities can support their sense of agency. Acknowledging and honoring their marginal spaces responds to bell hooks' (2004) call for resistance and liberation from hegemonic forces in our institutions and society.

Liberatory projects to support faculty in promoting the inclusion of IMBS practice in social work curricula include (1) conference presentations and publications of critical reflections on the continued dominance of Western ways of knowing and potential constraints on the content and process of our teaching; (2) conference sessions that present the growing evidence base for the efficacy of many IMBS modalities, invite dialogue about IMBS practice, and explore strategies for IMBS inclusion in social work curricula; and (3) research projects to identify IMBS content in social education literature and social work programs. An example of the second type of liberatory project is a National Association of Deans and Directors of Schools of Social Work (NADD)-sponsored "think tank" at the CSWE 59th annual meeting. This session invited dialogue among participants about IMBS practice as an emerging paradigm in social work (Raheim, Lee, & Tebb, 2013). NADD also supported the third type of project noted previously by funding a systematic review of IMBS literature and a survey of US MSW programs to identify current IMBS curricular content, intentions for future inclusion, and barriers to course development (Lee, Raheim, & Tebb, 2014).

Findings from Lee and colleagues' (2014) report can serve as a re-membering process for faculty who may be teaching IMBS content in isolation of other colleagues and create the possibility for connection that did not previously exist. In addition, the report's systematic literature review is a resource for social work educators who are seeking information about the efficacy of specific IMBS practices. These data can aid faculty who may be struggling with issues of credibility for their inclusion of IMBS content in courses.

CSWE could play a central role in advancing IMBS practice in social work education by sponsoring an IMBS curriculum project. Similar to the "Social Work and Integrated Behavioral Healthcare Project," such an initiative could include development of IMBS courses, a learning network for faculty and students using these course materials, and development of field placements (CSWE, 2014a). If funding were not available for a project of this magnitude, CSWE could sanction the development of IMBS model syllabi and the development of an IMBS practice clearinghouse, similar to its web-based "Religion and Spirituality Clearinghouse" (CSWE, 2014b). Any of these CSWE-sponsored initiatives would add legitimacy and support for faculty to incorporate IMBS practice into the content and pedagogical strategies in social work courses, thereby advancing holistic social work education.

This chapter's analysis and discussion support the effectiveness of a critical pedagogical approach to create a liberatory space for social work educators and students to reflexively examine the continued dominance of Western ways of knowing, including the scientific paradigm, and potential constraints on IMBS practice. To make informed choices about what we teach and assist students to make informed choices about how they practice, faculty must promote a critical understanding of the philosophical and theoretical foundations of practice paradigms; their underlying values, sociopolitical, economic, and historical contexts; and the power and privilege dynamics they perpetuate. Faculty can create a safe, collaborative learning environment to promote critical analysis by maintaining an accepting, nonjudgmental, respectful stance in response to students' contributions; encouraging intellectual curiosity, self-reflection, and examination of multiple perspectives; inviting rather than demanding participation; and embodying the role of co-learner by listening to and expressing value of students' knowledges and experiences.

Beyond curricular content, IMBS practice can inform pedagogical strategies in any social work course. Mindfulness and other approaches that invite faculty and students to be fully present support a productive learning environment. IMBS practice principles regarding the importance of internal and external balance, harmony, and connectedness, along with ways we can energetically impact each other, invite faculty to consider their influence on students beyond intellectual development. These principles suggest that faculty self-care is an essential part of being an effective social work educator. Informed by IMBS practice approaches, faculty can design learning processes that encourage students to be active participants in maintaining their well-being while experiencing the stressful demands of graduate education and often challenging demands of field education.

CONCLUSION

This exploration was intended to illuminate forces that facilitate and inhibit incorporating IMBS practice in the content and process of social work education. We hope that our reflections in this chapter will engage others in understanding and, perhaps, changing the phenomena that may silence social work educators who could advance knowledges of IMBS practice. Advancing this emerging paradigm in social work education will promote the profession's inclusion of practices that are supported by recent and exciting discoveries in affective neuroscience, epigenetics, psychoneuroimmunology, and spirituality and health. These discoveries are beginning to close the gap between Western science and indigenous and/or culturally grounded practices. The IMBS practice paradigm provides the foundation for holistic education. Both are essential to prepare social workers for practice in the 21st century.

REFERENCES

Barkin, S. L., Fuentes-Afflick, E., Brosco, J. P., & Tuchman, A. M. (2010). Unintended consequences of the Flexner report: Women in pediatrics. *Pediatrics, 126*(6), 1055–1057.

Bower, J. E., Kemeny, M. E., Taylor, S. E., & Fahey, J. L. (1998). Cognitive processing, discovery of meaning, CD4 decline, and AIDS-related mortality among bereaved HIV-seropositive men. *Journal of Consulting and Clinical Psychology, 66*(6), 979.

Bower, J. E., Kemeny, M. E., Taylor, S. E., & Fahey, J. L. (2003). Finding positive meaning and its association with natural killer cell cytotoxicity among participants in a bereavement-related disclosure intervent. *Annals of Behavioral Medicine, 25*(2), 146–155.

Canda, E. R. (1988). Spirituality, religious diversity, and social work practice. *Social Casework, 69*(4), 238–247.

Canda, E. R. (Ed.). (1998). *Spirituality in social work: New directions.* Binghamton, NY: Haworth.

Canda, E. R. (1999). Spiritually sensitive social work: Key concepts and ideals. *Journal of Social Work Theory and Practice, 1*(1), 1–15.

Canda, E. R., & Furman, L. D. (2010). *Spiritual diversity in social work practice: The heart.* New York, NY: Oxford University Press.

Cassidy, C. M. (2011). Social and cultural factors in medicine. In M. S. Micozzi (Ed.), *Fundamentals of complementary and alternative medicine* (pp. 42–60). St. Louis, MO: Elsevier.

Cohen, D. B. (2006). "Family constellations": An innovative systemic phenomenological group process from Germany. *The Family Journal, 14*, 226–233. doi:10.1177/1066480706287279

Council on Social Work Education (CSWE). (2014a). *Social work and integrated behavioral healthcare project.* Retrieved from http://www.cswe.org/CentersInitiatives/DataStatistics/IntegratedCare.aspx.

Council on Social Work Education (CSWE). (2014b). *Religion spirituality clearinghouse.* Retrieved from http://www.cswe.org/CentersInitiatives/CurriculumResources/50777.aspx.

Cross, T. L. (2013). *Relational world view model. National Indian Child Welfare Association.* Retrieved from http://www.nicwa.org/relational_worldview.

Curley, J. P., Jensen, C. L., Mashoodh, R., & Champagne, F. A. (2011). Social influences on neurobiology and behavior: Epigenetic effects during development. *Psychoneuroendocrinology, 36*(3), 352–371. doi:10.1016/j.psyneuen.2010.06.005

Davis-Floyd, R. E. (2003). *Birth as an American rite of passage* (2nd ed.). Berkeley, CA: University of California Press.

Earls, L. T., & Korr, W. S. (2013). Does social work have a signature pedagogy? *Journal of Social Work Education, 49*(2), 194–206.

Flexner, A. (1910). *Medical education in the United States and Canada: A report to the Carnegie Foundation for the Advancement of Teaching* (No. 4). Stanford, CA: Carnegie Foundation for the Advancement of Teaching.

Flexner, A. (1915). *Is social work a profession?* (Official Proceedings of the National Conference on Social Welfare annual meeting). Retrieved from http://www.social-welfarehistory.com/programs/is-social-work-a-profession-1915.

Freedman, J., & Combs, G. (1996). *Narrative therapy: The social construction of preferred realities.* New York, NY: Norton.

Freire, P. (2000). *Pedagogy of the oppressed.* New York, NY: Bloomsbury.

Garland, E. L., & Howard, M. O. (2009). Neuroplasticity, psychosocial genomics, and the biopsychosocial paradigm in the 21st century. *Health Social Work, 34*(3), 191–199.

Gerhards, J., & Hans, S. (2009). From Hasan to Herbert: Name-giving patterns of immigrant parents between acculturation and ethnic maintenance. *American Journal of Sociology, 114*(4), 1102–1128.

Goldstein, E. G. (2008). The psychosocial framework. In T. Mizrahi & L. E. Davis (Eds.), *The encyclopedia of social work* (20th ed., pp. 462–467). Washington, DC/New York, NY: National Association of Social Workers/Oxford University Press.

Gregory, S. T. (1999). *Black women in the academy: The secrets to success and achievement.* Lanham, MD: University Press of America.

Harding, S. G. (Ed.). (2004). *The feminist standpoint theory reader: Intellectual and political controversies.* New York, NY: Routledge.

Hollis, F. (1964). *Casework: A psychological therapy.* New York, NY: Random House.

hooks, b. (2004). Choosing the margin as a space of radical openness. In S. Harding (Ed.), *The feminist standpoint theory reader: Intellectual and political controversies* (pp. 153–159). New York, NY: Routledge.

Inhorn, M. C. (1994). *Quest for conception: Gender, infertility, and Egyptian medical traditions.* Philadelphia, PA: University of Pennsylvania Press.

Irwin, M. R. (2008). Human psychoneuroimmunology: 20 years of discovery. *Brain, Behavior, and Immunity, 22*(2), 129–139.

Ives, J. A., & Jonas, W. B. (2011). Energy medicine. In M. S. Micozzi (Ed.), *Fundamentals of complementary and alternative medicine* (pp. 130–142). St. Louis, MO: Elsevier.

Jones, L. (Ed.). (2001). *Retaining African Americans in higher education: Challenging paradigms for retaining students, faculty, and administrators.* Sterling, VA: Stylus Publishing.

Lee, M. Y., Ng, S., Leung, P. P. Y., & Chan, C. L. W. (2009). *Integrative body–mind–spirit social work: An empirically based approach to assessment and treatment.* New York, NY: Oxford University Press.

Lee, M. Y., Raheim, S., & Tebb, S. (2014). *Integrative mind–body–spirit social work initiative.* National Association of Deans and Directors of Schools of Social Work. Retrieved from http://www.naddssw.org/resources/monographs.

Lee, V., Cohen, R., Edgar, L., Laizner, A. M., & Gagnon A. J. (2006). Meaning-making intervention during breast or colorectal cancer treatment improves self-esteem, optimism, and self-efficacy. *Social Science Medicine, 62*(12), 3133–3145.

Micozzi, M. S. (2011) (Ed.). *Fundamentals of complementary and alternative medicine.* St. Louis, MO: Elsevier.

National Center for Complementary and Integrative Health. (2014). *Complementary, alternative, or integrative health: What's in a name?* Retrieved from https://nccih.nih.gov/health/whatiscam.

Raheim, S. (2013, March). *Grandma was a healer: Re-storying to liberate subjugated healing practices.* Paper presented at the 11th annual International Narrative Therapy and Community Work Conference, Adelaide, Australia.

Raheim, S., Lee, M. Y., & Tebb, S. (2013, November). *Integrative mind–body–spirit practice: Where is social work education in this emerging paradigm?* Paper presented at the 59th annual program meeting of the Council on Social Work Education, Dallas, TX.

Raheim, S., & Lu, J. J. (2014). Preparing MSW students for integrative mind–body–spirit practice. *Clinical Social Work Journal, 42*(3), 288–301. doi:10.1007/s10615-014-0484-3

Rodwell, M. K. (Ed.). (1998). *Social work constructivist research* (Vol. 1134). New York, NY: Taylor & Francis.

Rossi, E. L. (2002a). Psychosocial genomics: Gene expression, neurogenesis, and human experience in mind–body medicine. *Advances in Mind Body Medicine, 18*(2), 22–30.

Rossi, E. L. (2002b). *The psychobiology of gene expression.* New York, NY: Norton.

Siegel, D. J., Fosha, D., & Solomon, M. F. (Eds.). (2010). *The healing power of emotion: Affective neuroscience, development and clinical practice.* New York, NY: Norton.

Schwartz, S. A., & Dossey, L. (2010). Nonlocality, intention, and observer effects in healing studies: Laying a foundation for the future. *Explore: The Journal of Science and Healing, 6*(5), 295–307.

Smith, L. T. (1999). *Decolonizing methodologies: Research and indigenous peoples.* London, England: Zed books.

Snow, L. F. (1998). *Walkin' over medicine.* Detroit, MI: Wayne State University Press.

Stahnisch, F. W., & Verhoef, M. (2012). The Flexner report of 1910 and its impact on complementary and alternative medicine and psychiatry in North America in the 20th century. *Evidence-Based Complementary and Alternative Medicine, 2012,* Article 647896. Retrieved from http://dx.doi.org/10.1155/2012/647896.

Sue, C. A., & Telles, E. E. (2007). Assimilation and gender in naming. *American Journal of Sociology, 112*(5), 1383–1415.

Sullivan, L. W., & Mittman, I. S. (2010). The state of diversity in the health professions a century after Flexner. *Academic Medicine, 85*(2), 246–253. doi:10.1097/ACM.0b013e3181c88145

Swigonski, M. E. (1994). The logic of feminist standpoint theory for social work research. *Social Work, 39*(4), 387–393.

Taylor, S. E., Kemeny, M. E., Reed, G. M., Bower, J. E., & Gruenewald, T. L. (2000). Psychological resources, positive illusions, and health. *American Psychology, 55*(1), 99–109.

Turner, F. J. (1974). *Social work treatment.* New York, NY: Free Press.

Ursin, R., Tiefenbacher, F., Schmitt-Manderbach, T., Weier, H., Scheidl, T., Lindenthal, M., ...Zeilinger, A. (2007). Entanglement-based quantum communication over 144 km. *Nature Physics, 3*(7), 481–486.

Wheatley, S. C. (1989). *The politics of philanthropy: Abraham Flexner and medical education.* Madison, WI: University of Wisconsin Press.

White, M. (2002). Addressing personal failure. *International Journal of Narrative Therapy and Community Work,* No. 3, 33–76.

White, M. (2005). *Michael White workshop notes.* Adelaide, Australia: Dulwich Centre.

White, M., & Epston, D. (1990). *Narrative means to therapeutic ends.* New York, NY: Norton.

Wiegman, R. (Ed.). (2002). *Women's studies on its own: A next wave reader in institutional change.* Durham, NC: Duke University Press.

Williams, D. R., & Sternthal, M. J. (2007). Spirituality, religion and health: Evidence and research directions. *Medical Journal of Australia, 186*(10), S47.

CHAPTER 13

Pedagogy for an Integrative Practice

Experiential Unity Theory and Model

ALYSON QUINN

INTRODUCTION

Contemporary societal trends—namely busyness, speed-filled living, overworking, the influence of technology, and obeisance to materialism—are having an increasingly negative impact on people and cultures. In addition, numbing and the use of mind-altering substances encourage and perpetuate the disconnection from self (Quinn, 2014); these conditions make it vital that schools of social work, responsible for educating and equipping the next generation of social workers, role model a teaching style and a "way of being" that is counter to the dominant disconnecting strategies. Thomas Moore, in his book *Care of the Soul* (1992), believes the distress seen in this century is related to the "loss of soul." He believes "when the soul is neglected it doesn't just go away; it appears symptomatically in obsessions, addictions, violence, and loss of meaning" (p. xi). Disconnection in the classroom is evident with students' limited attention span, inability to name their feelings and relate to the feeling world of another, and a tendency toward cerebral communication and intellectualization of counseling. Faculty may find it is not just clients in the agencies but also the student population, undermined by cultural trends and meeting demands of the Academy, who are often exhibiting serious signs and symptoms of disconnection. It is incumbent on professors of social work to incorporate new modalities that counteract these undermining habits and to offer healing for those whose souls are disconnected.

Some professors of social work are turning to mindfulness-based para-digms, experiential processes, and holistic models of healing as a way to include the biopsychosocial–spiritual self in their teaching. For instance, Lee, Ng, Leung, and Chan (2009), in their book *Integrative Body–Mind–Spirit Social Work*, state,

> Integrative therapy focuses on the mind–body–spirit relationship, recognizes spiri-tuality as a fundamental domain of human existence, acknowledges and utilizes the mind's power as well as the body's, and reaches beyond self-actualization or symp-tom reduction to broaden a perception of self that connects individuals to a larger sense of themselves and to their communities. (introduction)

Teaching therapeutic techniques that are integrative requires students to learn in an experiential way. The professors' use of mindfulness techniques helps social work students experience the importance of being mindful of their own emo-tional state, and maintain a deep self-connection, in order to do holistic work with their clients.

An example of a theoretical and therapeutic approach that requires an inte-gration of mindfulness by social work students is *Experiential Unity Theory and Model: Reclaiming the soul* (Quinn, 2012). In this chapter, I review my pedagogic style in teaching this model and demonstrate the importance of incorporating a mindfulness and experiential teaching milieu. My intent in devising this thera-peutic model was to educate clients about the importance of feelings, the impact of cultural trends when appropriate, and offer a pathway for the essential engage-ment of the soul. The model requires the practitioner to be deeply connected and self-aware.

INDIGENOUS HEALING AND EXPERIENTIAL LEARNING

In the process of devising the model and theory, it was vital to draw on the wis-dom of indigenous healers for their insight and ideas on how we heal and reclaim the soul. Connor (2008) explains:

> Healing in an indigenous culture is inextricably tied to that culture and its world-view. Often, healers are the leaders of their communities. Their worldview is one in which body, spirit, and mind are not separate parts, nor are cultural practices sepa-rated from healing practices or language. (p. 7)

A common thread from indigenous healers throughout the world is that heal-ing and integrated learning requires engagement of the soul and a milieu whereby the learning can be experienced, rather than taught in a disembodied way, in order to affect change. One such example is offered by Lynn Andrews (1989), who states,

> Many of my friends were psychiatrists. I had seen people go through one or another of the leading therapies, sometimes an extraordinary process. Often they come out knowing why they were doing something, yet continue in their old patterns. I asked a friend, a well-known therapist, why he thought this occurred. He said, "We can help people to understand why they do the thing they do, but we can't necessarily change people." That statement was a real eye opener for me. I thought if therapy doesn't change you, then what is the point of it? To understand it intellectually is just one part of the process. I had to find a way to go on from there. (p. 42)

Andrews drew on the wisdom of a Native American healer, Agnes Whistling Elk, who taught her how critical both spirit and experiential processes are to healing and transformation. Agnes Whistling Elk stated (as quoted in Andrews, 1989),

> So often in your society, much of the knowledge given to people is borrowed knowledge. . . . Experience is really the link. If you could somehow experience what that person was telling you, then it would become real to you, instead of just being part of an intellectual process. (p. 43)

Given how important "experiencing" is to integration, it is critical that social work schools incorporate these "other ways of knowing" into pedagogy, integrating experiential methodologies in the classroom, exploring soul-based processes, and moving away from the professor as the expert on how to effectively counsel all clients. Students then are more likely to come away with the knowledge that they are not the experts for the clients whom they serve but, rather, trained professionals who draw on their own deep self-connection to facilitate a healing milieu for clients in distress. According to Napoli and Bonifas (2011), "Evidence also suggests that when social work students are taught to mindfully reflect upon their experience without judgment their capacity for empathy can increase" (p. 638).

In my experience as an educator, I have developed a strong bias toward experiential learning. When teaching counseling skills, experiential learning is particularly critical because the experience of learning can become integrated into the personality of the student (Gibbons & Grey, 2002; Goldstein, 2001; Horwarth & Thurlow, 2004; Quinn, 1999; Rocha, 2000). Young (2007) states, "There has been extensive literature on experiential learning as a preferred approach in social work education and particularly in clinical skills education" (p. 28). Many times in the field of social work, the social worker is confronting situations of such complexity and magnitude that there is little time to reflect on theories and models in the moment. The social worker has at those pressing moments his or her internalized beliefs and values and his or her ability to process how to proceed in challenging situations. Also, a social worker's ability to empathize, reflect, stay centered in times of grave distress, guide, and provide insightful feedback is directly related to the integration of learning, in which experiential processes play a major role.

David Kolb (1984), an American educational theorist drawing on work of other theorists, notes several factors that are relevant to an experiential learning process. They are summarized as follows:

> First is the emphasis on the process of adaptation and learning as opposed to content of outcomes. Second is that knowledge is a transformation process, being continuously created and re-created, not an independent entity to be acquired or transmitted. Third, learning transforms experience in both its objective and subjective forms. Finally, to understand learning, we must understand the nature of knowledge, and vice versa. (p. 38)

The experiential unity model mimics some of these processes. For example, it requires continuous learning from the clients in the "here and now" so that a social worker can effectively reflect their current inner state. It also puts emphasis on ongoing clinician adaptation to changing environments and circumstances.

EXPERIENTIAL UNITY THEORY AND MODEL: RECLAIMING THE SOUL AND PEDAGOGY

The overall premise of the "experiential unity theory and model" is that it incorporates the soul, as well as the mind, body, and emotional content, which is explored at a deep level by highlighting a client's current emotional state. The model was devised to address the consequences of the dominant cultural trends mentioned previously that are impacting clients, professionals, educators, and students in a profound way. The experiential unity model demands a different pedagogy in order to be taught successfully. The model also requires those learning it to develop their intuition, deepen self-connection, work holistically, and incorporate mindfulness skills into their practice. The model consists of seven different processes in a *group* setting, namely breathing and visualization, feeling rounds, check in, feedback on strengths, a visual tool derived from an overriding theme, movement, yoga, emotional freedom technique, and wrap-up. For an *individual* counseling session, the model includes five steps: breathing and visualization, feeling rounds, client process and emotional freedom technique, a visual tool based on an overriding theme in the client process, and wrap-up of the session.

Each step in both group and individual counseling is taught to social work students using an experiential learning format. This approach focuses on students' experiences in the "here and now"; role models a new way of working with clients in the field that is holistic in nature; places the client in an expert role on his or her situation; and is inclusive of mind, body, emotions, and spirit. It also incorporates right-brain orientation with the use of visuals, supported in the latest findings from the field of neuroscience. According to Allan Schore (2009),

> The essential roles of the right brain in the unconscious processing of emotional stimuli and in emotional communication are directly relevant to recent clinical models of an affective unconscious and a relational unconscious, whereby one unconscious mind communicates with another unconscious mind. In a number of writings I have described in some detail the fundamental role of right-brain to right-brain communications across an intersubjective field embedded within the therapeutic alliance. (p. 115)

The drawing of a visual or tool in the experiential unity model provides an opportunity for both the counselor and the client to engage in a right-brain orientation.

The experiential unity model incorporates other findings in neuroscience in the past decade. For instance, Siegel and Solomon (2003) emphasize that therapy informed by neuroscience "has a bottom-up processing approach of experiential therapies rather than top-down approach of cognitive and insight focused therapy" (pp. 229–230). This approach, for instance, in group therapy is focused on the client's present experience rather than deciding pre-group the topic for the session. The evidence from neuroscience is suggesting a new way of working with clients, bringing in the body, working holistically, and putting emphasis on right-brain methodologies in order to heal past trauma. It, too, is focused on the "here and now," using mindfulness and breathing techniques to resource the client. Other characteristics of trauma therapy informed by neuroscience and attachment studies advocated by Siegel and Solomon include the premise that emotional experience is not processed through language and logic. They emphasize the role of right-hemisphere language, which is a language of images, sensations, impressions, and urges toward action. They highlight techniques that should be reliving and picturing, rather than interpreting, narrating, and analyzing (pp. 229–230). The experiential unity model uses this bottom-up processing approach; for instance, for a client's present preoccupations, a right-brain orientation is activated by creating visual depictions of his or her present concerns. The visual is inclusive of mind, body, spirit, and emotions in the "here and now."

PEDAGOGY FOR AN EXPERIENTIAL MODEL: CASE EXAMPLE OF THE EXPERIENTIAL UNITY MODEL

Experiential learning requires the learner to be actively involved in the experience. Therefore, to facilitate students' whole self-presence, it is important for students to explore cultural trends that are affecting their ability to be fully present in the classroom. The connection/disconnection tool is a helpful group

educational tool and can be used in class to highlight cultural trends of disconnection and assist students in understanding that self-connection is vital to any
counseling work.

In demonstrating the tool, I first ask students to brainstorm current stressors
and past events that have caused distress. This list is captured in a stress/pain
container and includes current stressors in their life as well as their own unresolved childhood experiences. Students are then asked to weight the heaviness of
their container. Students then reflect on feelings they experience by the items in
the stress/pain container, and we draw connections between these feelings and
embodied tension.

As a class, we then list all those activities that encourage the students to dis-
connect from the feelings generated by the container. A typical list from students
includes busyness, academic demands, drugs and alcohol, excessive partying and
socializing, television, social media, and excessive cell phone use. We then make
connections between disconnection and an increase in heaviness of their stress/
pain container and consequent numbing.

The class then focuses on connecting to the container and exploring ways of
discharging the stressors and the heavy feeling. This list typically includes exercise, yoga, spending time in nature, taking breaks, sharing feelings with friends
and family, journal writing, meditation, writing letters to those who hurt them
in the past, attending counseling, and other activities that uplift them. We then
make connections between these activities and their ability to be present with
clients. An option to the stress/pain container is for professors to require students to highlight their feelings and self-connection in their journal writing; this
home assignment assists in tracking students' ability to engage holistically.

When using an experiential pedagogy, I consider the setup of the classroom.
When the students' desks are all facing the front of the room and the professor
is sitting or standing at the front, the paradigm of the professor being the "all-
knowing expert" is reinforced. When the desks and chairs are placed in a circle or
a horseshoe, the traditional pedagogic style is challenged. The professor's role is
then more aligned to guiding, facilitating, and instigating experiential learning.
The professor is also learning alongside the students, and there is an underlying
assumption that all contributions are valuable in an experiential process.

Another premise of teaching experientially is that the end product is not fully
known; this brings an energy and excitement to the class. Through the process of
learning in the "here and now," undiscovered processes will emerge; creativity is
likely unleashed; and through the mindful engagement of both the professor and
the students, learning is more likely to be integrated. For instance, I pair students
up for a role-play counseling session. The student counselor is asked to design a
visual for her or his student–client to assist in her or his self-awareness process.
The material for the visual derives from the student–client's concerns. Students
take turns in the role of counselor. All students then share their drawings and the
emotional processes contained in the visual to the class. In one class, a student

role modeled how to include the body in the process by locating anxiety in the stomach of the student's image and then exploring the impact of anxiety. Overall, students tend to be impressed with their peers' creativity.

In 2013, I taught an advanced interviewing class of both undergraduate and graduate students. We covered a number of modalities, including a sensorimotor approach, somatic experiencing, and the experiential unity model, as case examples of both integrative and experiential work. In my opinion, the challenge of teaching experientially is that it is critical to have consistent student engagement and participation. Therefore, it is important to be receptive to the emotional states of the class and resolve any tension directed toward the professor. On meeting the class for the first time, there was a misunderstanding regarding the volume of required reading. I encouraged students to vent their frustration while clearing up the misunderstanding. This conflict resolution work assisted in keeping the students engaged and active in the class processes. My personal experience of teaching experientially is that it requires a greater degree of vulnerability on my part in taking risks to resolve class tension and more work to improve class participation and cohesion. The teaching requires significant and intimate student engagement throughout the semester and a willingness to be open emotionally to students.

In teaching the experiential unity model, the first task for students to learn is to calm and center the client through a breathing and/or visualization exercise. This helps the client bypass cerebral processes, access his or her feeling state, and become more aware of his or her mind–body connection and unconscious material. A by-product of this process is that it also assists in centering and calming the clinician, and it facilitates his or her presence for the session. The teaching method for this task is based on the idea that the best way for students to learn is by experience. As part of their assignments for the class, each student has to guide the class, including the professor, through a breathing/visualization exercise. Students are encouraged to use their intuition, conduct research if necessary, and find a tool or technique that is a good fit for them. If there are not enough weeks in the semester, students double up and share the time slot for this assignment. This mode of learning helps students gain confidence in calming and centering themselves and their clients; they are able to experience a wide range of relaxation techniques and are educated about what works best from their standpoint. The emphasis at the beginning of class sends a strong message about the importance of mind–body work for clients at the outset of a session. A by-product is that students appear much more relaxed and grounded after this intervention, and anecdotally it seems to make a difference to their engagement in class. After each relaxation/visualization, students comment on the strengths of their peers' work. This helps boost their confidence, and it incorporates another step of the experiential unity model, namely feedback on strengths.

The second task for an experiential unity model is accessing and acknowledging feelings. In teaching this part of the model, I again assume the most powerful way of teaching "the feeling rounds" is for students in the counseling class to learn by example. After the breathing and/or visualization, students name one feeling word that they are feeling in the moment. This helps students learn the importance of acknowledging their own feelings. In addition, many learn how difficult it is to bypass their intellect and be present, thus bringing that experience into their future work. It also contributes to their self-awareness regarding their own degree of self-connection or disconnection and ability to concentrate. A consequence is that this process also educates the professor regarding the students' emotional health. For instance, if a student is unable to name a feeling or identifies as feeling numb, it is an indicator of some degree of disconnection.

Another way I have assisted students in learning about this particular skill was in the situation in which the majority arrived to class upset, angry, and unable to concentrate. They were unhappy with marks they had received, and they perceived a grave injustice. Their tendency was to discuss all the details, common in a client's experience, and stay with a cerebral communication process. I stopped them and asked them to take calming breaths, ground themselves, and then access one feeling word each. We went around for as many times as they needed to get all of their feelings out. The longer the process proceeded, the calmer they became. A number of students commented on how powerful the experience was in teaching them the importance of stating feelings and moving away from the dominance of cerebral communication. They also realized how naming feelings was critical to cultivating a calmer state and engaging in deeper work, and it also reinforced dramatically how much the torrent of cognitively derived detail can get away from healing and accessing one's inner world.

The next step in teaching the experiential unity model for both group and individual counseling is the construction of a tool. This is essentially a visual depiction, often a metaphor for the soul, that is an overall theme with which the client is presently struggling. For the classroom experience, I give students examples I have used in my own sessions; for instance, a client was feeling lost and directionless, so I described and drew a log floating down the river going this way and that with no direction. The client and I then explored the metaphor at a deeper level to ascertain more fully what her soul was experiencing in the moment.

Before students try to intuit a tool for each other in their role plays, a helpful next step is for them to elicit a drawing for themselves. Initially, I ask the students to close their eyes. I guide them through a visualization in which they are relaxing in a safe place in a home, and they hear a knock on the door. They are asked to open the door, and when they open it, they are looking at "stress." What does "stress" look like, feel like, smell like, and so on? Once they have taken a good look at "stress," they close the door, go back to their safe place, and draw what they saw. The students are impressed with how much the visual deepens their experience and illuminates unconscious processes.

To expand the students' experience of devising visual tools in the moment, during a counseling process, I read a quote from the *Tao of Leadership*, recorded in a manual by John Heider titled "Knowing What Is Happening" (1986). It states,

> When you cannot see what is happening in a group, do not stare harder. Relax and look gently with your inner eye. When you do not understand what a person is saying, do not grasp every word. Give up your efforts. Become silent inside and listen with your deepest self. When you are puzzled by what you see or hear, do not strive to figure things out. Stand back for a moment and become calm. When a person is calm, complex events appear simple. To know what is happening, push less, open out and be aware. See without staring. Listen quietly rather than listening hard. Use intuition and reflection rather than trying to figure things out. The more you can let go of trying, and the more open and receptive you become, the more easily you will know what is happening. Also stay in the present. The present is more available than either memories of the past or fantasies of the future. So attend to what is happening now. (14,1)

This quote is helpful for students because it reinforces present-centered skills—the need to ground, calm, and be mindful in order to discover deeper material from their fellow students' experience. It also reminds them of how critical it is to hone their intuition in both individual and group counseling work. The students spend a number of weeks in role-play counseling sessions, devising tools, noting mind–body reactions in their work with each other, and also practicing calming techniques and accessing feelings in their sessions. Their confidence in working holistically increases dramatically, and they are able to weave these ideas into other methodologies they are learning about.

To aid in learning experientially, and to increase integration for students, a course assignment is to hand in weekly journal writing; these are reflections on the content of the class and how it is impacting them. This is both beneficial to the student and for me as an educator. For me, it is helpful in tracking emotional themes; these themes can be utilized in a tool for a future class for awareness building and addressing any personal barriers to learning along the way. In the process of learning to use the experiential unity model, I highlight certain personal character traits and skills that can assist students in building their competencies in experientially oriented counseling. These include the ability to let go of content, self-awareness, intuition, self-trust, humility, vulnerability and not knowing, listening deeply, curiosity, courage in communication, creativity and imagination, and self-compassion. Students occasionally wrestle with these themes in their journals. Another critical piece of student learning is for many of these characteristics to be evident in the professor.

The last step to teach in the experiential unity model is the yoga and movement section along with some emotional freedom techniques (Ortner, 2014). Emotional freedom techniques are utilized in the field of energy psychology.

The methodology uses the tapping of acupuncture points to address psychological issues. I use a tapping CD called *Tapping for Stress Relief* (Ortner, 2014). The instructions on the CD guide the class through a tapping exercise; the students tap on key energy points, such as the chin, in order to release embodied emotions. Energy psychology has been researched "as a potent intervention that facilitates shifts in emotions, cognitions, behaviors, and physiology" (Mason, 2012, p. 224). Again, students have the opportunity to experience this themselves.

For the yoga and movement section, students choose some music and play it while I lead them through some shaking movements, followed by some kundalini yoga poses. In their book *Overcoming Trauma Through Yoga*, Emerson and Hopper (2011) state, "One of the profound lessons from contemporary neuroscience research is that our sense of ourselves is anchored in a vital connection with our bodies" (p. xxiii). Regarding trauma, they state, "People who are traumatized need to have physical and sensory experiences to unlock their bodies, activate effective fight/flight responses, tolerate their sensation, befriend their inner experiences, and cultivate new action patterns" (p. xxiv). Thus, physical exercises such as yoga can prove vital to the process of reconnecting to the self. In my class, I draw the yoga exercises from Yogi Bhajan's kriyas, which are known as holistic healing recipes. Yogi Bhajan brought kundalini yoga to the Western Hemisphere in 1968 in the form of holistic recipes for physical, emotional, and spiritual health. According to Shamanoff-Khalsa (2007), Yogi Bhajan taught between 1968 and 2004 "approximately 5,000 different meditation techniques as well as hundreds of different sets of yoga exercises, each set with a specific sequence, and all claiming to have a unique therapeutic value" (p 2). The poses chosen are intended to detoxify the body, drain fear, and bolster the nervous system. Students have commented how they feel more alive and their heads feel more clear. We talk about movement and yoga being another way to reconnect with self and the body and to protect oneself from unhealthy cultural trends of disconnection, such as busyness, speed-filled living, excess behavior, and cerebral communication. Some students elect to continue with the yoga and movement during their break in the middle of the class.

Students have completed evaluations of the class, and it has been successful on many fronts, particularly in its ability to engage the whole selves of the students. One student commented,

> Alyson continually asked us to move beyond our intellectual selves towards a new way of thinking and learning that engaged our whole selves. She integrated movement, self-reflection, and meditation into her classes, which allowed us to explore new communication and counseling skills from a very grounded and authentic place. With her focus on holistic engagement, she adapted her teaching style to honor our experiences and address our needs as individual students and as a class. Working with Alyson was, by far, one of the most valuable experiences during my social work degree.

It is clear that students find the class helpful, enlightening, and enjoyable. It also makes a significant contribution to their confidence in working holistically and increases their general competency in counseling. Overall, their progress has shown me how critical it is to teach in an experiential way as they are able to experiment, get comfortable with a new set of skills, learn to ground and remain self-connected, and build confidence by becoming their own experts on what works and what does not in their counseling processes. One of the challenges in teaching holistically is that when a student is skeptic of holistic processes, he or she may believe there is an excessive focus on integrative counseling. In this particular class, other modalities, such as narrative therapy, were taught experientially, and so this was not an issue in this class.

SELF-CARE AND ITS ROLE IN
HOLISTIC ENGAGEMENT

Self-care is a vital aspect of social work practice, as well as teaching and learning holistically. Researchers Moore, Bledsoe, Perry, and Robinson (2011) noted,

> The intensity and severity of client problems encountered by social work students can at times seem overwhelming. This professional stress coupled with the responsibilities of student life and the activities of daily living that they encounter make the need for the inclusion of self-care in social work curriculum all the more crucial. (p. 8)

As such, it is crucial for the professor to role model self-care in his or her own life and to demonstrate this with emotional connectedness, empathic attention, whole self-inquiry, healthy boundary setting, assertiveness skills, and healthy lifestyle choices. Often, students have asked me what I do for self-care, and I am able to produce a long list of how I go about looking after myself. Living in Southern Africa for 25 years inspired my own commitment to self-care. I observed "other ways of being" and "other ways of knowing" and noted a clear link between healing abilities and a grounded presence. This heightened my awareness around the importance of self-connection. I explain to students that part of my own self-care commitment has been not working full-time in the field of social work. This has demanded a simpler lifestyle, and it is only possible if one does not have dependents. Time for reflection is critical if one chooses a holistic therapeutic approach. Students need to understand fully that unless one is committed to self-care, it is very challenging to counsel holistically.

Another way to demonstrate the importance of self-care is for the professor to be alert to the emotional undercurrent in the class and to use this material to develop a tool with the class. This is putting into practice how critical it is to pay attention to emotional content and for the students to be the participants. For instance, one week I devised a tool based on my perception that the students appeared overwhelmed and buried by their present demands. The title of the tool was "How do I hold onto myself with all these personal, practicum, and academic demands?" We also devised a self-awareness tool for their personal learning, which focused on the following:

- How do we know we have self-awareness?
- What takes it away?
- How do we benefit from it?
- How do we know when it is high or low?

In working holistically, it is imperative that professors pay attention to the students' emotional experiences and not attempt to educate on top of their despair, apathy, and boredom, for example, because these emotional states will also be relevant to their work as clinicians in the future. Including this learning experientially in the course content by devising tools, or opening a discussion, can provide a critical piece of learning. It is demonstrating how vital it is to acknowledge our own and our clients' emotional undercurrent for effective and holistically oriented counseling.

REFLECTIONS FOR SOCIAL WORK PEDAGOGY IN THE FUTURE

Given the current societal trends of disconnection—for example, busyness, overworking, excess activity, excess materialism, technology's increasing influence, speed-filled living, and the use of mind-altering substances—it is critical that the social work profession develop new pedagogies, paradigms, and methodologies to equip social work students with effective healing modalities for individuals and communities throughout the world. "Social work can enhance its potential for change by not only reflecting on its unexamined support of modernism, but also by re-defining its foundational beliefs and values" (Coates, Gray, & Hetherington, 2006, p. 18). Coates et al. affirm what they call "alternative foundational beliefs" that are grounded in "a belief that humans are part of the web of life and share a common destiny with the Earth, and in this context seek a new understanding of what it means to be human" (p. 18). They expand: "The principles of Indigenous cultures such as wholeness, harmony, balance, and a close relationship of the physical and spiritual are consistent with the foundational beliefs of interdependence and emergence" (p. 18). In this light, it is critical that social work educators role model a commitment to these emerging principles and find ways of teaching new modalities that authentically represent a paradigm shift and are inclusive of mind, body, spirit, and emotions in the counseling process.

REFERENCES

Andrews, L. (1989). Mirroring the life force. In R. Carlson & B. Shield (Eds.), *Healers on healing* (pp. 42–47). New York, NY: Penguin Putnam.
Coates, J., Gray, M., & Hetherington, T. (2006). An ecospiritual perspective: Finally, a place of Indigenous approaches. *British Journal of Social Work, 36,* 381–399.
Connor, N. (2008). *Shamans of the world.* Boulder, CO: Ringing Rocks Foundation.
Emerson, D., & Hopper, E. (2011). *Overcoming trauma through yoga: Reclaiming your body* (pp. xxiii–xxiv). Berkeley, CA: North Atlantic Books.
Fosha, D., Siegel, D. J., & Solomon, M. (Eds.). (2009). *The healing power of emotion: Affective neuroscience, development and clinical practice.* New York, NY: Norton.
Heider, J. (1986). *The Tao of leadership: Lao Tzu's* Tao Te Ching *adapted for a new age.* Atlanta, GA: Humanics.
Kolb, D. A. (1984). *Experiential learning: Experience as the source of learning and development.* Mahwah, NJ: Prentice Hall.
Lee, M. Y., Ng, S., Leung, P. P. Y., & Chan, C. L. W. (2009). *Integrative body–mind–spirit social work: An empirically based approach to assessment and treatment.* New York, NY: Oxford University Press.
Mason, E. (2012, September). Energy psychology and psychotherapy: A study of the use of energy psychology in psychotherapy practice. *Counseling and Psychotherapy Research, 12*(3), 224–232.
Moore, S., Bledsoe, L. K., Perry, A. R., & Robinson, M. A. (2011). Social work students and self care: A model assignment for teaching. *Journal of Social Work Education, 47,* 1–8.
Moore, T. (1992). *Care of the soul: A guide for cultivating depth and sacredness in everyday life.* New York, NY: HarperCollins.
Napoli, N., & Bonifas, R. (2011). From theory toward empathic self-care: Creating a mindful classroom for social work students. *Social Work Education, 30*(6), 635–649.
Ortner, N. (2014). *The tapping solution.* Carlsbad, CA: Hay House.
Quinn, A. (2012). *Experiential unity theory and model: Reclaiming the soul.* Lanham, MD: Aronson.
Quinn, A. (2014). *Reclaim your soul: Your path to healing.* Lanham, MD: University Press of America.
Shamanoff-Khalsa, D. (2007). *Kundalini yoga meditation: Techniques specific for psychiatric disorders, couples therapy, and personal growth.* New York, NY: Penguin Compass.
Siegel, D., & Solomon, M. (2003). *Healing trauma attachment, mind, body and brain.* New York, NY: Norton.
Young, E. J. (2007). *The effectiveness of a virtual learning environment on student learning.* Doctoral dissertation, University of Texas at Arlington, Arlington, TX.

CHAPTER 14

Reconstructing Social Work Education

The Path Forward for Holistic Pedagogies

LORETTA PYLES AND GWENDOLYN J. ADAM

INTRODUCTION

The holistic engagement pedagogies presented in this text offer a compelling invitation to co-construct an innovative approach to evolving social work educa-tion to more directly address the whole person, with the whole person, in context, even and especially in the classroom. We have put forth an initial conceptualiza-tion of how holistic pedagogies can work, without dismissing traditional social work content. This vision can enhance the capacities of students to access many sources of knowing, and integrate and synthesize these (dynamic attunement)— body, mind, heart, culture, and spirit—with theory and research, to help inform and improve their practice (integrative capability).

In environments in which modern education, including social work educa-tion, emphasizes cognition over whole self knowing, outcomes over process, and status quo over social change, the use of holistic pedagogies can offer a vital anti-dote that can propel transformative social work practice (Barbezat & Bush, 2014; Pyles, 2013; Reisch, 2013). Furthermore, given the impacts of globalization as presented in Chapter 1, such as increased social disparity, overemphasis on tech-nology for problem-solving, and a sense of disconnection and isolation, such approaches to education are necessary for the transformation of the profession and the individuals and communities we which work (Coates, 2003; Hick, 2009). Indeed, the authors of this volume are trailblazers who are beginning to lay philo-sophical, analytic, and empirical foundations for what holistic pedagogies can be for transformative social work practice. In so doing, they also acknowledge limits and challenges, recognizing that any pedagogical change happens within diverse institutional contexts.

In this chapter, we highlight some of the common core themes addressed by the authors, especially the idea that social work education is a parallel process to social work practice, and that the creation of democratic classrooms requires openness to a different kind of educational experience—one that values spontaneity and loosening of control. We then consider the diverse pedagogies and methods presented by contributing authors utilizing the Center for Contemplative Mind and Society's Tree of Contemplative Practice image and categories juxtaposed with the four core holistic engagement skills—presence with the whole self, whole self-inquiry, empathic connection, and compassionate attention.

Although the potential impact on students and ultimately the capacity of social workers to utilize holistic engagement skills is clear, this shift requires changes and challenges at multiple levels. We consider the barriers to this change and invite social work educators to utilize organizing and advocacy skills within the Academy to overcome some of these barriers. Thus, we conclude this chapter by offering implications and calls to action at all relevant levels: individual educator, curricular, administrative, and national accrediting bodies. We offer suggestions for further inquiry into the scholarship of holistic engagement and pedagogy that are needed to reconstruct social work education into an endeavor that can nurture transformative practice.

EDUCATION AS PARALLEL PROCESS AND DEMOCRACY

The educator–authors of this volume have revealed that social work pedagogy and social work practice are parallel processes. This means that what happens in the classroom is a microcosm of practice, implying that social work students and educators must indeed embody the change they wish to see in the world (Sloan-Power, 2013). This insight makes it incumbent upon educators to model social work practice in the classroom and beyond through the skills of holistic engagement, such as whole self presence and empathic connection. Whether it is being willing to sit face-to-face with the discomforts of racism in the classroom (e.g., Burghardt, Chapter 4) or to try new methods that feel risky (e.g., Walter, Chapter 8), these authors confirm that the social work classroom is becoming a place where holistic engagement happens in real time.

It is clear that the internal life of the educator is central to holistic pedagogy and, by extension, that the internal life of the practitioner is fundamental to transformative social work practice (Lee, Ng, Leung, & Chan, 2009; Pyles, 2013). Whether it is feeling into the experience of vulnerability or lack of confidence (e.g., Quinn, Chapter 13), or just dealing with the realities of being a human being such as experiencing a loss of a loved one on the day one is teaching a class (e.g., Shepard, Chapter 5), these social work educators are bringing authenticity to their teaching in a way that is resonating with students. As educators model these actions, they invite students to take risks and seize opportunities to take the social work values of self-awareness, empathy, and relationship (Hardina, 2013) to heart and into their future practice.

Social workers know that sustainable personal and social change must co-occur with consciousness-raising about what kinds of beliefs, patterns, and energies are blocking the change, whether it be some form of social oppression, unhealthy relationship patterns, or counterproductive personal habits (Pyles, 2013; White, 2002). Thus, this kind of deconstructive and reconstructive practice is critical to foster among social work students, and it is a lifelong process that can be nurtured in the classroom. As such, it necessitates individualized self-inquiry, as well as collective examination of the cultural and socioeconomic structures that stand in the way of liberation (e.g., Svistova et al., Chapter 9). This requires that students have the opportunity to hear each other's stories in ways that feel safe (e.g., Quinn, Chapter 13) while still pushing the boundaries of comfort (e.g., Walter, Chapter 8). As Shepard (Chapter 5) and Pettie (Chapter 10) detailed, this level of introspection and the safety around sharing one's story is equally pivotal for instructors to learn, and Burghardt's (Chapter 4) assertions on the value of mindfulness to discomforts in the classroom point to challenges and tools in making this transition. The authors of this text have offered many examples of such processes, from group dialogue (Shepard, Chapter 5) to psychodrama (Pettie, Chapter 10), and highlight the strength of international frameworks and tools such as Christiansen's (Chapter 6) discussion of the European social pedagogy's Common Third. Multiple chapters address context-driven moments of sharing feelings, and authors assert the importance of diverse student responses to these methods, ethical considerations, and complications that can arise unexpectedly, as articulated by Lynn, Mensinga, Tinning, and Lundman (Chapter 11).

We have also learned from many of these authors that utilizing holistic pedagogy and practice may require us to interrogate and unpack the narratives of traditional education and practice (e.g., Raheim & Lu, Chapter 12). In addition, it can mean that the tables in the classroom are turned. A traditional classroom in which a professor stands at the front of the room while students are lined up as docile, passive recipients of the professor's words is giving way to more democratic spaces. A democratic classroom, in part initiated by faculty and in part demanded by students, entails much more than changing the physical environment of the classroom. It means that students become the central subjects and actors in their own learning and step into their own power in the classroom. This can manifest in infinite ways from students grading each other's work (Mizrahi, Martell, Cavanaugh, & Weingarten, Chapter 3) to faculty shifting the class plan in a way that honors the moment and their journeys (Shepard, Chapter 5). This transformation requires evolving skills by educators, including the necessity of instructor improvisation skills such as those presented by Walter (Chapter 8).

HOLISTIC ENGAGEMENT SKILLS MEET PEDAGOGICAL METHODS

The authors of this text have discussed a wide range of teaching methods that they have employed in their classes, with the goal of developing what we are calling holistic engagement skills as a way to support transformative social work practice. Some of these methods are group dialogue, deep listening, mindfulness meditation, psychodrama, theatrical games, outdoor team-building activities, community engagement, drawing, tai chi, emotional freedom techniques, and yoga. Making sense of these varied activities and their goals in relation to whole self-development, relationship building, and social change is challenging. However, the Center for Contemplative Mind in Society (n.d.), an organization that envisions higher education as "an opportunity to cultivate deep personal and social awareness . . . [and] an exploration of meaning, purpose and values in service to our common human future," has put forth a model reflecting many of the methods used by our authors and more. Thus, we present the Tree of Contemplative Practices (Figure 14.1) as a way to help social work educators visualize the possibilities that holistic pedagogies can offer.

The practices presented in the visual model are grounded in two key orientations: communion/connection and awareness. We believe that these key orientations resonate with the messages of this text, particularly as they relate to the holistic engagement skills to be developed—whole self presence and inquiry, empathic connection, and compassionate attention. For the purposes of a profession oriented toward social justice, and our keen concern with the radical changes needed for a world in crisis, we add to these two orientations the concept of "transformation." For us, this concept has two basic, and necessarily interconnected, dimensions. First, the idea is concerned with the personal transformation necessary for social workers to undergo as they come to social work practice, including enhanced awareness of personal strengths and a greater understanding of the role that culture and internalized oppression play in who they are. This process requires attending to the whole self and a willingness to let go of that which does not serve their highest good. Second, transformation refers equally to the *social* transformation that we are seeking to effect in our communities and classrooms, particularly as it relates to undoing the global socioeconomic and cultural oppression that manifests at the individual, organizational, and community levels.

The Tree of Contemplative Practices is divided into seven categories: stillness, generative, creative, activist, relational, movement, and ritual/cyclical. Examples

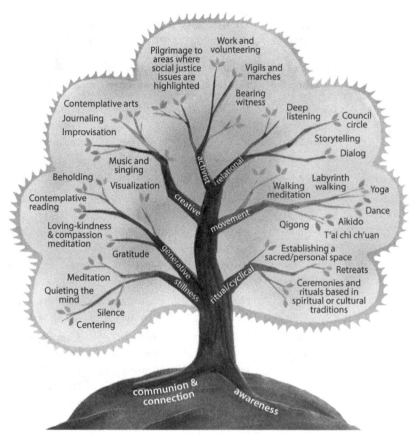

Figure 14.1:
Tree of Contemplative Practices
Source: Center for Contemplative Mind in Society

of stillness practices are meditation, quieting the mind, silence, and centering, many of our authors have practiced these with students. Although not previously considered through this lens, these kinds of activities have been discussed and utilized by the educators represented in this volume with the intent for students to practice gathering the full range of information from all the ways of knowing and to develop more empathic connections.

Given these categories of contemplative practices, coupled with a thorough analysis of the chapters in this text, we put forth a matrix (Table 14.1) that situates each of the chapters in relation to two key axes—namely the pedagogical (contemplative) practices and the holistic engagement skills that these practices seek to develop. Thus, the Matrix of Holistic Engagement Skills and Pedagogical Methods reveals the places where this sample of social work educators are strong in terms of both methods utilized and skills developed. Although there appears to be equal billing to all four holistic engagement skills, the educators seem to have an affinity for creative practices and relational practices. There is moderate

Table 14.1. MATRIX OF HOLISTIC ENGAGEMENT SKILLS
AND CONTEMPLATIVE/PEDAGOGICAL METHODS[a]

	Presence With the Whole Self	Whole Self-Inquiry	Empathic Connection	Compassionate Attention
Stillness	Lynn et al. (11)	Lynn et al. (11)		Lynn et al. (11)
	Pettie (10)			Pettie (10)
	Quinn (13)			Quinn (13)
	Raheim & Lu (12)			Raheim & Lu (12)
Generative	Pyles & Adam (1)	Pyles & Adam (1)	Pyles & Adam (1)	
Creative	Christiansen (6)	Lynn et al. (11)	Christiansen (6)	Mizrahi et al. (3)
	Mizrahi et al. (3)	Pettie (10)	Mizrahi et al. (3)	Quinn (13)
	Pettie (10)	Quinn (13)	Pettie (10)	Walter (8)
	Quinn (13)	Svistova et al. (9)	Svistova et al. (9)	
	Svistova et al. (9)	Walter (8)	Walter (8)	
	Walter (8)			
Activist		Mizrahi et al. (3)	Christiansen (6)	Christiansen (6)
			Mizrahi et al. (3)	Mizrahi et al. (3)
Relational	Burghardt (4)	Burghardt (4)	Burghardt (4)	Burghardt (4)
	Christiansen (6)	Dybicz (7)	Christiansen (6)	Christiansen (6)
		Mizrahi et al. (3)	Mizrahi et al. (3)	Dybicz (7)
		Lynn et al. (11)	Shepard (5)	Mizrahi et al. (3)
		Pettie (10)		Shepard (5)
		Shepard (5)		
		Svistova et al. (9)		
		Walter (8)		
Movement	Christiansen (6)	Quinn (13)	Christiansen (6)	Quinn (13)
	Quinn (13)	Raheim & Lu (12)	Walter (8)	Walter (8)
	Walter (8)	Walter (8)		
Ritual/ Cyclical	Mizrahi et al. (3)	Mizrahi et al. (3)	Mizrahi et al. (3)	Mizrahi et al. (3)

[a]Numbers in parentheses refer to the chapter numbers of the respective authors in this book.

attention to stillness and movement practices, and the least focus is on generative, activist, and ritual/cyclical practices.

IMPLICATIONS AND CALLS TO ACTION

Based on the lessons learned from the innovative authors in this text who are bravely forging new territory in their respective institutions and communities, we believe there are significant implications for social work education and, in some areas, equally significant barriers to making these shifts. Holistic and transformative social work education is a new and emerging field of practice and inquiry, requiring specific actions and change for it to be fully implemented and effective, while recognizing these actions must occur within highly diverse institutional cultures (Kelly & Horder, 2001). These implications and actions are relevant to social work educators, curriculum developers, scholars of pedagogy, social work educational leaders, and leaders of national accrediting bodies. Within each level, there are specific calls to action in moving this from a model in a book to an expected part of social work education. We also identify potential barriers to these shifts and possibilities that may help.

Individual Educator

First and foremost, integrating holistic pedagogies calls on the individual educator to engage in personal inquiry and ongoing research about holistic engagement skills and the pedagogies that can help students come to learn them. This may include becoming more aware of personal internal cues about agreement or resistance to the pedagogical practices, as well as studying the science supporting holistic engagement. As educators ask "What will this require of me?" many may fear taking risks to teach in a way they are not accustomed. Furthermore, acknowledging that these methods invite greater awareness of one's vulnerability as an educator, holistic engagement beckons the educator to develop holistic engagement skills, such as whole self presence and inquiry, as much as the students.

Some may welcome these shifts toward enhanced connection within the classroom, and some may see this as a problematic blurring of professional boundaries. Perhaps it could be both, but this approach to learning most certainly requires flexible agendas and the explicit valuing of class processes as content for learning about oneself and each other. Furthermore, contemplating this change positions the educator to share responsibility for class experiences and the requisite power shifts that go along with this. Student variation from week to week is likely to shift if students' roles include bringing their whole selves. Indeed, the intensity of class discussions and unspoken dynamics, both welcome and unwelcome, will flow with the emotional waves of the group that are in part a function of the environments that they are studying and working in.

These implications invigorate and reinforce some and frighten others because change in *how* we teach presents much more threat than change in *what* we teach. Not every educator is interested in orchestrating psychodrama or yoga poses, nor should they be. Holistic engagement does not require that level of expertise, but it does require intentionally taking risks, large and small, and using whatever happens as part of the learning and inherent to meaning-making. In short, holistic pedagogies more directly fuse social work practice skills with teaching skills, resulting in a shared valuing of process, relationship, and experience. Much like the beginning clinician often spends more time staffing a case with a supervisor than in the session itself, so too does the educator who wants to integrate holistic pedagogies need support and resources.

Recognizing this need for support, we encourage those most skeptical to start slowly—perhaps with a moment of silence during class, a deliberate pause, and see how it feels. Try inviting students to experience a song played in the classroom rather than just thinking about it, or invite them to stop abruptly mid-class to identify a feeling word that describes them at that very moment. The call to action for the individual educator begins with an intention, not a fully holistic curriculum. It can be as simple as inviting all to take a deep breath and notice it.

As educators explore holistic pedagogies that fit them or that they might grow into, we encourage them to seek out a new kind of professional development to reinforce these methods. Finding a community of like-minded or like-intended educators within the field of social work may be possible, and sometimes going beyond social work to other disciplines such as performing arts, integrative medicine, or contemplative studies can offer important resources. I (LP) have been fortunate to find a supportive community through a grassroots group called Capital Region Contemplative Network, which includes interdisciplinary college and university educators from the capital region of New York state who are interested in contemplative and transformative classrooms. This group includes several social work educators, and although I always learn new ideas and skills at our monthly meetings, I find its greatest use for me is that it is a safe place where faculty embrace a culture of presence, inquiry, and connection in a higher education setting. In addition, becoming a student of non-Western, globalized healing methods or global social movements can spark creativity. Beyond academia, local practitioners of somatic therapies, martial arts, and the creative arts, as well as Theatre of the Oppressed trainers, can provide other resources for activities and strategies to support experiential work within the classroom, as well as the educator's use of self.

Some may wonder how these methods could be applied to large classes, perhaps those of 50 or 100 students or more. Others may point out that distance and online learning methods now channel much energy and resources across institutions, whereas the proposed holistic engagement model seems to rely on small groups and direct connections (Henderson, 2010). Although we acknowledge that smaller groups (20 or fewer) and face-to-face contact may offer the most diverse options for experiential activities, holistic engagement does not rely on these. Instead, we begin with the premise that how the instructor chooses to engage catalyzes the process, regardless of what comes next. When we as educators embrace the notion that these skills matter, we show up with more of ourselves present and more of ourselves accessible, which inherently changes the connections with students no matter the distance or size of the group. Although smaller groups may support some of the experiential activities more easily, splitting large groups into several smaller groups is possible. Similarly, simple mindfulness activities, such as asking large groups or even distance learners to pause, intentionally, and take three breaths while paying full attention to experiencing, work no matter the setting.

Holistic engagement invites using the challenges of the transition as part of the context for learning. If that distance learner skips the breathing exercise, later in the session we can mention how some students might have found difficulty engaging in the activity because "no one will know." In so doing, we meet the learner with compassion and recognition that the distance invites disengagement but does not have to stay there. We can go on to invite the learner to examine how the challenges of even taking three breaths when not supported, or accountable and connected to others, can be challenging. When we greet reality with wonder and those in it with compassion and see all of it as education, we are using holistic engagement skills. Indeed, it is our belief that the larger the group, or the more distant or disconnected, the more these types of skills become crucial to forging effective relationship as part of learning. Holistic engagement empowers educators to begin differently, offer themselves and activities to connect, and welcomes all of what comes next as part of the process.

Finally, these implications and calls to action come with the reality that skepticism among peers or students can happen, but that this signifies that people are noticing what you are doing or saying and are interested enough to make comments. One of the virtues of engaging holistically is that the skills can help us even with our skeptics—notice with the whole self, inquire, and invite empathic connection. These skills can make the halls and meeting rooms of our academic institutions into places where we offer each other our compassionate attention as a hallmark of transformative social work practice.

We also recognize that at this time, there are institutions in which this type of student engagement and instructor activity may be rejected outright or feared or mocked. In contexts in which traditional methods prevail, or rigid definitions of acceptable pedagogy squeeze out most of the experiential, we can look to our profession for tools of strategic advocacy and effective social action, realizing that large-scale change sometimes takes a while. Although holistic engagement may never be the prominent pedagogy of the STEM professions, and it may be difficult even in some of our very own social work programs, we know firsthand how small changes create momentum for a more holistically engaged learning environment. A case example from my (GA) university illustrates this point. After beginning each class I teach with a short 1-minute or less mindfulness activity (often to grimaces or befuddled looks from my students), I learned how these simple activities cultivate students' willingness to take the risks we sometimes fear. A colleague who teaches research told me that one of our students in common, a rather shy African American young man, raised his hand at the beginning of his research midterm. He asked politely if he could lead the group in a brief mindfulness activity because they were all so nervous about the exam and he thought it might help them focus. Stunned, my colleague graciously offered him the room to lead. Several students subsequently told me similar stories of the use of mindfulness in and out of the classroom, in part entertained and in part proud of themselves. I realized that we may anticipate resistance and we may collide with it at the institutional level at times. Inasmuch as we empower social change through the efforts of one, so, too, we can empower our profession to welcome holistic engagement skills-building through small changes until we can claim larger ones.

Curriculum Design

Social work academic programs are forever being created, re-created, and modified. With an opportunity to be intentional about this creation, curricula evolution can begin by moving from a preoccupation with setting expectations and evaluating (Barter, 2012) to focusing on creating experiences within the classroom that will allow students to become more self-aware, connected social workers. This can involve setting program content to include experiential activities beyond analyzing thoughts in reaction to something done in class. Similarly, with a focus on holistic engagement, course work can balance traditional writing assignments with assignments that emphasize doing and experiencing (Christopher, Christopher, & Dunnagan, 2006).

Curriculum planning can grow to include a designated class or classes to develop these skills, such as a required generalist course on "Self-Care" or "Holistic Engagement," in order to set the stage for their integration in diverse ways across the program. Furthermore, as social work grapples with online or other distance methods for teaching traditionally, the potential for incorporating holistic pedagogies complicates planning further. Although there is only a very small body of research devoted to integrating holistic methods within the distance environment (Henderson, 2010), scholars have argued that there are several ways that instructors can create more connected online communities of learners. This requires attending to the cultivation of a mindful relationship with technology, addressing the presence/absence of the body in online courses, responding to issues of social isolation, nurturing interactivity, and enhancing the aesthetic environment of online education (Douglass, 2007). The last consideration, for instance, can be addressed by something as simple as changing the computer desktop background and playing music on the computer to reflect the kind of environment that the instructor and students want to foster together.

Curriculum changes need to be addressed at the doctoral level such that doctoral students practice teaching this way from the beginning. Indeed, in our experience, doctoral students appear to be quite eager and driven to find different ways of doing pedagogy and to forge paths that invite them to make teaching a meaningful part of their lives. This is consistent with findings by

Oktay, Jacobson, and Fisher (2013), who explored doctoral social work student needs in transitioning into the teaching role. Learning through experience, utilizing everything that happens as a learning experience, recognizing the emotional component to receiving feedback on teaching, reflecting on experiences, and discovering that "what might feel comfortable to them was not necessarily effective for their students" (p. 213) were all emphasized throughout their study results. Creating a course, or perhaps a series of workshops, in social work doctoral programs that invites doctoral students to learn about and develop their own skills related to teaching in a holistic, transformative way could help to create the kind of momentum that such a major shift in social work pedagogy requires.

Often, shifts in curricula are driven as much by what is not working as by what is, and holistic pedagogies are no exception. As the curriculum teams grapple with students' perceived lack of investment, or texting in class, for example, key strategies in holistic engagement offer antidotes that can solve problems as well as enhance skills. Instead of the traditional dictum of "no cell phone use in class" or "please refrain from texting," holistic methods could position this as an activity. As the instructor invites each student to hold a phone or other object in hand silently and examine it intently—the buttons, the screen, its texture, its color, its weight, considering its relationship with the person, and so on—the phone becomes a part of connecting with the self, each other, and the environment rather than a tug of war. Furthermore, assessing student evaluations from the recent past can also be helpful because students often cite versions of disconnection in courses they evaluate poorly.

It is important to remember that integration of holistic pedagogies at the program level also implies a certain level of buy-in from faculty. Sharing stories about the impact of using holistic pedagogies can make the methods more palpable. Organizing a subset of faculty to explore integration of holistic pedagogies in core courses or electives can be a beginning point in the journey. Not every faculty member will be interested or even tolerant, and that is fine. When we greet these faculty with the same presence and empathic connections as our supportive colleagues, we have opportunities to build our own skills.

Finally, the implications for curricular change also include faculty identification of and advocacy for realistic workloads to support holistic pedagogy efforts. Revamping curricular activities takes time, and purposively engaging in change to one's teaching does also. This may initially mean the need for designated course planning time and increased time designated for office hours or advising. The model emphasizes connection between teacher and student and sometimes results in more direct requests for individual mentoring. Similarly, programs with multiple faculty engaged in this level of self-awareness and self-care may result in different personal limit setting. As faculty increase their awareness of their stress or fatigue, the result may be a needed shift in program expectations.

Leadership in Social Work Education

Working with the whole person in context is a cornerstone of the social work person in environment identity. As Larrison and Korr (2013) note, the role of professional education is "socializing students into the ways, practices, and habit of a discipline" (p. 195). They further question whether social work's signature pedagogy, currently identified as field education by the Council on Social Work Education (2008), adequately includes what happens in the classroom to foster this socialization. Holistic pedagogies offer a bridge between classroom and field, with focus on developing student capacities to recognize, experience, assess, and articulate complex happenings within and around them.

If our social work practice prioritizes working with the whole person, how can we socialize students to the profession without teaching to and with the whole person? We call on social work leaders to contemplate this and identify how our profession stands out relative to other disciplines that offer field-based learning, such as teacher education (Hart, 2014). Holistic pedagogies offer not only classroom-based fusion of the discipline's practice and knowledge but also the explicit invitation to the whole person experience and critical inquiry we value and strive to meet. Leaders in social work education have the unique opportunity to set the course for training social work professionals and for continuing to differentiate social work as a unique profession. The holistic engagement model serves as one catalyst for these considerations, in the hope of claiming and promoting pedagogies that remain distinctly social work.

This movement requires that social work leaders support faculty in seeking the continuing education and time they need to develop these holistic engagement skills themselves. These can be fostered through retreats, where those experienced with holistic pedagogies can be brought in to facilitate; this also presents a powerful way to partner with community practitioners who are skilled in various transformative, embodied, or contemplative practices. In addition, faculty will need environmental supports for holistic pedagogies, where classroom spaces are accessible and set up for multiple uses—for example, including open space conducive to movement, movable chairs for group circles, and accessibility for community members. Finally, social work leaders can explicitly integrate discourse about the value of holistic pedagogies into program information given to students in order to raise awareness and expectations that faculty will be utilizing numerous experiential and reflective methods.

To engender a supportive team and infrastructure, leaders can specifically highlight faculty innovation in this area and build in group discussion at faculty meetings around the experiences happening in class. Similarly, leaders can benefit from these methods as promoting self-awareness and self-reflection among faculty en route to burnout prevention; they can model this behavior by beginning faculty meetings with an activity that invites presence, connection with each other, and/or deep self- or collective inquiry.

Social Work Educational Organizations and Accrediting Bodies

Implications for accrediting bodies for social work education and practice include expanding the understanding of social work practice skills to include holistic engagement skills and dynamic attunement. It is indeed possible to integrate holistic engagement skills within existing competency and capability measures to support faculty in initiating or expanding related efforts (Kelly & Horder, 2001). Similarly, based on the research reviewed in Chapter 1, holistic pedagogies not only offer skills development but also impact the overall learning environment within the classroom, thus affecting the implicit curriculum (Bogo & Wayne, 2013).

We recommend that these organizations (e.g., the Social Work Reform Board in Britain) emphasize *integrative capability* as a potential evolving measure of student proficiency. Recall from Chapter 2 that integrative capability is defined as using the dynamic process of engaging fully, responding, and learning through dynamic attunement, experience, and context to continually improve professional practice. Regarding scholarship and educational practice in holistic pedagogies, national leadership organizations are encouraged to invite innovation studies of holistic pedagogies and provide a platform for wide distribution of faculty activities and ideas on holistic pedagogies. Highlighting holistic pedagogies, interactive whole person teaching methods, or holistic practice methods through breakout sessions and special commissions of national conferences would also begin to provide a clearinghouse for educators already employing related methods and establish a resource network for those wanting to learn.

Scholarship of Pedagogy

As more holistic pedagogies are utilized within social work education, the network of people, resources, and research will expand. Until then, as the authors of this volume have done, it is incumbent upon all of us to write about what we are doing, share innovation, and engage in collaborative research to assess the impacts of holistic pedagogies on our students, our field, and ourselves. The profession needs faculty who are engaged in the use of holistic pedagogies to conduct research to assess their impact on student learning and experience, wellness, and retention, as well as practice in the field.

Although there is a growing body of evidence on the uses of mindfulness and other like practices in the social work classroom (Gerdes, Segal, Jackson & Mullins, 2011; Lynn, 2010; Mishna & Bogo, 2007), our specific model of holistic engagement must be explored and assessed for its relevance and resonance and to further articulate the skills as measurable if it is to be valued within the current academic standards. As the skills of presence, using the whole self, and being immersed fully in context and connection begin to be expressly developed, pedagogical scholars will explore the impact on students, instructors, and programs, as well as clients and communities.

Ongoing tension and debate exist within social work and among other professional disciplines as to whether and how much social work needs to be a "science-based discipline." Sommerfield (2014) articulates this debate internationally and offers ideas on how to conceive social work as an action science that is "trans-disciplinary" (p. 586) and cites the importance of developing a "consolidated knowledge base of social work" (p. 586). Related to these assertions, scholars of holistic pedagogies are called to begin to conceive of studies of comparative outcomes and cohort studies on holistic engagement skills as well as the broad range of holistic pedagogies. This may involve key partnerships with other disciplines in which the science is further along, such as integrative medicine, in addition to some of the scholarship relative to mind–body practices, meditation, and somatic therapies (Garland & Howard, 2009; Lee et al., 2009; McCall, 2007; Micozzi, 2011; Sharma, 2014; Siegel, Fosha, & Solomon, 2010). Doing so could also involve disciplines that utilize biological markers of impact (e.g., functional magnetic resonance imaging studies) such that a more objective measure of impact on the self physically can be assessed, in addition to experiential ones.

There is also a call for scholarship to assess both the needs of the existing workforce and the educator workforce for barriers and opportunities toward implementation of holistic pedagogies. These studies should emphasize the organizational cultures that may be supporting and hindering self-care, conscious communication, and transformative practice. The findings could inform educational programming for continuing education as well as educator training programs. Studies are also needed to explore the developmental trajectory of comfort and skill for educators transitioning to holistic methods in teaching and to develop curricula to support educator preparation that can facilitate ongoing growth and support.

CONCLUSION

The specific implications cited previously establish a strong foundation for growth in practice, teaching, scholarship, leadership, and accountability for social work education while considering some of the inherent challenges. Based on these, we can, as a profession, rethink and re-create what happens in our classrooms and impact what happens in ourselves as we teach and in our students as they learn. Ultimately, we can decide whether our signature pedagogy is *field education* or whether we will adopt signature pedagogies of *holistic practices in classroom and field*. We invite engagement in this discourse, from all of us to all of you.

REFERENCES

Barbezat, D., & Bush, M. (2014). *Contemplative practices in higher education: Powerful methods to transform teaching and learning.* San Francisco, CA: Jossey-Bass.

Barter, K. (2012). Competency-based standards and regulating social work practice: Liabilities to professional sustainability. *Canadian Social Work Review, 29*(2), 229–245.

Bogo, M., & Wayne, J. (2013). The implicit curriculum in social work education: The culture of human interchange. *Journal of Teaching in Social Work, 33,* 2–14.

Center for Contemplative Mind in Society. (n.d.). Retrieved September 24, 2014, from http://www.contemplativemind.org.

Christopher, J., Christopher, S., & Dunnagan, T. (2006). Teaching self-care through mindfulness practices: The application of yoga, meditation, and qigong to counselor training. *Journal of Humanistic Psychology, 46*(4), 494–509.

Coates, J. (2003). Exploring the roots of the environmental crisis: Opportunity for social transformation. *Critical Social Work, 4*(1). Retrieved from http://www1.uwindsor.ca/criticalsocialwork/exploring-the-roots-of-the-environmental-crisis-opportunity-for-social-transformation.

Council on Social Work Education. (2008). *Educational policy and accreditation standards.* Retrieved September 29, 2014, from http://www.cswe.org/File.aspx?id=13780.

Douglass, L. S. (2007). Contemplative online learning environments. *Journal of Online Education.* Retrieved from http://www.nyu.edu/classes/keefer/waoe/douglass.htm.

Garland, E. L., & Howard, M. O. (2009). Neuroplasticity, psychosocial genomics, and the biopsychosocial paradigm in the 21st century. *Health Social Work, 34*(3), 191–199.

Gerdes, K. E., Segal, E. A., Jackson, K. F., & Mullins, J. L. (2011). Teaching empathy: A framework rooted in social cognitive neuroscience and social justice. *Journal of Social Work Education, 47*(1), 109–131.

Hardina, D. (2013). *Interpersonal social work skills for community practice.* New York, NY: Springer.

Hart, T. (2014). *The integrative mind: Transformative education for a world on fire.* Lanham, MD: Rowman & Littlefield.

Henderson, J. (2010). *An exploration of transformative learning in the online environment.* Paper presented at the 26th Annual Conference on Distance Teaching & Learning. Board of Regents of the University of Wisconsin System. Retrieved from http://www.uwex.edu/disted/conference/Resource_library/proceedings/28439_10.pdf.

Hick, S. F. (2009). Mindfulness and social work: Paying attention to ourselves, our clients and society. In S. F. Hick (Ed.), *Mindfulness and social work* (pp. 1–30). Chicago, IL: Lyceum.

Kelly, J., & Horder, W. (2001). The how and the why: Competences and holistic practice. *Social Work Education, 20*(6), 689–699.

Larrison, T., & Korr, W. (2013). Does social work have a signature pedagogy? *Journal of Social Work Education, 49,* 194–206.

Lee, M. Y., Ng, S., Leung, P. P. Y., & Chan, C. L. W. (2009). *Integrative body–mind–spirit social work: An empirically based approach to assessment and treatment.* New York, NY: Oxford University Press.

Lynn, R. (2010). Mindfulness in social work education. *Social Work Education, 29*(3), 289–304.

McCall, T. (2007). *Yoga as medicine.* New York, NY: Bantam Dell.

Micozzi, M. S. (Ed.). (2011). *Fundamentals of complementary and alternative medicine.* St. Louis, MO: Elsevier.

Mishna, F., & Bogo, M. (2007). Reflective practice in contemporary social work classrooms. *Journal of Social Work Education, 43*(3), 529–541.

Oktay, J., Jacobson, J., & Fisher, E. (2013). Learning through experience: The transition from doctoral student to social work educator. *Journal of Social Work Education, 49*(2), 207–221.

Pyles, L. (2013). *Progressive community organizing: Reflective practice in a globalizing world* (2nd ed.). New York, NY: Routledge.

Reisch, M. (2013). Social work education and the neo-liberal challenge: The US response to increasing global inequality. *Social Work Education, 32*(6), 715–733.

Sharma, M. (2014). Yoga as alternative and complementary approach for stress management: A systematic review. *Journal of Evidenced-Based Complementary and Alternative Medicine, 19*(1), 59–67.

Siegel, D. J., Fosha, D., & Solomon, M. F. (Eds.). (2010). *The healing power of emotion: Affective neuroscience, development and clinical practice.* New York: Norton.

Sloan-Power, E. (2013). Diversity education and spirituality: An empirical reflecting approach for MSW students. *Journal of Religion and Spirituality in Social Work, 32*(4), 330–348.

Sommerfield, P. (2014). Social work as an action science: A perspective from Europe. *Research on Social Work Practice, 24*(5), 586–600.

White, M. (2002). Addressing personal failure. *International Journal of Narrative Therapy and Community Work,* No. 3, 33–76.

INDEX

accepting (improvisational
practice), 161–62
activist lessons, 86–91
advancing (improvisational practice), 162
advancing relationships (improvisational
practice), 162–63
advancing story (improvisational
practice), 163
affirmation circle, 67
African Americans, 241–42
Agency Sort, 203
Agnes Whistling Elk, 257
Alighieri, Dante, 111
Alinsky, Saul, 88
allopathic medicine. *See* biomedicine
alternative medicine, 245
Andrews, Lynn, 257
Aristotle, 144–45, 175
art class syllabus, 201
Askeland, G. A., 167
Association for Contemplative Mind in
Higher Education (ACMHE), 206
attending (improvisational practice), 161
attention. *See* compassionate attention
attunement
defined, 32, 47
dynamic, 47
holistic engagement, integrative
capability, and, 32–33, 33f
awareness, 109–10, 272. *See also* self-
awareness; tactical self-awareness

Babbie, E., 142
banking approaches to education, 7
moving beyond, 11
banking education
criticisms of, 7, 61, 180
vs. problem-posing education, 71–72

banking model of education, 164
critical pedagogy and, 238
banking system of education, 95, 99, 182
criticisms of, 61
Barbezat, D., 11, 14
Barretti, M., 119–20
Bartlett, L., 75–76
Bateson, Gregory, 36
Berry, Wendell, 25
binary thought, 95
biomedicine, 239, 240, 244–48
biopsychosocial-spiritual approach and
model, 5–6, 11, 19, 36, 71, 103,
236, 256
Birnbaum, A., 216
Birnbaum, L., 216
blaming the victim, 123
Bledsoe, L. K., 265
"bluffing," 123
Boal, Augusto, 182–87, 191. *See also* Theatre
of the Oppressed
Paulo Freire and, 72, 163, 179, 182, 191
Bodhi, B., 226–27
Bonifas, R., 257
Bowles, S., 120, 134
breaking the silence, 123
bricolage, 160
Brookfield, S., 124–25
Buddhism and mindfulness, 215–20,
222, 225–27
Burghardt, Steve, 76
Bush, Mirabai, 11, 14, 212

Cameron, Claire, 126–27, 131, 132, 134
Capital Region Contemplative
Network, 276
Cassidy, C. M., 240
celebrations, 65–67